Law for Purchasing and Supply

We work with leading authors to develop the
strongest educational materials in Law and
Business, bringing cutting-edge thinking and
best learning practice to a global market.

Under a range of well-known imprints, including
Financial Times Prentice Hall, we craft high-
quality print and electronic publications which
help readers to understand and apply their content,
whether studying or at work.

To find out more about the complete range of our
publishing, please visit us on the World Wide Web at:
www.pearsoneduc.com

Law for Purchasing and Supply

Third Edition

Margaret Griffths and Ivor Griffths

University of Glamorgan

FINANCIAL TIMES

Prentice Hall

An imprint of **Pearson Education**

Harlow, England · London · New York · Reading, Massachusetts · San Francisco · Toronto · Don Mills, Ontario · Sydney
Tokyo · Singapore · Hong Kong · Seoul · Taipei · Cape Town · Madrid · Mexico City · Amsterdam · Munich · Paris · Milan

Pearson Education Limited
Edinburgh Gate
Harlow
Essex CM20 2JE
England

and Associated Companies throughout the world

Visit us on the World Wide Web at:
www.pearsoneduc.com

First published in 1994
Second edition published under the Financial Times/Pitman Publishing imprint 1996
Third edition 2002

ISBN 0 273 64679 6

British Library Cataloguing-in-Publication Data
A catalogue record for this book is available from the British Library

10 9 8 7 6 5 4 3 2 1
06 05 04 03 02

Typeset in 10/12.5pt Sabon Roman by 35
Printed in Great Britain by Henry Ling Ltd, at the Dorset Press, Dorchester, Dorset

Contents

Preface   xv
Table of cases   xvii
Table of legislation   xxix

Part I   The law of contract   1

1   Contract formation   3

1.1   Introduction   3
1.2   Offer and acceptance   3
1.3   Invitations to treat   3
1.4   Status of tenders   4
1.5   Offers   4
        1.5.1 Termination of offers   5
1.6   Tenders   7
        1.6.1 Compulsory competitive tendering   9
1.7   Acceptance   9
        1.7.1 Certainty of terms   9
        1.7.2 Letters of intent   9
        1.7.3 Battle of the forms   10
        1.7.4 Communication of acceptance   10
1.8   Consideration   12
        1.8.1 Consideration must move from the promisee   13
        1.8.2 Past consideration is no consideration   13
        1.8.3 Consideration must be sufficient but need not be adequate   14
1.9   Intention to create legal relations   17
        1.9.1 Domestic agreements   17
        1.9.2 Commercial agreements   17
1.10   Contractual capacity   18
        1.10.1 Corporate capacity   18
        1.10.2 Minors   19
1.11   Privity of contract   20
        1.11.1 Traditional approach   20
        1.11.2 Contracts (Rights of Third Parties) Act 1999   20
        1.11.3 Mitigation of the privity rule   21

        Question and answer   22
        Further reading   23

2 Contractual terms and formalities   24

2.1	Formalities	24
2.2	Terms of the contract	25
2.3	Express and implied terms	26
	2.3.1 Express terms	26
	2.3.2 Implied terms	29
2.4	Conditions, innominate terms and warranties	30
	Question and answer	32
	Further reading	33

3 Vitiating factors   34

3.1	Mistake	34
	3.1.1 Common mistake	35
	3.1.2 Mutual mistake	36
	3.1.3 Unilateral mistake	36
	3.1.4 Mistake in documents	39
3.2	Misrepresentation	39
	3.2.1 A misrepresentation of fact	39
	3.2.2 The misrepresentation must be material	40
	3.2.3 The misrepresentation induced the contract	41
	3.2.4 Remedies for misrepresentation	41
3.3	Duress and undue influence	43
3.4	Illegality and invalidity	46
	3.4.1 Ousting the jurisdiction of the court	46
	3.4.2 Contracts in restraint of trade	46
	Question and answer	48
	Further reading	49

4 Exclusion clauses   50

4.1	Common law control	50
	4.1.1 Incorporation	50
	4.1.2 Interpretation	52
	4.1.3 Doctrine of fundamental breach	53
4.2	Statutory control	53
4.3	Unfair Contract Terms Act 1977	53
	4.3.1 Dealing as a consumer	54
	4.3.2 Reasonableness	55
	4.3.3 Section 2 – Negligence liability	56
	4.3.4 Section 3 – Contractual liability	56
	4.3.5 Section 4 – Unreasonable indemnity clauses	56
	4.3.6 Section 5 – Manufacturer's guarantees	56
	4.3.7 Section 6 – Sale of goods and hire-purchase	57
	4.3.8 Section 7 – Contracts for the supply of goods	57
	4.3.9 Section 8 – Liability for misrepresentation	58

4.4	Unfair Terms in Consumer Contract Regulations 1999	58
	4.4.1 The terms covered	58
	4.4.2 Unfair terms	59
	4.4.3 Role of the Director General of Fair Trading	60
4.5	Criminal control	61
	Question and answer	61
	Further reading	62

5 Termination and remedies — **63**

5.1	Introduction	63
5.2	Performance	63
	5.2.1 Substantial performance	63
	5.2.2 Part performance	64
	5.2.3 Divisible contracts	64
5.3	Agreement	64
5.4	Frustration	65
	5.4.1 Impossibility of performance	65
	5.4.2 Restrictions on application	66
	5.4.3 The effect of frustration	66
5.5	Breach	66
	5.5.1 Anticipatory breach	66
	5.5.2 Effect of the breach	67
5.6	Remedies	67
	5.6.1 Damages	68
	5.6.2 Specific performance	69
	5.6.3 Injunctions	70
	5.6.4 Limitation of actions	70
	Question and answer	71
	Further reading	72

6 The law of agency — **73**

6.1	Introduction	73
6.2	The role of an agent	73
6.3	The creation of an agency	74
6.4	Authority	74
	6.4.1 Actual authority	74
	6.4.2 Apparent authority	76
	6.4.3 Agency by ratification	77
	6.4.4 Agency of necessity	78
6.5	Duties arising from agency	80
6.6	The principal/agent relationship	80
	6.6.1 Duties owed by the agent	80
	6.6.2 Duties owed by the principal	83
6.7	The principal/third party relationship	84
	6.7.1 Financial settlement with the agent	85

6.8	The agent/third party relationship	86
6.9	Termination of agency	86
	6.9.1 Termination by the parties	86
	6.9.2 Termination by operation of law	86
6.10	Commercial Agents (Council Directive) Regulations 1993	87
	Question and answer	91
	Further reading	91

Part II   The supply of goods and services   **93**

7   Implied conditions in the sale of goods   **95**

7.1	Introduction	95
7.2	A 'contract of sale'	96
7.3	The right to sell	97
7.4	Sale by description	99
	7.4.1 What constitutes a 'sale by description'	100
	7.4.2 Descriptive words	100
7.5	Satisfactory quality	102
	7.5.1 In the course of a business	103
	7.5.2 The scope of the section	104
	7.5.3 The meaning of satisfactory quality	105
7.6	Fitness for purpose	110
	7.6.1 Particular purpose	111
	7.6.2 Reliance	111
7.7	Sales by sample	112
7.8	Acceptance	113
7.9	Modification of remedies	113
7.10	Exclusion of liability	114
7.11	European reform	115
	Question and answer	118
	Further reading	119

8   The supply of goods and services   **120**

8.1	Introduction	120
8.2	Part I – implied conditions	120
8.3	Implied terms in services	122
	8.3.1 Care and skill	122
	8.3.2 Time	124
	8.3.3 Consideration	124
	8.3.4 Exclusion	125
	Question and answer	125
	Further reading	126

9   Delivery and payment   127

9.1   Introduction   127
9.2   Delivery and payment   127
     9.2.1 Delivery   127
     9.2.2 Examination and acceptance   131
     9.2.3 Payment   134
9.3   Remedies   134
     9.3.1 Seller's remedies   135
     9.3.2 Buyer's remedies   138

     Question and answer   139
     Further reading   140

10   Passage of title and risk   141

10.1   Introduction   141
10.2   Specific, ascertained and unascertained goods   141
10.3   Passage of title   142
     10.3.1 Section 17   142
     10.3.2 Section 18 rules   143
     10.3.3 Retention of title   147
10.4   The passage of risk   149
10.5   Sale by a non-owner   151
     10.5.1 Estoppel   151
     10.5.2 Market overt   152
     10.5.3 Voidable title   153
     10.5.4 Seller in possession   154
     10.5.5 Buyer in possession   155
     10.5.6 Mercantile agent   156
     10.5.7 Hire Purchase Act 1964   157

     Question and answer   158
     Further reading   159

Part III   The law of tort   161

11   Negligence   163

11.1   Introduction   163
11.2   Duty of care   163
     11.2.1 Standard of care   165
     11.2.2 Breach of the duty   167
11.3   Causation   167
11.4   Defences   167
11.5   Recoverable damage   168
     11.5.1 Nervous shock   169
     11.5.2 Economic loss   171

11.6	Negligent misstatement	172
	11.6.1 Liability for services	174
11.7	Vicarious liability	175
	Question and answer	176
	Further reading	176

12	**Product liability**	**177**
12.1	Introduction	177
12.2	The American experience	177
12.3	Consumer Protection Act 1987	179
	12.3.1 'Producer' and 'product'	179
	12.3.2 Who is liable	180
	12.3.3 Defective	181
	12.3.4 Defences	183
	12.3.5 Recoverable damage	185
	12.3.6 Time limits	186
	12.3.7 Global limits	187
	12.3.8 Exclusion	187
	12.3.9 Reform	187
	Question and answer	188
	Further reading	189

Part IV	**Consumer protection**	**191**

13	**Criminal liability for false statements**	**193**
13.1	Introduction	193
13.2	Trade Descriptions Act 1968	193
	13.2.1 Goods	193
	13.2.2 In the course of a trade or business	194
	13.2.3 Trade description	195
	13.2.4 False trade description	196
	13.2.5 Applying	197
	13.2.6 Supplies or offers to supply	199
	13.2.7 Disclaimers	199
	13.2.8 Services	201
	13.2.9 Defences	204
	13.2.10 Enforcement	206
13.3	Prices	207
13.4	Property misdescriptions	211
	Question and answer	212
	Further reading	213

14 Product safety   214

14.1	Introduction	214
14.2	General Product Safety Regulations	214
	14.2.1 'Product' and 'safe product'	215
	14.2.2 Obligations of 'producers' and 'distributors'	216
	14.2.3 Offences and defences	217
14.3	Consumer Protection Act 1987	218
	14.3.1 The general safety requirement	218
	14.3.2 Safety regulations	220
	14.3.3 Enforcement	222
	14.3.4 Enforcement powers	224
14.4	Health and Safety at Work etc Act 1974	224
	14.4.1 Defences	226
	14.4.2 Enforcement	226
	14.4.3 Civil liability	226
	14.4.4 Recent regulations	227

| | Question and answer | 227 |
| | Further reading | 228 |

15 Food safety   229

15.1	Introduction	229
15.2	Food	229
15.3	Sale and commercial operations	230
15.4	Food safety offences	231
	15.4.1 Rendering food injurious	232
	15.4.2 The food safety requirement	232
	15.4.3 Enforcement of s 8	234
15.5	Notices and orders	234
	15.5.1 Improvement notice	235
	15.5.2 Prohibition orders	235
	15.5.3 Emergency prohibition notices and orders	236
	15.5.4 Emergency control orders	236
15.6	Consumer protection	237
	15.6.1 Food not of the nature or substance or quality demanded	237
	15.6.2 Falsely describing or presenting food	238
15.7	Regulations	239
15.8	Codes of practice	239
15.9	Defences	240
15.10	Enforcement	241
15.11	Food Standards Agency	241
	15.11.1 The functions of the Agency	242
	15.11.2 Enforcement	243

| | Question and answer | 244 |
| | Further reading | 244 |

16   Weights and measures   245

16.1   Introduction   245
16.2   Offences of short weight or measure   245
       16.2.1 Goods sold by weight, measurement or number   245
       16.2.2 Defences   247
16.3   Regulated packages   248

       Question and answer   250
       Further reading   250

Part V   Related legislation   251

17   Legal aspects of outsourcing   253

17.1   Introduction   253
17.2   Tenders   253
17.3   Letters of intent and letters of comfort   255
17.4   EU Public Procurement Directives   256
       17.4.1 Open procedure   259
       17.4.2 Restricted procedure   259
       17.4.3 Negotiated procedure   260
17.5   Compulsory competitive tendering   260
17.6   Transfer of undertakings   262
       17.6.1 Transfer of Undertakings (Protection of Employment)
               Regulations 1981   263
       17.6.2 Unfair dismissal   264
       17.6.3 Redundancy   265

       Question and answer   266
       Further reading   267

18   Competition law   268

18.1   Introduction   268
18.2   Competition Act 1998   269
18.3   Part I of the 1998 Act   269
18.4   Chapter I   269
       18.4.1 The prohibition   269
       18.4.2 Exclusions   271
       18.4.3 Exemptions   272
       18.4.4 Notification   274
18.5   Chapter II   274
       18.5.1 The prohibition   274
       18.5.2 Exclusions   275
       18.5.3 Notification   276
       18.5.4 Investigation and enforcement   276

18.6   Fair Trading Act 1973   276
        18.6.1 Monopolies   277
        18.6.2 Mergers   278
18.7   Articles 81 and 82 EC   279

        Question and answer   281
        Further reading   282

19   Intellectual property   283

19.1   Introduction   283
19.2   Breach of confidence and passing off   283
        19.2.1 Breach of confidence   283
        19.2.2 The tort of passing off   285
19.3   Patents   286
        19.3.1 A patentable invention   287
19.4   Copyright   290
19.5   Designs   294
        19.5.1 Design right   294
        19.5.2 Registered designs   296
19.6   Trade marks   296
        19.6.1 Trade Marks Act 1938   296
        19.6.2 Trade Marks Act 1994   297

        Question and answer   306
        Further reading   306

20   International trade   307

20.1   Introduction   307
20.2   Bills of lading   308
        20.2.1 Obligations of shipper and carrier   309
        20.2.2 Claims against the carrier   310
        20.2.3 Multi-modal transport   311
20.3   C.i.f. and f.o.b. contracts   312
        20.3.1 C.i.f. contracts   312
        20.3.2 F.o.b. contracts   313
        20.3.3 The passage of risk   314
20.4   Documentary credits   314

        Question and answer   316
        Further reading   316

21   Insurance   317

21.1   Introduction   317
21.2   Types of insurance   317
21.3   Insurable interest   318
21.4   The contract   319

21.5	Terms of the contract	322
21.6	The role of agents	323
21.7	Claims	323
21.8	Subrogation	325
	Question and answer	326
	Further reading	326
	Index	327

Preface

In the five years since the publication of the second edition of this text, the law has moved on apace. There have been many significant new judicial decisions that impact upon the subject matter of this text including **Commission of the European Communities *v* United Kingdom** (1997), **White *v* Chief Constable of South Yorkshire** (1998), **Stevenson *v* Rogers** (1999) and **St Albans City and District Council *v* International Computers Ltd** (2000). Equally, there have been major legislative developments including, *inter alia*, the Competition Act 1998, the Food Standards Act 1999, the Contracts (Rights of Third Parties) Act 1999 and the Unfair Terms in Consumer Contracts Regulations 1999.

Changes in the CIPS syllabus, which are due to come into effect in September 2001, have been reflected in the content of this edition. Thus, there is a new chapter looking at Legal Aspects of Outsourcing, while the chapters on Consumer Credit and Employment Law have been removed although some aspects of Employment Law have been retained in the chapter on outsourcing. Given the breadth of the CIPS syllabus that this text addresses, the authors have necessarily drawn on a wide range of sources. All the texts that have been used as resource materials have been acknowledged at the end of the relevant chapters.

As with the second edition, we must thank our colleagues at the University of Glamorgan for permitting us to pick their brains and for commenting on some of the chapters. Thanks are also due to David Dunleavy and Theresa Graves at the Food Standards Agency for their comments on the chapter on Food Safety.

On a personal level, we would like to record our thanks to family and friends for their support and encouragement during the drafting of this new edition, with particular thanks to our daughter, Charlotte, for her considerable patience during the latter stages of writing when the whole world seemed to revolve around Mum and Dad finishing the book.

The law stated is as we believe it to be on 12 May 2001.

Margaret Griffiths
Ivor Griffiths
Caerphilly

Table of cases

Abernethie *v* A M & J Kleinman Ltd [1969] 2 All ER 790 *195*

Abouzaid *v* Mothercare (UK) Ltd (2001) *The Times*, 20 February *185*

Adams *v* Lindsell (1818) 1 B & Ald 681 *12*

A G Stanley Ltd *v* Surrey County Council Trading Standards Office (1995)
159 JP 691 *210*

Aliakmon, The [1986] 2 All ER 145 *311*

Alcock *v* Chief Constable of South Yorkshire [1991] 4 All ER 907, HL *170*

Alf Vaughan & Co Ltd (in receivership) *v* Royscott Trust plc [1999] 1 All ER
(Comm) 856 *44*

Ali *v* Christian Salvesen Food Services Ltd [1997] 1 All ER 721 *29*

Allen *v* Redbridge Borough Council [1994] 1 All ER 728, DC *211*

Alliance & Leicester Building Society *v* Edgestop Ltd [1994] 2 All ER 38 *42*

Alpha Trading Ltd *v* Dunnshaw-Patten Ltd [1981] QB 290 *84*

Aluminium Industrie Vaassen BV *v* Romalpa Aluminium Ltd [1976]
2 All ER 552 *147, 148, 149*

Amstrad plc *v* Seagate Technology Inc (1998) 86 BLR 34 *106, 139*

Anderson *v* Britcher (1913) 78 JP 65 *238*

Andrews Bros (Bournemouth) Ltd *v* Singer & Co [1934] 1 KB 17 *52*

Anness *v* Grivell [1915] 3 KB 685 *238*

Anton Piller KG *v* Manufacturing Processes Ltd [1976] Ch 55 *81*

Arcos *v* Ronaasen & Son [1933] AC 470 *100*

Armour *v* Thyssen Edelstahlwerke AG [1990] 3 All ER 481 *148*

Armstrong *v* Jackson [1917] 2 KB 822 *82*

Arthur *v* Barton (1840) 6 M & W 138 *79*

Ashington Piggeries Ltd *v* Christopher Hill Ltd [1972] AC 441 *101, 111*

Ashley *v* Sutton London Borough Council (1995) *Trading Law* 350 *202*

Associated Japanese Bank (International) Ltd *v* Crédit du Nord [1988]
3 All ER 902 *35*

Aswan Engineering Establishment Co *v* Lupdine Ltd [1987] 1 All ER 135 *106*

Atari Corpn (UK) Ltd *v* Electronics Boutiques Stores (UK) Ltd [1998]
QB 539 *145*

Atlas Express Ltd *v* Kafco (Importers and Distributors) Ltd [1989]
1 All ER 641 *43*

Attorney-General *v* Guardian Newspapers Ltd [1999] EMLR 904, DC *283*

Banco Exterior Internacional *v* Mann [1995] 1 All ER 936 *45*

Bannerman *v* White (1861) 10 CBNS 844 *26*

Banque Financière de la Cité SA *v* Westgate Insurance Co Ltd [1990] 1 QB 665   *40, 321*

Barclays Bank *v* O'Brien [1994] 1 AC 180   *44*

Barry *v* Davies (t/a Heathcote Ball & Co) (2000) *The Times*, 31 August   *138*

Bartlett *v* Sydney Marcus [1965] 2 All ER 753   *105*

Barton *v* County Natwest Ltd [1999] Lloyd's Rep Bank 408   *41*

Bastin *v* Davies [1950] 1 All ER 1095   *238*

Beale *v* Taylor [1967] 2 All ER 253   *100, 102*

Beckett *v* Cohen [1973] 1 All ER 120   *203*

Beecham (H) & Co Pty Ltd *v* Francis Howard & Co Pty Ltd [1921] VLR 428   *108*

Bell *v* Lever Bros [1932] AC 161   *35*

Berkshire County Council *v* Olympic Holidays Ltd [1994] Crim LR 277, DC   *209*

Bernstein *v* Pamson Motors (Golders Green) Ltd [1987] 2 All ER 220   *96, 107, 109, 113, 118, 131, 139*

Best Travel Co *v* Patterson (1986) 151 JP 619   *202*

Betts *v* Willmott (1871) 6 Ch App 259, CA   *290*

Bettini *v* Gye (1876) 1 QBD 183   *31*

Bibby-Cheshire *v* Golden Wonder Ltd [1972] 3 All ER 738   *248*

Birkenhead & District Cooperative Society *v* Roberts [1970] 3 All ER 391   *204*

Birkett *v* Acorn Business Machines Ltd [1999] 2 All ER (Comm) 429   *46*

Blakemore *v* Bellamy [1982] RTR 303   *104, 195*

Blackpool & Fylde Aero Club Ltd *v* Blackpool BC [1990] 3 All ER 25   *7, 253*

Boardman *v* Phipps [1967] 2 AC 46   *82, 83*

Bolam *v* Friern Hospital Management Committee [1957] 1 WLR 582   *166*

Bolitho *v* City and Hackney Health Authority [1998] AC 232   *166*

Borden (UK) Ltd *v* Scottish Timber Products Ltd [1981] Ch 25   *148*

Brander *v* Kinnear [1923] JC 42   *237*

Brinkibon *v* Stahag Stahl und Stahlwarenhandelsgesellschaft mbH [1983] AC 34   *12*

Bristol-Myers Squibb *v* Paranova A/S (C-427, 429, 436/93) [1996] ECR 1-3457, ECJ   *303*

British Airways Board *v* Taylor [1975] 3 All ER 307   *203*

British Steel Corpn *v* Cleveland Bridge and Engineering Co Ltd [1984] 1 All ER 504   *10, 255*

Brown *v* Craiks [1970] 1 All ER 823   *108*

Bunge Corpn *v* Tradax Export SA [1981] 2 All ER 513   *32*

Butler Machine Tool Co Ltd *v* Ex-Cell-O Corpn [1979] 1 All ER 965   *10, 23, 26*

Butterworth *v* Kingsway Motors [1954] 2 All ER 694   *98*

Byrne *v* Van Tienhoven (1880) 5 CPD 344   *6, 12*

CBS Songs Ltd *v* Amstrad Consumer Electronics Ltd [1988]   *292*

CIBC Mortgages plc *v* Pitt [1994] 1 AC 200   *44*

CPC Consolidated Pool Carriers GmbH *v* CTM CIA Transmediterranea SA [1994] 1 Lloyd's Rep 68   *9*

CTN Cash & Carry *v* Gallagher Ltd [1994] 4 All ER 714   *43*

CTN Cash & Carry Ltd *v* General Accident Fire & Life Assurance Corpn plc [1989] 1 Lloyd's Rep 259   *323*

Cadbury Ltd *v* Halliday [1975] 2 All ER 226   *196*

Cammell Laird *v* Manganese Bronze & Brass [1934] AC 402   *112*

Caparo Industries plc *v* Dickman [1990] 2 AC 605   *172, 173*

Car and Universal Finance Co Ltd *v* Caldwell [1964] 1 All ER 290, CA   *41*

Carlill *v* Carbolic Smoke Ball Co [1893] 1 QB 256   *4, 5, 6, 11*

Carlos Federspiel & Co SA *v* Charles Twigg & Co Ltd [1957] 1 Lloyd's Rep 240   *147*

Casey's Patents, Stewart *v* Casey, *Re* [1892] 1 Ch 10   *14*

Castellain *v* Preston (1883) 11 QBD 380   *324*

Cavendish Funding Ltd *v* Henry Spencer & Sons Ltd [1998] PNLR 122   *167*

Cavendish Woodhouse Ltd *v* Wright (1985) 149 JP 497   *198*

Cehave NV *v* Bremer Handelsgesellschaft mbH, The Hansa Nord [1975] 3 All ER 739   *31*

Centrafarm BV and Adriaan De Peijper *v* Sterling Drug Inc (15/74) [1975] FSR 161, ECJ   *149, 300, 303*

Centrafarm BV *v* American Home Products Corpn (3/78) [1979] FSR 189, ECJ   *303*

Centrafarm BV and De Peijper *v* Winthrop BV [1976] 1 CMLR 1   *303*

Central London Property Trust Ltd *v* High Trees House Ltd [1947] KB 130   *16, 17*

Central Newbury Car Auctions *v* Unity Finance [1956] 3 All ER 905   *152*

Chadwick *v* British Railways Board [1967] 1 WLR 912   *170*

Chaigley Farms Ltd *v* Crawford Kaye & Grayshire Ltd [1996] BCC 957   *148*

Chapelton *v* Barry UDC [1940] KB 532   *51*

Chappell & Co Ltd *v* Nestlé & Co Ltd [1960] AC 87   *14*

Charnock *v* Liverpool Corpn [1968] 3 All ER 473   *124*

Chaudhry *v* Prabhakar [1988] 3 All ER 718   *81*

Citibank NA *v* Brown Shipley & Co Ltd [1991] 2 All ER 690   *38*

Close Asset Finance *v* Care Graphics Machinery Ltd (2000) *The Times*, 21 March   *156*

Clough Mill Ltd *v* Martin [1984] 3 All ER 982   *148*

Coca-Cola Trade Marks, *Re* [1986] RPC 351   *298*

Coco *v* AN Clark (Engineers) Ltd [1969] RPC 41   *284*

Coles *v* Enoch [1939] 3 All ER 327   *84*

Collins *v* Godefroy (1931) 1 B & Ad 950   *14*

Colwyn Bay Motorcycles *v* Poole (2000) unreported   *153, 157*

Commission for the New Towns *v* Cooper (GB) Ltd [1995] Ch 259   *36*

Commission of the European Communities *v* United Kingdom (C300/95) [1997] All ER (EC) 481   *185*

Consorzio del Prosciutto Di Parma *v* Marks and Spencer plc [1991] RPC 351   *286*

Cottee *v* Douglas Seaton (Used Cars) Ltd [1972] 3 All ER 750   *196*

Coupe *v* Guyett [1973] 2 All ER 1058   *206*

Couturier *v* Hastie (1856) HL Cas 673   *24, 35*

Cox *v* Phillips Industries Ltd [1976] 3 All ER 161   *69*

Credit Lyonnais Bank Nederland NV *v* Burch [1997] 1 All ER 144   *45*
Cundy *v* Lindsay (1878) 3 App Cas 459, HL   *37, 38*
Curtis *v* Chemical Cleaning & Dyeing Co [1951] 1 KB 805   *52*
Cutter *v* Powell (1756) 6 Term R 320   *63*

D & F Estates Ltd *v* Church Commissioners for England [1988]
   2 All ER 992, HL   *171*
Davies *v* Sumner [1984] 3 All ER 831   *194*
Dawson (G J) (Clapham) Ltd *v* H & G Dutfield [1936] 2 All ER 232   *96*
Dawsons Ltd *v* Bonnin [1922] 2 AC 413   *322*
Denard Burton Retail Ltd (1997) *The Times*, 19 November   *207*
Dennant *v* Skinner & Collom [1948] 2 KB 164   *143*
Department of the Environment *v* Thomas Bates & Son [1990]
   2 All ER 943, HL   *171*
Derry *v* Peek (1889) 14 App Cas 337, HL   *42*
Devlin *v* Hall [1990] Crim LR 879   *195*
Dick Bentley Productions Ltd *v* Harold Smith (Motors) Ltd [1965]
   2 All ER 65   *26*
Dickinson *v* Dodds (1876) 2 Ch D 463, CA   *6*
Director General of Fair Trading *v* First National Bank plc [2000]
   2 All ER 759   *59*
Dixons Ltd *v* Roberts (1984) 148 JP 513   *203*
Doble *v* David Greig Ltd [1972] 2 All ER 195   *200, 208*
Donoghue *v* Stevenson [1932] AC 562   *163, 164, 177*
Drummond *v* Van Ingen (1887) 12 App Cas 284   *112*
Duffen *v* FRA BO SpA (1998) *The Times*, 15 June   *28, 89*
Dunlop Pneumatic Tyre Co Ltd *v* New Garage & Motor Co Ltd [1915]
   AC 79   *27, 28, 68*
Dunlop Pneumatic Tyre Co Ltd *v* Selfridge & Co Ltd [1915] AC 847   *20*

Eagle Star Life Assurance Co Ltd *v* Griggs (1997) *The Independent*,
   20 October   *125*
East *v* Maurer [1991] 2 All ER 733   *42*
Eastern Distributors Ltd *v* Goldring [1957] 2 All ER 252   *152*
Economides *v* Commercial Union Assurance Co plc [1997] 3 All ER 636   *320*
Edgington *v* Fitzmaurice (1885) 29 Ch D 459   *40*
Elafi, The [1982] 1 All ER 208   *146, 147*
Elder *v* Crowe [1996] SCCR 38   *195*
Elvis Presley Trade Mark, *Re* [1999] RPC 567, CA   *286*
Entores Ltd *v* Miles Far East Corpn [1955] 2 QB 327   *12*
Errington *v* Errington & Woods [1952] 1 All ER 149   *6*
Esso Petroleum Ltd *v* Customs and Excise Commissioners [1976]
   1 All ER 117   *5, 96*
Esso Petroleum Co Ltd *v* Harper's Garage (Stourport) Ltd [1967]
   1 All ER 699   *47*
Esso Petroleum Ltd *v* Mardon [1976] 2 All ER 5   *39, 173*

Faccenda Chicken *v* Fowler [1986] 1 All ER 617   *285*
Felthouse *v* Bindley (1862) 11 CBNS 869   *11*
Ferguson *v* Davies [1997] 1 All ER 315   *16*
Few *v* Robinson [1921] 3 KB 504   *238*
Financings Ltd *v* Stimson [1962] 1 All ER 386   *7*
Fisher *v* Bell [1961] 1 QB 394   *199*
Fitzgerald *v* Dressler (1859) 7 CBNS 374   *24*
Fletcher *v* Budgen [1974] 2 All ER 1243   *195*
Formula One Autocentres Ltd *v* Birmingham City Council [1999] RTR 195   *198*
Forsikringsaktieselskapet Vesta *v* Butcher [1986] 2 All ER 488   *123*
Forster & Sons Ltd *v* Suggett (1918) 35 TLR 87   *47*
Francis Day & Hunter Ltd *v* Bron [1963] Ch 587   *292*
Frank H Mann (Torquay) Ltd *v* Womersley (1972) unreported   *246*
Freeman & Lockyer *v* Buckhurst Park Properties (Mangal) Ltd [1964]
   2 QB 480   *76*
Fry *v* First National Leasing Ltd (2000) unreported   *122*

Galoo Ltd *v* Bright Grahame Murray [1995] 1 All ER 16   *173*
Galloway *v* Guardian Royal Exchange (UK) Ltd [1999] Lloyd's Rep 209   *321*
Garrett *v* Boots Cash Chemists Ltd (1980) unreported, 16 July, DC   *205,*
   213, 248
Gibbon *v* Mitchell [1990] 3 All ER 338   *39*
Glasbrook Brothers Ltd *v* Glamorgan County Council [1925] AC 270   *14*
Glaxo Group Ltd *v* Dowelhurst (No 2) Ltd [2000] 2 CMLR 571   *304, 305*
Glengate-KG Properties Ltd *v* Norwich Union Fire Insurance Society Ltd [1996]
   2 All ER 487   *319*
Glicksman *v* Lancashire & General Insurance Co [1927] AC 139   *321*
Godley *v* Perry [1960] 1 WLR 9   *108*
Goodwill *v* British Pregnancy Advisory Service [1996] 2 All ER 161   *174*
Gran Gelato Ltd *v* Richcliff (Group) Ltd [1992] 1 All ER 865   *42*
Grant *v* Australian Knitting Mills [1936] AC 85   *100, 106, 108, 111*
Great Northern Railway *v* Swaffield (1874) LR 9 Ex 132   *79*
Great Northern Rly Co *v* Witham (1873) LR 9 CP 16   *8, 255*
Greaves & Co Contractors Ltd *v* Baynham, Meikle & Partners [1975]
   3 All ER 99   *123*
Green (R W) Ltd *v* Cade Bros Farm [1978] 1 Lloyd's Rep 602   *55*
Greenman *v* Yuba Power Products 59 Cal 2d 57 (1963)   *177, 178*
Greig (David) Ltd *v* Goldfinch (1961) 105 Sol Jo 307   *233*
Griffiths *v* Peter Conway Ltd [1939] 1 All ER 685   *111*
Grimshaw *v* Ford Motor Co 119 Cal App 3d 757 (1981)   *178*

H (A Child) *v* Merck & Co Inc (2001) WL 98168   *187*
Hadley *v* Baxendale (1854) 9 Exch 341   *68, 136, 139*
Hardy Lennox (Industrial Engines) Ltd *v* Puttick Ltd [1984] 2 All ER 152   *147*
Harlingdon & Leinster Ltd *v* Christopher Hull Fine Art Ltd [1990]
   1 All ER 737   *101, 112*

Harris (L S) Trustees Ltd *v* Power Packing Services (Hermit Road) Ltd [1970]
  2 Lloyd's Rep 65   *81*
Hartley *v* Ponsonby (1857) 7 E & B 872   *15*
Hartog *v* Colin & Shields [1939] 3 All ER 566   *36*
Harvela Investments Ltd *v* Royal Trust Co of Canada Ltd [1986] AC 207   *8,*
  23, 254
Havering London Borough Council *v* Stevenson [1970] 3 All ER 609   *54, 194*
Hawkes & Son (London) Ltd *v* Paramount Film Services Ltd [1934]
  RPC 31, CA   *292*
Healy *v* Howlett & Sons [1917] 1 KB 337   *146, 147*
Heath *v* Parkinson (1926) 42 TLR 693   *81*
Hedley Byrne & Co Ltd *v* Heller & Partners Ltd [1963] 2 All ER 575, HL   *42,*
  172, 173, 174
Helby *v* Matthews [1895] AC 471   *96, 156*
Hely Hutchinson *v* Brayhead Ltd [1968] 1 QB 549   *75*
Henderson *v* Merrett Syndicates Ltd [1995] 2 AC 145   *174*
Hepburn *v* A Tomlinson (Hauliers) Ltd [1966] AC 451   *319*
Herne Bay Steamship Co *v* Hutton [1903] 2 KB 683   *65*
Hillas & Co Ltd *v* Arcos Ltd (1934) 38 Com Cas 23   *9*
Hiranchand Punamchand *v* Temple [1911] 2 KB 330   *16*
Hochester *v* De La Tour (1853) 2 E & B 678   *66, 67*
Hoenig *v* Isaacs [1952] 2 All ER 176   *63, 64, 70*
Hollier *v* Rambler Motors (A M C) Ltd [1972] QB 71   *52*
Holwell Securities Ltd *v* Hughes [1974] 1 All ER 161   *12*
Hong Kong Fir Shipping Co Ltd *v* Kawasaki Kisen Kaisha Ltd [1962]
  1 All ER 474   *31*
Humble *v* Hunter (1848) 12 QB 31   *85*
Hussain *v* Brown (1995) *The Times*, 15 December   *320*
Hutton *v* Warren (1836) 1 M & W 466   *30*
Hyde *v* Wrench (1840) 49 ER 132   *5*

IHT Internationale Heiztechnik GmbH and Danziger *v* Ideal-Standard GmbH and
  Wabco Standard GmbH (C-9/93) [1995] FSR 59, ECJ   *304*
Interfoto Picture Library *v* Stiletto Visual Programmes Ltd [1988]
  1 All ER 348   *51*
Island Records Ltd *v* Tring International plc [1995] 3 All ER 444   *292*

JEB Fasteners Ltd *v* Marks Bloom & Co [1983] 1 All ER 583   *40, 41*
Jackson *v* Horizon Holidays Ltd [1975] 3 All ER 92   *21*
Jackson *v* Rotax Motors [1910] 2 KB 937   *131, 134*
Jackson *v* Union Marine Insurance Co Ltd (1874) LR 10 CP 125   *27*
Jarvis *v* Swans Tours [1973] 1 QB 233   *69*

Keighley Maxted & Co *v* Durant [1901] AC 240   *77*
Kelner *v* Baxter (1866) LR 2 CP 174   *78*
Kendall (Henry) & Sons *v* William Lillico & Sons Ltd [1969] 2 AC 31   *52, 106,*
  109, 110

Kent County Council *v* Price (1993) 8 CL 102   *183, 200, 201*

Keppel *v* Wheeler [1927] 1 All ER 577   *81*

Kinchin *v* Ashton Park Scooters Ltd (1984) 148 JP 540   *202*

Kings Norton Metal Co Ltd *v* Edridge, Merrett & Co Ltd (1897)
    14 TLR 98, CA   *38, 48*

Kirwin *v* Anderson (1991) 156 JP 301   *195*

Kleinwort Benson Ltd *v* Lincoln City Council [1998] 3 WLR 1095   *34*

Kleinwort Benson Ltd *v* Malaysian Mining Corporation Bhd [1989]
    1 All ER 785   *18, 255, 256*

Kler Knitwear Ltd *v* Lombard General Insurance Co Ltd [2000]
    Lloyd's Rep IR 47   *322*

Kpohraror *v* Woolwich Building Society [1996] 4 All ER 119   *68*

Krell *v* Henry [1903] 2 KB 740   *65*

Kursell *v* Timber Operators & Contractors Ltd [1927] 1 KB 298   *142*

LA Gear Inc *v* Hi-Tec Sports Ltd [1992] FSR 121, CA   *292*

Lambert *v* Fry (2000) Current Law, October   *79*

Lampleigh *v* Braithwait (1615) Hob 105   *14*

Lancashire & Cheshire Association of Baptist Churches Inc *v* Howard & Seddon
    Partnership [1993] 3 All ER 467   *124*

L'Estrange *v* Graucob [1934] 2 KB 394   *50*

Legal and General Assurance Society Ltd *v* Drake Insurance Co Ltd [1922]
    1 All ER 283   *325*

Lewin *v* Barratt Homes Ltd [2000] Crim LR 323   *203*

Lewin *v* Fuell [1990] Crim LR 323   *200*

Lewis *v* Averay [1971] 3 All ER 907   *38*

Lill (K) (Holdings) Ltd *v* White [1979] RTR 120   *198*

Limpus *v* London General Omnibus (1862) 1 H & C 526   *175, 176*

Lister *v* Romford Ice & Cold Storage Co Ltd [1957] AC 555   *30*

Liverpool City Council *v* Irwin [1977] AC 239   *30*

Lloyd *v* Grace Smith & Co [1912] AC 716   *175*

Lloyds Bank Ltd *v* Bundy [1975] QB 326   *46*

London Borough of Barking & Dagenham *v* Jones (1999) LTL 30 July   *206*

Lucena *v* Craufurd (1806) 2 B & PNR 269   *318, 319*

Lumley *v* Gye (1852) 1 De GM & G 604   *70*

Luque *v* McLean 8 Cal 3d 136 (1972)   *178*

Luxmoore-May *v* Messenger May Baverstock [1990] 1 All ER 1067   *166*

MFI Warehouses Ltd *v* Nattrass [1973] 1 All ER 762   *202*

MGN Ltd *v* Ritters (1997) 16 Tr LR 427   *208*

M & S Drapers (a firm) *v* Reynolds [1956] 3 All ER 814   *47*

McArdle, *Re* [1951] Ch 669, CA   *13*

McCann (John) & Co *v* Pow [1974] 1 WLR 1643   *80*

McFarlane *v* Wilkinson; Hegarty *v* EE Caledonia Ltd [1997] 2 Lloyd's
    Rep 259   *169*

Macaura *v* Northern Assurance Co Ltd [1925] AC 619   *318, 319*

Mann (Frank H) Torquay Ltd *v* Womersley (1972) unreported   *246*

Mansfield *v* Weetabix Ltd [1998] 1 WLR 1263   *165*

Maple Flock Co Ltd *v* Universal Furniture Products (Wembley) Ltd [1934]
1 KB 148, CA   *131, 134*

Marshall (Thomas) (Exports) Ltd *v* Guinle [1978] 3 All ER 193   *285*

Massey *v* Midland Bank plc [1995] 1 All ER 929   *45*

May *v* Vincent (1990) 154 JP 997   *200*

Meah *v* Roberts [1978] 1 All ER 97   *238*

Mercantile Credit Co *v* Hamblin [1965] 2 QB 242   *152*

Merck & Co Inc *v* Stephar BV and Petrus Stephanus Exler (187/80) [1981]
ECR 2063, ECJ   *290*

Michael Gerson (Leasing) Ltd *v* Wilkinson [2001] 1 All ER 148   *155*

Microbeads AG *v* Vinehurst Road Markings Ltd [1975] 1 All ER 529   *97*

Midland Bank Trust Co Ltd *v* Hett, Stubbs and Kemp [1979] Ch 384   *123*

Mihalis Angelos, The [1971] 1 QB 164   *32*

Moore, *Re* & Landauer [1921] 2 KB 519   *100*

Moore *v* Piretta PTA Ltd [1999] 1 All ER 174   *89*

Morris Angel & Son Ltd *v* Hollande [1993] 3 All ER 569   *69, 306*

Mountstephen *v* Lake (1874) LR 7 HL 17   *24*

Mullin *v* Richards [1998] 1 WLR 1304   *165*

Murphy *v* Brentwood DC [1990] 2 All ER 908   *171, 186*

N *v* United Kingdom Medical Council *sub nom* Creutzfeld-Jakob Disease
Litigation [1996] 7 Med LR 309   *166*

Nahum *v* Royal Holloway and Bedford New College (1998) *The Times*,
19 November   *84*

Nanka-Bruce *v* Commonwealth Trust [1926] AC 77, PC   *144*

National Employers Mutual General Insurance Association Ltd *v* Jones [1990]
1 AC 24   *156*

Naughton *v* O'Callaghan [1990] 3 All ER 191   *139*

Nettleship *v* Weston [1971] 2 QB 691   *165*

Newcastle-upon-Tyne City Council *v* Safeway plc (1994) unreported,
27 June, DC   *205, 209*

Newell *v* Hicks (1983) 148 JP 308   *202*

Newsholme Bros *v* Road Transport & General Insurance Co [1929]
2 KB 356   *323*

Newtons of Wembley Ltd *v* Williams [1964] 3 All ER 532, CA   *156*

Niblett Ltd *v* Confectioners' Materials Co [1921] 3 KB 387   *97*

Nicholson *v* Harper [1895] 2 Ch 415   *154*

Nordenfelt *v* Maxim Nordenfelt Guns and Ammunition Co [1894] AC 535   *47, 70*

Norman *v* Bennett [1974] 3 All ER 351   *200*

Norwich Union Life Insurance Co Ltd *v* Qureshi [1999] 2 All ER
(Comm) 707   *320*

Nurdin & Peacock plc *v* D B Ramsden & Co Ltd [1999] 1 All ER 941   *35*

Nutting *v* Baldwin [1995] 2 All ER 321   *28*

Ojjeh *v* Galerie Moderne Ltd (1998) unreported   *101*

Ojjeh *v* Waller (1998) unreported   *101*

Olgeirsson *v* Kitching [1986] 1 All ER 746   *206, 217*

Olley *v* Marlborough Court Ltd [1949] 1 All ER 127   *29, 50*

Oscar Chess Ltd *v* Williams [1957] 1 All ER 325   *26*

Overseas Tankship (UK) Ltd *v* Morts Dock and Engineering Co Ltd, The Wagon
   Mound [1961] 1 All ER 404, PC   *168*

Page *v* Combined Shipping and Trading Co Ltd [1997] 3 All ER 656   *90*

Page *v* Smith [1995] 2 All ER 736   *169*

Pan Atlantic Insurance Co Ltd *v* Pine Top Insurance Co Ltd [1994]
   3 All ER 581   *320*

Panatown Ltd *v* Alfred McAlpine Construction Ltd [2000] 4 All ER 97   *21*

Panorama Developments (Guildford) Ltd *v* Fidelis Furnishing Fabrics Ltd [1971]
   3 All ER 16, CA   *75*

Partridge *v* Crittenden [1968] 2 All ER 421   *4*

Pau On *v* Lau Yiu Long [1979] 3 All ER 65   *14, 43*

Peachdart, *Re* [1983] 3 All ER 204   *148*

Pharmaceutical Society of Great Britain *v* Boots Cash Chemists (Southern) Ltd
   [1953] 1 QB 394   *4*

Pharmacia and Upjohn SA (formerly Upjohn SA) *v* Paranova A/S (C-379/97)
   [2000] Ch 571, ECJ   *303*

Photo Production Ltd *v* Securicor Transport Ltd [1980] AC 827   *53*

Pinnel's Case (1602) 5 Co Rep 117a   *15, 16*

Pitt *v* PHH Asset Management Ltd [1993] 4 All ER 961   *6*

Planche *v* Colburn (1831) 8 Bing 14   *64*

Poussard *v* Spiers and Pond (1876) 1 QBD 410   *31*

Prager *v* Blatspiel Stamp & Heacock Ltd [1924] 1 KB 566   *79*

Priest *v* Last [1903] 2 KB 148   *111*

Printpak *v* AGF Insurance Ltd [1999] 1 All ER (Comm) 466   *322*

R *v* A F Pears Ltd (1982) 90 *ITSA Monthly Review* 142   *197*

R *v* Avro (1993) 12 Tr LR 83   *203*

R *v* Birmingham City Council, *ex parte* Ferrero Ltd [1993] 1 All ER 544   *223*

R *v* Breeze [1973] 2 All ER 1141   *202*

R *v* Carl Bull (1996) 160 JP 240   *200*

R *v* Ford Motor Co [1974] 3 All ER 489   *196*

R *v* Haesler [1973] RTR 486   *197*

R *v* Hammerton Cars Ltd [1976] 3 All ER 758   *200*

R *v* Inner London Justices, *ex parte* Another [1983] RTR 425   *196*

R *v* Liverpool City Council, *ex parte* Baby Products Association (1999) *The Times*,
   1 December   *223*

R *v* Richards [1999] Crim LR 598   *206*

R *v* Secretary of State for Health, *ex parte* US Tobacco International Inc [1992]
   3 All ER 212   *221*

R *v* Southwood [1987] 3 All ER 556   *198, 199*

R *v* Thomson Holidays Ltd [1974] 1 All ER 823   *202*

R & B Customs Brokers Co Ltd *v* United Dominions Trust Ltd [1988]
   1 All ER 847   *54*

Raffles v Wichelhaus (1864) 2 H & C 906   *36*

Reardon Smith Line Ltd v Yngvar Hansen-Tangen [1976] 3 All ER 570   *31, 32, 101*

Reckitt & Coleman Products Ltd v Borden Inc [1990] RPC 341   *285, 298*

Regal (Hastings) Ltd v Gulliver [1942] 1 All ER 378   *83*

Regina Fur Co Ltd v Bossom [1957] 2 Lloyd's Rep 466   *321*

Richardson v LRC Products Ltd [2000] Lloyd's Rep Med 280   *183*

Rickards v Oppenheim [1950] 1 All ER 420   *129*

Rimeco Riggelsen & Metal Co v Queenborough Rolling Mill Co [1995] CL 110   *10*

Roberts v Leonard (1995) *The Times*, 10 May   *195*

Roberts v Severn Petroleum & Trading Co Ltd [1981] RTR 312   *197*

Robins & Day Ltd v Kent Trading Standards Department (1996) unreported   *198*

Roe v Minister of Health [1954] 2 All ER 131   *166, 182*

Rogers v Parish (Scarborough) Ltd [1987] 2 All ER 232   *107, 108, 109, 113*

Romalpa, *see* Aluminium Industrie Vaasen BV v Romalpa

Rose & Frank Co v J R Crompton & Bros [1925] AC 445   *18*

Roselodge Ltd v Castle [1966] 2 Lloyd's Rep 113   *321*

Rousell Uchaf SA v Hockley International Ltd [1996] RPC 441   *290*

Routledge v McKay [1954] 1 All ER 855   *26*

Rowland v Divall [1923] 2 KB 500   *98*

Royal Bank of Scotland v Etridge [1998] 4 All ER 383   *45*

Royscott Trust Ltd v Rogerson [1991] 3 All ER 294   *42*

Rubicon Computer Systems Ltd v United Paints Ltd (2000) 2 TCLR 453   *99*

Ruxley Electronics and Construction Ltd v Forsyth [1995] 3 All ER 268   *69*

SA Cnl–Sucal NV SA v HAG Gf Ag (C-10/89) [1991] FSR 99, ECJ   *304*

Sabir v Tiny Computers (1999) unreported   *132*

Saunders v Anglia Building Society [1970] 3 All ER 961, HL   *39*

Scally v Southern Health and Social Services Board [1992] 1 AC 294   *29, 30*

Scammel v Ouston [1941] AC 251   *9*

Secretary of State for Employment v Spence [1986] IRLR 248   *263*

Selectmove Ltd, *Re* [1995] 2 All ER 531   *15, 16*

Shanklin Pier Ltd v Detel Products Ltd [1951] 2 KB 854   *21*

Sherratt v Gerald's The American Jewellers Ltd (1970) 114 Sol Jo 147   *205, 213, 248*

Shine v General Guarantee Corpn [1988] 1 All ER 911   *107, 109*

Shipton, Anderson & Co v Weil Bros & Co [1912] 1 KB 574   *129*

Silhouette International Schmied GmbH & Co KG v Hartlauer Handelsgesellschaft mbH (C355196) [1998] FSR 729, ECJ   *304, 305*

Simpkins v Pays [1955] 3 All ER 10   *17*

Sindell v Abbott Laboratories 26 Cal 3d 588 (1980)   *178, 187*

Slater Finning Ltd [1997] AC 473, HL   *111*

Smith v Baker & Sons [1891] AC 325, HL   *168*

Smith v Eric S Bush [1990] 1 AC 831   *172*

Solley v Wood (1852) 16 Beav 370   *80*

South Yorkshire Transport Ltd v Monopolies and Mergers Commission [1993] 1 All ER 289   *278, 281*

Sovereign Finance Ltd *v* Silver Crest Furniture Ltd [1997] CCLR 76   *55*

Spalding (AG) & Bros *v* A W Gamage Ltd and Benet Fink & Co Ltd (1915) 32 RPC 275, HL   *285*

Spartan Steel & Alloys Ltd *v* Martin & Co (Contractors) Ltd [1973] 1 QB 27 *171, 172*

Spencer *v* Harding (1870) 23 LT 237   *7, 254*

Spice Girls Ltd *v* Aprilia World Service BV [2000] EMLR 478   *40*

Spiro *v* Lintern [1973] 3 All ER 319   *76*

Spring *v* Guardian Assurance plc [1995] 2 AC 296   *30, 174*

Springer *v* Great Western Railway [1921] 1 KB 257   *79*

Spurling *v* Bradshaw [1956] 2 All ER 121   *51*

St Albans City and District Council *v* International Computers Ltd [1996] 4 All ER 481   *53, 56, 103, 180*

Stadium Finance Ltd *v* Robbins [1962] 2 All ER 633, CA   *157*

Stainethorpe *v* Bailey [1980] RTR 7   *199*

Stevenson *v* Rogers [1999] QB 1028   *55, 104, 194*

Stevenson *v* McLean (1880) 5 QBD 346   *6*

Stilk *v* Myrick (1809) 2 Camp 317   *15*

Sunair Holidays Ltd *v* Dodd [1970] 2 All ER 410   *202*

Surrey County Council *v* Bredero Homes Ltd [1993] 3 All ER 705   *68*

Swizzels Matlow Ltd's Three Dimensional Trade Mark Application [1999] RPC 879   *298*

TSB Bank plc *v* Camfield [1995] 1 All ER 951   *45, 46*

Tarleton Engineering Co Ltd *v* Nattrass [1973] 3 All ER 699   *200*

Taylor *v* Caldwell (1863) 3 B & S 826   *65*

Taylor *v* Combined Buyers Ltd [1924] NZLR 627   *107*

Tehran-Europe Co Ltd *v* S T Belton (Tractors) Ltd [1968] 2 QB 545   *112*

Tesco Supermarkets Ltd *v* Nattrass [1972] AC 153   *204, 205, 248*

Thake *v* Maurice [1986] 1 All ER 497   *123*

Thornton *v* Shoe Lane Parking Ltd [1971] QB 163   *51*

Toyota (GB) Ltd *v* North Yorkshire CC (1998) 162 JP 794   *208*

Toys 'R' Us *v* Gloucestershire County Council (1994) 158 JP 338, DC   *209*

Trentham (G Percy) Ltd *v* Archital Luxfer [1993] 1 Lloyd's Rep 25   *11*

Truk (UK) Ltd *v* Tokmakidis GmbH [2000] 1 Lloyd's Rep 543   *132, 133*

Tsakiroglou & Co Ltd *v* Noblee Thorl GmbH [1962] AC 93   *65*

Tweddle *v* Atkinson (1861) 1 B & S 393   *13, 20*

Underwood Ltd *v* Burgh Castle & Cement Syndicate [1922] 1 KB 343   *143*

Union Eagle Ltd *v* Golden Achievement Ltd [1997] 2 All ER 215   *27*

United Biscuits (UK) Ltd *v* Asda Stores Ltd [1997] RPC 513   *286*

Van Zuylen Bros *v* Hag AG :192/73 [1974] ECR 731, ECJ   *304*

Varley *v* Whipp [1900] 1 QB 513   *142*

Victoria Laundry (Windsor) Ltd *v* Newman Industries Ltd [1949] 2 KB 528   *68*

Vitol SA *v* Norelf Ltd, The Santa Clara [1996] AC 800   *67*

Wadham Kenning Motor Group Ltd *v* Brighton and Hove Council (1997)
  unreported *199*
Wagon Mound, The, *see* Overseas Tankship (UK) Ltd
Wait, *Re* [1927] 1 Ch 606 *142, 145*
Walford *v* Miles [1992] 1 All ER 453 *6*
Walker *v* Simon Dudley Ltd; *sub nom* Shropshire CC *v* Simon Dudley Ltd [1997]
  16 Tr LR 69 *206*
Wardar's (Import and Export) Co Ltd *v* Norwood & Sons Ltd [1968]
  2 All ER 602 *147*
Warner Bros Inc *v* Nelson [1937] 1 KB 209 *70*
Warwickshire County Council *v* Johnson [1993] 1 All ER 299 *207*
Watteau *v* Fenwick [1893] 1 QB 346 *76*
Westminster City Council *v* Ray Allan (Manshops) Ltd [1982] 1 All ER 177 *202*
White and Others *v* Chief Constable of South Yorkshire [1998] 3 WLR 1510
  169, 170
White *v* John Warwick & Co Ltd [1953] 2 All ER 1021 *52, 62*
White *v* Jones [1995] 2 AC 207 *174*
Whitehouse *v* Jordan [1981] 1 All ER 267 *123, 166*
William Sindall plc *v* Cambridgeshire County Council [1994] 3 All ER 932 *42*
Williams *v* Roffey Bros & Nicholls (Contractors) Ltd [1990] 1 All ER 512 *15, 16*
Williams and Reid *v* Natural Life Health Foods Ltd and Mistlin [1998]
  1 WLR 830 *173*
Wilson *v* Best Travel Ltd [1993] 1 All ER 353 *123*
Wilson *v* Rickett, Cockerill & Co [1954] 1 All ER 168 *105*
Wings Ltd *v* Ellis [1984] 3 All ER 577 *202*
Woolcott *v* Sun Alliance & London Alliance Ltd [1978] 1 All ER 1253 *321*
Worcester Works Finance Ltd *v* Cooden Engineering Ltd [1972] 1 QB 210 *154*
Workman Clark & Co Ltd *v* Lloyd Brazileno [1908] 1 KB 968 *135*
Wormell *v* R H M Agriculture (East) Ltd [1986] 1 All ER 769 *105*
Worsley *v* Tambrands Ltd [2000] PIQRP 95 *183*
Wycombe Marsh Garages Ltd *v* Fowler [1972] 3 All ER 248 *198*

Yasuda Fire and Marine Insurance Co of Europe Ltd *v* Orion Marine Insurance
  Underwriting Agency Ltd [1995] 3 All ER 211 *83*

Zawadski *v* Sleigh [1975] RTR 113 *200*
Zino Davidoff SA *v* A & G Imports [2000] Ch 127 *289, 305*

Table of legislation

Statutes

Agriculture Act 1970 *218, 243*
Assize of Bread and Ale 1266 *229*
Bills of Lading Act 1855 *310*
  s 1 *310*
Carriage of Goods by Sea Act 1971 *307*
Carriage of Goods by Sea Act 1992 *310*
  s 1(2) *310*
    (3) *310*
  s 1(4) *310*
  s 2 *308, 310*
    (1) *311*
  s 4 *309*
Civil Jurisdiction and Judgments Act 1982 *314*
Companies Act 1985 *19*
  s 35 *19*
  s 36(4) *74, 78*
  s 395 *148*
Companies Act 1989 *19*
  s 108(1) *19*
Competition Act 1980 *268*
  s 2 *268*
  s 10 *268*
Competition Act 1998 *47, 268, 277, 279, 280, 281*
  s 2 *269, 270*
  s 3 *269, 271, 272*
  s 4 *272*
  s 5 *273*
  s 6 *273*
    (6) *273*
  s 7 *273*
    (2) *273*
  s 8 *273*
  s 9 *272, 273*
  s 10(5) *273*
  s 11 *272, 274*

s 12   274
s 13   274
s 14   274
s 15   274
s 16   274
s 18   274
s 19   275
s 22   276
s 25   270
s 26   276
s 30   276
s 42   276
s 44   276
s 45   269
s 50(2)   272
s 60(1)   268
Sched 1   271, 275
Sched 2   271
Sched 3   271, 275
Sched 4   271
Consumer Credit Act 1974   24
s 61   39
s 137   46
s 138   46
Consumer Protection Act 1987   110, 204, 214
s 1(1)   179
s 2(2)   180, 184
   (3)   180, 184
s 3(1)   182
   (2)   182
s 4(1)   183, 184, 185
s 5   185
s 6(6)   186
s 7   187
s 10(1)   214, 218, 219, 220
    (2)   219
    (3)   219
    (4)   220
s 11(1)   220, 221, 222
    (2)   220
s 12   221, 222
    (1)   221
    (2)   221
    (3)   221
    (4)   221
s 13(1)   218, 222

s 14   *222, 223*

s 15   *223*

s 16   *223, 224*

   (5)   *224*

s 17   *223, 224*

s 19   *219*

s 20(1)   *207, 208, 209*

   (2)   *207*

   (6)   *207, 208*

s 24   *210*

s 25   *210*

s 26   *210*

s 27   *224*

s 35   *224*

s 39   *209, 220*

s 41   *221*

Sched 1   *186*

Sched 2   *222*

Sched 3   *224*

Consumer Safety Act 1978   *221, 222*

Contracts (Rights of Third Parties) Act 1999   *13, 20, 73, 95*

s 1(1)   *20, 21*

s 2   *21*

Copyright Act 1956   *292*

Copyright, Designs and Patents Act 1988   *284, 286, 290*

s 1   *290*

s 3(1)   *291*

  (b)   *290*

s 4(1)   *291*

s 16   *291*

s 24   *292*

s 28   *293*

s 50A   *292*

s 50B   *292*

s 50C   *292*

ss 77–89   *293*

s 84   *293*

s 107   *293*

s 107A   *294*

s 171   *284*

s 213   *294, 295*

s 227   *295*

s 237   *295*

Data Protection Act 1998   *243*

Development of Tourism Act 1969   *211*

s 18   *211*

Employment Rights Act 1996   *263, 265*
Factors Act 1889   *154*
  s 2(1)   *156*
  s 8   *154*
  s 9   *155*
Fair Trading Act 1973   *61, 268, 271, 276*
  s 2   *277*
  s 6   *277*
  s 7   *277*
  s 8   *277*
  s 9   *277*
  s 44   *276*
  s 46   *276*
  s 56   *278*
  s 56A   *278*
  s 81   *278*
  s 84(1)   *278*
Family Law Reform Act 1969   *18*
Financial Services Act 1986   *82*
Financial Services and Markets Act 2000   *82*
Food Safety Act 1990   *218, 224, 226, 229, 243, 247, 248*
  s 1   *229, 230*
  s 3   *230*
  s 7   *232, 233*
    (1)   *232, 233*
  s 8   *232, 233, 234, 238*
    (2)   *233*
  s 9   *241*
    (2)   *234*
  s 10   *233, 234, 235*
  s 11   *234, 235*
  s 12(1)   *236, 241*
    (2)   *236*
  s 13   *234, 236*
  s 14(1)   *233, 237, 238, 240*
    (2)   *237*
  s 15   *238, 240*
    (3)   *238*
  s 16   *239*
  s 17   *239*
  s 18   *239*
  s 19   *239*
  s 20(1)   *241*
  s 21   *240*
    (2)–(4)   *240, 241*
  s 22   *241*

s 40   *239*
s 53   *230*
Food Standards Act 1999   *241, 242*
  s 5(1)   *242*
  s 6   *242*
  s 7   *242*
  s 8   *242*
  s 10   *242, 243*
  s 11   *242*
  s 12   *243*
  s 13   *243*
  s 14   *243*
  s 17   *236, 243*
  s 19   *242*
Gaming Act 1845   *318*
Health and Safety at Work etc Act 1974   *224*
  s 6(1)   *224, 225*
    (2)   *225*
    (3)   *225*
    (4)   *225*
    (5)   *225*
    (6)   *226*
    (7)   *226*
    (8)   *226*
  s 47   *226*
Hire Purchase Act 1964   *157*
  s 27   *157*
Insurance Brokers (Registration) Act 1977   *323*
Law of Property (Miscellaneous Provisions) Act 1989   *24*
  s 2   *24*
Law Reform (Contributory Negligence) Act 1945   *42, 167*
Law Reform (Frustrated Contracts) Act 1943   *66*
  s 1   *66*
Limitation Act 1980   *70, 186, 187*
  s 5   *70*
  s 8   *70*
  s 11A   *186*
  s 14(1A)   *186*
  s 29   *71*
  s 32   *71*
Local Government Act 1972   *206*
  s 222   *206*
Local Government Act 1988   *261*
  s 1   *261*
  s 2   *261*
  s 3   *261*

s 4   *261*
s 7   *261*
s 13   *262*
s 14   *262*
Sched 1   *261*
Local Government Act 1992   *262*
  s 8   *262*
  s 9   *262*
Local Government, Planning and Land Act 1980   *260*
  s 7   *261*
Misrepresentation Act 1967   *25*
  s 2(1)   *42*
    (2)   *42*
  s 3   *58*
Patents Act 1977   *286, 287*
  s 39   *289*
  s 40   *289*
  s 50(2)(a)–(c)   *288*
  s 60   *288*
    (1)   *288*
    (5)   *288*
Pharmacy and Poisons Act 1933   *4*
Powers of Attorney Act 1971   *74*
Powers of Criminal Courts (Sentencing) Act 2000   *193*
  s 130   *193*
Prices Act 1974   *210*
  s 4   *210*
Property Misdescriptions Act 1991   *194*
  s 1   *211, 212*
  s 2(1)   *212*
    (2)   *212*
Registered Designs Act 1949   *296*
  s 8(2)   *296*
Resale Prices Act 1976   *47, 268*
Restrictive Practices Courts Act 1976   *47, 268*
Restrictive Trade Practices Act 1976   *47, 268, 271*
Restrictive Trade Practices Act 1977   *47, 268*
Sale of Goods Act 1893   *95*
Sale of Goods Act 1979   *30, 31, 95, 231, 312, 313*
  s 2(1)   *96*
  s 3(3)   *19*
  s 5   *142*
  s 10   *134*
  s 11(2)   *96, 113*
  s 12   *30, 31, 57, 96, 97, 98, 114, 116, 117, 120, 121, 151*
    (1)   *37, 97*
    (2)   *99*

(3) *97, 99*
(5) *99*
s 13 *30, 36, 99, 100, 101, 102, 114, 115, 116, 120, 121, 130*
(1) *99*
(2) *100*
(3) *100*
s 14 *30, 31, 32, 102, 103, 104, 114, 121, 122, 186, 194*
s 14(2) *102, 105, 107, 110, 114, 121*
(2A) *102, 107, 108, 121*
(2B) *102, 108, 109*
(2C) *103, 104, 113*
(3) *54, 109, 110, 111, 121*
(6) *103, 110*
s 15 *30, 31, 57, 96, 110, 113, 114, 115, 116, 117, 120*
(1) *112*
(2) *112, 113*
s 15A *31, 96, 109, 114, 116, 117*
s 16 *141, 145*
s 17 *142, 145*
s 18 *142, 143, 146*
Rule 1 *143, 149*
Rule 2 *143, 144*
Rule 3 *143, 144*
Rule 4 *143, 144, 145*
Rule 5 *143, 145, 146, 147*
s 19 *141, 143, 147*
s 20 *141, 149, 314*
(2) *149*
(3) *149*
s 20A *128, 149, 150, 151*
s 20B *128, 150*
s 21(1) *98, 151*
s 22(1) *152*
s 23 *37, 153*
s 24 *154, 155*
s 25(1) *155, 157*
(2) *156*
s 28 *127*
s 29(3) *129*
(4) *128*
s 30(1) *129, 130, 246*
(2) *129, 130*
(2A) *129, 130*
(2B) *129, 130*
(2C) *129, 130*
(2D) *129, 130*
(2E) *130*

(3)   *130*
(5)   *130*
s 31   *130*
s 32(1)   *128*
(3)   *128*
s 33   *128*
s 34(1)   *105, 113, 131*
s 35(1)   *121, 131, 132, 133*
(2)   *113, 131, 133*
(4)   *131, 132, 133*
(6)   *132, 133*
(7)   *133*
s 35A   *134*
s 36   *134*
s 37   *135*
s 38   *134*
s 39(1)   *136*
s 47(2)   *137*
s 48   *137, 155*
s 49(1)   *135*
(2)   *135*
s 50   *135*
(3)   *136*
s 51   *138*
(3)   *138*
s 53   *96, 139*
(3)   *139*
s 61   *96, 104, 128, 141*
Sale of Goods (Amendment) Act 1994   *153*
Sale of Goods (Amendment) Act 1995   *146, 149*
Sale and Supply of Goods Act 1994   *95, 120*
Statute of Frauds 1677   *24*
s 4   *24*
Supply of Goods (Implied Terms) Act 1973   *57, 121*
s 8   *57, 121*
s 9   *121*
s 10   *121*
s 11   *57, 121*
Supply of Goods and Services Act 1982   *30, 32, 97, 120, 201*
s 2   *120, 121*
s 3   *120, 121*
s 4   *120, 121*
(2A)   *121*
s 5   *120, 121*
s 5A   *121*
s 7   *120, 121, 122*
s 8   *120, 121*

s 9   *103, 120, 121*
  (2A)   *121*
s 10   *120, 121*
s 10A *121*
s 12   *122*
s 13   *32, 122, 123, 174*
s 14   *32, 124*
  (1)   *124*
s 15   *32, 122*
  (1)   *124*
s 16   *125*
Trade Descriptions Act 1968   *25, 104, 130, 193, 224, 286, 301*
  s 1   *36, 54, 183, 193, 194, 238, 240, 241*
   (1)(a)   *197, 198*
    (b)   *195, 199, 200, 201, 205*
  s 2(1)   *101, 195, 196, 197, 199, 200*
  s 3(1)   *196*
   (2)   *196*
   (3)   *196, 197*
   (4)   *197*
  s 4(1)   *197*
   (2)   *198*
   (3)   *198*
  s 6   *199*
  s 11   *200, 208*
  s 12   *195*
  s 14(1)   *54, 194, 201, 202, 203*
  s 20   *204*
  s 23   *206, 217, 241*
  s 24   *204, 205, 206, 209, 217, 218, 226*
  s 25   *205*
  ss 27–29   *301*
  s 33   *301*
  s 39   *194*
Trade Marks Act 1938   *296, 297, 298*
  s 9   *297*
Trade Marks Act 1994   *184, 286, 296, 297, 298*
  s 1(1)   *298*
  s 3   *299*
  s 5   *299*
   (1)   *299*
   (2)   *299*
   (3)   *299*
  s 10   *300*
   (1)   *300*
   (2)   *300*
   (3)   *300*

s 12(1)   *303*
s 49   *298*
s 92   *201, 301, 302*
   (1)   *301*
   (2)   *301*
   (3)   *302*
s 93   *301*
Trade Union Reform and Employment Rights Act 1993   *263*
Trade Union and Labour Relations (Consolidation) Act 1992   *265*
  s 188   *265*
Unfair Contract Terms Act 1977   *50, 53, 54, 55, 58, 61, 122*
  s 2   *56, 125*
  s 3   *56*
  s 4   *56*
  s 5   *56*
  s 6(1)   *57, 58, 61, 111*
   (2)   *57*
   (3)   *55, 57*
  s 7(2)   *57, 61, 122*
   (3)   *55, 58*
  s 8   *58*
  s 11   *55*
  s 12   *54, 115*
  Sched 2   *55, 57*
Weights and Measures Act 1985   *130, 224, 245*
  s 28(1)   *245, 246*
  s 29   *247*
  s 30(1)   *247*
   (2)   *247*
  s 31(1)   *247*
  s 33   *245, 247*
  s 34   *247*
  s 35(2)   *248*
   (3)   *248*
  s 36   *248*
  s 37   *245*
  s 41   *246*
  s 50(5)   *249, 250*
  s 51   *250*
  Sched 1   *245*

Statutory instruments

All-Terrain Motor Vehicles (Safety) Regulations 1989 (SI 1989/2288)   *221*
Commercial Agents (Council Directive) Regulations 1993 (SI 1993/3053)   *73, 87*

reg 2(1)   *87*
reg 3(1)   *87, 88*
    (2)   *87*
reg 4   *84, 88*
reg 5(1)   *88*
reg 6   *88*
reg 7   *88*
reg 10   *88*
reg 12   *88*
reg 13   *88*
reg 14   *88*
reg 15   *89*
reg 17   *89*
reg 20   *91*
Chemical (Hazard Information and Packing for Supply) Regulations 1994
    (SI 1994/3247)   *227*
Cigarette Lighter Refill (Safety) Regulations 1999 (SI 1999/1844)   *221*
Civil Procedure Rules 1998 (SI 1998/3132)   *187*
Collective Redundancies and Transfer of Undertakings (Protection of Employment)
    (Amendment) Regulations 1995 (SI 1995/2587)   *263, 265*
Consumer Protection (Distance Selling) Regulations 2000 (SI 2000/2334)   *11*
Consumer Protection Act 1987 (Product Liability) (Modification) Order 2000
    (SI 2000/2771)   *180*
Consumer Transactions (Restrictions on Statements) Order 1976
    (SI 1976/1813)   *61*
Control of Substances Hazardous to Health Regulations 1994
    (SI 1994/3246)   *227*
Cosmetic Products (Safety) Regulations 1996 (SI 1996/2925)   *221*
Dangerous Substances and Preparations (Nickel) (Safety) Regulations 2000
    (SI 2000/1668)   *221*
Dangerous Substances and Preparations (Safety) (Consolidation) Regulations 1994
    (SI 1994/2844)   *221*
Fireworks (Safety) Regulations 1997 (SI 1997/2294)   *221*
Food Labelling Regulations 1996 (SI 1996/1499)   *238*
Food Safety (Northern Ireland) Order 1991 (SI 1991/762 (NI 7))   *243*
Furniture and Furnishings (Fire) (Safety) Regulations 1988 (SI 1988/1324)   *221*
Gas Cooking Appliances (Safety) Regulations 1989 (SI 1989/149)   *221*
General Product Safety Regulations 1994 (SI 1994/2328)   *110, 214, 222*
  reg 7   *215, 216, 217*
  reg 8   *216*
  reg 9   *215, 216, 217*
  reg 12   *217*
  reg 13   *217*
  reg 14   *217*
  reg 15   *217*
Health and Safety (Display Screen Equipment) Regulations 1992
    (SI 1992/2792)   *227*

Heating Appliances (Fireguards) (Safety) Regulations 1991 (SI 1991/2693)   *221*
Low Voltage Electrical Equipment (Safety) Regulations 1989 (SI 1989/728)   *221*
Management of Health and Safety at Work Regulations 1992
    (SI 1992/2051)   *227*
Manual Handling Operations Regulations 1992 (SI 1992/2793)   *227*
Motor Vehicles Tyres (Safety) Regulations 1994 (SI 1994/3117)   *221*
Oral Snuff (Safety) Regulations 1989 (SI 1989/2347)   *221*
Pencils and Graphic Instruments (Safety) Regulations 1998 (SI 1998/2406)
    205, 221
Personal Protective Equipment at Work Regulations 1992 (SI 1992/2966)   *227*
Price Indications (Bureaux de Change) (No 2) Regulations 1992
    (SI 1992/737)   *210*
Price Indications (Method of Payment) Regulations 1991 (SI 1991/199)   *210*
Price Indications (Resale of Tickets) Regulations (SI 1994/3248)   *210*
Price Marking (Food and Drink on Premises) Order 1979 (SI 1979/361)   *211*
Price Marking Order 1991 (SI 1991/1382)   *211*
Price Marking Order 1999 (SI 1999/3042)   *211*
Property Misdescriptions (Specified Matters) Order 1992 (SI 1992/2834)   *212*
Provision and Use of Work Equipment Regulations 1992 (SI 1992/2932)   *227*
Public Contracts (Works, Services and Supply) (Amendment) Regulations 2000
    (SI 2000/2009)   *257, 259*
Public Services Contracts Regulations 1993 (SI 1993/3228)   *257*
Public Supply Contracts Regulations 1995 (SI 1995/2679)   *257*
Public Works Contracts Regulations 1991 (SI 1991/2680)   *256, 257*
Tourism (Sleeping Accommodation Price Display) Order 1999
    (SI 1977/1877)   *211*
Toys (Safety) Regulations 1989 (SI 1989/1275)   *221*
Transfer of Undertakings (Protection of Employment) Regulations 1981
    (SI 1981/1794)   *263*
  reg 5   *264*
    (2)   *264*
  reg 10   *264*
Transfer of Undertakings (Protection of Employment) (Amendment) Regulations
    1987 (SI 1987/442)   *263*
Unfair Terms in Consumer Contracts Regulations 1999 (SI 1999/2083)   *53*
  reg 3   *58*
  reg 5(1)   *59*
    (3)   *59*
  reg 6   *59*
  reg 10   *60*
  reg 12   *61*
  Sched 1   *60*
  Sched 2   *60, 61*
Utilities Contracts Regulations 1996 (SI 1996/2991)   *257*
Weights and Measures (Packaged Goods) Regulations 1986 (SI 1986/2044)   *248*
Workplace (Health, Safety and Welfare) Regulations 1992 (SI 1992/3004)   *227*

EU legislation

Treaties

EC Treaty
art 28 (previously art 30)   *289, 302*
art 30 (previously art 36)   *290, 303*
art 81 (previously art 85)   *268, 269, 270, 279, 280, 281*
art 82 (previously art 86)   *268, 269, 270, 279, 280, 281*

Directives

Directive 75/106/EEC   *248*
Directive 76/211/EEC   *248*
Directive 77/187/EEC   *263*
Directive 85/374/EEC   *179, 184, 187*
   art 16   *187*
Directive 86/653/EEC   *87*
Directive 89/104/EEC   *297*
Directive 89/665/EEC   *256*
Directive 92/13/EEC   *257*
Directive 92/50/EEC   *257*
Directive 92/59/EEC   *214*
Directive 93/36/EEC   *257*
Directive 93/37/EEC   *257*
Directive 93/38/EEC   *257*
Directive 93/98/EEC   *291*
Directive 98/50/EC   *263*
Directive 98/71/EC   *296*
Directive 99/34/EC   *179, 180*
Directive 1999/44/EC   *115*
   art 1   *115*
   art 2   *115*
   art 3   *115, 117*
   art 4   *117*
   art 5   *117*
   art 6   *117*

International legislation

Berne Convention for the Protection of Literary and Artistic Works 1886
   290, 291

Convention on the Contract for the International Carriage of Goods by Rail
(CMI)   *312*
Community Patent Convention (CPC) 1975   *286*
Convention on the Contract for the International Carriage of Goods by Road
(CMR) (1956)   *312*
European Patents Convention 1973   *286*
General Agreement on Tariffs and Trade (GATT) – Uruguay round 1994   *291*
Madrid Protocol 1989   *297*
Paris Convention on the Protection of Industrial Property 1883   *297*
Patent Cooperation Treaty 1970   *286*
Restatement of Torts (2d)   *178*
  s 402A   *178*
Trade Related Aspects of Intellectual Property Rights (TRIPS) 1994   *291*
Universal Copyright Convention 1952   *290*

In loving memory of Ivor Griffiths
Husband, Father and Friend
1947–2001

Part I The law of contract

1 Contract formation

1.1 Introduction

Given the pivotal role of contract law in purchasing, it is vital to have a clear understanding of the elements that create a legally binding contract enforceable under English law. These elements are threefold: agreement (offer and acceptance), consideration (the price of the contract) and contractual intention (the intention of the parties to be contractually bound). These elements have developed through many decades of judicial interpretation with the resultant evolution of a relatively certain body of rules governing the creation of legally binding, enforceable contracts.

1.2 Offer and acceptance

Agreement between the contracting parties, the *consensus ad idem*, is crucial to a contract. Thus, for example, if A is going to sell a quantity of gravel to B, they will need to agree on the quantity, quality, price, delivery date and place of delivery. Only when all these details have been agreed will it be possible for a contract to come into being.

In practice, agreements come about when one of the contracting parties (the offeror) makes an offer which the other contracting party (the offeree) accepts. It is possible that the offer will be accepted immediately without any further discussion, as, for example, when a consumer pays the fixed price for a bar of chocolate, but, in a business context, it is more likely that some negotiation about terms will take place before agreement is finally reached.

1.3 Invitations to treat

It is important to distinguish at this preliminary stage between an offer and an invitation to treat, for the acceptance of one will result in a contract, whereas the other is incapable of acceptance at all. Invitations to treat have no binding effect and are really a means of seeking information and inviting a prospective offeror to make a contractual offer. As such, they are in the nature of precontractual negotiations or statements.

Invitations to treat may arise in a variety of circumstances. It is well recognised that newspaper advertisements for the sale of goods and services are usually, though not always (**Carlill** *v* **Carbolic Smoke Ball Co** (1893)), invitations to treat, this being held to be so in the case of **Partridge** *v* **Crittenden** (1968). Similarly, the display of goods in a self-service shop (**Pharmaceutical Society of Great Britain** *v* **Boots Cash Chemists (Southern) Ltd** (1953)) and the display of goods in a shop window (**Fisher** *v* **Bell** (1961)) have both been held to constitute invitations to treat only and not contractual offers. In both of these situations the display is merely the seller displaying the goods that he has available for purchase. The contractual offer is made by the prospective purchaser when he offers to buy the goods, the seller then being at liberty to accept the offer and sell the goods, or alternatively to refuse the offer and retain the goods.

In **Pharmaceutical Society of Great Britain** *v* **Boots Cash Chemists (Southern) Ltd,** the defendants ran a retail self-service chemist's shop in which customers selected the items they wished to purchase from display shelves and took them to a cash desk to pay. Among the products on display in the shop were 'over the counter' drugs which could only be sold legally under the supervision of a registered pharmacist, who was stationed near the cash desk. At issue was whether the display of the drugs on the shelves was a contractual offer or merely an invitation to treat. If it was an offer, the defendants would be guilty of an offence against the Pharmacy and Poisons Act 1933, which required any sale to be 'effected by, or under the supervision of, a registered pharmacist'. The Court of Appeal held that the display was merely an invitation to treat, the contractual offer being made by the customer at the cash desk under the supervision of the pharmacist.

The most recent development in this area is undoubtedly e-commerce and the sale of goods and services via the Internet. Though this development relies on recent technology, the law underlying the contractual position is the same as that applicable to more traditional methods of selling. Thus, the advertisement on the Internet would constitute an invitation to treat with the contractual offer occurring when the prospective purchaser registers their wish to buy.

1.4 Status of tenders

The status of tenders illustrates well the distinction between invitations to treat and contractual offers. Any invitation inviting prospective contracting parties to submit a tender is an invitation to treat. The tender itself forms the contractual offer, which is capable of acceptance or rejection. Tenders are discussed later in the chapter.

1.5 Offers

A contractual offer exists when an offeror makes known the terms upon which he is prepared to contract and promises to be bound by those terms if they are accepted by the offeree. An offer can be made to an individual person or company (a bilateral offer) or alternatively can be made to the world at large (a unilateral offer), in which case it can be accepted by anyone who knows of the offer and who complies with its terms. The validity of unilateral offers was established in **Carlill v Carbolic Smoke Ball Co**, in which the defendants were the manufacturers of a medicinal product called 'The Carbolic Smoke Ball'. They placed an advertisement in a newspaper stating that they would pay £100 to any person who contracted flu after buying and using the smoke ball correctly. They further stated that, as a token of their sincerity, they had put £1,000 on deposit in the bank. The plaintiff purchased a smoke ball and used it according to the instructions but nonetheless contracted flu. She claimed £100 from the defendants, who refused to pay arguing that the advertisement was merely an advertising puff and that it was impossible to contract with the world. In an action to recover the £100, the Court of Appeal held that Mrs Carlill was entitled to the money. The company had made an offer to the world at large which Mrs Carlill had accepted by her conduct.

The same principle would hold true for 'free offers' linked to the purchase of an item. Thus, for example, if a retailer places an advertisement stating that he will provide a free item to anyone purchasing his product, he is legally obliged so to do. Any person may accept his offer by conduct through the purchase of the product in question and thereafter is legally entitled to receive the free item as held in **Esso Petroleum Ltd v Commissioners of Customs and Excise** (1976).

1.5.1 Termination of offers

An offer may come to an end in one of seven ways.

Acceptance
The offer ripens into a contract when it is accepted unconditionally by the offeree.

Rejection
The offeree may reject the offer, after which he cannot seek to revive it.

Counter-offer
An offer exists only as long as the terms of it remain unchanged. Thus a counter-offer proposed by the offeree in which he seeks to alter a term of the original offer will destroy the original offer. Once destroyed, the offer cannot be revived, as held in **Hyde v Wrench** (1840), in which the defendant offered to sell some real estate to the plaintiff for £1,000. Two days later, the plaintiff made a counter-offer of £950, which the defendant refused. Subsequently, the plaintiff contacted the defendant agreeing to purchase the land for £1,000 and sought an order of specific performance. The court refused to grant one finding that the offer to pay £950 was a counter-offer that had permanently destroyed the original offer and rendered it incapable of acceptance.

When considering counter-offers, it is important to remember two things: first, that a counter-offer may be clothed in the garb of an acceptance and, second, that an inquiry for further information is not a counter-offer and does not affect the continued existence of the offer. In respect of the first, where an offeree seeks to accept the offer while stipulating some amendment to a term of the offer, it is really a counter-offer and not an acceptance. In respect of the second, the case of **Stevenson *v* McLean** (1880) is instructive. The defendants offered to sell a quantity of iron to the plaintiffs for 40s net cash, the offer being held open for two days. On the second day, the plaintiffs sent a telegram to the defendants asking if it was possible to have credit terms over two months. Not receiving a reply to their first telegram, the plaintiffs sent a second telegram to the defendants three hours later accepting the original offer. In the intervening period, the defendants had sold the iron to a third party. It was held that the defendants were in breach of contract as the first telegram was only seeking additional information and was not a counter-offer. As such, the original offer was still open at the time that the plaintiff purported to accept it.

Revocation

The offeror can withdraw the offer at any time prior to acceptance, as held in **Byrne *v* Van Tienhoven** (1880). This is so even if the offer was stated to be available for a specified period unless the offeree has provided consideration for the offer to remain open until the specified deadline. The provision of such consideration would create a separate collateral contract under which the offeror is contractually bound to keep the offer open for the agreed period and may require that the offer be restricted to one particular offeree. Such 'lock out' agreements, which prevent anyone else from accepting the offer for the period of agreement, were considered in **Walford *v* Miles** (1992) and **Pitt *v* PHH Asset Management Ltd** (1993). The net effect of the decisions was to confirm that 'lock out' agreements are enforceable provided that valuable consideration has been paid and that the agreement is for a specified period. A 'lock out' agreement for an unspecified period will not be enforced.

The issue of revocation is of particular relevance in respect of those offers when acceptance will be by conduct as, for example, in unilateral offers such as in **Carlill *v* Carbolic Smoke Ball Co**. It would be unfair to allow the offeror to revoke the offer once the offeree has, in good faith, started but not yet completed the acceptance by conduct. This was the decision in **Errington *v* Errington & Woods** (1952), in which a father promised his son and daughter-in-law that if they (the son and his wife) paid all the mortgage payments, then he (the father) would give them the house. The Court of Appeal held that the father could not revoke the offer as long as the children kept up the payments.

A revocation of the offer is not effective until the offeree receives actual notice of it. However, the offeror is not required personally to inform the offeree of the revocation; it is sufficient if the offeree receives the information from a reliable third party. In **Dickinson *v* Dodds** (1876) the defendant offered to sell a house to the plaintiff, the offer to remain open for a specified period. The day before the period was due to expire, the defendant sold the house to a third party, the plaintiff hearing of this fact that evening from another reliable person. The following day, the plaintiff delivered a letter of acceptance to the defendant. The Court of Appeal held that there was no contract as the offer had been validly revoked. The plaintiff had been aware of the sale before the attempted acceptance.

Failure of a precondition

The existence of the offer may be subject to the offeree satisfying some precondition. If the offeree fails to satisfy the condition, the offer will fail to take effect, as in

Financings Ltd *v* **Stimson** (1962), in which a customer intended to buy a car and duly completed a hire-purchase proposal form. The car was subsequently stolen from the dealer's premises and was badly damaged. The following day the hire-purchase company purported to accept the offer. The Court of Appeal held that there was no contract as there was a condition precedent in the offer that the goods on acceptance would be in the same condition as at the time of the offer. As they were not, the offer was incapable of acceptance.

Lapse of time

If an offer is stated to be for a specific period, it will lapse automatically when that period expires. Otherwise, it will lapse after a reasonable time.

Death

The death of the offeror will terminate the offer automatically as long as the offeree was aware of the death prior to acceptance. If he was not, it seems that the offeror's estate will be bound by the contract unless the offer necessarily involved some element personal to the offeror, for example painting a portrait. The death of the offeree terminates the offer.

1.6 Tenders

The distinction between invitations to treat and contractual offers is most pertinent in respect of tenders, a matter of particular interest to both private businesses and those operating in the public sector. The legal status of tenders is important. Suppose, for example, that a company issues a circular inviting tenders for a contract to supply and fit carpeting to be laid in its 60 retail premises. Is the company bound to consider any tender that it receives and accept the highest, lowest or, indeed, any bid? The case of **Blackpool & Fylde Aero Club Ltd** *v* **Blackpool BC** (1990) suggests that there is a contractual obligation to consider all tenders that are received by any deadline set and which comply with all the requirements of the invitation to submit such tender. In that case Blackpool Borough Council invited tenders for a concession to run pleasure flights from Blackpool airport. The terms of the invitation were that tenders were to be submitted sealed in the envelope provided before 12 noon on a date specified. The plaintiff's tender, which complied with the prescribed form, was placed in the council's letterbox at 11 am on the relevant day. However, council staff failed to clear the letterbox at noon resulting in the plaintiff's tender being deemed late and not considered. The court held the council liable for breach of contract holding that the plaintiff had a contractual right to have its tender considered as it had complied in every respect with the terms of the invitation.

While there may be an obligation to consider all tenders validly submitted, the decision in **Spencer** *v* **Harding** (1870) suggests that there is no obligation to accept the highest bid or indeed any bid at all. There may be good reasons for deciding not to proceed with the contract or alternatively to accept a bid which, though not the highest, may offer other attractions. It is clear that the wording of the circular may be crucial. In **Spencer** *v* **Harding**, the defendants issued a circular stating that they had been instructed to offer for sale by tender to the wholesale trade, the stock-in-trade of Messrs G Eilbeck & Co. The plaintiffs submitted the highest tender, which the defendants refused to accept. The plaintiffs alleged that the circular constituted a contractual offer with the implication that the highest tender would be accepted. The plaintiffs had lodged the highest tender. The Court of Common Pleas held that the defendants were not liable to the plaintiffs and that the circular merely constituted an invitation to treat with no implication that they would necessarily accept any tender.

However, the court considered that the position would have been different if the circular had continued by making a statement that the highest tender would be accepted. In that situation, the circular would have constituted a unilateral contractual offer capable of acceptance by the highest bidder. The key issue appears to be whether the circular is merely seeking information or whether it evinces a definite intention to contract on specified terms with an appropriate bidder. The distinction is illustrated in the decision of **Harvela Investments Ltd** *v* **Royal Trust Co of Canada Ltd** (1986), which dealt with the issue of competitive tendering. In that case, the defendants wanted to sell some shares, the two obvious prospective purchasers being the plaintiffs and the second defendants. Both were invited to tender for the shares by a sealed competitive tender, the defendants confirming that 'if the offer made by you is the highest offer received by us, we bind ourselves to accept such offer providing that such offer complies with the terms of this telex'. In the event, the plaintiffs bid $2,175,000, while the second defendants bid $2,100,000 or $100,000 more than any other higher bid, a 'referential bid'. The defendants sold the shares to the second defendants. The House of Lords held that the defendants were obliged to sell the shares to the plaintiffs as their statement amounted to a contractual offer to accept the highest bid, i.e. that of the plaintiffs. To accept the 'referential bid' of the second defendants was contrary to the offer to accept the highest of the sealed competitive bids.

As explained earlier, if a circular or advertisement inviting tenders is merely an invitation to treat, any resultant tender is a contractual offer which the offeree can accept or reject. If accepted, the offer matures into a contract capable of enforcement.

The resultant contract may be of two types, either for the immediate supply of goods or for the supply of goods usually at a fixed price as and when ordered during a contractually agreed period, a 'standing offer'. Thus, for example, in a contract to supply a local authority with 1,000 tons of rock salt to be spread on the roads in winter, the successful supplier would be obliged to provide 1,000 tons of rock salt on the due delivery date. By contrast, if the contract was to supply up to 1,000 tons as and when ordered by the local authority during a period of 12 months, there would be no guarantee that any order would actually be placed. Nonetheless, there would be a contractual obligation to satisfy any order placed up to a total of 1,000 tons during the agreed period as indicated in the case of **Great Northern Rly Co** *v* **Witham** (1873).

Other established invitations to treat include the issue of company prospectuses for the sale of shares, in which the contractual offer is made by the prospective purchaser, and auctions, where the auctioneer merely invites prospective bidders to make bids, which constitute the contractual offers.

1.6.1 Compulsory competitive tendering

The volume and significance of tendering has increased with the advent of compulsory competitive tendering (CCT) in the public sector. This topic is considered at length in Chapter 17 on aspects of outsourcing.

1.7 Acceptance

A contract comes into being when the offer has been validly and unconditionally accepted by the offeree.

1.7.1 Certainty of terms

The underlying rationale of contract is *consensus* between the contracting parties. Thus, the acceptance must match the offer with both parties certain of the contractual terms. The contract is of no use if there is uncertainty over essential terms contained therein. Nonetheless, it is clear that an apparent uncertainty may be acceptable within a valid, legally binding contract in situations where the parties might be assumed to know the contractual terms either because of previous dealings or because of accepted business practice as in **Hillas & Co Ltd *v* Arcos Ltd** (1934). However, if neither of these aids to construction exists, the court will have no option but to consider the terms of the agreement as they appear, and if they are too speculative or ambiguous then it would seem that no contract will exist, as in **Scammel *v* Ouston** (1941), in which the respondent wanted to buy a motor-van on hire-purchase terms from the appellants. After some negotiations, the buyers placed an order containing the statement 'This order is given on the understanding that the balance of purchase price can be had on hire-purchase terms over a period of two years'. The hire-purchase terms were never agreed. The buyers sued the seller, who appealed, the case ultimately reaching the House of Lords. The court held that there was no contract as the financial terms were not sufficiently certain. The court further held that there was insufficient evidence of contractual intention.

This approach was reaffirmed in the decision of **CPC Consolidated Pool Carriers GmbH *v* CTM CIA Transmediterranea SA** (1994), in which the Commercial Court considered the alleged existence of an international contract of carriage and confirmed that as a major term of the contract had not been finalised, the contract did not exist for want of *consensus*.

1.7.2 Letters of intent

A related issue is letters of intent whereby one party issues a document to another party making clear their intention to enter a contract with them at some point in the future. This would arise, for example, where a building company tendering to a local authority for a contract to build a new school might issue letters of intent to sub-contractors that they would wish to employ if they gained the contract. There is no intention to be bound contractually at that stage and no contractual agreement reached and yet it is possible for work to begin on the strength of a letter of intent. The leading case is **British Steel Corpn *v* Cleveland Bridge and Engineering Co Ltd** (1984), in which the defendants negotiated with the plaintiffs for the latter to manufacture some specialist steel nodes to be used in the construction of a bridge. During negotiations, the defendants sent a letter of intent to the plaintiffs proposing that any contract would be on the defendants' standard terms. The plaintiffs were not prepared to contract on those terms. Work was completed and the plaintiffs sued for the price, the defendants counterclaiming for damages for late delivery. The court held that there was no contract, merely a letter of intent, final terms not having been agreed. Nonetheless, the plaintiffs were entitled to claim a *quantum meruit* for the goods supplied.

1.7.3 Battle of the forms

Certainty of terms is of particular significance in the business world because of the widespread use of standard form contracts. The offeror may wish to contract on his standard terms, while the offeree may want to accept on his own standard terms. This is the so-called 'battle of the forms'. The leading authority on this issue is the decision in **Butler Machine Tool Co *v* Ex-Cell-O Corpn** (1979). The plaintiff sellers offered to sell a machine tool to the defendants for £75,535 with delivery ten months later. The offer was on the plaintiff's standard terms, which included a price variation clause under which the plaintiff could charge the price prevailing at the time of supply. Resultant upon this offer, the defendant buyers placed an order using their own standard form of contract, the terms of which did not contain a price variation clause. The order form contained a tear-off slip at the bottom confirming agreement with the buyer's terms, which the sellers duly completed and returned. The sellers attempted to charge the buyers an extra £2,892 relying on the price variation clause but the Court of Appeal held that the plaintiff sellers could not charge the additional sum as their return of the tear-off slip signified an agreement to contract on the buyer's terms.

Discussions about the case suggest that the party who 'fires the last shot' will win the day. This would accord with the traditional approach by holding that the submission of each standard form is, in effect, a counter-offer and thus that the last form submitted contains the final contractual terms. In practice, it is often not as clear-cut as this and will depend upon the facts of the individual case, as in **Rimeco Riggelsen & Metal Co *v* Queenborough Rolling Mill Co** (1995).

1.7.4 Communication of acceptance

Acceptance must be communicated to be effective, with the contract coming into being at the time and place where the offeror receives the communication. Certain rules apply relating to the validity and communication of acceptance.

Knowledge of the offer

Acceptance cannot take place where the offeree did not know of the offer. There is no *consensus*.

Silence is not acceptance

The offeror cannot stipulate that silence by the offeree will constitute acceptance, as demonstrated in **Felthouse *v* Bindley** (1862), in which the plaintiff was negotiating the purchase of a horse from his nephew. Finally, he wrote to his nephew stating that if he did not hear further he would assume that he could buy the horse. The nephew decided to sell the horse to the plaintiff but failed to withdraw it from an auction. The defendant auctioneer, unaware of this, sold the horse and was sued in conversion by the plaintiff. The court held that mental acceptance by the nephew was not sufficient to constitute contractual acceptance. As such, the plaintiff had not bought the horse and thus could not sue the defendant in conversion.

This provision also covers the situation of unsolicited goods in which sellers of goods send unsolicited goods to prospective purchasers stipulating that unless the goods are returned within a specified period the seller will assume that the recipient wants to buy them. Typically, the goods are followed a short time later by an invoice. On the basis that the seller cannot stipulate that silence is assent, no contract exists, but many consumers, unaware of their rights, would feel obliged to pay if they had not returned the goods within the specified period. This abuse is currently dealt with by the Consumer Protection (Distance Selling) Regulations 2000.

Acceptance can be by conduct

The offeror may waive his right to receive communication of acceptance and allow acceptance to occur by the offeree's conduct, as in a unilateral offer such as in **Carlill**. Further, acceptance by conduct may occur through the facts of the situation. In **Trentham Ltd *v* Archital Luxfer** (1993), Steyn LJ was prepared to hold that a contract had come into existence through conduct even though it was difficult to analyse the contract in terms of offer and acceptance or identify the moment at which the contract was created. Trentham Ltd were building and civil engineering contractors who had been engaged as the main contractors for a building contract. They negotiated with Archital Luxfer for the latter to install aluminium windows, doors and screens in the premises. Work began before the negotiations were complete although both parties clearly intended to create an agreement and work was paid for. Trentham Ltd alleged that there were defects in the window works and claimed damages for breach of contract. Archital Luxfer denied liability stating that no contract had been concluded. The Court of Appeal held that a binding contract existed that 'came into existence during performance even if it cannot be precisely analysed in terms of offer and acceptance'.

Method of communication

If the offeror has stipulated that a particular manner of communication must be used, it may be that any acceptance communicated by an alternative method may not be valid. However, it will depend on all the circumstances with the court considering the true intention of the offeror.

Communication must be received

Thus, where the parties are dealing face to face or by telephone, the offeror must hear the acceptance for it to be valid. Likewise, if instantaneous communications such as telex are used, the acceptance occurs where the message is received, this being decided in **Entores Ltd v Miles Far East Corpn** (1955) and confirmed by the House of Lords in **Brinkibon v Stahag Stahl** (1983). In the **Entores** decision, the plaintiffs made an offer by telex to the defendants' agents in Amsterdam seeking to buy goods from them. The defendants accepted by a telex received by the plaintiffs in London. The latter subsequently wished to sue the defendants for breach of contract but their ability to issue a writ was dependent on whether the contract had been made in London or Amsterdam. The Court of Appeal held that the contract was agreed in London when the telex was received by the plaintiffs.

While there is no doubt about the place of acceptance, there has been debate about the timing of the acceptance given that instantaneous acceptance can take place worldwide and thus in different time zones. The offeree sent the acceptance during working hours for him but what may be the middle of the night for an offeror on the other side of the world. It is accepted however, that the contractual acceptance will occur either at the time it is received or, at the latest, at a time when it is reasonable for the offeror to have had the opportunity to read it.

This approach holds true for all forms of instantaneous communication and, thus, would apply to acceptance via the Internet. As explained previously, an advertisement on the Internet constitutes an invitation to treat with the contractual offer occurring when the prospective purchaser registers their wish to purchase. It follows that the contractual acceptance occurs when the Internet seller accepts the offer and confirms the sale.

Postal acceptance

When acceptance is communicated by post, the acceptance occurs when the letter is posted. There is no requirement that it be received by the offeror, who is contractually bound from that moment even though he does not know of the acceptance and may never receive it. This was established by the decisions of **Byrne v Van Tienhoven** (1880), see above, and **Adams v Lindsell** (1818). However, the offeror can countermand the normal 'postal rules' by stipulating that a letter of acceptance must be received to be valid, as occurred in **Holwell Securities Ltd v Hughes** (1974), in which the offeror had granted an option to the offeree relating to the purchase of some land. The terms of the offer were that the acceptance had to be by 'notice in writing'. In the event, the offeree had posted the acceptance before the deadline but it had not been received by the offeror. The Court of Appeal held that there was no contract as the offeror had made it clear that the acceptance had to be received and this overruled the normal application of the postal rule.

1.8 Consideration

The concept of a bargain is central to English contract law, a mere agreement between the parties being insufficient. A bargain must have been struck. As such, consideration is necessary in all contracts other than specialty contracts and is essentially the 'price' of the contractual promise. It may consist of payment, either monetary or in kind, the doing of some action or, alternatively, the forbearance from enforcing some right.

Consideration may be classed as either executed or executory. Executed consideration occurs where the promise is made in return for the doing of an act. The most common example of this is the 'reward' situation, where the offeror promises to pay money for the return of a lost item. When the offeree finds and returns the item, the monetary consideration must change hands. By contrast, executory consideration is a promise in exchange for a promise, any action being in the future. An example might be where A, a building contractor, promises to pay £1,000 to B, a plant hire company, if B will promise to supply A with the use of a fork-lift truck for five days. The actual provision of the truck is in the future with only promises taking place at the time that the contract is made.

As with offer and acceptance, there are certain rules relating to the provision of consideration.

1.8.1 Consideration must move from the promisee

Only a person who has provided consideration for the contractual promise has the *locus standi* to enforce it. Thus, a third party cannot enforce the contract even if it was made for his benefit, as held in the case of **Tweddle v Atkinson** (1861), in which the plaintiff's father and future father-in-law agreed to pay the plaintiff a sum of money prior to his marriage. His father-in-law died without making the payment and the plaintiff sued his estate for the outstanding money. The court held that although the contract was made for his benefit, the plaintiff did not provide any consideration for the promise and thus could not sue to enforce it. However, this situation has been amended to some extent by the passage of the Contracts (Rights of Third Parties) Act 1999, where a third party for whose benefit a contract has been made may be able to enforce a contract despite the lack of consideration.

1.8.2 Past consideration is no consideration

The law will not enforce a promise when the consideration relates to a past action. In that situation, the consideration is not contractual payment but rather a subsequent *ex gratia* payment and, as such, is not enforceable. In the decision of **Re McArdle** (1951) Mr McArdle left his house to his widow for her lifetime and thereafter to his children. During the widow's lifetime, one of the children and his wife moved into the house and did some renovations costing £448. Subsequently, all the children signed a document agreeing to reimburse the wife when the deceased's estate was distributed finally. They failed to do so and the wife sued to enforce the promise. The Court of Appeal held that she could not enforce it as it was made after the work had been done. Hence, the consideration was in the past and did not support the promise.

However, if it can be shown that the plaintiff undertook the work at the request of the defendant and there was a reasonable assumption that payment would be made, the plaintiff can sue to enforce any promise of payment even if it was made after the work had been completed. This was the *dicta* of the decision of **Lampleigh *v* Braithwait** (1615), a similar finding occurring in **Re Casey's Patents, Stewart *v* Casey** (1892) and **Pau On *v* Lau Yiu Long** (1979).

1.8.3 Consideration must be sufficient but need not be adequate

While the law is concerned with the existence of a bargain, it is not interested in the value of it and will not aid a plaintiff merely because he has made a bad bargain. *Caveat emptor* (let the buyer beware) rules as regards the value of the deal.

Sufficiency versus adequacy

The distinction between sufficiency and adequacy is vital. Consideration will be sufficient if it is capable of legally constituting consideration, while adequacy is concerned only with the value of the consideration and thus is of no interest to the law. Thus, for example, if A agrees to sell his factory to B for £10, the agreement will be enforceable as the consideration is sufficient even if the average person would not consider it adequate. A practical example of this occurred in **Chappell & Co Ltd *v* Nestlé & Co Ltd** (1960), in which it was held that chocolate wrappers could constitute consideration if collected by purchasers as part of the 'payment' for a contractual offer contained on the wrapper. This was so despite the fact that the wrappers had no intrinsic value and would be thrown away upon receipt.

The performance of existing duties

Generally, the performance of an action which the plaintiff is already obliged to perform either as a matter of public duty or because of some pre-existing contractual duty cannot constitute consideration for a contractual promise. Examples of the first, performance of a public duty, occurred in **Collins *v* Godefroy** (1831) and **Glasbrook Brothers Ltd *v* Glamorgan County Council** (1925). In the **Collins** decision the defendant, Godefroy, offered to pay Collins the sum of six guineas to give evidence in a court case. In fact, Collins had been subpoenaed to attend court and thus was under a public duty to do so. His action to recover the six guineas failed for lack of consideration.

The **Glasbrook** decision concerned the duty owed by a police authority to provide sufficient police officers to protect premises. The respondent requested the police to provide security for his mine during a strike. The police were satisfied that a unit of men patrolling outside the premises would be sufficient for the purpose. However, the colliery manager wanted to have a force of officers billeted at the premises. The police authority agreed to this request with the colliery manager agreeing to pay for the additional service. He subsequently refused to pay the bill and was sued for the cost of the additional cover, £2,300. The House of Lords held that the police authority was able to recover the cost. While they were under a public duty to provide protection for premises, the level of such protection fell within their discretion. A charge could be made for any additional service provided.

A pre-existing contractual duty will also be insufficient to constitute consideration for a contractual promise unless it can be shown that the promisee has received some benefit or avoided some loss. The traditional approach to pre-existing contractual duty is to be found in the decisions of **Stilk *v* Myrick** (1809) and **Hartley *v* Ponsonby** (1857). In the **Stilk** case the plaintiff was employed as a sailor and was under contract to man a ship of which the defendant was the captain. During the voyage, two seamen deserted and the captain promised the remaining crew that, if they manned the ship home shorthanded, he would divide the wages of the two seamen between them. Subsequently, he refused to do so and was sued. The court found for the defendant, holding that the plaintiff and the remainder of the crew were already contractually bound to man the ship back home and had not provided any consideration for the promise of the extra money.

The facts in **Hartley *v* Ponsonby** were very similar to those in **Stilk *v* Myrick** except that nearly half of the crew had deserted. This had the effect of making the voyage considerably more hazardous for the remaining crew members. They sued to recover the £40 per man that they had been promised for bringing the ship home. The court held that they were entitled to recover the additional money as the nature of the voyage had altered so drastically that their original contract had effectively been terminated leaving them free to make a new contract on different terms.

The position was reconsidered and **Stilk *v* Myrick** refined in the 1990 Court of Appeal decision of **Williams *v* Roffey Bros & Nicholls (Contractors) Ltd** (1990). However, the **Roffey** decision did recognise a situation in which an existing contractual duty can constitute consideration for a new contractual promise. The defendants were building contractors who gained a contract to refurbish a block of flats. They sub-contracted some joinery work to the plaintiff for £20,000, the arrangement being that payment would be made in instalments as the work was completed. In practice, £16,200, over 80 per cent of the price, was paid to the plaintiff although he had not completed 80 per cent of the work. At this point, he got into financial difficulties due partly to his price being too low and partly to a failure to provide proper supervision for his workmen. The defendants, aware of his financial problems and anxious to avoid a penalty clause if the major contract was not completed on time, agreed to pay the plaintiff an additional £575 per flat on completion, a total of £10,300. The plaintiff completed a further eight flats and received a further £1,500 before stopping work. The Court of Appeal, upholding the decision of the lower court, held that the plaintiff was entitled to recover the additional money due for the completed flats less a small deduction for defective or incomplete items. They held that the defendants had acquired a benefit by having the plaintiff complete the contract on time in exchange for the additional payment, namely that the defendants had avoided the penalty clause under the main contract.

The **Williams *v* Roffey Bros** decision was reconsidered by the Court of Appeal in **Re Selectmove Ltd** (1995) (see below) when the court held that the principle should not be extended to situations of part payment of a debt.

Part payment of a debt

Generally, part payment of a debt is not sufficient consideration for a promise to accept the payment as full settlement of the debt, this rule being known as the rule in **Pinnel's case** (1602). Suppose, for example, that a main contractor and a sub-contractor have agreed that the latter will undertake some work for £1,000. Upon completion of it, however, the main contractor, pleading cash flow problems, offers the sub-contractor £800 in full settlement of the contract debt. The sub-contractor, needing the money quickly to settle immediate commitments, accepts but later thinks better of it. Will the sub-contractor be bound by his acceptance of the lower sum? **Pinnel's case** would say not, a position reaffirmed by the Court of Appeal in **Ferguson** *v* **Davies** (1997), in which it was held that the acceptance and cashing of a cheque by the plaintiff for £150 which the defendant acknowledged he owed did not prevent the plaintiff seeking to recover the remainder of the contract debt through the courts.

Rules relating to part payment were revisited in the decision of **Re Selectmove Ltd** (1995) when the Court of Appeal was required to consider whether the principle of **Williams** *v* **Roffey Bros** could be extended to situations of part payment of a debt. In **Re Selectmove Ltd** a company owed a substantial number of tax and national insurance contributions to the Revenue. During negotiations with the collector of taxes, the company proposed that it should pay off its arrears at the rate of £1,000 per month. The collector of taxes stated that such a proposal would need the approval of his superiors. Nothing further was heard but the Revenue subsequently served a demand for the whole outstanding sum and sought to have the company wound up. The company argued, amongst other things, that its promise to pay off its existing debt was good consideration as the Revenue gained practical benefits from the proposed payment system. The Court of Appeal held, dismissing the company's argument, that the principle of **Williams** *v* **Roffey Bros**, namely that a promise to perform an existing obligation could amount to good consideration as long as the promisee acquired a benefit, was limited to situations for the supply of goods and services and would not be extended to situations relating to the part payment of a debt.

Nonetheless, there is a variety of situations in which lesser payment will suffice. Thus, if the payment were made at an earlier date, or in a different place, or in a different form at the payee's request, the payment of the lesser sum would be binding. The payee has received a benefit by receiving payment in a way other than that to which he was contractually entitled and thus consideration has been provided for his promise to accept a lesser sum. Acceptance of a lesser sum will also be binding if the part payment is made by a third party on condition that the original debt will be extinguished, as was shown in the decision of **Hiranchand Punamchand** *v* **Temple** (1911), in which the defendant's father offered part payment of the defendant's debt in full settlement.

Of more concern in a business context is the position regarding composition agreements whereby a debtor seeks to settle all his debts by agreeing to pay each creditor a percentage of the due debt in full settlement. Parties to such an agreement cannot sue later for the balance of the debt owed to them as this would amount to a fraud on the creditors who had accepted part payment.

The final situation in which part payment may be binding is that of promissory estoppel, as enunciated in the decision of **Central London Property Trust Ltd** *v* **High Trees House Ltd** (1947). It must be stressed that this doctrine can only be used as a defence to an action and never as a cause of action. Hence, it is 'a shield and not a sword'. In the **High Trees** case, the plaintiffs entered into a lease with the defendants whereby the latter leased a block of flats in London from the plaintiffs for a term of

99 years at an annual ground rent of £2,500. The lease was effective from September 1937. In January 1940, as a result of the outbreak of the war and the consequent difficulties of letting property in London, the plaintiffs wrote to the defendants agreeing to reduce the ground rent to £1,250 per annum. The defendants paid rent at the reduced rate from the beginning of 1941 until 1945, when the flats were fully occupied. The plaintiffs sought to recover the difference between the rent agreed in the lease and that actually paid for the last two quarters of 1945 with the clear intention that, if the claim was successful, a further claim would be made relating to the whole of the period during which the reduced rent had been paid. Denning J held that the agreement about the reduced rent was intended to apply only for the duration of the war and, thus, that the plaintiffs were entitled to recover for the last two quarters of 1945, the war being over. However, no claim would be permitted in respect of the period 1941 to 1945 while hostilities existed.

The use of the doctrine as a defence requires that the plaintiff made a promise intending it to be relied upon and that the defendant acted in reliance upon it. There is no requirement that the defendant has suffered any detriment by his reliance, merely that he has altered his position. As is evident from the **High Trees** decision, the rule will suspend the plaintiff's rights for the period during which the reliance occurred but will allow them to be revived thereafter.

1.9 Intention to create legal relations

Not all agreements are legally enforceable. Many situations occur in which people make agreements never intending that any legal liability will arise. Thus, for example, an agreement to go to the cinema with a friend would not be actionable if you fail to turn up.

The major factor in deciding whether a promise is actionable is whether the agreement is of a domestic nature or a commercial one.

1.9.1 Domestic agreements

There is a presumption at law that agreements of an essentially domestic or social nature will not be binding. Naturally, the presumption will be overruled if evidence is adduced demonstrating an intention to be bound as occurred in the decision of **Simpkins** *v* **Pays** (1955), in which the three tenants of a house jointly entered a competition agreeing to share any winnings.

1.9.2 Commercial agreements

There is a rebuttable presumption in commercial dealings that the parties do intend to be contractually bound. It is possible, however, to rebut this presumption by the inclusion of a statement in the agreement to the effect that there is no intention to create a binding contract.

In **Rose & Frank Co** *v* **J R Crompton & Bros** (1925) an agreement between the parties, an English company and an American company, contained an 'honourable pledge clause' which provided that the agreement 'was not entered into . . . as a formal or legal agreement and shall not be subject to legal jurisdiction in the law courts either of the United States or England, but is only a definite expression and record of the purpose and intention of the parties concerned, to which they each honourably pledge themselves'. Under the agreement, the plaintiffs were to act as the sole American agents for the sale of the defendants' products. The defendants terminated the agreement without giving the agreed period of notice and refused to fulfil orders placed by the plaintiffs prior to the date of termination. The Court of Appeal held that the defendants were obliged to fulfil outstanding orders in respect of which a contract had arisen but that, because of the 'honourable pledge clause', there was no contractual obligation on the defendants to continue with the agreement or accept any further orders.

A recent development with regard to intention in the commercial context has been the recognition of 'letters of comfort', most notably in the decision of **Kleinwort Benson Ltd** *v* **Malaysian Mining Corporation Bhd** (1989), in which the plaintiff bank agreed to provide a loan to the defendants' wholly owned subsidiary, MMC Metals Ltd, which traded in tin on the London Metal Exchange. The defendants refused to provide a guarantee for the loan but did provide two 'letters of comfort' each of which read 'It is our policy to ensure that the business of MMC Metals Ltd is at all times in a position to meet its liabilities to you under the (loan facility) arrangements'. Due to the collapse of the tin market, MMC Metals Ltd went into liquidation while still owing the plaintiff the whole of the sum borrowed. The plaintiff sued the defendants for the amount owing relying on the 'letters of comfort'. The Court of Appeal held that the defendants were not liable, the 'letters of comfort' merely being statements of fact about the defendants' present intentions and not contractual promises as to their future conduct. There was no intention to create a legal relationship, as evidenced by the defendants' refusal to provide a guarantee.

Clearly, a business issuing a letter of comfort must ensure that their intention is beyond doubt because of the presumption that businesses intend to contract.

1.10 Contractual capacity

A person of full legal age, 18 by virtue of the Family Law Reform Act 1969, has the legal capacity to enter any contract other than those which are void or illegal either at common law or by statute. The position with regard to companies and minors is not so clear-cut.

1.10.1 Corporate capacity

Suppose, for example, that firm A supplies £20,000 worth of timber to firm B but does not receive payment. It transpires that firm B was established for the purpose of breeding pigs. Can firm A sue for the money or is firm B able to avoid the debt?

The majority of commercial companies, both public and private, are incorporated under the provisions of successive Companies Acts, the current statute being the Companies Act 1985 as amended. Traditionally, the legal capacity of companies has been governed by the doctrine of *ultra vires*, which stipulates that any action by a company which falls outside the provisions of the company's 'objects clause' will be invalid. The 'objects clause' is to be found in the memorandum of association, the major corporate document registered at the time of incorporation, and specifies those areas of business in which the company will be involved. The *ultra vires* doctrine at its most draconian provided that contracting parties had constructive notice of the contents of any company's 'objects clause' and thus were bound by its contents. Hence, in the example above, firm A would be unable to sue firm B for the £20,000 as the latter was acting outside its declared object of pig breeding and thus was acting *ultra vires*.

The *ultra vires* doctrine, intended to protect third parties, shareholders and investors in their dealings with companies, was heavily criticised with consequent calls for its abolition. Section 35 of the Companies Act 1985, as enacted by s 108(1) of the Companies Act 1989, while not abolishing the doctrine has severely limited its impact. Section 35(1) provides:

> The validity of an act done by a company shall not be called into question on the ground of lack of capacity by reason of anything in the company's memorandum.

In the example quoted above, therefore, firm A would now be able to recover the £20,000 for the timber from firm B, the latter being unable to plead *ultra vires*. This is clearly an advantage for anyone dealing with the company. Nonetheless, while s 35 now prevents a company hiding behind the *ultra vires* doctrine in its relationships with third parties, the doctrine has been retained as a means of internal corporate control. Thus, any shareholder may seek an injunction to prevent a company from acting *ultra vires* and restrain the directors from acting in excess of their powers.

1.10.2 Minors

Minors – anyone under the age of 18 – possess restricted legal capacity, the underlying rationale being to protect them from full legal liability. Contracts with minors are void with the exception of two groups of contracts, the first of which are binding while the second group are voidable.

Binding contracts with minors comprise those for the purchase of necessaries, as defined in s 3(3) of the Sale of Goods Act 1979, and contracts of service beneficial to the minor. This includes contracts of employment, apprenticeship and education, but does not include trading contracts. Thus, a minor running his own business will not be bound by the contracts that he makes, though they will be voidable. While such trading contracts are likely to be relatively few in number, they do pose a risk in the commercial context.

Voidable contracts, i.e. those that can be ratified or avoided by the minor on attaining his majority, include trading contracts and those where he has gained an interest in something such as shares or land. A voidable contract that has been ratified becomes binding. A minor wishing to repudiate a voidable contract must do so within a reasonable period of gaining his majority, the exact length of the period depending on the facts of each individual case.

1.11 Privity of contract

1.11.1 Traditional approach

If A and B enter into a contract, can C enforce it in the event of either of the contracting parties going into breach? The traditional answer has been 'no', the doctrine of privity of contract providing that only a party to a contract may sue upon it, for only the contracting parties will have provided consideration, as in **Dunlop Pneumatic Tyre Co Ltd v Selfridge & Co Ltd** (1915), a case which revolved around the issue of resale price maintenance whereby goods would be provided through a chain of distribution but subject to a contractual term whereby contracting parties would agree not to resell the goods at less that the prescribed resale price. This prevented sellers selling goods at a discount and undercutting other suppliers in the market. In the **Dunlop** decision, Dunlop supplied tyres to a third party, Dew & Co, subject to a resale price maintenance contract. Dew & Co then sold them to Selfridge, also subject to a resale price maintenance contract. When selling the tyres, Selfridge breached the resale price maintenance provision and Dunlop tried to enforce it against them. It was held that Dunlop could not enforce the term as they were not privy to the contract between Dew & Co and Selfridge.

The strict application of the rule of privity of contract has meant that a third party cannot sue on a contract even if he is the intended beneficiary of it. This traditional view was set out in the decision of **Tweddle v Atkinson** (1861) (above), in which a bridegroom could not enforce a contract entered into by his father and prospective father-in-law, despite the fact that he was an intended beneficiary of the contract. He was not a party to the contract and, in the absence of privity, could not enforce it.

1.11.2 Contracts (Rights of Third Parties) Act 1999

The restrictions of the traditional approach to privity of contract have been significantly reduced by the impact of the Contracts (Rights of Third Parties) Act 1999. Section 1(1) provides:

> (1) Subject to the provisions of this Act, a person who is not a party to a contract (a 'third party') may in his own right enforce a term of the contract if—
> (a) the contract expressly provides that he may, or
> (b) subject to subsection (2), the term purports to confer a benefit on him.

In order to take advantage of this provision, the third party must be expressly identified by name in the contract or be a member of a class or answer a particular description. There is no requirement that the third party be in existence at the time that the contract was made and thus potential beneficiaries could include children not yet born and companies not yet incorporated at the time that the contract was made. However, third parties cannot take advantage of s 1(1)(b) if, on a proper construction of the contract, it appears that the parties did not intend the term to be enforceable by the third party. Where a third party possesses a right of enforcement, s 2 provides that the contracting parties cannot, by agreement, rescind the contract or vary it in such a way as to affect the third party's rights if the third party has communicated his acceptance of the term to the promisor and either the promisor is aware that the third party has relied on the term or he should reasonably be expected to have foreseen that the third party would rely on the term and has in fact done so. The assent may be by words or conduct but if sent by post is not to be regarded as communicated until it has been received by the promisor. However, s 2 will not be effective if the contract includes an express term allowing for it to be altered without the consent of the third party.

Where a third party has been given express rights to enforce a contract between two contracting parties, it follows that the third party must take any legal action to enforce its rights and the two contracting parties cannot sue on its behalf, as held in the decision of **Panatown Ltd v Alfred McAlpine Construction Ltd** (2000), in which the defendant building contractor had contracted with the plaintiff to construct a building on a site owned by a third party, Unex Investment Properties Ltd. Under the terms of a deed, Unex was expressly given a right to pursue direct remedies against the defendant in the event of breach. When a delay occurred, Panatown Ltd sought to claim damages from the defendant on behalf of Unex, which had suffered damage as a consequence of the breach. The House of Lords held that Panatown could not claim compensation on behalf of Unex, which must exercise its own contractual right of action for any loss that they had suffered.

1.11.3 Mitigation of the privity rule

In addition to the new rules relating to third party rights, there are a few situations in which the harshness of the privity rule may be mitigated by some other factor.

Contracting on behalf of a group
In **Jackson v Horizon Holidays Ltd** (1975) the plaintiff, who had booked a holiday on behalf of his family, was entitled to claim compensation for all of them when the holiday proved unsatisfactory. However, the application of this exception is restricted to situations where there is a clear presumption that the plaintiff was acting on behalf of the group as a whole.

Collateral contracts
This occurs where a separate contract related to the main contract exists between a third party and one of the main contracting parties, as in **Shanklin Pier Ltd v Detel Products Ltd** (1951), in which a contract existed between the plaintiff and a contractor for the painting of a pier. The plaintiff, relying on representations made by the defendant paint manufacturer, insisted that the defendant's paint should be

used for the job. The contractor purchased the paint, which proved unsatisfactory and did not match up to specification. It was held that the plaintiff was entitled to recover damages from the defendant manufacturer of the paint on the basis of a collateral contract.

Assignment

This occurs where one of the contracting parties enters an agreement to transfer his rights and liabilities under a contract to a third party, who may enforce it on his own behalf. Thus, if in a contract between A and B, B were to assign his contractual rights to C, the contract would then be between A and C and enforceable by both. Strictly speaking, this is not an exception to the privity rule, since the contract is still a bilateral one enforceable by the parties; it is merely the identity of the parties that has changed.

Agency

In an agency agreement an agent will contract on behalf of his principal. Thus, for example, B, acting on behalf of A, will negotiate a contract with C. While C may be aware of the fact that B is acting as an agent for A, it is equally possible that he is not and that he will assume that he is contracting with B personally. In fact, the privity of contract will be between A and C even though they may not have had any direct dealings and C may not even be aware of A's existence. Agency will be considered in detail in Chapter 6.

Question

Ace Ltd, a manufacturing company, wanted to replace all the computers in their offices with a new comprehensive system. They invited tenders for the provision and installation of the equipment from various computer companies with whom they had dealt before. The letter inviting the tenders included the statement 'if the offer made by you is the lowest offer received by us, we bind ourselves to accept such offer'. In response to the letter Niger Computers Ltd bid £360,000, while Congo Computers Ltd bid £375,000 or £5,000 less than any lower bid. The contract was awarded to Niger Computers Ltd.

Ace Ltd then placed the order stating that the contract was to be on the basis of their standard terms and conditions. However, Niger Computers Ltd purported to accept the offer but on a contract form comprising their own standard terms, which included a price variation clause. On the bottom of Niger Computer Ltd's contract was a tear-off slip acknowledging the agreement to the terms. An employee of Ace Ltd duly signed and returned the slip. Advise:

(a) Congo Computers Ltd, who feel that they should have been awarded the contract as they made the lowest bid.
(b) Niger Computers Ltd, who want to raise the contract price to £370,000, which Ace Ltd are refusing to pay.

Answer

This question raises two issues: first, the question of competitive tendering and any obligation on the person seeking the tender to accept one of the tenders, and, second, the battle of the forms.

(a) Congo Computers Ltd feel that they should have been awarded the contract as their referential bid was lower than the tender of £360,000 made by Niger Computers Ltd. Certainly, Ace Ltd had committed themselves to accepting the lowest offer and thus would be bound to do so in accordance with the decision in **Harvela Investments Ltd *v* Royal Trust Co of Canada Ltd** (1986). However, the **Harvela** case also held that a referential bid is not legitimate in that situation. Therefore, Ace Ltd were right to award the contract to Niger Computers Ltd and Congo Computers Ltd have no grounds for complaint.

(b) Niger Computers Ltd want to raise the contract price from £360,000 to £370,000. Whether they can do this will depend on whose standard terms were adopted as the contract. It is a battle of the forms situation in which both Ace Ltd and Niger Computers Ltd have each attempted to contract on their own standard terms. Applying **Butler Machine Tool Co *v* Ex-Cell-O Corpn** (1979), Niger Computers will win as their terms were the last ones proposed and were accepted by Ace Ltd when their employee signed and returned the tear-off slip. Therefore, the price variation clause is enforceable and Niger Computers Ltd can raise the price.

Further reading

Adams, A (2000). *Law for Business Students*, 2nd edn (Longman)

Bradgate, R (2000). *Commercial Law*, 3rd edn (Butterworth)

Dobson, P (1997). *Charlesworth's Business Law*, 16th edn (Sweet & Maxwell)

Downes, T A (1997). *Textbook on Contract*, 5th edn (Blackstone Press)

Keenan, D (2000). *Smith and Keenan's Advanced Business Law*, 11th edn (Longman)

Keenan, D and Riches, S (2001). *Business Law*, 6th edn (Longman)

Richards, P (2001). *Law of Contract*, 5th edn (Longman)

Stone, R (2000). *Principles of Contract Law*, 4th edn (Cavendish)

Contractual terms and formalities

2.1 Formalities

The law stipulates few formalities in the creation of legally binding contracts. They do not even need to be in writing although there are some exceptions to this general rule. Oral contracts are equally as valid as written ones although, naturally, their terms may be more difficult to prove. Consequently, it is common sense for business contracts and any contract involving a large sum of money to be written.

In contrast to the general rule, certain contracts of interest to businesses must be written. First, regulated agreements under the Consumer Credit Act 1974 must be written and in a prescribed format or they will be unenforceable against the debtor or hirer without a court order (s 65). Second, s 2 of the Law of Property (Miscellaneous Provisions) Act 1989 requires that any contract for the sale or other disposition of land must be in writing, contain all the terms agreed by the parties and be signed by both parties. A contract not in this form will be void.

Contracts of guarantee are slightly different. While the contract itself does not need to be written, s 4 of the Statute of Frauds 1677 requires that there must be some written evidence of the terms of the agreement. A contract of guarantee occurs where the guarantor promises to pay the debts of a second person if that other should default. The promise must be made to the third party to whom the debt is owed. It is important to note that the guarantor is accepting liability only upon the debtor's default and not in any other situation. The written evidence of the agreement can be contained in a note but must stipulate all the terms of the guarantee and have been signed by the guarantor. There are two situations involving contracts of guarantee which fall outside the requirements of s 4. The first is where the guarantee forms part of a larger transaction, for example where the guarantor is a *del credere* agent. This occurs when an agent, usually in exchange for a larger commission, agrees to guarantee a debt owed to his principal by a third party. Here, the guarantee forms part of a larger contract of agency and falls outside the statute, as held in **Couturier *v* Hastie** (1852), in which the defendant, acting as a *del credere* agent, was held liable to his plaintiff principal on an oral contract of guarantee. The second exception occurs when the guarantee is provided by the guarantor as a way of securing property which he owns, as in **Fitzgerald *v* Dressler** (1859).

It is vital to distinguish between contracts of guarantee, where written evidence is essential, and contracts of indemnity, where there is no such requirement. Unlike contracts of guarantee, which involve secondary liability, indemnity occurs where the defendant has assumed the debt in his own right. The case of **Mountstephen *v* Lakeman** (1874) illustrates the point well. Mountstephen, the plaintiff builder, was to undertake some work for a Local Board of Health. In a discussion about the method of payment, Lakeman, the Chairman of the Board, stated 'Go on, Mountstephen, and do the work, and I will see you paid'. The Board refused to pay for the work on the basis that they had not made any agreement with the plaintiff. The court held that, in the absence of an agreement, the Board could not be regarded as a debtor and hence Lakeman was personally liable having provided an indemnity.

In a business context, the distinction is important to contractors seeking a guarantee from a parent company that they will receive payment for goods or services provided to a subsidiary business or, alternatively, a financial institution seeking guarantees for a business loan. The agreement will need to be considered carefully as the terminology used will not necessarily determine whether the parent is merely acting as a guarantor or is providing an indemnity. Further, note the distinction between a guarantee, which gives rise to legal liability, and a letter of comfort (as discussed in the previous chapter), which does not.

Lastly, there are some contracts which must be made by deed and 'signed, sealed and delivered'. Of prime concern are conveyances for the sale of land or the creation of a lease lasting more than three years. Of lesser interest are contracts lacking consideration, which will be enforceable if made by deed.

2.2 Terms of the contract

Precontractual discussions are a normal part of the business of contracting. But it would be naive to assume that all the statements made during those negotiations will necessarily become embedded in the contract. Precontractual statements can best be divided into three groups: advertising puffs, representations and contractual terms. The first group involves those statements that are so wildly exaggerated that there is clearly no intention that they should be relied upon. Examples might include 'a good little runner' when applied to a car, or 'smells like spring' when applied to washing powder or other similarly exaggerated claims. For the purposes of legal liability such statements are discarded easily. By contrast, representations, sometimes termed 'mere representations', are those statements which invite reliance and are intended to induce one of the parties to enter the contract. This might, for example, include general statements about reliability or efficiency. Lastly, contractual terms are those statements that both parties intend should form an integral part of their agreement and be actionable if untrue.

It is the distinction between misrepresentations and contractual terms that is of most import. Either can give rise to legal liability if they prove to be untrue, a false representation being actionable under the Misrepresentation Act 1967 (see next chapter) while a false term will give rise to an action for breach of contract. Likewise, both may give rise to some criminal liability under the Trade Descriptions Act 1968 (see Chapter 13). It is often difficult to draw the dividing line between the two but various guidelines have been established. Thus the timing of the statement in the process of negotiation, whether it was later reduced into any written contract, the relative expertise of the contracting parties and the importance of the term to them all play a part in deciding the status of the relevant statement. Two contrasting decisions illustrate this.

In **Bannerman** *v* **White** (1861) a buyer of hops asked during the precontractual negotiations whether the hops had been treated with sulphur, making clear that he would not buy any hops that had been so treated. The seller confirmed that the crop had not been treated. It subsequently transpired that a small proportion of the hops had been treated with sulphur, the buyer consequently refusing to pay. The court held that the statement that the hops were untreated was a condition of the contract having been made at a significant point in the negotiations with both parties aware of its importance.

By contrast, in **Routledge** *v* **McKay** (1954), the parties, both private individuals, were negotiating the sale of a motorcycle. The defendant, relying on the registration document, stated that the bike was registered in 1942. This information was not included in the written contract concluded a week later. In fact the bike dated from 1930. The court held that the statement was sufficiently remote from the final contract not to be classed as part of it. It was a mere representation.

The **Routledge** decision is also good authority for the proposition that the statement may be classed as a mere representation if it is not contained in any later written contract.

The relevance of the skill and expertise of the contracting parties is demonstrated by the contrasting cases of **Oscar Chess Ltd** *v* **Williams** (1957) and **Dick Bentley Productions Ltd** *v* **Harold Smith (Motors) Ltd** (1965), both of which involved the sale of a car. The cases suggest that if the more experienced or knowledgeable of the two contracting parties makes the statement it may be classed as a term whereas if the less experienced of the two makes the statement, it is likely to be classed as a representation. It would seem that this may be so irrespective of whether the experienced party is the seller or the buyer.

One potential solution to the difficulty of deciding the status of a statement may be to class representations as collateral contracts.

2.3 Express and implied terms

Thus far we have assumed that the parties are of equal bargaining power and have freedom of contract, i.e. the ability to decide for themselves what terms are to be included in their contract. In practice, this is not so.

2.3.1 Express terms

The express terms of a contract are those terms agreed upon by the parties and which form the nub of the contract, be it written, oral or a mixture of both. Thus, for example, the express terms might include details of the subject matter, the price, any price variation clause of the type discussed in the **Butler Machine Tool Co** *v* **Ex-Cell-O Corpn** case, any permitted exclusion clauses, a *force majeure* clause, a liquidated damages clause, a clause governing arbitration in the event of a dispute and the time of performance. If the time of performance is considered to be important, the parties must expressly agree upon this as the general contractual rule is that time is not of the essence. However, in commercial contracts, the courts may be prepared to imply that time is of the essence in order to give the contract business efficacy. Where the parties have included an express term in the contract stipulating a time for contractual performance and thus making time of the essence, the courts will enforce it. Hence, in **Union Eagle Ltd** *v* **Golden Achievement Ltd** (1997) the purchaser entered into a written contract for the purchase of a piece of property in Hong Kong paying a 10 per cent deposit of $HK4.2 million. The contract provided that completion had to take place by 5 pm on the specified date or the deposit would be forfeited as liquidated damages. The purchaser tried to complete at 5.10 pm but the seller refused. The Privy Council held that the purchaser could not claim specific performance of the contract or recover the deposit as the contract had clearly made time of the essence and the purchaser had not complied with that term.

A *force majeure* clause, invariably included in business contracts for the supply of goods, constitutes an attempt by the contracting parties to stipulate what will happen if some event beyond their control interferes with contractual performance. Thus, for example, the clause might stipulate that if the supplier is prevented from delivery in accordance with the contract because of some specified supervening event additional time for performance is to be allowed, or that the supplier can delay further performance without penalty or even terminate the contract forthwith. Supervening events outlined in *force majeure* clauses typically include acts of God, delays in manufacture and problems with sub-contractors. The courts tend to construe such clauses narrowly but if the term does cover the event that actually occurs the term will take effect. If it does not, the contract will be frustrated instead. Thus, in **Jackson** *v* **Union Marine Insurance Co Ltd** (1874) a ship was chartered to sail from Liverpool to Newport 'with all possible despatch' to load cargo for San Francisco 'dangers and accidents of navigation excepted'. The ship ran aground in Caernarvon Bay on her way to Newport and was not repaired for eight months. The court held that the clause did not cover the accident that actually occurred and that the contract was frustrated.

The parties to a commercial contract may try genuinely to calculate their likely losses in the event of contractual breach. Where agreement is reached, a liquidated damages clause may be included in the contract and will take effect when relevant. This can be used, for example, as a method for settling damages for late performance by specifying that a given percentage of the contract price is payable for each day, week or month by which delivery or completion is delayed. When a liquidated damages clause takes effect the parties receive the amount agreed by way of damages, no more and no less, irrespective of the actual damage suffered. It is vital to distinguish between liquidated damages clauses, which are a genuine pre-estimate of losses and are enforceable, and penalty clauses, which seek to use punishment to force compliance by the contracting parties and are void. This distinction was considered in **Dunlop Pneumatic Tyre Co Ltd** *v* **New Garage & Motor Co Ltd** (1915), in which the House of Lords established guidelines for identifying penalty clauses. A clause will be a penalty clause if:

1 the amount to be paid on breach is extravagant as compared with the maximum loss that could be suffered as a result of the breach;
2 the contractual performance required consists of paying a sum of money and the clause requires the payment of a larger sum of money on breach;
3 the clause stipulates one sum to be paid as damages in the event of a variety of possible breaches of differing significance, some serious and some trivial. The sum cannot possibly be a realistic pre-estimate in respect of all the specified breaches.

The recent Court of Appeal decision of **Duffen *v* FRA BO SpA** (1998) demonstrates the application of the **Dunlop** principles. The plaintiff, Duffen, was employed as FRA's agent, the agency contract providing that, upon termination of the contract, Duffen would receive £100,000 by way of liquidated damages, this being a genuine pre-estimate of the loss. When the contract was terminated, Duffen sought to enforce this clause and recover £100,000 but the validity of the clause was challenged by FRA. The Court of Appeal held that the clause was a penalty clause as it allowed Duffen to receive £100,000 irrespective of the unexpired term of the contract and could provide him with a windfall rather than genuine compensation.

The court will decide whether the clause is a penalty clause or not; the nomenclature used by the parties to the contract is irrelevant. It is the responsibility of the party who is liable to pay to establish that the clause is a penalty clause.

The **Dunlop** decision and what does or does not constitute a penalty clause was considered by the Chancery Division in **Nutting *v* Baldwin** (1995). The case concerned the rules of an association formed for the purpose of permitting Lloyd's Names to launch the prosecution of claims against the managing agents of two Lloyd's syndicates and 81 members' agents in respect of losses caused by them to the members of the association. The association decided to levy a charge against all its members to finance the prosecutions, the members sharing in the monies recovered through such actions. Such a levy was legitimate within the rules of the association. Nineteen of the members failed to pay the levy, were declared to be 'defaulting members' and precluded from sharing in any proceeds. The Chancery Court was asked to consider whether the association rule permitting such an exclusion was a penalty clause and therefore unenforceable. The court held that the rules of the association constituted a contract among the members to share the burdens and the benefits of enforcing their claims. The rule permitting the exclusion of members was not a penalty clause effective for breach of contract but rather part of the scheme for sharing the benefits and burdens.

A prime example of express contractual terms in the business context is standard form contracts in which a business lays down the terms and conditions on which it is prepared to contract. Clearly, for a company contracting on a regular basis this is sound business practice for it prevents the need to negotiate a new contract with every client while also allowing it to stipulate terms that are protective of its own position (subject to statutory controls on exclusion clauses). Further, it permits relatively junior members of staff to contract on the company's behalf. A potential difficulty with standard form contracts arises, of course, when two businesses contract together and each wants to use its own standard form contract. Hence the 'battle of the forms' as discussed in the previous chapter.

The valid incorporation of any express term must be established if it is to be enforceable. This must have occurred prior to the conclusion of the contract. Thereafter any additional term can be added to the contract only with the agreement of both parties. Unilateral alteration of the contract is not permitted, as illustrated by the decision of **Olley** *v* **Marlborough Court Ltd** (1949), which concerned the incorporation of an exclusion clause. The plaintiffs, Mr and Mrs Olley, booked into a hotel for the first time, the contract for the stay being finalised at the reception desk. On their bedroom wall was a notice which read 'the proprietors will not hold themselves responsible for articles lost or stolen unless handed to the manageress for safe custody'. In their absence, a third party took the key from the reception and used it to enter the plaintiffs' bedroom and steal some furs. The defendant hotel attempted to deny liability relying on the exclusion clause. The Court of Appeal held that the exclusion clause had not been incorporated validly as it had not been included at the time that the contract had been concluded and had only come to the notice of the plaintiffs later. The hotel could not rely on it.

2.3.2 Implied terms

The ability of the parties to decide all the contractual terms is restricted both by the insertion of implied terms either statutorily or judicially and by the exclusion of terms that are void or illegal. Further, an inequality of bargaining power may lead to one party having terms imposed upon him with which he is not happy. This problem has been addressed to some extent by the inclusion of protective implied terms as detailed below and partly by statutory controls over exclusion clauses. Implied terms can be subdivided into those relating to fact and those relating to law.

Implied terms relating to fact will be those terms that a court may imply into a particular contract in order to give it business efficacy. The court's role is to imply those terms that the contracting parties have genuinely overlooked and not to include terms that might improve the contract. The implied terms should complete the contract intended by the parties and not add to it, as reconfirmed in the Court of Appeal decision of **Ali** *v* **Christian Salvesen Food Services Ltd** (1997).

The test to be applied is whether, had the presence of the term been queried, both contracting parties would have agreed to its inclusion without hesitation. An unwillingness by one party to include the term would be fatal. This approach was specified in the House of Lords decision of **Scally** *v* **Southern Health and Social Services Board** (1992), in which Lord Bridge opined that the test for an implied term of fact is whether it is 'necessary to give business efficacy to a particular contract'. The same requirement of necessity exists in respect of implied terms of law, Lord Bridge stating that such a term should 'based on wider considerations . . . [be] . . . a necessary incident of a definable category of contractual relationships'. In short, the court should consider it necessary as a matter of public policy to include an implied term of the type proposed into all contracts of a particular defined group. Such terms are implied into all appropriate contracts irrespective of the wishes of individual contracting parties although reserving the right of those parties expressly to exclude the implied term to the extent that such an exclusion is legal.

Implied terms as to law may be implied by common law or statute or custom. Terms implied by the courts may cover a variety of situations. In the decision of **Lister _v_ Romford Ice and Cold Storage Co Ltd** (1957), in which Lister, a driver, was being sued by his employer for breach of contract, the court implied a term that an employee would use reasonable care and skill when performing his duties. The case resulted from Lister driving his lorry negligently and injuring a workmate, his father. A similar approach was adopted in **Liverpool City Council _v_ Irwin** (1977), in which the House of Lords held that in relation to a block of flats owned by the council, there was an implied term that the council would take reasonable care to maintain the common areas of the property including the stairs and lifts in a reasonable condition. In the **Scally** decision the House of Lords implied a term into contracts of employment to the effect that the employers had a duty to inform their staff of the possibility of purchasing added years to gain the full benefit of a statutory superannuation scheme. The implied rights of employees received a further boost in the 1994 decision of **Spring _v_ Guardian Assurance plc** (1995). In that case, the House of Lords confirmed that the law imposes a duty on employers to ensure that reasonable care and skill should be used in the preparation of references for employees. This duty would arise from an implied term in the contract of employment and would be similar to the normal duty of care arising in negligence.

Arguably the most significant statutory implied terms are those contained in ss 12–15 of the Sale of Goods Act 1979 as amended. Sections 12, 13 and 15 are implied into all contracts of sale, while s 14 is restricted to those contracts of sale in which the seller sells in the course of a business. The terms govern the seller's right to sell, sales by description, the concepts of satisfactory quality and fitness for purpose and sales by sample. These implied conditions are considered in depth in Chapter 7. Similar terms are implied into contracts for the supply of services together with additional terms governing the care and skill to be exhibited in the performance of contracts for services, the time of performance and a right to payment by the Supply of Goods and Services Act 1982. These terms are considered in Chapter 8.

Terms implied by custom may be of significance in particular industries where neither contracting party would expressly include a term as both would assume that they would be bound by custom, as in **Hutton _v_ Warren** (1836), in which it was held that a farm tenant was entitled to receive some allowance for the seeds and labour that he had spent on the land.

2.4 Conditions, innominate terms and warranties

Not all contractual terms are of equal significance. A longstanding distinction exists between conditions and warranties. Conditions are those terms that go to the heart of the contract, the breach of which effectively destroys the contract. By contrast, a warranty is a lesser term, the breach of which would not have a major impact upon the continued existence of the contract. This distinction is reflected in the remedies available for breach, the breach of a condition giving the innocent party a right to terminate the contract whereas a breach of warranty only attracts an action for damages. In respect of a breach of condition, the injured party can elect to continue with the contract and sue for damages instead. The distinction between conditions and warranties is amply illustrated by two contrasting decisions involving similar contracts for services.

In **Poussard v Spiers and Pond** (1876) the plaintiff, Madame Poussard, was under contract to the defendant to appear in an operetta. She was taken ill five days before the first performance and was not available until a week after the show had started. It was held that her failure to appear for the first performance was a breach of condition as it effectively rendered the contract incapable of performance. The defendant had been within his rights to terminate her contract and engage another singer. By contrast, in **Bettini v Gye** (1876), in which the plaintiff, Bettini, was required to be present for rehearsals six days before the first performance, it was held that his arrival three days late was only a breach of warranty for which damages were payable. He was present for the opening night and thus the substantial performance of the contract was possible. The term relating to rehearsal time was of lesser significance.

The parties may themselves decide the status of any particular term for which they are responsible. In respect of statutory implied terms, the statute may stipulate the nature of the term as, for example, in s 14 of the Sale of Goods Act 1979, which states that the term regarding the satisfactory quality of goods is a condition. The obvious advantage of the nature of the term being made clear at the outset is that both parties are aware of the significance of any breach. There is certainty. In practice, the effect of a breach of s 14 of the Sale of Goods Act 1979 has been amended by the provisions of the Sale and Supply of Goods Act 1994. Section 15A of the Act, effective from 3 January 1995, now provides that while consumers retain a right of repudiation in respect of a breach of any of the implied conditions contained in ss 12–15, non-consumer buyers may be restricted to a remedy in damages for minor breaches. Remedies for such breaches are considered in detail in Chapter 7.

A more recent concept, first discussed in **Hong Kong Fir Shipping Co Ltd v Kawasaki Kisen Kaisha Ltd** (1962), is that of the innominate term. These terms fall midway between conditions and warranties with the outcome of any breach being uncertain. The court has the ability to render the contract terminated or alternatively to award damages, whichever is the more appropriate remedy given the effect of the breach. It will depend upon whether the injured party has effectively been denied the benefit of the contract. The **Hong Kong Fir Shipping** case involved a contract to charter a ship 'being fitted in every way for ordinary cargo service' for 24 months from the date of delivery. Due to the condition of the engines and the ineptitude of the crew, the ship was delayed for 20 weeks for repair. The charterers repudiated the contract and the shipowners sued for wrongful termination. The Court of Appeal held that although the ship had been unseaworthy at the outset of the contract, there were still 20 months of the charter to run at the time that the ship was ready. The contract was not frustrated, being capable of substantial performance. In the circumstances, the charterers were only entitled to claim damages.

This approach of considering the effect of the breach has been followed in two other notable decisions, **Cehave NV v Bremer Handelsgesellschaft mbH, The Hansa Nord** (1975) and **Reardon Smith Line Ltd v Yngvar Hansen-Tangen** (1976). In the **The Hansa Nord** decision, the sellers sold a cargo of citrus pellets to the buyers subject to a term that they would be shipped 'in good condition'. On arrival, part of the cargo was damaged and the buyers rejected the whole consignment. Subsequently, the original buyer bought the cargo at a substantially reduced price and used it for the original purpose of making animal feed. The Court of Appeal, rejecting the argument that all express terms about quality must be classed as conditions because of the impact of s 14 of the Sale of Goods Act 1979, held that this particular clause was an innominate term and that as the damage to the goods had not been significant, the buyer did not have a right to reject them.

Similarly, in the **Reardon Smith Line** decision, the House of Lords held that a term of the contract identifying the yard where a ship under construction would be built was an innominate term, the breach of which would give rise only to damages. It was a technical breach. The contract identified the ship as Osaka No 354 (Osaka being the yard at which it would be built). Because of a reallocation of work to the Oshima yard, the ship was actually built as Oshima 004. Nonetheless, the ship was built according to the agreed specifications.

It is important not to extend the principle of innominate terms too far, for in cases such as **The Mihalis Angelos** (1971) and **Bunge Corporation** *v* **Tradax Export SA** (1981) the courts, in the pursuit of certainty, have expressed a preference for stipulating that a particular term is either a condition or a warranty.

On a statutory level, innominate terms are to be found in ss 13–15 of the Supply of Goods and Services Act 1982, where the implied terms about skill and care, the time of performance and the right to payment are expressed to be implied terms as opposed to implied conditions or warranties.

Question

Speakeasy Telephones Ltd contracted to supply and install a new telephone system in the premises of Bloggs Manufacturing Co. The contract included two terms:

(a) the supplier would be liable for any delay in installing the system unless such delay was due to act of God, war, industrial action or some other reason beyond the control of the supplier;

(b) in the event of non-completion by the due date, contractual damages would be assessed at a rate of 1 per cent of the contract price for each week or part of a week by which installation was delayed.

Some of the essential component parts for the system could be purchased only from Tele-Electronics Ltd, the sole supplier in the UK, with whom Speakeasy Telephones Ltd duly contracted for the purchase of sufficient parts for the system. However, due to industrial action at Tele-Electronics Ltd, the relevant component parts were not delivered on time with the result that Speakeasy Telephones Ltd could not complete the system by the due date of 1 March. Contractual completion finally occurred on 15 May.

Bloggs Manufacturing Co are seeking to enforce the clause relating to contractual damages.

Discuss.

Answer

The question relates to the use of two types of express clause in contracts: *force majeure* clauses and liquidated damages clauses. A *force majeure* clause stipulates what will happen if certain contingent events occur, while a liquidated damages clause seeks to agree a genuine enforceable pre-estimate of contractual loss in the event of a breach. In the question, the *force majeure* clause has included industrial action and thus covers the situation in hand. Hence the supplier Speakeasy Telephones Ltd will not be liable for the delay in completion of the contract. However, if Speakeasy Telephones Ltd had been, the validity of the liquidated damages would have become an issue and whether 1 per cent of the contract price for each week's delay was a genuine pre-estimate of loss or a penalty. Only the former is enforceable.

Further reading

Adams, A (2000). *Law for Business Students*, 2nd edn (Longman)

Bradgate, R (2000). *Commercial Law*, 3rd edn (Butterworth)

Dobson, P (1997). *Charlesworth's Business Law*, 16th edn (Sweet & Maxwell)

Downes, T A (1997). *Textbook on Contract*, 5th edn (Blackstone Press)

Keenan, D (2000). *Smith and Keenan's Advanced Business Law*, 11th edn (Longman)

Keenan, D and Riches, S (2001). *Business Law*, 6th edn (Longman)

Richards, P (2001). *Law of Contract*, 5th edn (Longman)

Stone, R (2000). *Principles of Contract Law*, 4th edn (Cavendish)

3 Vitiating factors

Apparently valid contracts agreed upon by the contracting parties may subsequently be rendered either void or voidable by some extenuating factor that existed at the time that the contract was finalised.

The effect of a contract being rendered void *ab initio* is that the contract is deemed never to have existed. It follows that neither party can acquire any rights or incur any liability under the contract and that the contracting parties must be returned to the position they occupied before the contract was concluded, the *status quo ante*. Thus, any goods that have changed hands under the contract must be returned to the original owner and any monies paid must be refunded.

By contrast, the consequences of a contract being rendered voidable are less clear-cut. The contract in question remains legal and enforceable until such time as it is avoided by the innocent party. The effect of the avoidance is *prima facie* to terminate the contract *ab initio* with all goods and monies being returned to their original owner. However, the right to rescind the contract may be lost if either full restoration of the *status quo ante* is not possible or an innocent third party has acquired any goods under the contract prior to the rescission or the innocent contracting party chooses to affirm the contract and carry on.

The events that may render a contract either void or voidable are:

(a) mistake;
(b) misrepresentation;
(c) duress;
(d) illegality.

3.1 Mistake

Only an operative mistake will have any effect upon the existence or continuance of a contract, the meaning of an operative mistake being far narrower than the meaning of mistake in common parlance. Thus, for example, in the absence of some misrepresentation by the seller, the mere fact that a purchaser has not bought what he intended to buy or has paid too much for it will not affect the validity of the contract. The basic rule of *caveat emptor*, let the buyer beware, will apply unchallenged. However, two recent decisions have recognised a new situation whereby a plaintiff can recover for overpayment on a contract if the overpayment has resulted from a mistake of law. In **Kleinwort Benson Ltd *v* Lincoln City Council**

(1998), the House of Lords ruled, in a situation in which a local authority had entered an agreement which was *ultra vires* and therefore void, that money paid under a mistake of law can be recovered if to do otherwise would lead to the recipient of the money being unfairly enriched.

This decision was followed in 1999 in the decision of **Nurdin & Peacock plc *v* D B Ramsden & Co Ltd** (1999), in which the tenant of some commercial property overpaid rent having been wrongly advised by its solicitor that it could recover the overpayment through the courts. The court held that the overpayment was recoverable as the mistake of law induced the plaintiff to make the overpayment.

Operative mistakes fall into one of two categories:

1   Common mistake where both parties have made the same mistake about some fundamental aspect of the contract. They have made an agreement but based on a false premise.
2   Comprising both mutual mistake and unilateral mistake, this occurs where the mistake means that there is no true agreement between the parties.

3.1.1 Common mistake

The essential feature of common mistake is that both parties have made the same mistake about a fundamental feature of the contract. A typical example might be where the parties have contracted for the supply and purchase of some identified goods, both unaware that the goods had perished prior to the contract being made. The decision of **Couturier *v* Hastie** (1856) is the most commonly quoted authority for this proposition. The parties contracted for the sale of some corn which was in transit aboard ship. Unknown to both parties, a few days before the contract was made the captain of the ship had sold the corn as it had started to deteriorate and he wished to avoid loss.

A later decision that reinforces the doctrine of common mistake is **Associated Japanese Bank (International) Ltd *v* Crédit du Nord SA** (1988), a decision of the Commercial Court. In that decision, the plaintiff bank, Associated Japanese Bank (International) Ltd, agreed a sale and leaseback transaction with B under which the bank bought four specified precision engineering machines from B and then leased them back to him. Under this arrangement, the plaintiff bank paid £1,020,000 to B. The agreement was subject to a condition that B's obligations were to be guaranteed by the defendant bank, Crédit du Nord. Both banks believed that the four machines existed and were in B's possession. When B defaulted on the agreement, the plaintiff bank sought to enforce the guarantee. It transpired that the machines did not exist and the defendants denied liability arguing that the contract was void *ab initio* for common mistake. The court held that there was both an express and implied condition in the guarantee that the machines did exist. As they did not the guarantee was void for common mistake.

It is vital to recognise the distinction between the non-existence of goods and the fact that they are of a different quality from that envisaged. The leading case is that of **Bell *v* Lever Bros** (1932) relating to the termination of a contract of employment, in which Lord Atkin propounded the view that a mistake about the quality of the subject matter of a contract will be an operative mistake only if it involves 'the existence of some quality which makes the thing without the quality essentially different from the thing as it was believed to be'.

In respect of the sale or supply of goods, if the goods have been described as possessing some quality which they do not and the seller has warranted the truth of the statement, then a contract action will lie for a breach of s 13 of the Sale of Goods Act 1979 (or other similar provision under another statute depending on the nature of the supply of the goods). A misdescription of this nature would also give rise to criminal liability under s 1 of the Trade Descriptions Act 1968 if applied in the course of a trade or business.

The third way in which common mistake may arise is where both parties have made the same mistake about the ownership of the subject matter of the contract, typically where the seller purports to sell or supply something which, unknown to both parties, already belongs to the buyer.

3.1.2 Mutual mistake

Mutual mistake occurs when the parties are dealing at cross purposes with no real *consensus*, as, for example, if there is confusion about the subject matter of the contract. Thus, in **Raffles** *v* **Wichelhaus** (1864), the buyer agreed to buy some cotton to be transported on the ship 'Peerless'. In fact, there were two ships of that name, one sailing in October and the other in December. The buyer believed that he was buying the cotton to be transported in October, while the seller believed that he was selling the December shipment. The court held the contract void for mistake. There was no agreement.

3.1.3 Unilateral mistake

Unilateral mistake occurs where one party has made a mistake about a fundamental facet of the contract with knowledge of the other party. This may arise in two situations: a mistake as to the terms of the contract or a mistake as to the identity of one of the contracting parties.

Mistake as to terms

This rare situation occurs when one of the parties has misunderstood a fundamental term of the proposed contract, this mistake being known to the other contracting party. Thus, in the decision of **Hartog** *v* **Colin & Shields** (1939) the defendants offered to sell some hare skins and negotiated on the basis of a unit price per piece as was the trade custom. Subsequently, the contract was for a sale at a unit price per pound, which the plaintiffs purported to accept. They were prevented from enforcing the contract on the basis that they must have been aware of the defendants' mistake.

The behaviour of the 'guilty party' was discussed in the 1995 decision of **Commission for the New Towns** *v* **Cooper (GB) Ltd** (1995). The defendant, Cooper (GB) Ltd, had acquired an underlease of business premises from the predecessor in title. The original agreement had been granted by the plaintiff's predecessor in title and included four agreements, one of which was a 'put option' whereby the plaintiff could be obliged to take an assignment of the underlease from the defendant upon receipt of notice of termination. The defendant company were in financial difficulties and decided to try to acquire the 'put option' and then exercise it against the plaintiff. However, the defendant wanted to acquire the option without the plaintiff realising it, and so in discussions between the parties the defendant always concentrated on some other aspect of the agreement and never mentioned the option. Once the agreement had been signed, the defendant gave notice of its intention to exercise the option. The plaintiff sought to have the agreement rectified on the basis of unilateral mistake arguing that he had made a mistake as to the content of the agreement about which the defendant knew. The Court of Appeal held that the agreement should be rectified. Rectification can be granted on the basis of unconscionable behaviour by the defendant. The defendant intended the plaintiff to be mistaken about the terms of the agreement and had diverted the plaintiff's attention away from discovering the mistake by making false and misleading statements. The defendant had intended to deceive.

Mistake as to identity

Identity cases are most likely to arise when one of the contracting parties has been the victim of a fraud. The typical scenario is that the plaintiff seller has sold goods to a fraudster, who has in turn sold them to the defendant purchaser, who has bought them innocently and in good faith unaware of the fraud.

Whether the contract will be void for mistake or merely voidable for fraudulent misrepresentation will depend on the facts of the individual case and the extent to which the identity of the fraudster was central to the negotiations. Clearly, whether the contract is void or voidable has a significant impact on the rights of the innocent seller and purchaser and upon the ownership of the goods. If the contract is void, the original owner, the plaintiff seller, will be able to recover the goods from the defendant on the basis that the fraudster never acquired any title to the goods and thus was incapable of passing title to the defendant buyer. The buyer is liable for conversion of the goods and is left with the unenviable task of locating the fraudster and suing him under s 12(1) of the Sale of Goods Act 1979 for breach of the implied condition of the right to sell (see Chapter 7). By contrast, if the contract is voidable, the plaintiff seller can recover the goods only if he has avoided the contract before the fraudster sold the goods to the innocent defendant buyer. Otherwise, the buyer will be protected under s 23 of the Sale of Goods Act 1979 and gain valid title to the goods, leaving the seller with the equally unenviable task of suing the fraudster for the purchase price (see Chapter 10 for a full discussion of the s 23 provision).

Identity cases are subject to a rebuttable presumption that the seller who was the victim of the fraud intended to deal with the person with whom he actually dealt, i.e. the fraudster. In practice, this presumption is extremely difficult to rebut. For the contract to be held void for mistake the seller must prove that the identity of the person with whom he was dealing was of fundamental importance to him and that he intended to deal only with the person of the specified identity. Further, he must show that he took reasonable steps to confirm the identity of the buyer. The case of **Cundy v Lindsay** (1878) is a rare example of the successful rebuttal of the presumption. The fraudster, Blenkarn, ordered some handkerchiefs from Lindsay. He signed the order in such a way that it looked like 'Blenkiron & Co', a reputable company known to Lindsay which traded from the same street as Blenkarn. Lindsay despatched the goods to Blenkarn, who duly sold them to Cundy. The court held that the contract was void for mistake as Lindsay had intended to sell only to Blenkiron & Co. Lindsay was able to recover the cost of the goods from Cundy.

This case is of particular interest in the business context given that a large percentage of contracts are negotiated by letter or fax without the parties ever meeting face to face. Nonetheless, the importance of the case should not be overstated and must be contrasted with the decision in **Kings Norton Metal Co Ltd** *v* **Edridge, Merrett & Co Ltd** (1897), in which the plaintiffs sold goods to a fraudster named Wallis, who for the purposes of perpetrating the fraud had letterheads printed with the name 'Hallam & Co'. He then ordered the goods on headed paper. He subsequently sold them to the defendant, who acted in good faith. The court held that the contract was not void. The plaintiffs had always intended to contract with the fraudster and had done so.

The distinction between the two cases is vital. While the identity was crucial in **Cundy** *v* **Lindsay**, in the **Kings Norton** decision it was held that it was merely his ability to pay that mattered. His true identity was irrelevant.

The difficulty of rebutting the presumption is demonstrated further by the decision of **Lewis** *v* **Averay** (1971), in which the parties dealt face to face, as well as in the Commercial Court decision of **Citibank NA** *v* **Brown Shipley & Co Ltd** (1991). In **Lewis** *v* **Averay**, Lewis sold his car to a fraudster who claimed to be Richard Greene, an actor and star of the television series 'Robin Hood'. When paying by cheque, the fraudster produced what appeared to be a pass to Pinewood Studios as proof of identity. He then sold the car to Averay. The court held that the contract was not void for mistake but voidable for fraudulent misrepresentation, the identity of the fraudster not being important to the seller at the time of the contract. As the fraudster had sold the car to Averay before Lewis avoided the contract, Averay had acquired good title to it.

In **Citibank NA** *v* **Brown Shipley & Co Ltd** a fraudster purporting to be a signatory of a company account at Citibank NA phoned the defendant, Brown Shipley, and ordered large amounts of foreign currency, payment to be made by a banker's draft drawn on Citibank NA. He then contacted Citibank and asked them to draw up a banker's draft in favour of the defendant bank and drawn on the company's account. Citibank handed the banker's draft to the fraudster, who cashed it with Brown Shipley. The Commercial Court held that the contract was not void for mistake, only voidable, and that Citibank could not recover the money from the defendant. The identity of the fraudster had not been fundamental in the contract and title to the draft had passed to the defendant.

As indicated earlier, the identity situation is most likely to arise where a fraud has been perpetrated. However, this is not necessarily so and it may occur quite innocently as, for example, where a business has changed hands and a buyer continues to order goods from the business unaware of the change of ownership. If the buyer can establish that the identity of the proprietor of the business was of particular importance to the contractual relationship, the contract with the new proprietor would be void for mistake.

3.1.4 Mistake in documents

There are two further situations in which it may be possible to plead mistake. The first is where a contract has been reduced into writing but does not accurately reflect the terms of the agreement. The parties can seek the equitable remedy of rectification to have the document amended to record the agreement accurately.

The second involves the plea of *non est factum* – it is not my deed. This exception is limited to those situations where the plaintiff can show that the document he signed is essentially different in nature and effect from that which he thought he was signing, as in the decision of **Gibbon** *v* **Mitchell** (1990). Generally, the rule is that any contracting party is bound by what he has signed and will not be relieved of his liabilities. Thus, in **Saunders** *v* **Anglia Building Society** (1970) an elderly widow was bound by the terms of a document which she had not bothered to read. Similarly, a plaintiff cannot plead mistake if he has signed a blank contract and allowed the blanks to be filled in later, although if such a contract falls within the provisions of s 61 of the Consumer Credit Act 1974, the contract will be unenforceable against the debtor without a court order.

3.2 Misrepresentation

As discussed previously, a representation is a statement that occurs prior to a contract and which induces one of the parties to enter the contract. Should the representation prove false, a remedy will lie for misrepresentation, the precise outcome depending on whether the misrepresentation was fraudulent, negligent or innocent.

Three factors must be established for an action in misrepresentation:

(a) a misrepresentation of fact not law;
(b) the misrepresentation was material;
(c) it induced the contract.

3.2.1 A misrepresentation of fact

The misrepresentation must involve some pertinent fact, must be distinguished from a mere 'advertising puff' and must be a verifiable statement about an existing fact. A misrepresentation of law will not suffice as everyone is assumed to have equal access to the law.

Further, a distinction must be drawn between statements of fact and mere expressions of opinion. There is no liability for opinion unless the person either did not genuinely hold that opinion or had no reasonable grounds on which to base it. Opinion includes statements that cannot be verified such as the projected turnover in a business or the likely sales figures for a new untried product. A seemingly good product may fail spectacularly.

The decision of **Esso Petroleum Ltd** *v* **Mardon** (1976) confirms the view that opinion must be held reasonably. Esso wanted to sell a petrol site to Mardon and stated that the petrol sales for the site should reach 200,000 gallons per year. However, due to restricted access to the site, actual sales never exceeded 78,000 gallons a year. Esso were held liable for misrepresentation, the Court of Appeal holding that given their experience and skill in market research, their expressed opinion of likely sales was not reasonable.

Similarly, a statement about future conduct is not actionable unless it can be shown that the person had no intention of acting that way, as in **Edgington v Fitzmaurice** (1885), in which the directors of a company stated in their prospectus that the money to be raised from the sale of debentures would be used to buy premises and develop the company. In fact, they intended to use it to pay off debts. The plaintiff subscriber was able to rescind the contract for misrepresentation as the directors had deliberately misled prospective subscribers as to their intentions. Naturally, this does not affect the situation where the statement about future conduct is a term of the contract and is actionable as such as, for example, terms about future manufacture or delivery of goods.

Generally, silence will not be classed as a misrepresentation. However, there are some exceptions to this, namely where any statement actually made reveals only half the truth, where a true statement subsequently becomes untrue and where the relationship is *uberrimae fidei* (of the utmost good faith). A prime example of the last situation would be an insurance contract where the policyholder is obliged to disclose all relevant matters to the insurance company with silence constituting a misrepresentation which could render the policy invalid (see Chapter 21). It was confirmed in the Court of Appeal decision of **Banque Financière de la Cité SA v Westgate Insurance Co Ltd** (1990) that the duty is reciprocal, being placed on both insurer and insured.

Thus far, we have considered misrepresentation in terms of words but it is equally possible for a misrepresentation to be made by actions, as in the recent decision of **Spice Girls Ltd v Aprilia World Service BV** (2000), a case involving a pop group, the Spice Girls, who were negotiating a contract with Aprilia whereby the pop group, of whom there were five members, would promote Aprilia's product. Before the contract was signed, the five group members made a promotional film for Aprilia but did not reveal that one of the group members was intending to leave the group, a fact known to Spice Girls Ltd. It was held that allowing the filming to go ahead amounted to a misrepresentation by conduct by Spice Girls Ltd.

3.2.2 The misrepresentation must be material

To be actionable, the misrepresentation must have related to a material fact rather than mere trivia. A statement will be classed as material if a reasonable man would have been affected by it when deciding whether to enter the contract. Note that the test is objective and is not concerned with whether the particular plaintiff was influenced. That factor is considered separately. **JEB Fasteners Ltd v Marks Bloom & Co** (1983) demonstrates the distinction. The plaintiffs wanted to launch a takeover bid for JEB Fasteners Ltd, largely to acquire the services of two of the directors. As part of the takeover bid, the plaintiffs looked at the company's accounts, which it transpired were inaccurate because of the negligence of the defendant accountants. It was held that the accounts were a material representation as a reasonable man would be influenced by them when deciding whether to launch a takeover bid. However, it was held on the facts that the plaintiffs could not recover as they had not relied on them, being interested only in the directors.

3.2.3 The misrepresentation induced the contract

It is here that subjective reliance must be shown. As demonstrated by the **JEB Fasteners** decision, it is insufficient merely to show that a reasonable man would have relied on the misrepresentation; the plaintiff must show that it actually induced him to enter the contract. However, the Court of Appeal held in **Barton** *v* **County Natwest Ltd** (1999) that where the misrepresentation is one upon which a reasonable man would have relied, there will be a rebuttable presumption that the plaintiff actually relied upon it. It is up to the defendant to rebut that presumption by demonstrating that reliance did not take place. Naturally, the plaintiff will fail to prove reliance if either he was unaware of the misrepresentation, or, alternatively, he knew it was untrue. However, it should be noted that, in the absence of a fiduciary relationship, there is no obligation to correct a misrepresentation known to be held by a person.

3.2.4 Remedies for misrepresentation

The available remedies for misrepresentation are rescission and damages although the availability of the latter will depend to some extent on whether the misrepresentation was fraudulent, negligent or innocent.

Rescission
When a misrepresentation is proved the contract is usually voidable and thus the innocent party can rescind it and seek to restore the *status quo ante*. As explained previously, the innocent party's ability to recover any goods that have been transferred under the contract will be defeated if an innocent third party has acquired the goods before the act of avoidance. An action for damages would then lie.

To constitute a valid rescission, the innocent party must take some positive action; mental rescission will not suffice. However, there is no obligation to contact the other contracting party directly; it is sufficient that the innocent third party has undertaken some action that demonstrates an intention to rescind. Thus in **Car and Universal Finance Co Ltd** *v* **Caldwell** (1964), a case involving a car obtained by fraudulent misrepresentation, it was held sufficient to have informed the police and the AA of the fraud.

Damages
The ability to claim damages for misrepresentation will depend on the nature of the misrepresentation.

Fraudulent misrepresentation occurs when the person making the statement either knows it to be false, or does not believe it to be true, or is reckless as to whether it is true. Damages are payable irrespective of the statement's impact on the contract. There must be clear evidence of dishonesty, as held in **Derry** v **Peek** (1889), in which the directors of a company were found not liable for fraudulent misrepresentation in respect of a statement in a prospectus which they had genuinely believed to be true. The plaintiff may claim all the losses resulting directly from the fraudulent misrepresentation. It is not open to the defendant to claim a defence based on the contributory negligence of the plaintiff, as confirmed in **Alliance & Leicester Building Society** v **Edgestop Ltd** (1994).

Damages for negligent misrepresentation arise in both contract and tort. Under s 2(1) of the Misrepresentation Act 1967 'where a person has entered into a contract after a misrepresentation has been made to him by another party' the innocent party can claim contractual damages as long as the guilty party would have been liable to pay damages if the misrepresentation had been made fraudulently.

The damages that can be claimed under s 2(1) do not include claims for any loss of profit suffered by the plaintiff as a result of the misrepresentation. However, it was made clear in the decision of **East** v **Maurer** (1991) that the plaintiff can claim for any 'lost opportunity' that the misrepresentation caused. Thus, in **East** v **Maurer** the plaintiff had bought a hairdressing business in reliance upon a fraudulent misrepresentation. The court would not award any damages for lost profits but did award a sum in lieu of the profit that the plaintiff would have made if he had bought a different hairdressing business in the area.

The right to damages under s 2(1) will be lost, however, if the defendant can show that 'he had reasonable grounds to believe up to the time the contract was made that the facts represented were true'. Thus if the defendant can establish that he was not negligent the claim will fail. Damages for a negligent misstatement can also be founded in tort under the authority of **Hedley Byrne & Co Ltd** v **Heller & Partners Ltd** (1963), which is discussed in Chapter 11. Where a plaintiff makes concurrent claims in negligence at common law and under the Misrepresentation Act 1967, any claim that the plaintiff was contributorily negligent such as to reduce damages under the Law Reform (Contributory Negligence) Act 1945 will apply both to the negligence claim and to the claim under the Misrepresentation Act, as held in **Gran Gelato Ltd** v **Richcliff (Group) Ltd** (1992).

Under s 2(1) of the Misrepresentation Act 1967, damages for innocent misrepresentation are available for any loss flowing from the misrepresentation even if that loss was not foreseeable, as held by the Court of Appeal in **Royscott Trust Ltd** v **Rogerson** (1991). Further, while the normal remedy for innocent misrepresentation is rescission, the court has the power under s 2(2) of the 1967 Act to declare the contract subsisting and award damages instead if it is of the opinion that it would be just in all the circumstances. Note that there is no right to damages under this section; it is merely a discretion available to the court. In exercising it, the court must balance the nature of the misrepresentation and the loss that would be caused by upholding the contract against the loss that rescission would cause to the other party, an approach confirmed in the 1994 decision of **William Sindall plc** v **Cambridgeshire County Council** (1994). This discretion can never be used in respect of fraudulent misrepresentations.

3.3 Duress and undue influence

Agreement assumes the voluntary consent of both contracting parties. Naturally, if the consent of one party is involuntary because his agreement has been induced by duress, the contract should be voidable. Originally duress was restricted to actual or threatened violence such as to cause fear of physical injury or death. More recently, duress has been extended to cover illegitimate threats to goods, i.e. economic duress. In **Pau On** *v* **Lau Yiu Long** (1979) Lord Scarman summarised the position thus:

> there is nothing contrary to principle in recognising economic duress as a factor which may render a contract voidable, provided always that the basis of such recognition is that it must always amount to a coercion of will, which vitiates consent.

It seems that there are two criteria which must be satisfied if the duress is to be actionable. First, did the victim of the duress complain at the time and, second, did the victim intend to repudiate the agreement. A more recent example of economic duress occurred in **Atlas Express Ltd** *v* **Kafco (Importers and Distributors) Ltd** (1989) and would suggest that the concept is now firmly established. The plaintiff company, Atlas Express Ltd, contracted with the defendants, Kafco, to transport cartons of basketware for them to retail premises nationwide. The agreed rate was £1.10 per carton, the plaintiffs' expectation being that each load would comprise 400–600 cartons. The first load contained only 200 cartons and the plaintiffs refused to carry any more loads unless the defendents agreed to a minimum price of £440 per load. Unable to find an alternative carrier and thus dependent on the plaintiffs, the defendants agreed reluctantly to pay the new rate. When they subsequently refused to pay, the plaintiffs sued to enforce the new agreement. The Commercial Court, dismissing the claim, held that the pressure applied by the plaintiffs to force the defendants to renegotiate the contract was economic duress which vitiated the contract.

It had long been accepted that duress comprised two elements: first, that there must be a coercion of the plaintiff's will, and second, that the pressure must be illegitimate. In practice, illegitimate pressure frequently arose from an unlawful act. However, in **CTN Cash & Carry** *v* **Gallagher Ltd** (1994) the Court of Appeal had to consider both whether a lawful act could constitute duress and the situation where the two parties were dealing at arm's length. The defendant was a distributor of cigarettes and contracted to sell cigarettes to the plaintiff on the defendant's standard terms of business. The defendant also provided credit facilities that could legally be withdrawn. The plaintiff cash and carry company, which had six warehouses, ordered cigarettes worth £17,000 from the defendant, which were delivered accidentally to the wrong warehouse. The defendant agreed to redeliver the goods to the correct warehouse but in the interim the goods were stolen. The defendant claimed the £17,000 purchase price from the plaintiff, making clear that the plaintiff's credit facilities would be withdrawn if it did not pay. The plaintiff paid but then attempted to recover the £17,000 pleading duress. The Court of Appeal held that it is possible for the threat of a lawful act to constitute duress. On the facts, however, no duress existed for the defendant was entitled to withdraw the credit facilities and had done so in the genuine and reasonable belief that it was owed the money. Further, the parties had acted at arm's length, which militated against duress.

This principle was applied recently in the decision of **Alf Vaughan & Co Ltd (in receivership) v Royscott Trust plc** (1999), in which goods subject to a hire-purchase agreement were reclaimed by the legal owner when the hirer (Alf Vaughan & Co Ltd) went into receivership. While the receiver offered to pay the outstanding payments on the hire-purchase agreement and exercise the option to purchase, the owner would only agree if a higher payment were made. It was held that they were entitled to recover their own property and could only be prevented from so doing if any pressure that was applied was unconscionable in all the circumstances.

It should be stressed that economic duress does not extend to situations where the contracting parties have voluntarily agreed to enter a contract, the terms of which seem unfair or unduly onerous to one party. The law will not interfere with bargains agreed voluntarily.

Allied to the concept of duress is that of undue influence and the inequality of bargaining power. Undue influence typically occurs where one of the contracting parties holds a position of influence over the other and thus is in a position to influence the weaker to enter a contract against his own best interests. This would include relationships such as doctor/patient, solicitor/client and priest/parishioner. Any contract entered as a result of undue influence is voidable.

The concept of undue influence was analysed further by the House of Lords in **Barclays Bank v O'Brien** (1994), which confirmed the division of undue influence into two classes; class 1, actual undue influence, and class 2, presumed undue influence. Presumed undue influence is further subdivided into class 2A, that arising from the type of relationship in question, and class 2B, that arising from the specific relationship of the plaintiff and the defendant as, for example, with a husband and wife.

In **Barclays Bank v O'Brien** a husband persuaded his wife to sign a mortgage on their jointly owned home as security for an overdraft for his company, telling her that the overdraft was for three weeks and limited to £60,000. In practice, it was unlimited in both time and amount. The bank sought to foreclose on the mortgage when the overdraft debt reached £154,000. It transpired that the bank branch concerned had not complied with company policy of recommending that each party take independent advice about the transaction. It was held that the bank had notice of the undue influence exercised by the husband and the failure to advise the wife to take independent advice meant that they failed to protect her. Consequently, she was entitled to rescind the agreement.

The existence of actual undue influence is a question of fact based on the individual situation. It was established in **CIBC Mortgages plc v Pitt** (1994), a case held to involve actual undue influence, that it equates with fraud. As such, there is no need for the plaintiff to demonstrate any special relationship between himself and the defendant, or that the act complained of caused any manifest disadvantage to the plaintiff.

Situations of presumed undue influence arising from a type of relationship, class 2A, would include relationships such as doctor/patient, solicitor/client etc, in which it can be presumed that the dominant party exerts a degree of influence by virtue of his relative position and the degree of trust and confidence vested in him. The undue influence arises from the abuse of that relationship. There is generally a presumption that some manifest disadvantage to the plaintiff must have been caused by the undue influence if it is to be actionable.

Even in the absence of a special relationship of the type discussed, it is still possible to demonstrate undue influence because of the *de facto* specific relationship between the plaintiff and the defendant: a class 2B relationship. Such relationships have been held to exist between banks and their customers, between employers and employees, between husband and wife and between long-term cohabitees. Again, some manifest disadvantage must have been suffered by the plaintiff to found an action.

In situations of presumed undue influence, the burden of proof is on the dominant person to show that there was no abuse of the position and no undue influence. In practice, this is best demonstrated by showing that the plaintiff's subservient partner in the relationship received independent advice concerning the transaction. Three recent cases – **Banco Exterior Internacional** *v* **Mann** (1995), **Massey** *v* **Midland Bank plc** (1995) and **TSB Bank plc** *v* **Camfield** (1995), all of which involved situations in which a wife or long-term partner acting under undue influence was persuaded to give a charge over her home to the bank as security for a loan to the husband/partner confirmed the importance of ensuring that independent advice is provided. Equally, the decision of **Credit Lyonnais Bank Nederland NV** *v* **Burch** (1997), a case involving undue influence by an employer and family friend, reinforced the importance of ensuring that appropriate independent advice has been sought. In the **Credit Lyonnais** decision, a junior employee, who was also a family friend of her employer, was persuaded by him to take out a mortgage on her flat as security for his company's overdraft. Neither the employer nor the bank told the plaintiff about the company's precarious financial position although the bank did advise her to take independent legal advice about the transaction. To the bank's knowledge, she did not get independent advice and entered the agreement. The Court of Appeal held that the bank could not enforce the security against her as they had constructive knowledge of the undue influence exercised by her employer, actual knowledge that she had not received independent advice, and were aware that the nature of the agreement was so inadvisable that it was reasonable to assume that she had only entered into it as a result of undue influence.

The undue influence cases raise the issues of what constitutes independent advice and when a bank will be deemed to have constructive knowledge that undue influence exists. The Court of Appeal revisited these issues in the 1998 decision of **Royal Bank of Scotland** *v* **Etridge** (1998) when it held that a bank is entitled to assume that a solicitor will always act professionally when giving legal advice even if the solicitor has been retained by the person allegedly exercising the undue influence. However, a bank will still be deemed to have constructive knowledge of undue influence if either the solicitor was not aware of all the relevant facts when giving the advice or, alternatively, no competent solicitor would have advised the client to proceed.

In summary, while a failure to show the existence of independent advice will not necessarily be fatal in undue influence cases, it is certainly easier for the bank enforcing the charge to overcome allegations of undue influence if independent advice can be demonstrated. Further, a third party such as a bank will be unable to enforce a contract resulting from undue influence if it has had actual or constructive notice of that undue influence.

A contract entered into as a result of undue influence is voidable not void. It is clear, however, that the transaction as a whole is avoided and that the defendant cannot argue – as was attempted in the **TSB Bank plc *v* Camfield** case – that the plaintiff should remain liable for that part of the contract/security which she would have undertaken willingly.

Despite Lord Denning MR's attempts in **Lloyds Bank Ltd *v* Bundy** (1975), inequality of bargaining power is not recognised as a ground for rendering contracts voidable. Nonetheless, in the area of consumer law, there are a few examples of statutory protective measures that rely on that general idea. The most notable is in ss 137–138 of the Consumer Credit Act 1974, in which the court has the power to reopen extortionate credit bargains if certain criteria are satisfied.

3.4 Illegality and invalidity

A total of nine different categories of contract are either illegal or void at common law. While void contracts will be of no legal effect, it was confirmed by the Court of Appeal in **Birkett *v* Acorn Business Machines Ltd** (1999) that the courts will refuse to enforce an illegal contract irrespective of whether that fact is actually pleaded in any court hearing involving a contract dispute.

Two forms of illegal contract are relevant here: contracts that oust the jurisdiction of the courts and contracts in restraint of trade.

3.4.1 Ousting the jurisdiction of the court

Contracts to oust the jurisdiction of the courts are void. However, contractual terms agreeing to submit disputes to arbitration are valid as are agreements to use some form of alternative dispute resolution. Such agreements are enforceable provided that they do not seek to oust the supervisory powers of the court.

3.4.2 Contracts in restraint of trade

Generally, it is in the public interest to allow individuals to follow their trade or profession, any contract that interferes with this freedom being *prima facie* void. Nonetheless, there are situations in which it may be reasonable to permit some fetter to be placed on an individual's ability to trade freely. These are:

1　the right of a purchaser of a business to protect the goodwill from abuse by the previous owner;
2　an employer's right to protect legitimate business interests, i.e. trade secrets and customer lists, from past employees (see also Chapter 19);

3   agreements whereby a trader agrees to restrict his sources to one manufacturer or wholesaler; and

4   contrary contracts to the Competition Act 1998 (see also Chapter 18).

A restraint of trade clause is *prima facie* void, it being the responsibility of the person relying on it to demonstrate its validity by showing that it is both in the public interest and reasonable as between the parties.

In respect of the first two types of clause listed above, their validity will depend largely on the geographic area of the restriction and its duration, although in respect of controlling past employees other factors such as their position in the firm may be relevant in determining their access to trade secrets or their ability to influence customers. The clause must not merely seek to prevent competition; it must protect some legitimate interest. In **Nordenfelt *v* Maxim Nordenfelt Guns and Ammunition Co** (1894) it was considered reasonable for an armament manufacturer to be bound by a clause agreed when he sold his business in which he promised not to deal in arms worldwide for a period of 25 years. Similarly, in **Forster & Sons Ltd *v* Suggett** (1918), a manager who had acquired trade secrets regarding the manufacture of glass, was prevented from being involved in glass making anywhere in Britain for five years. By contrast, in **M & S Drapers (a firm) *v* Reynolds** (1956) a five-year restraint against a salesman was not enforced.

Restraint of trade clauses preventing former employees of a company from soliciting customers of the company for a given period are capable of being enforced by a subsequent purchaser of the company. Thus, in **Morris Angel & Son Ltd *v* Hollande** (1993) the Court of Appeal held that where the plaintiff had purchased a company and then immediately sacked the defendant, the managing director of the company, the plaintiff was entitled to enforce the restraint of trade clause contained in the defendant's contract. The plaintiff had acquired all the rights and obligations of the company at the time of purchase including the right to enforce the restraint of trade clause. This would also be true of companies to which the Transfer of Undertakings (Protection of Employment) Regulations 1981 apply.

'Vertical agreements' or 'solus agreements' whereby a trader agrees to restrict his source of supply to one manufacturer may be upheld if their duration is reasonable and the trader derives some benefit from the contract. Thus, in **Esso Petroleum Co Ltd *v* Harper's Garage (Stourport) Ltd** (1967) Harper's entered into two agreements with Esso whereby Harper's agreed to buy all the petrol for two garages from Esso. They further agreed to keep the garages open at all reasonable hours and to ensure that anyone buying the garages would abide by the solus agreements. In return, Harper's received a discount on all their petrol and the second garage was mortgaged to Esso to cover a loan of £7,000. The agreements were to last for four and a half years for the first garage and 21 years (the term of the mortgage) for the second garage. The House of Lords held that the first agreement was valid but that the second one was unreasonable and hence void.

Contracts which are contrary to the Restrictive Practices Acts 1976 and 1977 and the Resale Prices Act 1976, both of which seek to control anti-competitive practices, are considered fully in Chapter 18.

Question

Hippo Ltd, wholesalers of clothing, entered two contracts:

(a) They contracted to sell 20 coats valued at £1,400 to Jones Bros. The order for the coats was received on paper headed 'Jones Bros, Wholesale Clothier, 15 Forest Hill, Blanktown'. Hippo Ltd had not dealt with Jones Bros in the past. Hippo Ltd have not received payment and an investigation has revealed that Jones Bros do not exist. The coats had actually been ordered by Jeremy, a fraudster.

(b) They contracted to buy designer lingerie from a distributor, Worm Silks Ltd, at a cost of £3,000, delivery to be made in five instalments. Hippo Ltd have already contracted to sell the lingerie to various retail outlets. After three instalments had been delivered, Worm Silks Ltd announced that they were raising the contract price to £3,800. Unable to get replacement goods elsewhere with which to fulfil the retail contracts, Hippo Ltd have had no alternative but to pay the extra £800.

Advise Hippo Ltd about possible remedies available to them in respect of each of the two contracts.

Answer

The two parts of this question deal with two different situations in which the consent to the contract has not been genuine.

(a) Part (a) deals with a situation in which the buyer of goods has misrepresented his identity so that the seller is not aware of the true identity of the purchaser. The solution depends on whether the identity of the buyer was essential to the formation of the contract. There is a presumption that the seller intended to deal with the person with whom he actually dealt and that the identity of the buyer did not matter. Where this is so, the contract will only be voidable. Where the identity was crucial the contract will be held void for mistake. In this question, applying **Kings Norton Metal Co Ltd v Edridge, Merrett & Co Ltd** (1897), it will be held that Hippo Ltd intended to deal with Jeremy. As such the contract is only voidable and if Hippo Ltd are to regain the coats they must avoid the contract before Jeremy sells the coats to an innocent third party.

(b) On the facts, Hippo Ltd have had no alternative but to complete the contract with Worm Silks Ltd despite the price being raised by £800 otherwise they will be in breach of their retail contracts. However, the decision to continue the contract with Worm Silks Ltd has resulted from duress and Hippo Ltd would be entitled to claim for a return of the £800.

Further reading

Adams, A (2000). *Law for Business Students*, 2nd edn (Longman)

Bradgate, R (2000). *Commercial Law*, 3rd edn (Butterworth)

Dobson, P (1997). *Charlesworth's Business Law*, 16th edn (Sweet & Maxwell)

Downes, T A (1997). *Textbook on Contract*, 5th edn (Blackstone Press)

Keenan, D (2000). *Smith and Keenan's Advanced Business Law*, 11th edn (Longman)

Keenan, D and Riches, S (2001). *Business Law*, 6th edn (Longman)

Richards, P (2001) *Law of Contract*, 5th edn (Longman)

Stone, R (2000). *Principles of Contract Law*, 4th edn (Cavendish)

4 Exclusion clauses

Inequality of bargaining power in a contract is at its most obvious in relation to limitation clauses and exclusion clauses, whereby the stronger party may seek to limit or totally exclude his liability to the weaker party in the event of breach. Such clauses, in common use in business contracts, have been subjected to control by common law and more recently and effectively by statute.

4.1 Common law control

Attempts by the common law to control exclusion clauses have revolved around three strategies: incorporation, interpretation and the now defunct doctrine of fundamental breach.

4.1.1 Incorporation

The same requirements for incorporation apply to exclusion clauses as to any other express clause, namely that the clause must be validly incorporated at the time that the contract is made, as in **Olley** *v* **Marlborough Court Ltd** (1949). Methods of incorporation vary along with the emphasis that any clause must receive for effective incorporation.

Signed documents
The parties to a signed agreement are bound by the terms of the agreement irrespective of whether they have read the document. It follows, therefore, that if the contract includes a limitation or exclusion clause the parties will be bound by it as it will have been validly incorporated. Thus, in **L'Estrange** *v* **Graucob** (1934) the plaintiff, Miss L'Estrange, bought a cigarette vending machine and signed a sales agreement. In the small print of the agreement was a clause reading 'Any express or implied condition, statement or warranty, statutory or otherwise, not stated herein is expressly excluded'. Miss L'Estrange signed the agreement without reading it. The machine proved unfit for its purpose but the court held that Miss L'Estrange was still liable to pay for it as she had signed away her rights. The draconian exclusion clause in this case is typical of those that led to a demand for the controls ultimately contained in the Unfair Contract Terms Act 1977.

The enforceability of a signed document would not extend, of course, to situations where *non est factum* has been pleaded successfully (see Chapter 3)

Notices

Where there is no signed contract, merely an unsigned notice or ticket, it is still possible to incorporate an exclusion clause as long as two criteria are satisfied. First, the person to whom the unsigned document was given either knew or should have realised that it had contractual effect and, second, sufficient notice of the exclusion clause has been given. The description given to the document by the parties, for example invoice, receipt etc, is not conclusive, the correct test being the objective one of whether the reasonable man would have assumed the document to contain contractual terms as opposed to being a mere acknowledgement or receipt for payment. In **Chapelton *v* Barry UDC (1940)** the plaintiff, Chapelton, was given a ticket when he hired a deck chair. There was an exclusion clause on the reverse of the ticket which read 'The Council will not be liable for any accident or damage arising from hire of the chair'. The canvas of the chair gave way and Mr Chapelton was injured. The court held the council liable, holding that the document was a mere receipt which no reasonable man would have considered to be a contract.

The issue of notice must be resolved on a case by case basis. Reasonable notice of the existence of the clause must have been given to the party bound by it with a greater degree of notice being demanded if the clause is particularly onerous or unusual in its effect. Thus, in **Thornton *v* Shoe Lane Parking Ltd (1971)** the plaintiff, Thornton, when parking his car in the defendant's car park received a ticket which stated on the reverse 'issued subject to the conditions of issue displayed on the premises'. Inside the car park was a separate notice purporting to exclude the defendant's liability for 'loss, mis-delivery of or damage to the vehicle or injury to the customer'. Mr Thornton was subsequently injured in an accident caused partly by the defendant's negligence. The Court of Appeal found the defendant liable, holding the exclusion clause ineffective as it was sufficiently unusual to justify it being explicitly drawn to the plaintiff's attention.

A similar approach was adopted in **Interfoto Picture Library *v* Stiletto Visual Programmes Ltd (1988)**, which related to an unusually onerous penalty clause. The Court of Appeal held that the clause contained in a standard form contract had not been incorporated due to a lack of appropriate notice. Nonetheless, the plaintiffs were awarded some damages on a *quantum meruit* basis.

The most telling and oft-quoted comment on the requirement of notice was given by Denning LJ in **Spurling *v* Bradshaw (1956)** when he stated that some clauses:

> . . . would need to be printed in red ink on the face of the document with a red hand pointing to it before the notice could be held to be sufficient.

Previous course of dealings

Trade custom or a longstanding course of dealing between two parties may give rise to the incorporation of a limitation or exclusion clause. In practice, this is more likely to arise in a commercial context where regular dealings between two parties are more likely to occur. The involvement of a consumer in a regular course of dealing is less likely.

This distinction is illustrated by contrasting the decisions of **Kendall (Henry) & Sons (a firm)** *v* **William Lillico & Sons Ltd** (1969) and **Hollier** *v* **Rambler Motors (AMC) Ltd** (1972). In the **Kendall** decision, a course of dealing involving over 100 transactions over a three-year period was held to be sufficient to incorporate an exclusion clause. The sellers sold some animal feed to the buyer in an oral contract followed up by a written 'sold note' containing an exclusion clause on the reverse. When the goods proved unfit, the House of Lords held that the exclusion clause protected the defendant from liability. Although the sold note had not been incorporated as it occurred after the oral contract, the previous course of dealing on the same terms demonstrated a preparedness by the parties to be bound by those terms, including the exclusion clause.

By contrast, in **Hollier** *v* **Rambler Motors (AMC) Ltd** three or four transactions in the previous five years was not sufficient to found a course of dealing. The plaintiff, Hollier, had left his car at the defendant's garage to be repaired. It was damaged in a fire caused by the defendant's negligence. The plaintiff had used the garage three or four times in the previous five years and on two occasions had signed invoices containing a clause excluding the defendant's liability in the event of fire. The Court of Appeal held that the exclusion clause had not been validly incorporated.

4.1.2 Interpretation

Traditionally, the courts have taken a strict view of the interpretation of exclusion clauses. The basic tenet of interpretation is that the clause will be construed *contra proferentum* (against the person seeking to rely on it). One effect of this approach is that the clause will apply only to matters expressly covered by it and any ambiguity will be construed in favour of the innocent party. Thus in **Andrews Bros (Bournemouth) Ltd** *v* **Singer & Co** (1934) the plaintiff entered a contract to buy 'new Singer cars' from the defendant. The contract contained an exclusion clause which excluded all liability for implied terms. One of the cars supplied was not new. The Court of Appeal held that the exclusion clause was not valid as the term 'new Singer car' was a condition of the contract and the exclusion clause only covered warranties.

A further effect of this approach is that where liability may arise under either contract or negligence, only the contractual liability will be covered by the clause unless it expressly refers to negligence. However, if the only liability that can arise is in negligence, no contract action being possible, the clause will be presumed to apply to the negligence claim. Hence, in **White** *v* **John Warwick & Co Ltd** (1953) White hired a bicycle from the defendants. The hire agreement included an exclusion clause stating 'nothing in this agreement shall render the owners liable for personal injury'. While riding the bike, White was injured when the saddle tipped forward. The Court of Appeal held that the defendants were liable in negligence and could not claim the protection of the exclusion clause. A contractual liability existed regarding the merchantability of the bike and the effect of the exclusion clause was limited to that liability.

Lastly, an exclusion clause will not be upheld if the party seeking to rely upon it misrepresented its effect to the other contracting party, as in **Curtis** *v* **Chemical Cleaning & Dyeing Co** (1951).

4.1.3 Doctrine of fundamental breach

The doctrine of fundamental breach stipulated that an exclusion clause could never negate liability for the breach of a fundamental term of the contract, i.e. a term going to the heart of the contract. This doctrine was finally and firmly laid to rest by the House of Lords in **Photo Production Ltd *v* Securicor Transport Ltd** (1980), Lord Wilberforce stating

> After [the Unfair Contract Terms Act 1977], in commercial matters generally, when the parties are not of unequal bargaining power, and when risks are normally borne by insurance . . . there is everything to be said . . . for leaving the parties free to apportion the risks as they think fit and for respecting their decisions.

This is of particular importance in contracts between businesses who are given the power to determine their own contract terms subject to the provisions of the Unfair Contract Terms Act 1977.

4.2 Statutory control

Since 1977 statutory control of exclusion clauses has been governed largely, though not exclusively, by the provisions of the Unfair Contract Terms Act 1977. This Act, which governs clauses used by businessmen, renders some clauses void and subjects others to a test of reasonableness. The Act's title is misleading in that it covers only limitation and exclusion clauses and not all contract terms that might be deemed unfair. Further, it extends to both contract and tort, notably negligence. The Act is now supplemented by the Unfair Terms in Consumer Contracts Regulations 1999, which will be considered later.

4.3 Unfair Contract Terms Act 1977

The 1977 Act applies to contracts entered into on or after 1 February 1978 and covers business liability, defined as being obligations or duties arising:

(a) from things done or to be done by a person in the course of a business (whether his own business or another's); or

(b) from the occupation of premises used for the business purposes of the occupier . . .

Business includes a profession and any activities of any government department or local or public authority. This position was confirmed in the decision of **St Albans City and District Council *v* International Computers Ltd** (1996), in which a local authority purchased a piece of computer software from International Computers Ltd to help them administer the collection of the community charge. They dealt on the defendant's standard contract terms. Because of an error in the software, the computer program overestimated the population liable to pay community charge and, in reliance upon this figure, the local authority set a community charge that was too low. The shortfall had to be recouped by setting a much higher charge the following year. The local authority claimed damages. Clause 9 of the contract was a limitation clause which sought to limit the defendant's liability to £100,000. In applying the Unfair Contract Terms Act 1977 to the case, both parties accepted that the local authority was acting in the course of a business and that the transaction was therefore a business to business sale.

4.3.1   Dealing as a consumer

The protection the Unfair Contract Terms Act 1977 provides to the other contracting party depends to a significant extent on whether that person is 'dealing as a consumer'. This status depends on three factors to be found in s 12, which states:

> A party to a contract 'deals as a consumer' in relation to another party if—
> (a) he neither makes the contract in the course of a business nor holds himself out as so doing; and
> (b) the other party does make the contract in the course of a business; and
> (c) in the case of a contract governed by the law of sale of goods or hire-purchase, or by section 7 of this Act, the goods passing under or in pursuance of the contract are of a type ordinarily supplied for private use or consumption.

This definition gives rise to two issues of interpretation: first, what does 'in the course of a business' mean and, second, when are goods 'of a type ordinarily supplied for private use and consumption'? In respect of the first, the courts, thus far, seem to be adopting the same approach as under the Trade Descriptions Act 1968 by holding that the mere fact that the purchaser is a business does not necessarily prevent it acting as a consumer in any particular transaction. The nature of the transaction will depend on whether the purchase was integral to the purchaser's business or merely incidental. Thus, in **R & B Customs Brokers Co Ltd** *v* **United Dominions Trust Ltd** (1988) the plaintiff company bought a second-hand car for one of their directors, to be used partly for business and partly for private motoring. The purchase was financed through the defendant finance company with an agreement which contained an exclusion clause. When the car leaked, the plaintiff sought to recover the purchase price. The Court of Appeal found that car was not fit for its purpose contrary to s 14(3) of the Sale of Goods Act 1979. Further, as the car was only the second or third bought by the plaintiff on credit terms, the practice was not integral to the business. As such, the plaintiff should be classed as a consumer, against whom the exclusion clause was void.

If the courts continue to adopt this approach, which is similar to that adopted in ss 1 and 14 of the Trade Descriptions Act 1968 and in the decision of **Havering London Borough Council** *v* **Stevenson** (1970), it would mean if taken to its logical conclusion that a business will act as a business only in respect of stock-in-trade items. All ancillary items not essential to the business would be bought 'as a consumer'. It seems likely that this situation will continue despite the decision of **Stevenson** *v* **Rogers** (1999), which seems likely to be restricted to cases under the sale of goods legislation.

Which goods are of a type 'ordinarily supplied for private use or consumption' is also not as clear-cut as might first appear. Heavy manufacturing plant is obviously not for private use, curtains for one's home clearly are. The difficulty lies with those items that straddle the divide such as company cars used for private purposes and personal computers/word processors used for both business and private correspondence. It can only be decided on a case by case basis.

4.3.2 Reasonableness

A recurring theme of the 1977 Act is that some exclusion clauses may be valid to the extent that they are reasonable. This clearly begs the question what is reasonable? There are no clear guidelines other than those contained in Schedule 2, which relate specifically to liability when goods are covered by ss 6 and 7, although s 11 does refer to some general factors that should be considered. These include that the burden lies on the person seeking to rely on the clause to show that it is reasonable, that reliance on a non-contractual notice should be fair and reasonable in all the circumstances and that where limitation clauses are concerned the court should consider the resources open to the contracting party to cover his potential liability and the availability of insurance. The more far-reaching an exclusion clause or limitation clause seeks to be, the less likely it is to be upheld as satisfying the 'reasonableness' requirement. Thus, in **Sovereign Finance Ltd** *v* **Silver Crest Furniture Ltd** (1997) an exclusion clause which purported to exclude all liability was held to be unreasonable and hence unenforceable.

Schedule 2 lays down five criteria to be considered in relation to liability under ss 6(3) and 7(3) when clauses are being used in business to business sale or supply. These are:

(a) The relative bargaining strength of the parties including any alternative means of satisfying the customer's requirements. This would be relevant if, for example, a multi-national company was imposing an exclusion clause on a small manufacturer.

(b) Whether the party received any inducement to accept the term or whether he had the opportunity to gain a similar contract elsewhere without the term. It may be that the customer received a discount on the price or the opportunity to buy on credit in exchange for accepting the exclusion clause.

(c) Whether the customer knew or ought to have known of the existence of the term. Was the term drawn to the customer's attention or was there a previous course of dealing such as to assume knowledge of incorporation?

(d) Where the clause excludes liability for non-compliance with a contractual term, whether such compliance was practical. For example, can a customer be required to give notice of any defect before it would become apparent, as in **R W Green Ltd** *v* **Cade Bros Farm** (1978), in which the buyer was required to inform the seller of seed potatoes of any defect in the product within three days of delivery?

(e)   Whether the goods were manufactured, processed or adapted to the special order of the customer. If this is so, it may be reasonable for the supplier to exclude liability for merchantability and/or fitness for purpose.

Whether any particular contract term is unreasonable will, of course, be a question of fact. For example, in the 1996 decision of **St Albans City and District Council** *v* **International Computers Ltd** (see above) the Court of Appeal held that the limitation clause which sought to limit the defendant's liability to £100,000 was unreasonable. The figure was too small relative to the potential and actual loss and also that, as the choice of providers was very limited, the defendant was in a very strong position when setting the contractual terms. Further, it was fairer to place liability on the defendant, who carried substantial product liability insurance, rather than on the local authority taxpayers.

4.3.3   Section 2 – Negligence liability

Section 2 of the 1977 Act prohibits the use of contract terms or notices to exclude liability for death or personal injury caused by negligence. In respect of any other loss or damage caused by negligence it is possible to exclude liability to the extent that the exclusion is reasonable.

4.3.4   Section 3 – Contractual liability

Section 3 covers two situations where there is potential for an inequality of bargaining power: first, where one of the contracting parties is dealing as a consumer and, second, where one of the parties deals on the other's standard terms. In either of these situations the other party cannot use a contract term to exclude or restrict his or her liability in the event of a breach of contract. Section 3 further provides that a trader cannot claim to be entitled to render either no contractual performance at all or a substantially different performance from that expected unless the contract term is reasonable.

4.3.5   Section 4 – Unreasonable indemnity clauses

Under s 4 a person dealing as a consumer cannot by reference to a contract term be made to indemnify another person (whether a party to the contract or not) in respect of liability that may be incurred in contract or negligence unless the term is reasonable.

4.3.6   Section 5 – Manufacturer's guarantees

Section 5 defines a guarantee as being 'anything in writing . . . if it purports to contain some promise or assurance (however worded or presented) that defects will be made good by complete or partial replacement, or by repair, monetary compensation or otherwise'. A manufacturer cannot use a contract term or notice related to the guarantee to exclude liability for loss or damage to goods ordinarily supplied for private use or consumption if the loss or damage has arisen from the goods proving defective while in consumer use and results from the negligence of the manufacturer or a person involved in the distribution process. This section resolves the problems caused by manufacturers using guarantees ostensibly to provide consumers with additional rights while actually using them to deprive the consumer of some of his legal rights, both contractual and tortious.

4.3.7 Section 6 – Sale of goods and hire-purchase

Section 6 contains some of the central provisions of the Unfair Contract Terms Act 1977. It concerns the extent to which it is possible to exclude liability for the implied conditions of title, description, satisfactory quality, fitness for purpose and sale by sample contained in ss 12–15 of the Sale of Goods Act 1979 and ss 8–11 of the Supply of Goods (Implied Terms) Act 1973. The former provisions relate to contracts for the sale of goods, while the latter imply the same terms into hire-purchase contracts. Section 6 deals with both categories of contract simultaneously.

The condition as to title receives separate treatment under s 6(1) of the Unfair Contract Terms Act 1977, which provides that it cannot be excluded by reference to any contract term.

The legitimacy of exclusion clauses relating to description, satisfactory quality, fitness for purpose and sale by sample depends upon whether the purchaser was 'dealing as a consumer'. If he was, s 6(2) provides that the implied terms cannot be excluded. While this protects the consumer from business sellers, it offers no protection at all if the item was sold by a private individual who would not satisfy the requirement of being 'in the course of a business' (Unfair Contract Terms Act 1977, s 12).

If the purchaser is not 'dealing as a consumer' because he is in the course of a business as is the seller, then exclusion clauses are permissible under s 6(3) to the extent that they are reasonable. This will depend upon the application of the Schedule 2 guidelines discussed above. Note, however, that a private seller can never be held liable in respect of the conditions of satisfactory quality and fitness for purpose as those conditions apply only if the seller sells 'in the course of a business' (see Chapter 7). As such, any discussion of the exclusion of that liability by private sellers is irrelevant.

4.3.8 Section 7 – Contracts for the supply of goods

Part I of the Supply of Goods and Services Act 1982 makes provision for the implied terms of title, description, satisfactory quality, fitness for purpose and sale by sample to be implied both into other contracts under which goods are supplied and into hire contracts. This covers, for example, contracts for the repair of goods under which spare parts are to be provided by the repairer together with contracts of barter for which the consideration is not money but in kind. In respect of contracts under which the ownership of goods will pass, any exclusion of the condition as to title is void. However, in hire contracts, it can be excluded to the extent that the exclusion is reasonable. The remaining implied conditions are dealt with in the same way as under s 6 of the Unfair Contract Terms Act 1977, namely that under s 7(2) of that Act they cannot be excluded against a person 'dealing as a consumer' but otherwise can be excluded under s 7(3) subject to the test of reasonableness.

4.3.9 Section 8 – Liability for misrepresentation

Section 3 of the Misrepresentation Act 1967 as amended by s 8 of the Unfair Contract Terms Act 1977 prevents the exclusion of liability for misrepresentation except to the extent that the exclusion is reasonable.

4.4 Unfair Terms in Consumer Contracts Regulations 1999

The Unfair Terms in Consumer Contracts Regulations 1999, which replaced the 1994 Regulations of the same name, came into force on 1 October 1999. The Regulations apply in addition to the Unfair Contract Terms Act 1977 and thus create an additional layer of protection in respect of those contracts governed by the Regulations. Both the Regulations and the Unfair Contract Terms Act must be satisfied if the clause is to be upheld.

4.4.1 The terms covered

The Regulations lay down new requirements for the control of unfair terms, including exclusion clauses, in contracts concluded between a seller or supplier and a consumer. For these purposes, a consumer is defined as 'any natural person who, in contracts covered by these Regulations, is acting for purposes which are outside his trade, business or profession'. Hence, given the reference to a natural person, it is clear that limited companies are not protected by these Regulations. By contrast, a sole trader or a partnership acting for purposes not connected with their business would attract protection. A 'seller or supplier' is defined as 'any natural or legal person who, in contracts covered by these Regulations, is acting for purposes relating to his trade, business or profession, whether publicly owned or privately owned'. It is clear that the definition of seller or supplier encompasses limited companies.

The rationale behind the Regulations is to protect consumers against unfair terms over which they have had no control. Thus, reg 3 provides that the Regulations will apply in relation to unfair terms in contracts concluded between a seller or supplier and a consumer. However, the Regulations do not apply to contractual terms which reflect mandatory statutory or regulatory provisions or the provisions or principles of international conventions to which the EEA member state or the European Community is party.

4.4.2 Unfair terms

Having identified those contract terms covered by the Regulations, the main thrust of the controls is to render 'unfair terms' in a contract concluded with a consumer by a seller or supplier not binding on the consumer. Such terms will be of no effect. However, the provision only impacts upon the unfair terms themselves and thus the remainder of the contract will continue to be binding as long as it is capable of subsisting without the unfair terms.

Regulation 5(1) provides the basic statement that:

> A contractual term which has not been individually negotiated shall be regarded as unfair if, contrary to the requirement of good faith, it causes a significant imbalance in the parties' rights and obligations arising under the contract, to the detriment of the consumer.

For these purposes, there is a presumption that a term has not been individually negotiated where it has been drafted in advance and the consumer therefore has not been able to influence the substance of the term. Naturally, this applies most easily to standard form contracts over which the consumer has had no control. Indeed reg 5(3) even provides that despite the fact that a specific term or certain aspects of it have been individually negotiated, these Regulations will still apply to the rest of the contract if an overall assessment of the contract indicates that it is a pre-formulated standard contract. The burden of proving that a term has been individually negotiated and thus falls outside the parameters of the Regulations lies on the seller or supplier who claims that it was.

Given that the purpose is to render unfair terms not binding on the consumer, the key question is, of course, how to identify an 'unfair term'. As stated above, reg 5(1) defines it as a term which, contrary to the requirement of good faith, causes a significant imbalance in the parties' rights and obligations under the contract to the detriment of the consumer. When assessing the potential unfairness of a contractual term, reg 6 requires that the nature of the goods or services for which the contract was concluded be taken into account as well as all the circumstances pertaining at the conclusion of the contract and all the other terms of the contract or any other contract upon which it is dependent. However, as long as the terms are expressed in plain intelligible language, the assessment of the fairness of a term will not include consideration of any term which defines the main subject matter of the contract or the adequacy of the price or remuneration as compared with the goods or services supplied in exchange. In short, the Regulations do not take account of whether the consumer has made a bad bargain.

Which clauses are subject to the test of fairness was considered in the Court of Appeal decision of **Director General of Fair Trading *v* First National Bank plc** (2000), which was decided on a similar provision in the 1994 Regulations. In that decision, the Director General of Fair Trading challenged a term contained in the standard contract terms upon which First National Bank conducted business. Clause 8 of the contract provided that if a debtor under one of their credit agreements were to default, the bank could claim the whole of the outstanding debt together with accrued interest. However, it also provided that the bank could claim additional interest on the outstanding debt to be charged at the contractual rate until payment, both before and after any court judgment. The Director General alleged that this clause was unfair within the meaning of the Regulations. The bank claimed that the fairness test could not be applied to this term as it was a 'core term' of the contract. However, the Court of Appeal held that the clause was subject to the fairness test as only clauses defining the main subject of the contract or the adequacy of the price were exempt from the fairness test. The court further held that the clause in question did not satisfy the requirement of good faith.

Regulation 7 provides that where the contract is provided in writing, the seller or supplier must ensure that it is written in plain intelligible language with any doubt about the meaning being construed in favour of the consumer.

Schedule 2 to the Regulations contains an indicative, illustrative and non-exhaustive list of 17 terms which may be regarded as unfair. Included amongst these are:

(a) terms that have the object or effect of excluding or limiting liability in the event of the death of or personal injury to the consumer;

(b) terms permitting the seller to retain money from the consumer should he cancel the contract while not permitting the consumer to receive an equivalent amount from the supplier should the supplier cancel;

(c) automatically extending contracts of fixed duration where the consumer has not indicated otherwise when the deadline fixed for the consumer to express his desire not to extend the contract is unreasonably early;

(d) enabling the supplier to alter the terms of the contract unilaterally without a valid reason being specified in the contract;

(e) providing for the price of goods to be determined at the time of delivery or allowing a seller of goods or supplier of goods or supplier of services to increase their price without in both cases giving the consumer the corresponding right to cancel the contract if the final price is too high in relation to the price agreed when the contract was concluded;

(f) giving the seller or supplier the right to determine whether the goods supplied or services provided are in conformity with the contract, or giving him the exclusive right to interpret any term of the contract; and

(g) obliging the consumer to fulfil all his contractual obligations while the supplier does not fulfil his.

4.4.3 Role of the Director General of Fair Trading

As a further measure of consumer protection, the Regulations provide for the Director General of Fair Trading and 'qualifying bodies' under Schedule 1 to the Regulations to consider complaints alleging that a contractual term drawn up for general use is unfair. Regulation 10 requires the Director General of Fair Trading to consider any complaint made to him about such a term unless the complaint appears to the Director to be frivolous or vexatious or a qualifying body notifies the Director General that it has agreed to consider the complaint. If, having considered a complaint, either the Director General or a qualifying body believes a term to be unfair they may, if appropriate, apply for an injunction under reg 12 against any person appearing to them to be using or recommending the use of such a term. In deciding whether to seek an injunction, the Director General can take into account any undertakings given to him by or on behalf of any person as to the continued use of such a term in contracts concluded with consumers. If he or a qualifying body decides to apply for an injunction, the court may grant one on such terms as it thinks fit and may relate it not only to the use of a particular term drawn up for general usage but also to any similar term or any term having a like effect used or recommended to be used by any person.

The 'qualifying bodies' under these Regulations are identified in Schedule 1 and include the Information Commissioner, the Gas and Electricity Markets Authority, the Directors General of Electricity Supply and of Gas for Northern Ireland, the Directors General of Telecommunications and of Water Services, the Rail Regulator, every weights and measures authority in Great Britain, the Department of Enterprise, Trade and Investment in Northern Ireland, and the Financial Services Authority.

4.5 Criminal control

Running parallel to the civil law controls over exclusion clauses found in the Unfair Contract Terms Act 1977 are criminal law controls promulgated under the Fair Trading Act 1973. It is an offence contrary to the Consumer Transactions (Restrictions on Statements) Order 1976 as amended for a trader to display a notice which would contravene ss 6 and 7 of the Unfair Contract Terms Act 1977. Thus an exclusion clause displayed in this way would be both void and illegal.

Question

Leopard Ltd, a manufacturer of electrical equipment, bought some new office furniture from Tiger Office Furniture Ltd. Among the items purchased were some chairs with upholstered seats and stainless steel frames. The contract of sale for the furniture included the term 'Tiger Ltd accept no liability for any damage howsoever caused'.

Emily, an employee of Leopard Ltd, was injured when one of the welds failed on the leg of the chair on which she was sitting. She fell to the floor and injured her back. It transpired that the weld was faulty because of negligent workmanship by an employee of Tiger Office Furniture Ltd.

Emily wishes to claim for the injury caused to her, while Leopard Ltd want to claim a refund for the faulty chair. Tiger Office Furniture Ltd are denying liability relying on the exclusion clause.

Discuss.

Answer

The exclusion clause in this contract must be examined from two perspectives: first, the type of damage that it seeks to exclude and, second, the nature of the injured person.

Emily wants to claim for the injury caused to her back by the fall. We are told that the chair broke because of negligent workmanship by an employee of Tiger Office Furniture Ltd. This is crucial, for s 2(1) of the Unfair Contract Terms Act 1977 forbids any exclusion which attempts to restrict liability for physical injury caused by negligence. Hence, the clause is invalid as regards Emily's claim and she can claim compensation.

Leopard Ltd's claim is for property damage. They have two potential causes of action. They can make a claim in negligence or, alternatively, they can claim for a breach of the implied condition of satisfactory quality in s 14(2) of the Sale of Goods Act 1979. Where there are two potential actions, one contractual and the other tortious, the exclusion clause will apply only to the contract action and not to the tort action, unless the clause specifically says so. Applying **White v John Warwick & Co Ltd** (1953) the clause can be pleaded for the claim under the Sale of Goods Act but will have to satisfy the test of reasonableness as required by s 6(3) of the Unfair Contract Terms Act 1977 as Leopard Ltd are not 'dealing as a consumer'. (If they were 'dealing as a consumer' the clause would be void under s 6(2) of the 1977 Act.) The clause cannot affect the negligence action.

Further reading

Adams, A (2000). *Law for Business Students*, 2nd edn (Longman)
Bradgate, R (2000). *Commercial Law*, 3rd edn (Butterworth)
Dobson, P (1997). *Charlesworth's Business Law*, 16th edn (Sweet & Maxwell)
Downes, T A (1997). *Textbook on Contract*, 5th edn (Blackstone Press)
Keenan, D (2000). *Smith and Keenan's Advanced Business Law*, 11th edn (Longman)
Keenan, D and Riches, S (2001). *Business Law*, 6th edn (Longman)
Richards, P (2001). *Law of Contract*, 5th edn (Longman)
Stone, R (2000). *Principles of Contract Law*, 4th edn (Cavendish)

5 Termination and remedies

5.1 Introduction

There are four methods by which a contract may be terminated: performance, agreement, frustration and breach.

5.2 Performance

The majority of contracts will be terminated by performance when both parties have completed successfully their contractual obligations as per the terms of the contract. Thus, in a contract for the purchase and delivery of a piece of machinery, the contract will be terminated by performance when the correct machine in working order has been delivered to the correct premises and the contractual price has been paid.

5.2.1 Substantial performance

Strictly, the law requires full performance of all the contractual obligations by both parties. Either party failing in any aspect of contractual performance would be sufficient to prevent the successful termination by performance of the agreement. This potentially draconian rule has been mitigated, however, by the evolution of the doctrine of substantial performance. Under this doctrine, a contract may be deemed concluded if substantial performance of the contractual obligations has occurred and the contractual price must be paid less an appropriate amount for the uncompleted work. This doctrine is a major step forward from the position that existed previously whereby nothing other than full performance would suffice to establish an action for the contract price, as evidenced in the decision of **Cutter** *v* **Powell** (1756).

Hoenig *v* **Isaacs** (1952) is the most commonly quoted decision demonstrating the impact of contractual substantial performance. The plaintiff agreed to decorate the defendant's flat and undertake some refurbishment including providing a wardrobe and bookcase at a total cost of £750. The defendant paid £400 but refused to pay the balance stating that the work was negligently done and that the wardrobe and the bookcase needed further work. The plaintiff sued for the remaining £350. The Court of Appeal found that the contract had been substantially performed and that the plaintiff was able to recover the £350 less a reduction of £55 to cover the cost of the remedial work necessary to the wardrobe and bookcase.

5.2.2 Part performance

It is important to distinguish between substantial performance as illustrated in the **Hoenig** decision and partial performance, which occurs when one of the parties fails to complete the contract. The innocent party has the option of rejecting the work performed or alternatively accepting the partial performance and paying for it on a *quantum meruit* basis.

The assumption has been made that the promisee is prepared to allow full contractual performance to take place. Clearly, it would be inequitable to allow him to avoid the contract or use non-performance as a defence in an action for the price if he has prevented performance taking place. In this situation, the promisor is entitled to treat the contract as terminated and sue for the value of the work actually performed on a *quantum meruit* basis, as in **Planche v Colburn** (1831), where an author was entitled to receive payment for the research and writing undertaken for a book before the publisher decided to abandon the project.

5.2.3 Divisible contracts

A further example of the mitigation of the performance rule is to be found with divisible contracts. A divisible contract is one whereby each stage of performance brings with it an entitlement to receive part of the contract price. Thus, for example, if a large quantity of goods is to be delivered in instalments over an extended period of time each instalment might carry a right to payment in respect of it. Where this is the case the contractor providing the goods would be entitled to receive payment for the deliveries actually made even if the contract is not fully performed.

5.3 Agreement

In the same way that the contracting parties agree to enter a contract so they can agree to terminate it. This may occur in two ways, either as a result of an express contractual term or because one or both of the parties wish to terminate the contract before performance has been completed.

The first situation would occur, for example, where the contract is for a fixed period, as in the hire of machinery for three months. At the conclusion of the period the contract will terminate automatically. Similarly, if the agreement was to last until some specified event took place, the occurrence of the event would cause automatic contractual termination. Lastly, it would also include contracts the terms of which provide for either party to terminate the contract by notice as, for example, in a tenancy agreement, a contract of employment or a hire agreement of indeterminate length.

Agreements to terminate once contractual performance has started but not been completed pose some difficulties, the major one being that the agreement to terminate must itself satisfy the requirements of a binding contract. In particular, this means that consideration must be present. When neither party has completed his contractual performance, i.e. a bilateral agreement, the consideration provided by each party which releases him from further contractual performance is the promise to release the other party from his remaining obligations. Both parties benefit from the new agreement.

By contrast, when only one party has outstanding contractual obligations, the other party having completed performance, i.e. a unilateral agreement, there is no consideration provided by the party who has not completed his contractual performance. While the parties may agree to terminate the contract and not require any further performance, the promise received by the party with outstanding obligations is gratuitous and, as such, not enforceable unless contained in a deed.

5.4 Frustration

5.4.1 Impossibility of performance

A contract is deemed to be frustrated when further performance becomes impossible due to some intervening factor beyond the control of the contracting parties. Examples would include the destruction of the subject matter of the contract, the cancellation of an event central to the contract and the contract subsequently becoming illegal. Decisions in which contracts have been frustrated include the decision of **Taylor *v* Caldwell** (1863), in which the plaintiff hired a music hall from the defendant in order to give some concerts. After the contract was agreed but before the date of the first concert, the hall was destroyed by fire. The plaintiff sued the defendant in an attempt to recover all the expenses that he had accrued in arranging the concerts. The Court of Appeal found the defendant not liable, the contract having been frustrated.

The so-called 'coronation cases' demonstrate that decisions as to whether any individual contract has been frustrated will depend on the particular facts. Thus, in **Krell *v* Henry** (1903) the plaintiff owned a flat which he hired to the defendant for Edward VII's coronation day to enable the defendant to watch the coronation procession. The coronation was cancelled due to the king's illness and the defendant refused to pay for the flat. The court held that the defendant was not liable for the hire fee as the primary purpose of the hire was to watch the coronation procession. As it did not take place the contract was frustrated. Contrast, however, the decision of **Herne Bay Steamship Co *v* Hutton** (1903), another of the 'coronation cases', in which a contract for the hire of a boat to watch the coronation review of the fleet at Spithead was not frustrated even though the review was cancelled, because it was still possible to view the fleet.

It is important to distinguish between those cases where further performance genuinely becomes impossible and frustration is likely to occur and those instances where performance merely becomes more expensive or time-consuming and frustration will not take place. An example of the latter situation occurred in **Tsakiroglou & Co Ltd *v* Noblee Thorl GmbH** (1962), in which a contract of shipment under which goods were to be transported from Port Sudan to Hamburg was not frustrated by the closure of the Suez Canal. Shipment would take longer and be considerably more expensive than envisaged originally by the seller but this was insufficient to frustrate the contract as delivery of the goods was still possible.

5.4.2 Restrictions on application

Application of the doctrine of frustration is restricted and will not occur if the parties have foreseen the frustrating event and made provision for it in the contract by, for example, the use of a *force majeure* clause as discussed in Chapter 2. Likewise, the contract will not be frustrated if the frustrating event has been induced by one of the contracting parties, for example a contract whereby A agrees to service B's car for a year would be terminated but not frustrated by B selling the car.

5.4.3 The effect of frustration

The effect of contractual frustration is that the contract is avoided from the date of the frustrating event and the parties are released from any further contractual performance. This leaves the issues about the possible recovery of monies paid before the event and payment for any contractual performance that preceded the frustrating event. This is governed by s 1 of the Law Reform (Frustrated Contracts) Act 1943, which provides that any monies paid before the frustrating event can be recovered subject to the payee's right to receive reimbursement in respect of any appropriate expenses incurred prior to the frustration. Similarly, where one of the contracting parties has received a valuable benefit under the terms of the contract before the contract was discharged, he is liable to pay the other contracting party a sum that the court considers fair in all the circumstances. In deciding a figure the court must take account of expenses incurred legitimately by the benefited party when seeking to perform the contract and the effect of the frustrating event upon the benefit received.

5.5 Breach

A failure by either contracting party to fulfil his contractual obligations either wholly or in part may cause the contract to be terminated by breach. This leaves the innocent party with the right to claim contractual damages and the potential to deem the contract at an end depending on the circumstances.

5.5.1 Anticipatory breach

Breach may occur during the lifetime of the contract or, alternatively, may happen after the contract has been agreed but before the date for performance. This latter possibility is termed anticipatory breach and gives the innocent party the right to seek contractual damages immediately as in **Hochester *v* De La Tour** (1853). For an action in anticipatory breach to succeed, it must be clear that the guilty party has decided irrevocably not to perform his contractual obligations. If there is any doubt about his intentions, the innocent party should wait until the date for contractual performance has passed before commencing any action. The facts of the **Hochester** case were that the plaintiff was employed by the defendant to act as a courier with effect from 1 June, the contract having been concluded in April. On 11 May, the defendant wrote to the plaintiff stating that his services would not be needed. The plaintiff sued on 22 May seeking contractual damages for the breach, the court holding in his favour on the basis that the plaintiff's letter was actionable as an anticipatory breach.

Once an anticipatory breach has occurred the aggrieved party can decide whether to accept the anticipatory breach and consequent repudiation or whether to affirm the contract. The House of Lords reconsidered the issue of anticipatory breach in the decision of **Vitol SA *v* Norelf Ltd, The Santa Clara** (1996) when the buyer of goods, having heard that delivery of the goods he had ordered would be later than the agreed contractual delivery date, sent a telex to the sellers rejecting the cargo and repudiating the contract. The seller did not respond to this telex but arranged for the resale of the goods to a third party. It was held that this resale constituted an acceptance by the seller of the buyer's anticipatory breach. It follows from this case that there is no requirement for formal notification by the aggrieved party of his acceptance of the anticipatory breach; his conduct will suffice. What matters is that the repudiating party knows unequivocally that the aggrieved party has accepted the repudiation.

5.5.2 Effect of the breach

The effect of the breach will be dictated by the status of the term breached. If the term is a condition, the breach of which has effectively destroyed the contract, the innocent party will have a right to repudiate the contract and seek damages. Alternatively, the innocent party may elect to continue with the contract and merely seek damages by way of compensation. If he chooses the latter option, he will himself continue to be bound by the terms of the contract and would be liable for breach if he failed to fulfil his contractual obligations properly. If the breached term is merely a warranty, damages are the only remedy available, there being no right of repudiation. The more complex position arises in respect of innominate terms where, ultimately, the court has the power to decide upon an appropriate remedy depending on the effect of the breach (see Chapter 2).

5.6 Remedies

Remedies for contractual breach fall into two categories: damages, the normal legal remedy, and the equitable remedies of specific performance and injunctions. The essential distinction is that while damages are awarded to the innocent party as of right, the award of the equitable remedies of specific performance and injunctions is discretionary with the plaintiff having no right to insist on them.

5.6.1 Damages

Liquidated damages

As discussed in Chapter 2, businesses may use a liquidated damages clause in a contract to stipulate the amount of damages payable in the event of breach. Such a clause is for an agreed sum and, provided that the court is satisfied that the clause is a genuine pre-estimate of loss and not a penalty clause as outlined in the decision of **Dunlop Pneumatic Tyre Co Ltd** *v* **New Garage & Motor Co Ltd** (1915), it will be upheld and enforced. Where a liquidated damages clause is upheld, the plaintiff will receive the agreed sum irrespective of the actual loss suffered.

Unliquidated damages

Where there is no agreed figure for the damages, the plaintiff will sue for unliquidated damages, this being the sum that the court considers appropriate to compensate the injured party for the loss that he has suffered as a result of the breach. If no loss has been sustained, the court will award nominal damages to acknowledge the breach. The Court of Appeal decision of **Surrey County Council** *v* **Bredero Homes Ltd** (1993) confirmed that the function of contractual damages is to compensate the victim for his loss, not to transfer to the victim the benefit which the wrongdoer gained by his breach.

To be recoverable the damages must relate to loss that was foreseeable at the time that the contract was made, as stipulated in **Hadley** *v* **Baxendale** (1854), in which the plaintiff mill-owner employed the defendant to transport a broken crankshaft to the shaft manufacturer to enable it to be used as a pattern for the construction of a new, replacement part. The defendant negligently delayed delivery of the shaft resulting in the mill being closed longer than would otherwise have been the case. The plaintiff sued for his loss of profits due to the mill being out of use. The court held that the defendant was not liable as there was nothing to suggest that he should have been aware of the special losses that the plaintiff would suffer as a result of the delay. The plaintiff might have had a spare shaft.

The rules emanating from the **Hadley** decision mean that recoverable damage is limited to that which falls within two specified criteria:

1 such damage as arises naturally from the breach, i.e. in the usual course of events, and
2 that which, while not arising naturally, 'may reasonably be supposed to have been in the contemplation of both parties at the time they made the contract' as being the probable result of the breach.

Applying these rules, it follows that the defendant in the **Hadley** decision would have been liable for the plaintiff's loss of profits if he had known that the plaintiff did not have a spare shaft and thus that any delay would cause increased damage.

This approach was subsequently approved and applied in the decision of **Victoria Laundry (Windsor) Ltd** *v* **Newman Industries Ltd** (1949) and, more recently, by the Court of Appeal in **Kpohraror** *v* **Woolwich Building Society** (1996).

If the damage is not too remote the plaintiff can recover for death and personal injury, damage to property, financial loss and, in some situations, distress and disappointment occasioned by the breach, as in **Jarvis *v* Swans Tours** (1973), in which the plaintiff was awarded damages for the disappointment he suffered when a holiday did not live up to the description applied in a holiday brochure. Similarly in **Cox *v* Phillips Industries Ltd** (1976) an employee was allowed to recover for the distress caused by his wrongful demotion.

The purpose of damages is to compensate the innocent party for the loss that he has sustained and attempt to put him in the same position he would have occupied but for the breach. Note, however, that while the innocent party has a right to receive appropriate compensatory damages, he is under a duty to mitigate (reduce) his loss as far as is reasonably possible. He cannot recover damages for losses that he could have avoided through reasonable actions.

Given that the function of damages is to put the plaintiff in the position he would have occupied but for the breach, one issue that does arise in relation to an award of damages for faulty goods is whether the plaintiff is entitled to the 'cost of the cure', i.e. the cost of remedying any contractual defect, or whether he is entitled merely to the difference in value between the goods actually supplied and those which should have been provided. In many situations the two are the same and thus the question is academic, but this is not always so, as illustrated in the decision of **Ruxley Electronics and Construction Ltd *v* Forsyth** (1995). Ruxley Electronics had contracted to construct a swimming pool for Mr Forsyth in his garden, the swimming pool to have a maximum depth of 7 feet 6 inches. When constructed, the maximum depth of the pool was actually 6 feet 9 inches. To remedy the defect would have involved rebuilding the pool at a cost of £21,560. It was found that the pool was still safe for diving and the court of first instance awarded Mr Forsyth £2,500 for lost amenity, holding that there was no difference in value between the pool as constructed and that which should have been built. The Court of Appeal overruled this decision and awarded Mr Forsyth the full cost of remedying the defect. The House of Lords, overruling the Court of Appeal and reinstating the original judgment, held that the plaintiff was entitled to receive compensation only for the loss of amenity and not for the cost of the cure.

It is clear from this judgment that the full cost of the cure can be claimed only where it would be reasonable to allow the plaintiff to make such a claim. While the personal preference of the plaintiff is a relevant factor, it is not the only factor that should be considered, other factors including, for example, the level of contractual liability accepted by the defendant.

Punitive or exemplary damages, the primary purpose of which is to punish the wrongdoer, are not normally awarded in contract actions.

5.6.2 Specific performance

An order of specific performance requires the defendant to perform his contractual obligations according to the terms of the contract. The order is discretionary and will be awarded only when the court considers it just and equitable so to do. Breach of such an order is actionable as a contempt of court. Certain criteria must be satisfied if specific performance is to be granted.

Damages must be inadequate as a remedy

In many contracts damages would suffice as a remedy but there are some contracts where mere money would prove inadequate. This situation is most likely to pertain where the subject matter of the contract is unique. A contract for the purchase of land is a prime example as all land is unique if only because of its location, thus the court would be likely to award specific performance to enforce a contract for the sale of land. Similarly, specific performance might be awarded to enforce a contract for the sale of goods if the goods are unique as, for example, if the contract were for the sale of the Mona Lisa. By contrast, if the contract were for the sale of an item that is widely available such as a washing machine, specific performance would be refused as damages would be sufficient to allow the innocent party to obtain the goods elsewhere. (Other remedies relating to contracts for the sale of goods are discussed in Chapter 7.)

Specific performance must be available to both parties

The court will not award specific performance to one contracting party if the remedy would not be open to the other party. Thus, for example, as specific performance cannot be awarded against a minor, a minor cannot claim it against an adult.

The court must be capable of supervising the order

The court will not award specific performance if it is incapable of supervising the enforcement of the order as this would bring the law into disrepute. Similarly, it is unlikely to award specific performance in respect of personal contracts such as employment contracts as it would be potentially inequitable to force an employee to work for an employer with whom he has disagreed in the past.

5.6.3   Injunctions

While specific performance enforces the positive terms of a contract, injunctions are used to enforce the negative ones, as, for example, to enforce a legitimate restraint of trade clause as in the **Nordenfelt** decision (see Chapter 3).

In respect of the use of injunctions in employment contracts, the decisions of **Lumley** *v* **Gye** (1852) and **Warner Bros Inc** *v* **Nelson** (1937) both support the notion that an injunction can be used against an employee to enforce a clause under which he has agreed not to work for someone else. However, the court will not allow an injunction to be used as a way of forcing an employee to continue working for his present employer. Lastly, injunctions may be used by an employer to protect confidential information by restraining an employee from disclosing it (see also Chapter 19).

5.6.4   Limitation of actions

Whether seeking damages or one of the equitable remedies, the plaintiff must commence his action within the appropriate time period as specified in the Limitation Act 1980. This is six years from the time of the breach for simple contracts (s 5) and 12 years in respect of contracts under seal (s 8).

Section 32 of the 1980 Act provides that where a fraud, concealment or mistake is alleged, the limitation periods will not begin to run until the plaintiff has discovered the fraud, concealment or mistake, or could with reasonable diligence have discovered it.

Of particular interest in the commercial context is that under s 29, when an action has accrued in respect of a debt or a liquidated damages claim, the limitation period begins afresh every time that the debt is acknowledged in writing by the debtor or his agent or a part payment is made in respect of it. This applies, however, only if the original claim was commenced within the appropriate limitation period.

Question

Danny, a house building contractor, entered three different contracts:

(a) To buy some window frames from Eric Ltd. The frames were to be delivered in six instalments, each instalment to be paid for on arrival. After four instalments had been delivered, Eric Ltd announced that they were in financial difficulties and did not intend to deliver the rest.

(b) Plumbers Ltd were employed to install all the plumbing in the houses at a total cost of £30,000. While they completed the job, some of the work was unsatisfactory and Danny had to get another plumber to remedy the defects at a cost of £350. Consequently, Danny has not paid the last £1,000 due on the original agreement.

(c) A contract with Flooring Ltd to supply ceramic floor tiles for the kitchen. The contract contained a liquidated damages clause stating that a payment of £100 would be due for every day by which delivery was delayed. The tiles were three days late arriving.

Advise Danny about his rights and liabilities in respect of each of the three contracts.

Answer

(a) Danny's contract with Eric Ltd for the purchase of the window frames is probably a divisible contract. While this issue is never clear-cut, the fact that each instalment carries with it a right to payment suggests that it is divisible. Despite their failure to complete the contract, therefore, Eric Ltd will be entitled to be paid for the four instalments that they have delivered. Danny should be advised to pay for them. However, he may be able to claim some compensation for the fact that Eric Ltd are not intending to complete the contract. Their statement means that there is an anticipatory breach and Danny can sue for damages immediately without waiting for the completion date of the contract.

(b) Plumbers Ltd have completed the contract by performance. However, the fact that Danny had to employ another plumber to do some necessary remedial work means that the performance was substantial rather than complete. As such, Danny is entitled to deduct the cost of the remedial work from the contract price but he is liable to pay the remainder. Applying **Hoenig** *v* **Isaacs** (1952) Danny must pay Plumbers Ltd the outstanding £1,000 less the £350 for the remedial work.

(c) The contract with Flooring Ltd contained a liquidated damages clause effective if the floor tiles were late in being delivered. The issue is whether the clause is a genuine pre-estimate of the loss or a penalty. If it is a genuine pre-estimate, Danny will be entitled to claim £300 from Flooring Ltd for the three-day delay, irrespective of whether his actual loss was more or less than £300.

Further reading

Adams, A (2000). *Law for Business Students*, 2nd edn (Longman)

Bradgate, R (2000). *Commercial Law*, 3rd edn (Butterworth)

Dobson, P (1997). *Charlesworth's Business Law*, 16th edn (Sweet & Maxwell)

Downes, T A (1997). *Textbook on Contract*, 5th edn (Blackstone Press)

Keenan, D (2000). *Smith and Keenan's Advanced Business Law*, 11th edn (Longman)

Keenan, D and Riches, S (2001). *Business Law*, 6th edn (Longman)

Richards, P (2001). *Law of Contract*, 5th edn (Longman)

Stone, R (2000). *Principles of Contract Law*, 4th edn (Cavendish)

6 The law of agency

6.1 Introduction

While the doctrine of privity stipulates that, with the exception of situations governed by the Contracts (Rights of Third Parties) Act 1999 (see Chapter 1), only the contracting parties have the right to enforce a contract, there is no requirement that they be the only people involved in the precontractual negotiations in which the terms of the contract are agreed. It is commonplace, particularly in business, for a contracting party to use another person, an agent, to negotiate on his behalf. Thus, an employee is the agent of his employer, an estate agent is the agent of the vendor and a stockbroker is an agent for the purposes of buying and selling stocks and shares. The use of agents by businesses and financial institutions to advise and act on financial matters, by market research agencies to advise on marketing trends and practice, and by advertising agencies to advise on popular presentation bears testimony to the continued importance of agents in the commercial sector.

The degree of formality needed to establish an agency will be dictated by the character of the relationship. While all agency situations are governed by the common law, agency situations involving a commercial agent must also comply with the Commercial Agents (Council Directive) Regulations 1993 (see later). The crucial factor central to the establishment of any agency arrangement is that the agent is acting on behalf of the principal with the latter's authority.

6.2 The role of an agent

The function of an agent is to bring about a valid, binding contract between his principal and a third party. Essentially, his role is that of negotiator, there being no intention that he should be bound contractually himself by the deal. The limit of the agent's contractual involvement is that a contract of agency exists between himself and his principal. It is from this contract that the agent derives his authority.

While in the vast majority of situations the agent drops out of the picture after arranging the contract, there are some exceptions, discussed later, in which the agent may become contractually bound to the third party.

The contractual relationships between the principal, the agent and the third party are as illustrated in Figure 6.1.

Figure 6.1   Agency/contractual relationship

6.3   The creation of an agency

There are no formal requirements at common law for the formation of an agency unless the principal wishes to give his agent the authority to enter deeds on his behalf, in which instance a power of attorney will need to be created under the provisions of the Powers of Attorney Act 1971.

The only restriction on an ability to appoint someone as an agent is that the principal must both exist and have the contractual capacity to enter the contract. Thus, a company cannot create an agency to enter a contract prior to its incorporation, s 36(4) of the Companies Act 1985 providing that where a company purports to enter a pre-incorporation contract, the person acting on behalf of the company, i.e. the supposed agent, will be personally liable on the contract unless it provides otherwise. Similarly, a minor cannot create an agency for a contract other than a contract for necessaries and any adult purporting to act as an agent in this situation would, in fact, enter the contract as a principal in his own right.

6.4   Authority

The scope of an agent's power is delineated by the level of authority that the principal has bestowed upon him. Authority may be actual or apparent, express or implied.

6.4.1   Actual authority

As the name suggests, this is the level of authority that actually exists between the principal and the agent and the authority for which the agent is entitled to receive his remuneration. If the agent acts in excess of this authority he may be liable to the principal for breach of agency, particularly as, depending on the circumstances, the principal may be bound by a contract negotiated by his agent when he was acting outside his actual authority.

Actual authority may be either express or implied.

Express authority

If the agency has been created by a written contract of agency, the scope of the express authority can be determined from the construction and wording of the document. In an oral agency agreement, it will depend on what the parties agreed the agent should have the authority to do.

Implied actual authority

The scope of implied actual authority is more difficult to determine as it must be deduced from all the surrounding circumstances. Typically, it will arise from the extension of a pre-existing express authority although this is not necessarily the case as, for example, in the implied authority existing between a husband and wife. **Hely Hutchinson v Brayhead Ltd** (1968), a Court of Appeal decision, examined the scope of implied authority. The chairman of the defendant company acted as its *de facto* managing director with the acquiescence of the other directors although he had not been formally appointed to that position. He issued two letters of guarantee to the plaintiffs, which they subsequently sought to enforce, the defendant denying liability on the grounds of lack of authority. The court held that the 'managing director' had implied actual authority exercised with the defendant's agreement.

An agent will also have implied authority for any acts that are necessarily incidental to the exercise of his express authority. Thus, for example, if an agent is instructed to buy an item for his principal, there would be an implied authority to pledge the principal's credit such as to bind him to the debt.

Usual authority

The exact location of usual authority within the law of agency has given rise to much academic debate, but the widely held view that it is a subdivision of implied actual authority is supported here.

Usual authority is the authority which an agent acquires by virtue of his profession. It results from an assumption that a principal, when appointing an agent to a recognised job or profession, impliedly provides him with the authority to undertake all the duties that would normally fall within such a job or profession. It follows that it does not have a general application but is limited to those situations where the agent occupies an identifiable job or profession. Hence, in **Panorama Developments (Guildford) Ltd v Fidelis Furnishing Fabrics Ltd** (1971) it was held that a company secretary has the implied authority to enter contracts 'dealing with the administrative side of the company's affairs'. This included the authority to hire cars and thus the company was liable in respect of such contracts even though the company secretary had hired the cars for his own purposes. From the **Panorama** decision, a company secretary would clearly also have authority to buy office equipment, hire staff, rent accommodation, etc.

Given the breadth of the powers that an agent might acquire under usual authority, it is appropriate that a principal should have the ability to limit the extent of those powers if he sees fit. Any such restriction will be binding on a third party only if he knows of it. If he is unaware of the restriction, the principal will be liable on any contract that the agent enters that falls within the usual authority. It is this aspect of usual authority that has given rise to debate, for this reliance on the way that the agency appears to a third party is very similar to the approach used in apparent authority. The decision of **Watteau *v* Fenwick** (1893) analysed the role of notice in usual authority. Fenwick employed Humble as the manager of his hotel and expressly forbade Humble to buy any cigars on credit. Watteau, unaware of the agency and of the restriction on it, supplied Humble with cigars. Fenwick was held liable for the debt as Humble was deemed to be acting within the usual authority of a hotel manager and Watteau, the third party, was ignorant of the restrictions.

The case has been subjected to much criticism since it held an undisclosed principal liable for an action that he had expressly forbidden. Nonetheless, while some commentators doubt whether this case will be followed strictly in the future, at the moment it is good law.

6.4.2 Apparent authority

Apparent authority, sometimes called 'ostensible authority', derives not from any agreement between the principal and agent but rather from the appearance of an agreement as seen from the third party's perspective. Hence, it is what appears to exist rather than what actually exists.

Clearly, there must be some reasonable foundation for the third party's belief. Three criteria must be established to prove apparent authority which effectively involve creating an estoppel. These are the existence of a representation, reliance on the representation and the third party altering his position.

Existence of a representation

To be effective the principal must have made a representation, whether by words or conduct, that the agent possesses a level of actual authority. The agent is not capable of making such a representation about his authority; it must come from the principal or from someone acting on his behalf who has the actual authority to make such a representation. This means that the existence of the principal must be known to the third party, it following that apparent authority cannot be created where the principal is undisclosed. The leading case is **Freeman & Lockyer *v* Buckhurst Park Properties (Mangal) Ltd** (1964). The defendant company, with the acquiescence of its other directors, allowed one of its directors to act as the *de facto* managing director and undertake the day to day management of the company. He instructed a firm of architects in connection with a property development plan in which the company was involved. Subsequently, the company refused to pay the architects' fee contending that the 'managing director' did not have any authority to engage them. The Court of Appeal held that the board of directors had by their acquiescence represented that the managing director had the authority to act on their behalf. As such, the company was liable.

It is possible for a representation to be made after the agent has agreed the contract with the third party if the principal by his actions has appeared to adopt or affirm it. Thus, in **Spiro *v* Lintern** (1973) the defendant instructed his wife to arrange for the sale of the house although she did not have the authority to enter a binding contract. Acting on her instructions the estate agent arranged a sale to the plaintiffs. Knowing of this supposed contract, the defendant allowed the plaintiffs to make arrangements for alterations to the premises. He subsequently refused to complete the sale relying on his wife's lack of authority. The court held the defendant was bound by the contract as his acquiescence in the plaintiffs' behaviour represented an affirmation of the contract.

Reliance on the representation

The existence of reliance is a question of fact in each case. To prove reliance, the third party will need to demonstrate that he had actual knowledge of the representation, constructive knowledge will not suffice. It follows that the third party cannot establish an apparent authority if either he was unaware of the principal's representation or, alternatively, he had actual or constructive knowledge that the agent did not possess any authority.

Alteration of the third party's position

Again, this is a question of fact. The third party must demonstrate that, in reliance on the representation, he has altered his legal position. It is generally believed that the third party must have acted to his detriment though there is some debate on this point.

6.4.3 Agency by ratification

If an agent has acted beyond his authority, or a person with no authority has purported to act as an agent, the principal may adopt or ratify any resultant contract and be bound by it. Ratification provides the agent with retrospective actual authority so that he will be deemed to have been acting within his authority at all times and the principal will be bound by the contract *ab initio*.

In order for a valid agency by ratification to be created, certain criteria must be met:

(a) *The agent must have contracted as an agent* When negotiating the contract, the agent must have purported to act as an agent for an identifiable principal. It follows that an undisclosed principal cannot ratify a contract as this would necessarily have involved the agency relationship being kept secret. Thus, in **Keighley, Maxted & Co v Durant** (1901) an agent exceeded his authority and bought corn at a price higher than that approved by his principal. The agent bought in his own name and did not disclose the agency although his intention was to buy on behalf of his principal. Initially the principal agreed to ratify the contract and accept the wheat but subsequently refused to take delivery. The third party sued the principal, who was held not liable by the House of Lords. As an undisclosed principal he was incapable of ratifying the contract.

In a situation such as this, there would be a strong argument for holding that the third party could sue the agent for a breach of warranty of authority. Remedies in agency are discussed later.

(b) *The principal can ratify any contract for which he was named* Once the principal has been named by the agent in a contract, the principal has the right to ratify it and receive any contractual benefits even if the agent used his name fraudulently and intended to gain the benefit of the contract for himself.

(c) *The principal exists* For ratification to be possible, the principal must have existed at the time that the contract was made. This is of most concern in relation to limited companies and pre-incorporation contracts. As explained previously, a company cannot enter a contract prior to its incorporation as it does not exist at law. For the same reason, it is incapable of ratifying any pre-incorporation contract purportedly made on its behalf. In **Kelner *v* Baxter** (1866) the plaintiff, Kelner, sold some wine to Baxter, who purported to act on behalf of a hotel company prior to its incorporation. The wine was consumed but not paid for. It was held that Baxter was personally liable as the company, not being incorporated at the time of the contract, could not ratify it.

This position has now been reinforced by s 36(4) of the Companies Act 1985 as mentioned earlier.

(d) *The principal had the contractual capacity* The ability of a principal to ratify is limited to those contracts for which he had the contractual capacity at the time that the contract was made. Thus, a minor would only be able to ratify contracts for necessaries.

(e) *The contract must be capable of ratification* The principal cannot ratify a contract which would be illegal or void *ab initio*. As such contracts would never have any effect, they cannot be ratified. A voidable contract, however, is capable of ratification because it is a valid binding contract until it is avoided.

(f) *The knowledge of the principal* The principal must have had knowledge of all the material facts prior to ratification if he is to be bound by it. The principal can, however, declare an intention to be bound irrespective of the material facts.

(g) *Reasonable time* Ratification must take place within a reasonable time, this being a question of fact in each individual case.

6.4.4 Agency of necessity

Agency of necessity is seldom used due to the difficulty of establishing the requisite criteria and the attitude of the courts. It is intended to cover those situations where in an emergency or crisis the agent acts on behalf of a principal from whom he does not have the relevant authority. The court will grant the agent appropriate authority but has restricted the application of the doctrine to situations where the agent and the principal have a pre-existing relationship.

Impossibility of contact

It must be impossible for the agent to contact his principal to gain instructions. This must be increasingly difficult to prove in this modern age of high-speed telecommunications. Even though it was easier to prove in bygone days, the burden of proof was still heavy. Two contrasting decisions are **Arthur** *v* **Barton** (1840) and **Springer** *v* **Great Western Railway** (1921). In the **Barton** case, the master of a ship validly created an agency of necessity when his ship was badly damaged during a voyage and was forced to put into port for crucial repairs. The master was unable to contact the ship's owners and pledged the ship for the value of the repairs. The owners were held liable for the debt.

By contrast, in **Springer** *v* **Great Western Railway** (1921) the railway company failed to establish an agency of necessity because they had not contacted the principal prior to acting. A consignment of tomatoes being sent from Jersey to London arrived in port three days late and was delayed a further two days prior to unloading. As the consignment was bad when unloaded, the railway company sold it locally. The company was held liable to the owner for failing to take instructions and wrongly selling his goods.

Actual and commercial necessity

The agent must demonstrate that there was an actual and commercial necessity for his actions. In the past, this tended to mean a need to show that his actions were necessary either to preserve or to avoid the physical destruction of the principal's goods. Acting to make a profit for the principal is not sufficient. The application of this requirement can be seen by comparing the following three decisions. As seen above, in **Arthur** *v* **Barton** the undertaking of repairs to a ship to render it seaworthy for the voyage home was a genuine necessity. Similarly, in **Great Northern Railway** *v* **Swaffield** (1874) a genuine necessity arose when the plaintiff railway company stabled a horse for the night after no one arrived at the station to collect it. The railway company was under an obligation to take care of the animal and hence the owner was liable for the costs of the stabling. By contrast, in **Prager** *v* **Blatspiel Stamp & Heacock Ltd** (1924) there was no agency of necessity. The case involved the purchase and subsequent sale of some animal skins. The agent purchased some skins for the principal in 1915 but because of the war was unable to send them to the principal or receive instructions. Two years later, the agent sold them at a handsome profit. However, the court held the agent liable to the principal as the sale had not been necessary. The skins would not have deteriorated if stored properly and the opportunity to make a financial gain was not commercial necessity.

The agent acted bona fide

The agent must show that he acted *bona fide* in the best interests of the principal. This is a basic requirement of any agency relationship as it is a relationship *uberrimae fidei* – of the utmost good faith. The existence of good faith is a matter of fact. The recent decision of **Lambert** *v* **Fry** (1999) reaffirmed that the agent must be acting on behalf of the principal. Lambert recovered a stolen vehicle acting on instructions from the police, who needed to recover the vehicle for evidential purposes. Lambert subsequently tried to claim fees for acting on behalf of the owner's insurance company under an agency of necessity but failed as, while the insurance company had benefited from the recovery of the vehicle, the work had been undertaken specifically on behalf of the police.

6.5 Duties arising from agency

There are three distinct relationships in the agency scenario: that between the principal and the agent, that between the principal and the third party and, lastly, that between the agent and the third party. Each of these relationships gives rise to rights and liabilities.

6.6 The principal/agent relationship

The relationship of the principal and agent is central to the whole concept of agency for it is on this relationship that the whole scenario depends. The relationship is a fiduciary one that confers a variety of rights and obligations on both principal and agent.

6.6.1 Duties owed by the agent

Underlying the duties owed by the agent to the principal is the fact that it is a relationship *uberrimae fidei*. As such, the good faith of the agent is paramount in establishing the nature and extent of his duties with a constant requirement that the agent acts in the best interests of his principal at all times.

The agent is required to act personally, reflecting the fact that the principal, in appointing him, necessarily places a degree of trust in him. The contract is personal in nature. Therefore, the agent is not permitted to delegate his duties to a subagent without the agreement of the principal, either expressly or impliedly. Any wrongful delegation of the agent's duties would be actionable as a breach of agency. Delegation in this context would not include the agent employing some other person to undertake a purely menial task.

Implied authority to delegate may arise from the surrounding circumstances. Thus, in **Solley** *v* **Wood** (1852) it was held that a provincial solicitor had the implied right to delegate his functions regarding High Court attendance to a London solicitor, this being the practice of the profession. By contrast, in **John McCann & Co** *v* **Pow** (1974) an estate agent who was appointed as a 'sole agent' had no implied authority to delegate his functions to a sub-agent.

The relationship between the principal and the sub-agent will depend on whether the agent's delegation of his functions was authorised by the principal. If it was, contractual privity would exist between the principal and the sub-agent such as to make the sub-agent liable directly to the principal for the performance of his functions. By contrast, if the delegation was not authorised, the agent would remain contractually liable to the principal for both his own actions and those of the sub-agent.

The agent is under a duty to obey the instructions that he receives from his principal, for if he acts outside his express or implied authority he may be liable to his principal for breach of agency. Should the instructions be ambiguous, he will not be liable if he has acted upon a reasonable interpretation of them, even though that interpretation was wrong.

The agent must exercise reasonable skill and care when performing his functions, the standard of this care depending upon factors such as the expertise of the particular agent, whether or not he was paid and the degree of reliance attached to his duties. Clearly, therefore, a higher standard of care would be expected of a professional agent as opposed to someone acting gratuitously, although the decision of **Chaudrhy** *v* **Prabhakar** (1988) held that a gratuitous agent does owe a duty to the principal to exercise reasonable skill and care in all the circumstances. Encompassed within the concept of skill and care is a duty on the agent to tell his principal of all relevant factors, to obtain the best deal possible for his principal if he is buying or selling goods, services or other property and a duty not to disclose his principal's confidential information, be it personal or business. A breach of any of these could attract liability as a breach of agency.

In **Keppel** *v* **Wheeler** (1927) the agent was employed to sell a house. He received an offer of £6,150 and the principal subsequently sold the property for this amount. Unknown to the principal, the agent received a second offer of £6,750 before the contract for the lower sum was finalised. The court held that the agent was liable to reimburse the principal for the difference between the two bids as he was in breach of his duty. Equally, in **Heath** *v* **Parkinson** (1926) the agent, Heath, was engaged by Parkinson to sell the lease of his premises. Parkinson believed that the landlord would not allow the premises to be used for business purposes. However, Heath gained an assurance from the superior landlords that they were prepared to allow the premises to be used for a tailor's business. This affected the desirability of the property and thereby increased the value of the lease. Heath did not disclose this fact to Parkinson and persuaded him to sell the lease for a lower sum than he would have gained otherwise. The court held that Heath was in breach of his agency and was not entitled to receive his commission.

L S Harris Trustees Ltd *v* **Power Packing Services (Hermit Road) Ltd** (1970) addressed the issue of confidentiality. The defendants suffered a fire at their warehouse and instructed the plaintiffs to prepare an insurance claim. In contravention of an express prohibition against disclosing any of the defendants' confidential information during their inquiries, the plaintiffs disclosed such information to one of the defendants' customers. The court held that the defendants were entitled to terminate their contract with the plaintiffs for breach of agency and seek damages.

The issue of confidentiality is clearly important to an agency relationship based, as it is, on good faith. While, as shown above, damages may be awarded for a breach of confidentiality by the agent, situations may arise in which this is deemed not to be a sufficient response and remedy for such a breach. In exceptional circumstances, when the principal feels that he may suffer loss if his agent disposes of or destroys confidential information, the court may grant a search order permitting a representative of the principal to enter the agent's premises and seize the confidential information in question. In **Anton Piller KG** *v* **Manufacturing Processes Ltd** (1976), the case upon which this approach is based, a German manufacturer of computer parts was concerned that his English agent would pass on confidential information to a competitor regarding a new range of products. The manufacturer obtained an order from the court against the agent permitting the manufacturer's solicitor to enter the agent's premises, inspect documents contained therein and remove the relevant ones.

The general duty to pursue the best interests of his principal and specifically to obtain the best price for him in any deal necessarily requires that an agent must not place himself in the position of conflict with his principal. The difficulty is obvious. If, for example, an agent is selling an item on behalf of his principal and the agent buys the item himself, a conflict is created. The principal, as seller, wants to sell for the highest price possible and his agent should work to that end. The agent, as purchaser, however, will want to buy for the lowest sum possible. The two are incompatible. Thus, there is an absolute prohibition against an agent contracting with his principal, a breach of which entitles the principal to rescind the resultant contract. Hence, in **Armstrong *v* Jackson** (1917) Armstrong employed Jackson, a stockbroker, to buy some shares for him. In fact, Jackson sold Armstrong his own shares but fraudulently provided contract notes suggesting that they had been bought elsewhere. The court held that Armstrong was entitled to rescind the contract of purchase.

While the decision of **Armstrong *v* Jackson** is clearly justifiable given the agent's fraud, the concept bites much deeper than that. Should the agent get into a position of conflict, he will be liable for breach, and thus liable to account to the principal for any profit that he has made, even if the agent has behaved in good faith and in the best interests of his principal. Therefore, in **Boardman *v* Phipps** (1967) two agents acting on behalf of the trustees of a trust fund purchased some shares for the fund. On the basis of the information they acquired, the agents also bought some of the shares for themselves, the purchase being made with the consent of the trustees. Both the trust fund and the agents made a profit on the shares. It was accepted that the agents had acted in good faith and that the principal had not suffered by the agents' actions. Nonetheless, the agents were held liable to account to the principal for the profit that they had made on their shares.

The **Boardman** decision may seem draconian given that the agents had acted in good faith and that the principal had not suffered. However, the approach of the English courts to situations of conflict is to construe them very strictly and not to allow the agent, however innocent, to retain any profit. The logic appears to be that if the agent knows that he will not be able to keep the profit in any circumstances, the temptation to place himself in a position of conflict for financial gain will be reduced or even eradicated. Some of the Commonwealth jurisdictions are less stringent in their approach and are prepared to allow an innocent agent to keep the profit in a situation such as **Boardman** provided that his actions have received the genuine consent of the principal. At the moment **Boardman** remains good law in England.

Preventing a conflict situation presents a dilemma if the agent acts in more than one capacity as, for example, in the buying and selling of shares on the Stock Exchange. Currently, it is possible for one stockbroking company to act as both buyer and seller in respect of an individual share transaction. The Financial Services Act 1986, as amended by the Financial Services and Markets Act 2000, attempts to control the potential conflicts this creates by requiring the different functions to be undertaken by different departments within the organisation, these being separated by so-called 'Chinese Walls' the purpose of which is to prevent the transfer of information. While the Stock Exchange presents a pertinent example of such conflict, the same scenario would arise if any agent, for example a solicitor, were to act for both the buyer and the seller in any transaction as he could not genuinely serve the interests of both parties.

The duty that attracts most attention is the duty not to make a secret profit, this description covering any unauthorised payment over and above the fee or commission to which the agent is entitled. It does not necessarily connote a bribe although clearly a bribe would be one form of secret profit. Essentially it means that the agent cannot use either the principal's property or any information gained in the course of the agency for the purpose of making a profit. The **Boardman** decision is a good example of this, as is the decision of **Regal (Hastings) Ltd** *v* **Gulliver** (1942), in which the plaintiff company wanted to buy two cinemas and decided to establish a new subsidiary company to undertake the deal. However, the company could not pay up all the share capital for the new company and the defendant directors agreed to purchase the shares themselves to allow the whole deal to go through. The plaintiff company duly bought the cinemas, which were sold subsequently at a handsome profit. The defendants made a profit of £2.80 per share but were held liable to account for it to the company.

If the existence of a secret profit is established the principal has a range of remedies available to him. He may choose to do nothing and allow the agent to keep the profit, particularly if the agent has acted in good faith and in the interests of the principal. Any suggestion of wrongdoing, however, may encourage the principal to take a far tougher line and exercise some of the other options open to him. These include the summary dismissal of the agent (justified on the grounds that the principal should not be compelled to retain an agent whom he can no longer trust), the recovery of the secret profit from the agent or the third party and a refusal to pay any commission due while recovering any already paid. Further, the principal can rescind the contract with the third party and sue both the agent and the third party in the tort of deceit for any losses that he has sustained as a result of the wrongdoing. It should be noted that these remedies are available irrespective of the effect, if any, that any bribe had upon the actions of the agent. Thus, an agent whose actions have not been affected by the bribe will still be held liable.

The final duty owed by the agent is to render account to the principal for his affairs whenever he so requests. This includes a duty to permit the principal to inspect the agent's records relating to the principal's business. In 1995, in **Yasuda Fire and Marine Insurance Co of Europe Ltd** *v* **Orion Marine Insurance Underwriting Agency Ltd** (1995), the Commercial Court held that the principal's right to inspect the records and the corresponding agent's duty to permit such inspection subsists even after the agency relationship has been terminated. On termination of the agency, the agent must give back to the principal all books, documents, accounts, etc belonging to him.

6.6.2 Duties owed by the principal

The principal owes two duties to the agent under the common law, namely to pay him his fee or commission when it is due and to reimburse the agent for any expenses incurred legitimately in the course of the agency.

The agent is entitled to receive payment for work carried out only under an express or implied authority, and only when the agency task is completed unless the agency agreement specifies otherwise. Further, the agent must have been the effective cause of the contract between the principal and the third party, as evidenced by the decision of **Coles _v_ Enoch** (1939) and, more recently, by the Court of Appeal decision of **Nahum v Royal Holloway and Bedford New College** (1998). In that case, Nahum, an art dealer, was employed as an agent by the defendant to find and introduce potential buyers for three paintings. Nahum introduced a purchaser who bought one painting and, some considerable time later, bought a second. The question arose as to whether he could recover commission for the sale of the second painting, it being held that he could as, although he had not been involved in the second sale to the same extent as in the first, the seller would not have known the buyer but for the original introduction by Nahum.

Normally the contract will specify the level of payment, but in the absence of a specific term the court may be prepared to imply a term for payment if the agent was acting in the course of his business. Such an implied term would provide for a _quantum meruit_ payment. The court will not intervene, however, if the contract includes a term providing for payment at a rate to be agreed but no rate has been agreed.

One difficulty facing an agent seeking payment arises if he is prevented by the principal from completing the agency task and is thereby denied the right to his remuneration. The courts have proved unwilling to imply any term into an agency agreement that gives the agent the right to complete his agency function as this interferes with the principal's right to deal with his property as he chooses. However, the courts have been willing to imply such a term where the principal has resorted to a deliberate breach of his contract with the third party as a means of denying the agent his right to payment, as in **Alpha Trading Ltd _v_ Dunnshaw-Patten Ltd** (1981).

When the agent is an employee of the principal, his commission is in the form of his salary, which he is entitled to receive for the duration of the contract of employment.

In addition to his fee, the agent has a right to be indemnified for legitimate expenses incurred in the course of the agency. This right is lost if the agent has incurred the expenses negligently or has acted illegally.

The agent has a lien over any of the principal's goods in his possession in respect of any monies owed to him by the principal.

Where the agency relationship involves a commercial agent and is governed by the Commercial Agents (Council Directive) Regulations 1993, additional duties are owed by the principal to the agent under reg 4. These will be considered later.

6.7 The principal/third party relationship

When the agent has acted within his actual authority or the principal has ratified his actions, the principal and the third party will have a normal contractual relationship with the ability to sue and be sued on their contract. As explained earlier, the agent having arranged the contract drops out of the picture.

A more interesting and complex situation arises when the principal is 'undisclosed'. This occurs where neither the existence nor the identity of the principal is made known to the third party, who believes that the agent is acting on his own behalf as a contracting party. By contrast, an 'unnamed' principal exists when the agent is known to be acting as an agent but the identity of his principal is unknown.

This situation would exist, for example, where an agent, in an auction room, receives his instructions from an anonymous telephone bidder.

When an agent has contracted for an undisclosed principal, the contract is enforceable between the third party and the agent. Should the existence of the principal become known, the third party can elect whether to retain his rights against the agent or enforce the contract against the principal instead. He is free to choose but his election is irrevocable. Alternatively, the principal may choose to make his presence known with the consequent right to enforce the contract, although this right is limited to situations where the agent was acting within his actual authority. Where the principal supplants the agent, the former takes the contract subject to any claims that the third party may have against the agent.

There are some restrictions upon the principal's right to adopt the contract if, for example, his intervention is expressly or impliedly prohibited by the contract. Thus, in **Humble v Hunter** (1848) the agent chartered a ship in his own name describing himself in the contract as her 'owner'. The court held that this implied that there was no other principal and thus the real principal was not liable on the contract.

The intervention of the principal may also be prevented if the third party had genuine reasons for wanting to deal with the agent personally or genuine objections to dealing with the principal. A desire to contract with the agent might arise, for example, if the agent owed money to the third party and the contract was to be used as a means of off-setting the debt. Objections to the identity of the principal are more difficult to substantiate. It must be more than a mere unwillingness by the third party to contract with the principal. He must demonstrate that the identity of the principal is a matter of real importance to him such as to mean that he would never have knowingly consented to contracting with the principal. If this can be established or the agent has misrepresented his position, the principal will lose the right to intervene with the result that the contract will subsist between the agent and the third party.

6.7.1 Financial settlement with the agent

Where agents are used in the commercial context, either party to the contract may wish to settle their contractual debts by paying the agent, particularly if the agent is the only person with whom they have had any actual contact. However, this is not, *prima facie*, an acceptable way of settling contractual debts.

The authority given to an agent by the principal to sell goods on his behalf does not include an authority to receive money on his account. Thus, the payment of a debt by the third party to the agent will not satisfy the third party's liability and he will remain liable if the agent fails to give the money to the principal. Naturally, the principal can give his agent actual authority to receive money on his behalf, in which case payment to the agent by the third party will suffice to extinguish the debt. However, the method of such payment must comply with the terms of the authority granted to the agent.

The agent also lacks authority to receive payment on behalf of the third party and so the giving of payment to the agent by the principal will not suffice to satisfy the debt. The third party can overrule this general position by indicating that he will accept payment via the agent.

6.8 The agent/third party relationship

While the intention in an agency scenario is for the agent to have no liability to the third party, there are some situations in which personal liability will follow the agent.

As seen above, the agent will be personally liable on the contract if he acts on behalf of an undisclosed principal until such time as the principal makes his presence known or the third party elects to be contractually bound to the principal. Also, the agent is personally liable on the contract if he has acted for a non-existent principal or has acted without authority in a situation where the principal cannot ratify the contract.

Liability of a different kind will be visited on the agent if, unknown to the third party, he has acted beyond his authority. In this situation he may be liable to the third party for a breach of warranty of authority. It is argued that such a breach is actionable as a breach of a collateral contract, the terms of the contract being that the agent warrants that he has the authority to act on behalf of the principal in return for the third party entering the main contract with the principal.

Misleading statements made by the agent during the negotiations may result in a tortious action for either misrepresentation or deceit.

6.9 Termination of agency

An agency may be terminated either by the parties themselves or by operation of law.

6.9.1 Termination by the parties

An agency relationship can, like any other contract, be terminated by agreement between the parties. The arrangements for the termination of the agency may be embodied within the agency agreement itself. Thus, for example, a fixed-term agency agreement will terminate upon the expiration of the term. Similarly, an agreement due to last until the commission of a specified act, for example the sale of a piece of property, will terminate when the sale is complete. Otherwise the parties may conclude the agency by agreement. Naturally, at the termination of the agency the agent is entitled to receive any remuneration or expenses owing to him for work done during the lifetime of the agency agreement.

6.9.2 Termination by operation of law

The law will effect the end of the agency agreement in four situations, these being where the principal has died, become insane, been declared bankrupt or become an enemy (for example following the outbreak of war). In addition, agency agreements may be frustrated in the same way as any other contract.

6.10 Commercial Agents (Council Directive) Regulations 1993

The common law position described above was strengthened by the passage of the Commercial Agents (Council Directive) Regulations 1993, which implement Directive 86/653/EEC on the coordination of the laws of member states relating to self-employed commercial agents. These Regulations, implemented on 1 January 1994, clarify the position regarding commercial agents. A 'commercial agent' is defined in reg 2(1) as being:

> a self-employed intermediary who has continuing authority to negotiate the sale or purchase of goods on behalf of another person (the 'principal'), or to negotiate and conclude the sale or purchase of goods on behalf of and in the name of that principal.

The definition appears to include limited companies although it continues by excluding from its provisions officers of a company, duly authorised partners and insolvency practitioners.

The first point to note is that the Regulations do not apply to commercial agents arranging for services rather than goods, and expressly do not apply to agents operating on commodity exchanges in the commodity market. Thus their impact is comparatively limited for they apply only to agents involved in the buying and selling of goods. Further, their impact is limited in that they do not apply to commercial agents whose activities are unpaid or whose activities are to be considered as secondary as defined in the Schedule to the Regulations.

The Regulations apply in their entirety to agency agreements entered into after 1 January 1994 and amended agreements concluded before that date. They do not apply to agency agreements where the parties have agreed that the agency contract is to be governed by the law of another member state.

Part II of the Regulations addresses the issue of the duties owed by both the commercial agent and the principal. As seen earlier, duty lies at the centre of the agent/principal relationship and many of the liabilities in agency arise from a breach of the respective duties. Regulation 3(1), which closely echoes the common law position, provides that an agent must look after the interests of his principal and act dutifully and in good faith. Regulation 3(2), which qualifies the general requirement, states that he shall:

(a) make proper efforts to negotiate and, where appropriate, conclude the transactions he is instructed to take care of;
(b) communicate to his principal all the necessary information available to him;
(c) comply with reasonable instructions given by his principal.

The duties imposed upon the principal by the 1993 Regulations exceed those formerly recognised by the common law, which relate merely to remuneration and the recovery of expenses. Under the Regulations, the principal is obliged to keep the agent provided with the necessary documentation relating to the goods and the necessary information to enable him to fulfil his duties. Further, the principal must inform the agent within a reasonable period of his acceptance or refusal of any commercial transaction negotiated by the agent and of the principal's failure to perform any transaction agreed upon by the agent.

Regulation 5(1) confirms the status of the aforementioned provisions by stating that the parties cannot derogate from regs 3 and 4 and that the law applicable to the contract will govern the consequences of breach.

Part III of the Regulations, regs 6–12, deals with the central issue of the agent's right to remuneration. Regulation 6 underlines his right to receive remuneration in the absence of any express term in the agreement. The essential provision (very similar in impact to s 15 of the Supply of Goods and Services Act 1982) is that the agent has a right to receive a level of remuneration that would customarily be received by agents in the same position and, where no such custom exists, that he should receive a reasonable remuneration.

Regulations 7 onwards deal with the agent's entitlement to commission and recognise the right of an agent to receive commission when a transaction has been concluded as a result of his actions (as under common law) or is concluded with a third party whom the agent had acquired previously as a customer for such transactions. Further, they recognise the right of a sole agent to receive commission when the agreement relates to a specific geographic area or a specific group of customers. These rights subsist after the termination of the agreement so that the agent has a right to recover commission if the transaction was attributable mainly to the actions of the agent during the period of the agency. Where a new agent has been appointed, the new agent shall not be entitled to any portion of that commission unless it is equitable that he should be so entitled.

Under reg 10 commission becomes due when either the principal executes the transaction or when he should have executed the transaction under the terms of the agreement or when the third party executes the transaction. It is payable at the latest when the third party either executes his part of the transaction or should have done so if the principal had complied with the agreement. The right to commission is lost if the major contract between the principal and the third party is not executed for reasons for which the principal is not to blame. If this occurs any commission already received by the agent must be refunded.

Lastly, under reg 12 the agent has the right to receive a statement about the commission due to him not later than the last day of the month following the quarter in which it was earned. The statement must set out the main components used in calculating the commission due, the agent having the right to demand access to the appropriate information to allow him to check the statement. This would include books, papers, accounts, deeds, writings and documents.

Part IV of the Regulations deals primarily, though not exclusively, with the conclusion and termination of the agency agreement. Regulation 13 contains an absolute right that cannot be waived whereby either party is entitled to receive from the other upon request a signed document setting out the terms of the agency agreement agreed at the outset of the contract and subsequently. Naturally, this would include any agreed provisions regarding termination of the agreement or, alternatively, rights of extension.

Regulation 14 deals specifically with the position when a fixed-term agency agreement (for example three years) reaches the end of the specified period and yet the parties continue to act as if the contract was subsisting. The regulation provides that the agency will continue on the same terms but be of an indefinite duration. Thus the agent will continue to exercise the level of authority existing previously and be entitled to remuneration.

Many agreements make suitable provision for the termination of the agreement either because it is for a fixed duration or, alternatively, by stipulating periods of notice. However, the position may arise whereby a commercial agent is employed under an indefinite contract in which no term exists regarding periods of notice. This position is rectified by reg 15, which stipulates that prescribed minimum periods of notice will apply in that situation, namely one month notice during the first year of the agreement, two months notice during the second year and three months notice during the third or any subsequent year all ending on the last day of the month unless otherwise agreed by the parties. This protection for the agent is reinforced by later provisions within reg 15, which provide that the parties may agree upon longer periods of notice but subject to the requirement that the period of notice that the agent is entitled to receive must not be shorter than that to which the principal is entitled. These provisions also apply to a fixed-term contract which has been rendered indefinite by the operation of reg 14 as discussed above.

If the agent suffers loss as a result of the termination he is entitled to receive either an indemnity or compensation under reg 17 as long as his claim is lodged within one year of termination. The Regulations facilitate either approach but stipulate that the agent will receive compensation unless the contract specifically refers to indemnity. It is important to recognise, however, that the function of both indemnity and compensation is not to compensate the agent for any breach of contract by the principal. That is the role of contractual damages, which can be claimed in addition to an indemnity or compensation under the Regulations, as in **Duffen v FRA BO SpA** (1998). The Regulations recognise that an agent has a valid interest in the continuation of the agency and the opportunity that it gives him to earn an income through fees or commission. To lose that opportunity is to lose a potentially valuable asset. The function of an indemnity or compensation under the 1993 Regulations is to compensate the agent for that loss of opportunity irrespective of why the agency has been terminated. Hence, the agent is entitled to indemnity or compensation when the agency contract has come to an end naturally as, for example, where a fixed-term contract has expired. This particular situation was considered in **Moore v Piretta PTA Ltd** (1999), where it was held that the termination of an agency should be construed as the termination of the agency relationship. Hence, where a series of fixed-term contracts between a principal and agent run consecutively, the agent will not be entitled to payment when each contract finishes but only when the final one expires and the agency relationship ceases to exist.

Where the contract provides for indemnity, under reg 17(3) the agent will be entitled to payment if and to the extent that

(a) he has brought the principal new customers or has significantly increased the volume of business with existing customers and the principal continues to derive substantial benefits from the business with such customers; and
(b) the payment of this indemnity is equitable having regard to all the circumstances and, in particular, the commission lost by the commercial agent on the business transacted with such customers.

The maximum amount payable by way of indemnity is the equivalent of the average annual income of the agent based on the last five years of the agency or, alternatively, the duration of the agency if it is less than five years. There is no obligation on the agent to try to mitigate the loss and, thus, any income that the agent may be receiving from a new agency will not be taken into account.

Where the agency contract does not provide for an indemnity, the agent may claim compensation instead where the termination of the agency is in circumstances which

(a) deprive the commercial agent of the commission which proper performance of the agency contract would have procured for him whilst providing his principal with substantial benefits linked to the activities of the commercial agent, or

(b) have not enabled the commercial agent to amortise the costs and expenses that he had incurred in the performance of the agency contract on the advice of his principal.

The meaning of 'proper performance' of the agency contract was considered in the decision of **Page _v_ Combined Shipping and Trading Co Ltd** (1997), when it was held to mean the 'normal' performance of the contract, i.e. the performance that the parties were expecting. In that case, the principal reduced the amount of business which the agent was able to perform to a minimum, thereby depriving him of the opportunity to earn his commission. The agent repudiated the contract and claimed compensation. The principal argued that, as the contract allowed him to control the amount of business that the agent undertook and thereby the amount of commission that the agent could earn, the agent could not complain if it was reduced and hence he had not suffered any loss. However, the Court of Appeal rejected this approach and concluded that the agent was entitled to expect 'normal' performance of the contract and, further, that the principal would act in good faith in that performance.

Naturally, following the common law approach, compensation is not recoverable if the termination was due to the agent's default. Thus, for example, if the agent had made a secret profit or breached the good faith requirement, the right to compensation would be lost. Further, compensation is not payable if the agent terminated the agreement unless it was due to his age, infirmity or illness rendering further performance unreasonable or was justified by the principal's behaviour. Lastly, the right to compensation ceases if the agent assigns his rights and liabilities to a new agent. The agent's estate can recover compensation if the termination was caused by the agent's death.

Unlike indemnity, there is no prescribed formula for calculating the amount that is payable by way of compensation. It falls to the parties to expressly agree that in the contract and they are free to decide for themselves what figure is appropriate. Given that compensation is not contractual damages, they are not subject to the normal rule against penalties.

Given the _uberrimae fidei_ nature of agency and the opportunity it provides for the agent to acquire knowledge of the principal's business, it is perhaps natural that a principal may want to insert a restraint of trade clause into an agency agreement. Such clauses are valid at common law, as discussed in Chapter 3, subject to certain criteria being satisfied. Regulation 20 of the 1993 Regulations reinforces this position by stipulating that restraint of trade clauses are valid only if and to the extent that two criteria are satisfied: namely, that the clause is written (this puts its scope beyond doubt) and that it relates both to the geographic area or to a group of customers and geographic area in which the agent works and to the type of goods covered by the agency. The maximum duration of a restraint of trade clause is two years after termination.

Question

Bloggs Ltd employ Charles as their agent for the distribution and sale of their computers. The agency agreement provides that the agency will last for a period of two years commencing on 1 January 1996 and that Charles will receive a 5 per cent commission on every computer sold.

Discuss the rights and liabilities of the parties in relation to this agency agreement.

Answer

This question considers the relationship between a principal and an agent, and the rights and liabilities created by that relationship. This agency will be governed by the Commercial Agents (Council Directive) Regulations 1993 as Charles appears to be an independent commercial agent authorised to negotiate the sale of goods on behalf of his principal. Charles must act in the best interests of Bloggs Ltd, his principal, communicating all necessary information to them and complying with reasonable requests. In return, Charles has the right to receive his commission on the due dates, receive statements about the amount of commission to which he is entitled, etc. The main point of interest in the question is that the agency is for a fixed period of two years. Under reg 14, if at the end of the period the parties continue to act as if the contract is subsisting, the contract will be deemed to continue on the same terms but for an indefinite period.

Further reading

Adams, A (2000). *Law for Business Students*, 2nd edn (Longman)

Bradgate, R (2000). *Commercial Law*, 3rd edn (Butterworth)

Dobson, P (1997). *Charlesworth's Business Law*, 16th edn (Sweet & Maxwell)

Keenan, D (2000). *Smith and Keenan's Advanced Business Law*, 11th edn (Longman)

Keenan, D and Riches, S (1998). *Business Law*, 5th edn (Longman)

Markesinis, B S and Munday, R J C (1998). *An Outline of the Law of Agency*, 4th edn (Butterworth)

Richards, P (2001). *Law of Contract*, 5th edn (Longman)

Stone, R (2000). *Principles of Contract Law*, 4th edn (Cavendish)

Part II   **The supply of goods and services**

7 Implied conditions in the sale of goods

7.1 Introduction

The quality and utility of goods is an issue of paramount importance to anyone involved in the regular sale and purchase of goods, whether in a professional capacity or a personal one. The law covering quality derives originally from nineteenth-century common law decisions. Indeed, there have only been two Acts of Parliament governing the quality of goods in contracts of sale: the Sale of Goods Act 1893, which codified the pre-existing common law, and the Sale of Goods Act 1979, which is a consolidation Act. The Sale of Goods Act 1979 has itself been amended with effect from 3 January 1995 by the Sale and Supply of Goods Act 1994.

The 1979 Act (hereafter the Act) seeks to control the relationship between sellers and buyers. Being contractual, the rules of contractual privity apply (subject to third party rights under the Contracts (Rights of Third Parties) Act 1999) and thus the manufacturer of a product will not have any direct liability to the ultimate consumer unless he sold the goods to him. Each member of the distributive chain will have contractual privity with the person next to him in the chain whether as seller or buyer and so acquire rights and obligations. A distributive chain might include a variety of persons such as appears in Figure 7.1, each of whom will have some contractual rights and responsibilities.

The Act protects the buyer of goods by a collection of implied terms contained in ss 12–15 that cover title, sales by description, satisfactory quality, fitness for purpose and sale by sample. Although the major provisions in the Act are stated to be implied

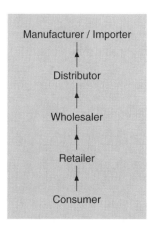

Figure 7.1   Distributive chain

terms (in order to avoid certain technical difficulties in Scotland), the Act provides that the terms are to be treated as 'conditions' in England, Wales and Northern Ireland. Being implied conditions any breach, however slight, gives a *prima facie* right to terminate the contract (but see s 15A regarding remedies). However, s 11(2) allows the buyer to treat a breach of condition as merely a breach of warranty. This involves the buyer forgoing his right to terminate and electing to continue with the contract while suing for contractual damages for the breach in accordance with s 53. This section provides that where the buyer elects or is forced to treat a breach of condition as a breach of warranty, he can use the breach as a means of either reducing or extinguishing the price or sue for damages. This solution will be forced upon a buyer if he is deemed to have 'accepted' the goods, as in **Bernstein** *v* **Pamson Motors (Golders Green) Ltd** (1987), in which case the buyer will lose his right of termination and be forced to rely on an action for damages.

7.2 A 'contract of sale'

The Sale of Goods Act 1979 applies only to contracts for the sale of goods as defined in the Act. It is important to understand the parameters of such contracts for there are many similar contracts involving the transfer of goods which do not attract the protection of ss 12–15. Arguably, the distinction is of less significance today as most of these contracts are now covered by similar provisions contained in other statutes. Nonetheless, it is important to establish the parameters of each classification of contract so as to identify which statute applies to any individual contract.

A 'contract of sale' is defined in s 2(1) as being 'a contract by which the seller transfers or agrees to transfer the property in goods to the buyer for a money consideration called the price'. Section 61 defines 'goods' as 'including all personal chattels other than things in action and money . . . [and] . . . emblements, industrial growing crops, and things attached to or forming part of the land which are agreed to be severed before sale or under the contract of sale'. The last clause of the definition would clearly include things such as timber, which can be severed from the land, but would not include buildings, which cannot. Analysis of s 2 permits identification of those contracts involving the transfer of goods which would not be covered by the 1979 Act. Hire-purchase contracts are not included for it was held in the case of **Helby** *v* **Matthews** (1895) that the hirer in a hire-purchase agreement has not bought or agreed to buy the goods.

The requirement for a money consideration necessarily excludes contracts of barter whereby goods are exchanged, as in **Esso Petroleum Ltd** *v* **Customs and Excise Commissioners** (1976), in which World Cup coins were provided as a special offer to customers who purchased four gallons of petrol. The House of Lords held that there was a contract but not a contract of sale. Note, however, that the decision of **G J Dawson (Clapham) Ltd** *v* **H & G Dutfield** (1936) held that a part-exchange agreement in which the goods are paid for partly by exchange goods and partly by money is a contract for the sale of goods. In that case, two lorries were to be paid for partly by a trade-in of two other lorries with the balance being payable in cash. The potential inclusion of contracts for the supply of work and materials will depend on the balance between the two elements of the contract. If the contract is primarily for the purchase of the goods, the service element being a mere incidental, as, for example, the sale of a take-away meal, the contract will be covered by the Act. By contrast, where the primary element of the contract is the provision of the service, as in a contract for the repair of a car or the interior decoration of premises, the contract will fall outside the provisions of the Act even though some goods will be transferred as an integral part of the contract. In the above examples, this would be the replacement parts for the car and the paint used for the decoration.

Contracts of bailment likewise fall outside the Act because there is no intention to pass the property in such contracts, merely to pass the temporary possession of the goods. This would include contracts of hire, whether short-term or long-term, and contracts for the repair of goods whereby the repairer takes temporary possession of the goods but surrenders them to the owner upon completion of the repairs.

The implied conditions of title, description, satisfactory quality, etc for the goods in contracts of barter, contracts for services and contracts of hire are contained in Part I of the Supply of Goods and Services Act 1982 (see Chapter 8).

7.3 The right to sell

When purchasing goods, the buyer naturally wishes to be assured that he is going to acquire good title to them. While this will be of importance to any purchaser, the significance in a commercial context may be overwhelming when any individual contract of purchase may potentially involve thousands or millions of pounds. There is little point in a buyer contracting to buy an extremely expensive piece of precision machinery only to discover that he has not acquired the title to it because the seller did not have the right to sell.

Section 12(1) of the Act addresses this problem and provides:

In a contract of sale, other than one to which subsection (3) below applies, there is an implied term on the part of the seller that in the case of a sale he has a right to sell the goods, and in the case of an agreement to sell he will have such a right at the time when the property is due to pass.

The term is to be treated as a condition in England and Wales and Northern Ireland. The requirement is that the seller will have the 'right to sell' at the appropriate time. It does not require that the seller has the title to the goods, although this is likely to be so, except in agency situations. The right to sell implies more than a mere ability to pass the property and has been construed to mean the freedom to sell the goods legally. Hence, in **Niblett Ltd** *v* **Confectioners' Materials Co** (1921) the defendants, an American company, sold 3,000 tins of 'Nissly Brand' condensed milk to the plaintiff. Nestlé obtained an injunction preventing the resale of the tins as they infringed Nestlé's copyright. The Court of Appeal held that the defendants had breached s 12 as they did not have the freedom to sell the product in England.

By contrast, in **Microbeads AG** *v* **Vinehurst Road Markings Ltd** (1975) Microbeads, a Swiss company, sold some road-marking machines to Vinehurst, who failed to pay. Subsequently, another company unconnected with the sale acquired a patent covering road-marking machines. This was enforceable against Vinehurst, who argued that this meant Microbeads were in breach of s 12 as they did not have the right to sell the machines in England. The court held that this argument failed as the patent was not effective at the time of sale.

If the buyer can show that there has been a total failure of consideration because the seller does not have the right to sell and cannot get it by the relevant time, then the buyer can terminate the contract and claim a total refund of the contract price. This is one of the few situations in English law where the buyer is provided with a windfall for he is entitled to reclaim the full contract price even though he may have had significant use of the goods meanwhile. Thus, in **Rowland v Divall** (1923), a case that has been criticised, Divall sold a car to Rowland, a car dealer, for £334. Rowland sold it to a third party for £400. Subsequently, the police took possession of the car, which had been stolen. Rowland refunded the £400 to his purchaser and sued Divall to recover his purchase price of £334. The Court of Appeal held that there had been a breach of the equivalent of s 12 of the Sale of Goods Act 1979 and that Rowland was entitled to recover the full £334. This was so despite the fact that Rowland and the third party between them had been using the car for four months and had effectively had this benefit free.

The **Rowland** decision cannot be followed unless the buyer can show a total failure of consideration; partial failure will not suffice. The decision of **Butterworth v Kingsway Motors** (1954) illustrates the distinction. Miss A, who had bought a car on hire-purchase, sold it to B before she had completed the hire-purchase payments. As instalments were owing, she did not have a right to dispose of the vehicle, which belonged to the finance company. B sold the car to C, who sold it to Kingsway Motors, who sold it to Butterworth. In practice, every sale of the car involved a breach of the equivalent of s 12 as none of the sellers had a right to sell. Some 11 months later, Butterworth discovered that he did not own the car and purported to terminate the contract with Kingsway Motors suing for a return of the purchase price. At this stage, Miss A completed her hire-purchase payments and the title fed down the line to Kingsway Motors. The court held that Butterworth could recover the full purchase price even though he had used the car for 11 months as there had been a total failure of consideration. However, B, C and Kingsway Motors could not recover the full purchase price for their respective purchases as they had not suffered a total failure of consideration. Each of them had acquired title to the goods eventually and before they had attempted to terminate their respective contracts. Therefore, they had suffered only a partial failure of consideration, for which a claim for damages would suffice.

Section 21 of the Act provides that a seller cannot pass better title than he possesses, summed up in the Latin maxim *nemo dat quod non habet*. Where a person who is not the owner of goods purports to sell them, it follows that the buyer cannot generally acquire good title. In such a situation, there has been an actionable breach of s 12 for the seller does not have the right to sell. In fact, there are some exceptions to the basic *nemo dat* rule which provide that in certain situations, the innocent buyer can acquire good title to the goods even though the seller did not have title. One of the statutory exceptions relates to motor vehicles on which there is outstanding hire-purchase. Given the current exception, Butterworth would now have acquired good title to the car. The *nemo dat* exceptions are considered fully in Chapter 10. Section 12(2)–(5) provides for the only implied terms (warranties) to be found in ss 12–15. Section 12(2) provides:

> In a contract of sale, other than one to which subsection (3) below applies, there is also an implied term that—
>
> (a) the goods are free, and will remain free until the time when the property is to pass, from any charge or encumbrance not disclosed or known to the buyer before the contract is made, and
>
> (b) the buyer will enjoy quiet possession of the goods except so far as it may be disturbed by the owner or other person entitled to the benefit of any charge or encumbrance so disclosed or known.

A breach of this warranty would occur if, for instance, the seller did not tell the buyer that he had used the goods as security for a loan he received from a third party. Being a breach of warranty, an action would lie for damages. The recent decision of **Rubicon Computer Systems Ltd *v* United Paints Ltd** (2000) considered the application of s 12(2). Rubicon had contracted with United Paints to provide and install a computer system for them. Following a dispute about payment, Rubicon installed a time-lock system into the computer and later activated it so that United Paints could not access their computer system. United Paints treated this as a repudiatory breach and deemed the contract to be at an end. The Court of Appeal held that repudiatory breach had occurred and also that, following delivery and installation, an implied term under s 12(2)(b) had arisen. Consequently, the installation of the time-lock constituted a wrongful interference with the goods which disturbed the buyer's right to quiet possession under s 12.

Section 12(3)–(5) provides for implied warranties in relation to contracts of sale where it appears from the contract, or can be inferred from the circumstances, that the intention is that the seller will transfer only such title as he or a third person may have. In such contracts, there is an implied warranty that all charges or encumbrances known to the seller and not known to the buyer have been disclosed to the buyer before the contract is made. Further, there are implied warranties that in such a contract none of the following will disturb the buyer's quiet possession:

(a) the seller, or

(b) where the seller is transferring the title belonging to a third person, that person, or

(c) anyone claiming through the seller or that third person other than under a previously disclosed charge or encumbrance.

7.4 Sale by description

Section 13 of the Act applies to sales by description and provides:

> (1) Where there is a contract for the sale of goods by description, there is an implied term that the goods will correspond with the description.

(2) If the sale is by sample as well as by description it is not sufficient that the bulk of the goods corresponds with the sample if the goods do not also correspond with the description.

(3) A sale of goods is not prevented from being a sale by description by reason only that, being exposed for sale or hire, they are selected by the buyer.

In England, Wales and Northern Ireland this term is a condition and applies to all sales of goods irrespective of the character of the seller. Thus, both business sellers and private sellers are potentially liable for breach, unlike the corresponding criminal law provision in s 1 of the Trade Descriptions Act 1968, which applies only where the seller sells in the course of a trade or business.

7.4.1 What constitutes a 'sale by description'

A sale by description for the purposes of s 13 will arise in any sale where the buyer has relied upon a description of the goods when selecting them. Thus, any sale of unascertained or future goods (see Chapter 10 for a definition of these terms) such as '10 tons of King Edward potatoes' or a 'cherry red Rover 2000' will necessarily be a sale by description for the goods are not to hand at the time of sale and the buyer must rely on the description applied to them by the seller. A prime example is any purchase made from a catalogue, where the description applied to the goods is the major selling technique and the seller and buyer may never meet.

Sales by description are not limited, though, to situations in which the goods are not present. It is equally possible for a sale by description to occur where the purchaser has seen and even handled the goods, a point confirmed in **Grant v Australian Knitting Mills** (1936), in which the sale of underwear was held to be a sale by description. Similarly, in **Beale v Taylor** (1967) the sale of a car described as a 'Herald, convertible, white, 1961' was a sale by description even though the buyer subsequently inspected the vehicle prior to purchase. In fact, the car was a 'cut and shut', the back half being from a 1961 car and the front half from an earlier model. Sales in supermarkets or in trade warehouses would be classed as sales by description if the goods were in any way described by, for example, labels or shelf edge tickets. Further, it is clear from s 13(3) that the self-selection of goods by the buyer does not prevent it being a sale by description.

7.4.2 Descriptive words

Not all words that might be classed as descriptive in the normal generic sense of the word will necessarily constitute descriptions for the purposes of s 13. Recently the courts have become more restrictive in their approach and some of the older cases such as **Re Moore and Landauer** (1921) are now criticised as being excessively technical. In **Re Moore** the buyers agreed to buy 3,000 tins of fruit to be packed in boxes, each containing 30 tins. The correct quantity was delivered but some of the tins were in boxes of 24. The court held that the buyer was entitled to reject the goods. Similarly, in **Arcos v Ronaasen & Son** (1933) the buyer was entitled to reject a consignment of wooden staves which should have been 1/2 inch thick but some of which were 9/16 inch thick. The House of Lords held that size is an enforceable part of the description.

The modern approach was summed up by Lord Diplock in **Ashington Piggeries Ltd v Christopher Hill Ltd** (1972), who stated that what really matters:

> is whether the buyer could fairly and reasonably refuse to accept the goods on the basis that their failure to correspond with what was said about them makes them goods of a different kind from those he had agreed to buy. The key to section 13 is identification.

Thus it is only those words that identify some essential characteristic of the product that will be classed as descriptions for this purpose. This would include factors such as size (including tolerances where appropriate), constituent elements, capacity, age, manufacturer and performance. This approach accords with that adopted under the Trade Descriptions Act 1968, where the factors subject to criminal control are listed in s 2 and are characteristics of the goods. Liability under s 13 will not arise in respect of general information such as the current location of the goods. In **Reardon Smith Line v Yngvar Hansen-Tangen** (1976) the buyer ordered a ship described in the contract as being No 354 from Osaka Zosen shipyard. The ship was built in another yard although it conformed with the buyer's specifications. The Privy Council held that the buyer could not reject the ship as the statements about the number and shipyard were not part of the description of the ship.

When drafting commercial contracts of sale close scrutiny must be given to the descriptions applied so that there can be no confusion about the precise details of the goods under contract. Traditionally, the courts have been reluctant to interfere in commercial contracts, being of the opinion that businessmen are in the best position to agree terms and decide what significance should be attached to them. It follows that the more precise the terms included, the more precise must be the performance. Thus, for example, if a contract detailing specifications of goods includes details of acceptable tolerances, then those should be enforced and goods failing to comply with such tolerances could be rejected as breaching s 13.

When enforcing s 13, there must also be proof that the description was influential in the sale in that the buyer did rely upon it, for liability will arise only if the sale was by reference to the contractual description. It must be clear that the description must form an essential part of the contract. This position was clarified in **Harlingdon & Leinster Ltd v Christopher Hull Fine Art Ltd** (1990), a Court of Appeal decision in which the seller sold a painting described as being by the German expressionist artist, Munter. The seller relied for this description on one previously applied to the painting in an auction catalogue. The seller made clear to the buyer that he was not an expert, unlike the buyer, who did specialise in German expressionist paintings. The buyer paid £6,000 for the painting, which subsequently proved to be a fake worth approximately £100. The Court of Appeal held that the buyer could not reasonably have relied on the description. As such, it was not influential in the sale and was not an essential term of the contract.

This approach was followed recently in the 1998 decision of **Ojjeh v Waller; Ojjeh v Galerie Moderne Ltd** (1998). Ojjeh, a collector, purchased 17 purple Lalique glass mascots from Galerie Moderne Ltd, of which Waller was a director. Waller, an expert and dealer in Lalique glass, had confirmed that the purple colouring of the glass had been done by the manufacturer. In reliance upon this, Ojjeh bought the mascots. It transpired subsequently that the statement was not true and the court held that there had been a breach of s 13 of the Sale of Goods Act 1979. The company was held liable, as was Waller because he had used his personal reputation in making the statement and had encouraged reliance upon it.

Section 13 is often viewed as being closely linked to the s 14 requirement of satisfactory quality. It should be remembered that while the two may go hand in hand on many occasions, this is not necessarily so. It is feasible that goods that comply with their contractual description are not of a satisfactory quality and vice versa. Nonetheless, there are examples where one section has been used when the other was more appropriate, the prime example of this being the decision of **Beale** *v* **Taylor** (above), in which the courts stretched the use of s 13 to provide the buyer with a remedy because it involved a private sale not amenable to s 14 liability.

7.5 Satisfactory quality

Section 14 is often viewed as the central plank of the 1979 Act, containing as it does the implied conditions of satisfactory quality and fitness for purpose. These two, when assessed alongside the price of the product, are the standard by which most purchasers would assess value for money.

From the passage of the original Sale of Goods Act in 1893 until 3 January 1995, when the reforms encompassed in the Sale and Supply of Goods Act 1994 became effective, the implied condition contained in s 14(2) of the Act referred to 'merchantable quality'. This phrase was much criticised over the years but reflected the rationale of the original section, which was to regulate contracts between merchants as opposed to traders and consumers. The section was originally drafted in a period of economic *laissez-faire* when the watchwords were *caveat emptor*, let the buyer beware.

The rise of consumerism in the latter half of the twentieth century led to a call for reform of this outdated term and its replacement with a phrase more appropriate to modern language and trading conditions. The Law Commission in its Report No 160 *Sale and Supply of Goods* advocated the adoption of the term 'acceptable quality'. However, in the event the phrase 'satisfactory quality' has been adopted.

Section 14 of the Sale of Goods Act 1979 provides:

(2) Where the seller sells goods in the course of a business, there is an implied term that the goods supplied under the contract are of a satisfactory quality.

(2A) For the purposes of this Act, goods are of a satisfactory quality if they meet the standard that a reasonable person would regard as satisfactory, taking account of any description of the goods, the price (if relevant) and all the other relevant circumstances.

(2B) For the purposes of this Act, the quality of the goods includes their state and condition and the following (among others) are in appropriate cases aspects of the quality of goods—

(a) fitness for all the purposes for which goods of the kind in question are commonly supplied,

(b) appearance and finish,

(c) freedom from minor defects,

(d) safety, and

(e) durability.

(2C) The term implied by subsection (2) above does not extend to any matter making the quality of goods unsatisfactory—

(a) which is specifically drawn to the buyer's attention before the contract is made,

(b) where the buyer examines the goods before the contract is made, which that examination ought to reveal, or

(c) in the case of a contract of sale by sample, which would have been apparent on a reasonable examination of the sample.

Although expressed as an implied term, the provision is rendered a condition by virtue of s 14(6).

Liability under s 14 is strict and thus traders who were not directly responsible for the creation and satisfactory quality of the goods will nonetheless be held liable for that quality and any direct consequential losses that may be suffered by a purchaser of the product if it should prove faulty. While at face value this appears to be a very onerous duty on retailers, the opportunity exists for them to pass liability back up the distributive chain subject, of course, to any valid exclusion clauses that may be contained in their contract of purchase.

The advent of computers has, of course, raised the issue of whether computer disks and programs are 'goods' for the purposes of the Act such as to give rise to implied conditions under ss 12–15. This issue was considered by the Court of Appeal in the decision of **St Albans City and District Council** *v* **International Computers Ltd** (1996), when a computer system supplied to St Albans City and District Council by International Computers Ltd contained a faulty program. Sir Iain Glidewell confirmed that a computer disk does fall within the definition of goods while a computer program, of itself, does not. However he continued that if a disk carrying a program which has been designed and encoded to achieve a particular function is transferred, by way of sale or hire, and the program is in some way defective so that it will not instruct or enable the computer to achieve the intended purpose, then this would constitute a breach of the implied conditions in s 14 of the Sale of Goods Act 1979 (or s 9 of the Supply of Goods and Services Act 1982 – see Chapter 8).

7.5.1 In the course of a business

The first significant point to note is that, unlike the other implied terms, s 14 applies only where the seller sells 'in the course of a business'. There is no liability visited upon private sellers and no protection for buyers in that situation. The dividing line between business and private sales is of paramount importance when considering potential liability and, for the business seller, the need to consider insurance against the risk of an item proving defective and causing injury, especially given that liability is strict. In practice, the distinction is often easy to draw. A cement company selling bags of cement is clearly acting in the course of a business, as is a wholesale greengrocer selling potatoes. Equally clear is the fact that a private individual selling his second-hand lawnmower through the small ads in the local paper is not selling in the course of a business. But what of a car-hire company selling off its old vehicles to replace them or a manufacturing company selling off old office furniture as part of a refurbishment plan. Until 1999, this was a grey area. The case law, which relied heavily on criminal law decisions under the Trade Descriptions Act 1968, tried to draw artificial boundaries between those sales that were integral to a company's business and those that were peripheral with liability only existing in relation to those sales that were integral to the seller's business. However, the Court of Appeal in **Stevenson v Rogers** (1999) held that this distinction is no longer relevant in civil law and that all sales conducted by a business, including the first such sale, should be deemed to be 'in the course of a business' for the purposes of civil law. The previous distinctions are now restricted to criminal law liability (see Chapter 13).

In Stevenson v Rogers Stevenson was the purchaser of a medium fishing vessel sold to him by Rogers, an experienced fisherman. Rogers was selling the vessel in order to replace it. The issue revolved around whether there was an implied condition about the satisfactory quality of the vessel, which itself depended on whether the vessel was sold in the course of a business. The Court of Appeal held that for the purposes of civil law the phrase should be construed both widely and at face value so as to give effect to Parliament's intention to protect consumers. As such, any sale by a business would be 'in the course of a business'. As such, the sale concerned had been conducted in the course of a business and, hence, there was an implied condition about the satisfactory quality of the goods.

There remains the issue of the hobbyist, such as occurred in **Blakemore v Bellamy** (1982), in which a postman used to refurbish cars as a hobby and then sell them. Here the crucial issue will still be whether the person is merely indulging in a hobby or has crossed the boundary into business, in which case all of the sales would attract liability under section 14. This dividing line has never been an easy one to draw and will depend on the facts in each case.

Lastly, s 61 of the Act defines a business as including 'a profession and the activities of any government department (including a Northern Ireland department) or local or public authority'.

7.5.2 The scope of the section

The wording of s 14(2C) imposes some limitations on the ambit of the implied condition of satisfactory quality. It provides that the condition will not extend to any matter making the quality of the goods unsatisfactory:

(a) which is specifically drawn to the buyer's attention before the contract is made,
(b) where the buyer examines the goods before the contract is made, which that examination ought to reveal, or
(c) in the case of a contract for sale by sample, which would have been apparent on a reasonable examination of the sample.

Paragraph (a) covers only defects drawn to the buyer's attention prior to the contract. This would be relevant, for example, in respect of second-hand goods which may already have a defect caused through previous usage, such as a second-hand car with a worn clutch. Similarly, it would cover new goods which are sold as 'seconds'. In either situation, the buyer is aware that the goods have a defect and thus is put on notice to ensure that the defect is such that he is still prepared to buy the goods despite the defect. In either of the above situations, it would be inequitable to hold the seller liable in respect of a defect of which the buyer had notice.

Paragraphs (b) and (c) both relate to defects that would be obvious upon an examination of the goods. However, it is important to consider each provision carefully for they provide different standards. Paragraph (b), which would apply in all sales other than sales by sample, provides for a subjective test referring to the examination which actually took place. Before the seller can evade liability, the buyer must have actually examined the goods and it must be shown that the defects should have revealed themselves during that particular examination. Arguably, a buyer is wiser not to examine the goods at all as in that way his protection against defects will not be removed. By contrast, paragraph (c), which applies only to sales by sample, provides for an objective test, namely that the defect would have been apparent on a reasonable examination of the sample. Note that in this situation there is no requirement that any examination actually took place, merely that the defect would have been apparent if a reasonable examination had taken place. Note, however, that under s 34 (to be discussed later) a seller must afford the buyer a reasonable opportunity to examine the goods for the purpose of ascertaining whether they are in conformity with the contract prior to acceptance occurring. The section applies to both new and second-hand goods although the extent of the liability for second-hand items will depend on a variety of factors including the age of the goods and the price paid for them, as seen in **Bartlett _v_ Sydney Marcus** (1965). Further, the implied condition applies to 'the goods supplied under the contract'. It follows that this includes packaging and instructions so that absent or faulty instructions could render the product unsatisfactory, as in **Wormell _v_ R H M Agriculture (East) Ltd** (1986), and faulty packaging such as a defective bottle would also breach s 14(2). This would be so even if the bottle is returnable as s 14(2) does not require the goods to have been sold, merely 'supplied under the contract'. Hence, a cracked milk bottle leaving splinters of glass in the milk would render the whole item unsatisfactory, as would a faulty pop bottle which explodes under the pressure of containing the carbonated drink. Similarly, any extraneous matter supplied with the goods will be covered by the section, as in **Wilson _v_ Rickett, Cockerill & Co** (1954), in which an explosive detonator was included with some coalite. Both the coalite and the detonator were merchantable (now satisfactory) as individual items but unmerchantable (now unsatisfactory) when sold together.

7.5.3 The meaning of satisfactory quality

In order to understand the likely meaning of 'satisfactory quality' it is as well to start by reviewing briefly the development and meaning of the concept of merchantable quality, the predecessor of the current provision, which had been in existence for over a century. Strictly speaking, of course, all the case law relating to the concept of merchantable quality is no longer relevant and a new body of case law relating to satisfactory quality will have to develop. However, in practice, it is likely that certain of the existing cases will be used as an aid to the interpretation of some aspects of the new implied condition of satisfactory quality.

Prior to 1979, two distinct approaches to merchantable quality developed: first, the 'acceptability' test and, second, the 'usability' test. The 'acceptability' test was summarised by Dixon J in **Grant *v* Australian Knitting Mills** (1936), who suggested that goods would be merchantable if they were:

> in such a state that a buyer, fully acquainted with the facts, and therefore knowing what hidden defects exist and not being limited to their apparent condition would buy them without abatement of price obtainable for such goods if in a reasonable sound order and condition and without special terms.

In the **Grant** decision, the plaintiff had purchased some underwear. He contracted dermatitis after wearing it because a quantity of excess sulphites had been left in the fabric of the garment after manufacture when they should have been removed.

The 'usability' test revolved around the question of whether the goods were fit for their purpose and provided that goods were of a merchantable quality if they were usable within their contract description. This approach was confirmed in the decision of **Henry Kendall & Sons *v* William Lillico & Sons Ltd** (1969), which held that if the item had more than one common purpose, it would be classed as merchantable if it could satisfy any one of those purposes. Thus, in the **Kendall** decision, adulterated animal feeding stuff that proved fatal to pheasants was still merchantable as it could have been fed safely to cattle, one of its other purposes. In 1979, a statutory definition was introduced by the Sale of Goods Act. This definition relied heavily on the concept of fitness for purpose while acknowledging that other factors such as contract description, price and other relevant circumstances had a part to play. Despite the introduction of this definition, the courts continued to refer to pre-1979 case law, and thus the court in **Aswan Engineering Establishment Co *v* Lupdine Ltd** (1987) relied heavily on the *Kendall* decision when holding that the goods in question were merchantable because they were fit for one of their common purposes. The plaintiff, Aswan Engineering, bought some waterproofing compound from the defendants. It was packed in heavy duty plastic pails, which on arrival in Kuwait were stacked five or six high on the dockside in extremely high temperatures. The pails collapsed and the waterproofing compound was lost. On a claim that the pails were unmerchantable, the Court of Appeal held that they were merchantable as they could have been stacked that way quite safely in many other countries and could have been used in Kuwait if stacked in a different way. By contrast, in the decision of **Amstrad plc *v* Seagate Technology Inc** (1998), a case involving the supply of computer hard drives by Seagate to Amstrad for use in the latter's computers, it was held that the goods did not comply with the contract description and that it was not open to the defendant to argue that it had been used by other manufacturers without trouble.

Meanwhile, in relation to 'consumer' cases as opposed to 'commercial' cases, the court expanded the concept of merchantable quality to include factors not previously considered such as the appearance of the goods, minor defects and the ease of repair.

The most notable of these cases, and the ones which seem destined to be used in interpreting satisfactory quality, are **Rogers v Parish (Scarborough) Ltd** (1987), **Bernstein v Pamson Motors (Golders Green) Ltd** (1987) and **Shine v General Guarantee Corpn** (1988).

In **Rogers v Parish (Scarborough) Ltd** (1987) the plaintiff bought a new Range Rover costing £16,000. It suffered from a variety of faults including faulty oil seals and defects in the engine, gearbox and bodywork. After driving it for 5,500 miles in six months the plaintiff sought to reject it as being unmerchantable. The Court of Appeal held that it was unmerchantable as the court should consider not merely the buyer's purpose of driving the car from one place to another but should also take account of other factors such as his ability to do so with the appropriate degree of comfort, ease of handling and pride in the vehicle's outward appearance.

Similarly, in **Bernstein v Pamson Motors (Golders Green) Ltd** (1987) a Nissan Laurel was held unmerchantable because some sealant blocked the oil supply, causing the car to break down while on a motorway some three weeks and 140 miles after purchase. The plaintiff actually lost the case because the court held that he had accepted the vehicle and so lost his right to terminate. The court felt that three weeks was a reasonable period in which to examine and reject the goods. As he had not done so, acceptance had occurred.

In **Shine v General Guarantee Corpn** (1988) this more liberal approach to merchantable quality was extended to cover second-hand goods when the Court of Appeal held that the consumer's expectations as related to the contract description were a relevant factor to consider when assessing merchantable quality. The car sold as 'a nice car, good runner, no problems' was in fact an insurance write-off that had been submerged in water for 24 hours and which 'no member of the public, knowing the facts, would touch with a barge pole unless they could get it at a substantially reduced price'.

To move to the new requirement of 'satisfactory' quality contained in s 14(2), the basic definition is contained in s 14(2A) and provides that goods are of a satisfactory quality if:

> they meet the standard that a reasonable person would regard as satisfactory, taking account of any description of the goods, the price (if relevant) and all the other relevant circumstances.

This definition is somewhat nebulous and owes much to the previous statutory definition of 'merchantable quality'. The test is objective, relying on the opinion that a reasonable person would hold about the goods taking account of any description, the price and other relevant circumstances. It should be noted that there is no prescribed lower threshold for satisfactory quality in the same way that none existed for merchantable quality. Thus, it may safely be assumed that satisfactory quality does not connote any particular level of quality and that the *dicta* of Salmond J in **Taylor v Combined Buyers Ltd** (1924) remain pertinent and can be applied to satisfactory quality:

> The term 'merchantable' does not mean good, or fair, or average quality. Goods may be inferior or even bad quality but yet fulfil the legal requirement of

merchantable quality. For goods may be in the market in any grade, good, bad or indifferent, and yet all equally merchantable. On a sale of goods there is no implied condition that they are of any particular grade or standard. If the buyer wishes to guard himself in this respect he must expressly bargain for the particular grade or standard that he requires. If he does not do so, *caveat emptor*; and he must accept the goods, however inferior in quality, so long as they conform to the description under which they were sold and are of merchantable quality – the term 'quality' including state or condition.

The contract description applied to the goods is significant for it is against this description that overall quality may be judged. Thus, for example, it would be ridiculous to hold that shoes were not of a satisfactory quality because they proved unsuitable for hillwalking when they were described as 'dance slippers'. Price may also be relevant. There is a general assumption that 'you get what you pay for' and certainly the courts have been prepared to consider the price as a relevant factor, holding in **Rogers** *v* **Parish (Scarborough) Ltd** (above) that in the case of a luxury car costing £16,000 the buyer had a right to expect to be able to take pride in the vehicle's appearance. By contrast, it is equally clear from the decision in **Godley** *v* **Perry** (1960) that the fact that an item is cheap does not permit it to be unmerchantable, or (one assumes) unsatisfactory. In the **Godley** decision, a six-year-old child was blinded in one eye when a cheap plastic catapult snapped. It had cost 6d (equivalent to 2.5p). It was held that there had been a breach of the requirements of merchantable quality and fitness for purpose and the plaintiff recovered £2,500 damages.

There have been several leading decisions in which price was the leading factor and which would appear to remain good authority for the interpretation of s 14(2A). In the decision of **Grant** *v* **Australian Knitting Mills** referred to above, price was relied on as a mechanism for assessing whether goods were merchantable based on whether the buyer knowing the facts would still buy the goods without a reduction in the price. A similar approach is apparent in the decision of **Brown** *v* **Craiks** (1970) and **H Beecham & Co Pty Ltd** *v* **Francis Howard & Co Pty Ltd** (1921).

In **Brown** *v* **Craiks** the buyer ordered some cloth to be used for manufacturing dresses. The contract description was sufficiently wide to cover both dress fabric and industrial fabric, the seller believing that the cloth was to be used for industrial purposes. The agreed price was marginally higher than the prevailing rate for industrial fabric. When delivered the fabric was suitable for industrial use but not for dressmaking. It was held that the cloth was merchantable. By contrast, in **H Beecham & Co Pty Ltd** *v* **Francis Howard & Co Pty Ltd**, wood purchased for the manufacture of pianos was held to be unmerchantable when it was found to have dry rot, which made it unsuitable for that purpose and reduced its value to 30 shillings per 100 feet as opposed to the 80 shillings per 100 feet that the buyer had paid.

'Other relevant circumstances', the concluding part of the definition referred to in s 14(2A), is very open-ended but some guidance as to appropriate factors is provided by the non-exhaustive list given in s 14(2B), which adopts the recommendations of the Law Commission. Section 14(2B) is set out at pages 102–3. The factors referred to are:

(a) *Fitness for all the purposes for which goods of the kind in question are commonly supplied* Fitness for purpose remains a key factor in determining whether goods are of a satisfactory quality. Of course, there is some overlap between s 14(2B) and s 14(3), which introduces a separate implied condition of fitness for purpose. It is generally thought, however, that s 14(2B) addresses the common uses and purposes to which the goods are likely to be put, while s 14(3) addresses the issue of particular purposes for which the buyer requires the goods and which he has made known to the seller. Nonetheless, the overlap may be significant. Section 14(2B) finally addresses the perceived weakness of the decisions of **Kendall** *v* **Lillico** and **Aswan Engineering** above in that the goods will not be considered of a satisfactory quality unless they are fit for all the puposes for which they are commonly supplied as opposed to merely one such purpose. This undoubtedly strengthens the position of the buyer.

(b) *Appearance and finish* This provision adds weight to the decisions of **Rogers** *v* **Parish (Scarborough) Ltd** and **Shine** *v* **General Guarantee Corpn** above, both of which supported the view that non-functional aspects of quality such as appearance and finish should be relevant in determining merchantable quality (and, one assumes, satisfactory quality). In the **Rogers** case, a decision of the Court of Appeal, Mustill LJ stated:

> starting with the purpose for which 'goods of that kind' are commonly bought, one would include in respect of any passenger vehicle not merely the buyer's purpose of driving the car from one place to another but of doing so with the appropriate degree of comfort, ease of reliability and, one may add, of pride in the vehicle's outward and interior appearance.

In the **Shine** decision the mere fact that the car had been submerged in water for 24 hours was sufficient to render the car unmerchantable even though no particular defects were being alleged.

(c) *Freedom from minor defects* Any breach of a condition entitles the buyer to repudiate the contract (but see s 15A later). This means that however slight the defect, the buyer could terminate the contract if the court held that this rendered the goods unmerchantable. In practice, the courts have at times seemed reluctant to grant a remedy for minor defects given the potentially far-reaching remedy. This new provision, however, reinforces the fact that minor defects may nonetheless render goods unsatisfactory such as to justify termination. This confirms the decision of **Bernstein** *v* **Pamson Motors** above in which a new car with a relatively minor defect, a piece of sealant in the lubricating system, caused major engine damage which cost £700 to repair. The car was held to be unmerchantable such as to justify termination. In practice, the right of termination had been lost because the buyer was deemed to have accepted the goods (see Chapter 9 for a full discussion of acceptance).

(d) *Safety* Safety has never been overtly considered as an aspect of merchantable quality but has been implicit in some decisions such as **Bernstein**. The inclusion of it in the new definition complies with the wishes of the Law Commission and elevates safety to a new level of significance.

Of particular interest are goods which have a hidden defect or characteristic which may pose a safety hazard. Under the Consumer Protection Act 1987 and the General Product Safety Regulations 1994 (see Chapter 14), it is a criminal offence to supply goods without adequate safety warnings. Section 14(2B)(d) now provides a civil law counterpart whereby the failure to provide adequate safety warnings or instructions for use may also render the goods not of a satisfactory quality and give the injured buyer a right to terminate the contract and seek damages for loss. This would accord with the minority judgment in **Kendall** *v* **Lillico**.

(e) *Durability* Durability is also a new factor included at the behest of the Law Commission. It has always been a moot point whether and to what extent durability was an issue in respect of merchantable quality. There is now no doubt, however, that durability is relevant in determining satisfactory quality. The requirement would appear to be that the goods must remain of a satisfactory quality for a reasonable period following purchase. What is a reasonable period is a question of fact dependent upon the nature of the goods, the price paid, whether they are second-hand, etc.

7.6 Fitness for purpose

Section 14(3) provides:

Where the seller sells goods in the course of a business and the buyer, expressly or by implication, makes known—
(a) to the seller, or
(b) where the purchase price or part of it is payable by instalments and the goods were previously sold by a credit-broker to the seller, to that credit-broker,
any particular purpose for which the goods are being bought, there is an implied condition that the goods supplied under the contract are reasonably fit for that purpose, whether or not that is a purpose for which such goods are commonly supplied, except where the circumstances show that the buyer does not rely, or that it is unreasonable for him to rely, on the skill or judgment of the seller or credit-broker.

This subsection again applies only where the sale is in the course of a business and governs all goods supplied under the contract. Thus, the same arguments considered in respect of s 14(2) would apply here. This implied term is rendered a condition in England, Wales and Northern Ireland by virtue of s 14(6).

The fitness for purpose requirement often overlaps significantly with the requirement of satisfactory quality. It is not unusual for a plaintiff to seek to enforce both conditions against a seller.

7.6.1 Particular purpose

For liability to arise under s 14(3) the buyer must demonstrate that the goods were not fit for the particular purpose for which they were bought, whether or not that is a normal usage of the goods. He can assume that the normal purposes of an item are self-evident and there is no liability on him to make those expressly known to the seller. Thus, in **Priest** *v* **Last** (1903) it was held that the purpose of a hot water bottle was obvious. Thereafter the buyer may assume that the goods are fit for that purpose. Thus, a local authority buying food for use in school dinners can assume that it is edible (even if the children do not think so!). Likewise, a car must be safe to drive, a chair safe to sit on and shampoo safe to apply to the scalp. The buyer may wish to use the goods for some particular purpose whether or not it is a normal purpose. He is then under an obligation to make this purpose known either to the seller or to his agent. Where goods are purchased on hire-purchase or credit sale, it will suffice to tell the supplier as opposed to the finance company. This obligation will arise between any buyer and seller in the distributive chain, customer and retailer or wholesaler and manufacturer. If the seller knowing of the particular purpose sells the goods to the buyer he is deemed to warrant that they are fit for that purpose or purposes. Thus, in the **Ashington Piggeries** case, the manufacturer was liable under s 14(3) for supplying meal not fit for the specified purpose of being compounded into animal feed.

However, it should be noted that the seller will not be liable if the lack of fitness for purpose of the goods is due to some idiosyncracy of the buyer or some idiosyncratic aspect of the purpose for which the goods are to be used. Naturally, this exception only applies if the seller was not aware of the relevant idiosyncracy. Thus, in **Griffiths** *v* **Peter Conway Ltd** (1939) the seller of a Harris tweed coat was not liable to a buyer who suffered dermatitis after wearing the coat when the buyer had failed to disclose that she had abnormally sensitive skin. The decision of **Slater** *v* **Finning Ltd** (1997) took this a stage further when the House of Lords held that the seller would not be liable to the buyer even if the buyer did not know of the idiosyncracy either. In that case, the seller, a marine engine supplier, installed a new camshaft in the buyer's motor fishing vessel. A similar camshaft had been used without problems in other vessels with the same engine. The camshaft failed, as did two replacements, causing the buyer substantial loss and delay in his fishing operation. It transpired that the camshafts were satisfactory and that the problem arose because of an unknown idiosyncracy in the vessel's engine. The House of Lords held that the seller was not liable.

7.6.2 Reliance

An essential element of s 14(3) liability is that the buyer has relied upon the seller's skill and judgment in selecting the appropriate goods. Lord Wright in **Grant** *v* **Australian Knitting Mills** (1936) made clear that general reliance on the seller's skill is to be assumed from the buyer's decision to do business with that seller. This would be so whether it is a consumer buying from a retail outlet or a business buying from a wholesaler or distributor. Other factors, including the relative expertise of the parties, may play a part in establishing reliance. If the buyer is more experienced than the seller, he may find it difficult to establish either that he did so rely or that any reliance was reasonable. In a situation such as occurred in **Harlingdon & Leinster Ltd** *v* **Christopher Hull Fine Art Ltd** (1990), discussed above, reliance would be virtually impossible to prove. Experience may relate equally to the market into which the goods are to be introduced. Thus in **Tehran-Europe Co Ltd** *v* **S T Belton (Tractors) Ltd** (1968) the buyer purchased tractors for sale in Persia. The tractors broke Persian criminal regulations and the buyer was convicted and fined. The seller was held not liable under s 14(3) as it was unreasonable for the buyer to rely on the seller's skill given that the buyer knew more about the Persian market.

Partial reliance is possible where the seller is liable for anything left to his discretion, but the buyer is responsible for any aspect in which he has relied on his own expertise. Thus, if the buyer supplies a specification for the goods to be manufactured but leaves the seller to decide some details and arrange for the purchase of appropriate components, the seller will be liable if the components are unsuitable, but the buyer will be liable for any deficiency arising from the specification. Thus, in **Cammell Laird** *v* **Manganese Bronze & Brass** (1934) the seller was to provide ships' propellers to be manufactured according to the buyer's specifications. Anything not included in the specification was to be left to the skill of the seller. The propellers were not fit for the purpose because they were not thick enough, a factor not covered by the specifications. The seller was liable.

Taken to its logical conclusion, if the buyer has relied totally on his own opinion, no reliance on the seller will have occurred and no liability will exist under s 14(3). Such lack of reliance might be evidenced by the buyer buying goods by a brand name or buying from a seller who stocks only one make of an item, this fact being known to the buyer.

7.7 Sales by sample

Section 15 governing sales by sample is applicable to both business and private sales. In practice, of course, it is rare for any private sale to involve the use of samples and, hence, the application of this section is really limited to business sellers.

The mere use of a sample when negotiating a contract of sale does not necessarily make it a contract of sale by sample. Section 15(1) stipulates that a contract of sale by sample occurs where there is an express or implied term to that effect in the contract. If the contract is written, it is easy to establish from the terms whether the parties intended it to be a contract of sale by sample. With an oral contract the court must try to establish the intention of the parties from all the circumstances. The purpose of a sample was defined in **Drummond** *v* **Van Ingen** (1887) as being:

> to present to the eye the real meaning and intention of the parties with regard to the subject-matter of the contract which, owing to the imperfection of language, it may be difficult or impossible to express in words. The sample speaks for itself.

Once it is established that a contract is one of sale by sample s 15(2) provides two implied conditions, namely:

(a) that the bulk will correspond with the sample in quality;

[. . .]

(c) that the goods will be free from any defect, making their quality unsatisfactory, which would not be apparent on reasonable examination of the sample.

The first is self-explanatory. Where the sample is being used as a physical description of the goods, the bulk of the goods supplied must correspond with that description. The second implied condition relates to freedom from inherent indiscernible defects in the goods. Note that there is no liability for defects that would have been apparent on a reasonable inspection of the goods irrespective of whether an examination actually took place. This test is both objective and more stringent than the standard test under s 14(2C)(b). Here, it is in the buyer's interests to ensure that he does inspect the goods thoroughly before acceptance. In the previous version of the section, there was a third implied condition which provided that the buyer would have a reasonable opportunity to compare the bulk with the sample. This condition really related to the issue of acceptance of the goods in a contract for a sale by sample. It has been deleted from s 15 with effect from 3 January 1995 and has been subsumed within a revised and extended version of s 35, which deals with acceptance. It now appears as s 35(2)(b) (see Chapter 9).

7.8 Acceptance

Whether the goods have been accepted is of crucial importance because, as can be seen from the **Bernstein** decision, acceptance of the goods will involve the buyer losing his right to terminate the contract. Thereafter, he will only be entitled to recover damages for a breach of ss 12–15. Case law does not provide any firm guidelines about when acceptance occurs, as can be seen from contrasting the decisions of **Bernstein** and **Rogers *v* Parish**, both of which related to the purchase of cars. In the former decision, acceptance was deemed to have occurred after three weeks and 140 miles, while in **Rogers *v* Parish** (1987) the buyer was still entitled to reject the goods after six months. Sections 34–35 of the Sale of Goods Act 1979 provide statutory guidance about acceptance and are considered fully in Chapter 9.

7.9 Modification of remedies

Thus far in this chapter, it has been assumed that a breach of an implied condition automatically gives rise to a right of repudiation unless the buyer has either accepted the goods or elected to treat the breach of condition as a breach of warranty under s 11(2) of the Sale of Goods Act 1979 and thereafter to claim damages rather than termination. This view would certainly accord with both the general rules about conditions and warranties and the pre-existing situation under the Sale of Goods Act 1979. However, the situation regarding remedies has been amended significantly by the introduction via the Sale and Supply of Goods Act 1994 of a new s 15A (s 15B in Scotland) to the Sale of Goods Act 1979, which provides that in specified situations a breach of condition is to be treated as a breach of warranty with a consequent change of remedy from repudiation to an action in damages. Section 15A states:

(1) Where in the case of a contract of sale—

(a) the buyer would, apart from this subsection, have the right to reject goods by reason of a breach on the part of the seller of a term implied by section 13, 14 or 15 above, but

(b) the breach is so slight that it would be unreasonable for him to reject them, then, if the buyer does not deal as a consumer, the breach is not to be treated as a breach of condition but may be treated as a breach of warranty.

(2) This section applies unless a contrary intention appears in, or is to be implied from, the contract.

(3) It is for the seller to show that a breach fell within subsection (1)(b) above.

There are a few factors to note about this provision. First, it applies only to breaches of ss 13, 14 and 15. It follows that it does not apply to breaches of s 12, the right to sell, breaches of this provision continuing to provide an automatic right of repudiation. This approach accords with the fact that s 12 is singled out for special treatment as regards exclusion clauses as well, evidencing both the gravity of a breach of the right to sell condition and a determination not to undermine the protection that the provision affords to the buyer.

The second point is that s 15A applies only to buyers who do not 'deal as a consumer' within the parameters attributed to that phrase by the Unfair Contract Terms Act 1977. Thus, the modification to the remedy that may be claimed upon breach is applicable only to non-consumer buyers. Consumer buyers continue to enjoy the higher level of protection commensurate with a right of repudiation.

The third factor is that the section covers only breaches which are 'so slight that it would be unreasonable for [the buyer] to reject [the goods]'. Naturally, this is a question of fact and a body of case law will have to evolve to demonstrate where the courts will draw the boundaries. The burden of proving that the breach was so slight falls on the seller who stands to benefit from s 15A. The effect of proving this fact means that the breach of condition will be treated as a breach of warranty and thus while the seller will be liable to pay damages the contract will continue. It should be noted that under s 15A(2) there is a presumption that this section applies to appropriate contracts unless a contrary intention appears in, or can be implied from, the contract.

7.10 Exclusion of liability

As discussed in Chapter 4, the seller's ability to exclude the implied conditions in ss 12–15 is governed by s 6 of the Unfair Contract Terms Act 1977. The implied condition of the right to sell cannot be excluded in any contract of sale. However, exclusion of liability under ss 13–15 will depend on the nature of the buyer. If he is 'dealing as a consumer' within the meaning of s 12 of the Unfair Contract Terms Act 1977, liability for the implied conditions contained in ss 13–15 of the Sale of Goods Act 1979 cannot be excluded. If the buyer is dealing otherwise than as a consumer, exclusion is possible to the extent that it is reasonable.

7.11 European reform

The law relating to contracts for the sale of goods is going to be amended as an inevitable consequence of Directive 99/44/EC on certain aspects of the sale of consumer goods and associated guarantees. This Directive, passed by the European Union in May 1999, must be given effect in the national legislation of member states no later than 1 January 2002. For the purposes of the Directive, contracts of sale are deemed to include contracts for the supply of consumer goods to be manufactured or produced.

While the effect of the Directive is limited to consumer contracts, it will make some significant changes to those contracts and also the legality and enforceability of manufacturers' guarantees. The purpose of the legislation is stated in art 1 as being the approximation of laws in member states 'to ensure a uniform minimum level of consumer protection in the context of the internal market'. As it only provides a minimum level of protection, member states are at liberty to adopt other measures which ensure a higher level of consumer protection. A consumer is defined as being a natural person who is acting for purposes which are not directly related to his trade, business or profession. Thus, for the purposes of this Directive, a company can never be a consumer. By contrast, a seller is defined as 'any natural or legal person, who, under a contract, sells consumer goods in the course of his trade, business or profession'.

The Directive is also restricted in effect to 'consumer goods', which means any tangible moveable items with three exceptions, namely, goods sold by way of execution or by authority of law, water and gas when they are not put up for sale in limited volumes or set quantities, and electricity. In respect of gas and water it is clear that while normal water and gas supplies would be excluded, pre-packed bottles of water or canisters of gas would be caught by this provision. Member states have the right to decide that 'consumer goods' will not cover second-hand goods sold at public auction where consumers have the opportunity of attending the sale in person.

The essential thrust of the Directive is contained in art 2.1, which requires the seller to deliver goods to the consumer which are in conformity with the contract of sale and provides the consumer with rights that cannot be excluded.

This provision begs the question of what constitutes conformity with the contract. Article 2.2 provides that goods will be presumed to be in conformity with the contract if they:

a) comply with the description given by the seller and possess the qualities of the goods which the seller has held out to the consumer as a sample or model

b) are fit for any particular purpose for which the consumer requires them and which he made known to the seller at the time of conclusion of the contract and which the seller has accepted

c) are fit for the purposes for which goods of the same type are normally used

d) show the quality and performance which are normal in goods of the same type and which the consumer can reasonably expect, given the nature of the goods and taking into account any public statements on the specific characteristics of the goods made about them by the seller, the producer or his representative, particularly in advertising or labelling.

At first glance these provisions tally closely with those contained in ss 13–15 of the Sale of Goods Act 1979 referring as they do to description, quality, fitness for purpose and samples. However, the scope and interpretation of the liability differs from ss 13–15 in significant ways. Article 2.3 provides that there is no lack of conformity if, at the time the contract was concluded, the consumer was aware of or could not reasonably have been unaware of the lack of conformity or alternatively that it was materials supplied by the consumer that caused the non-conformity. Article 2 also expressly addresses the liability of sellers for public statements made in respect of goods particularly in advertising and labelling. While under s 13 of the Sale of Goods Act 1979 there would be strict liability in respect of such statements, art 2.4 provides some protection for the seller providing that he will not be liable if he can show that he was not and could not reasonably have been aware of the statement and that by the time of the conclusion of the contract it had been corrected or that the consumer's decision to buy could not have been influenced by the statement. The final part of art 2 relates to the installation of goods, making clear that where installation is included in the contract, any lack of conformity due to incorrect installation shall be deemed to be a lack of conformity by the goods. The same will be true where the consumer has installed the goods and the incorrect installation is due to a shortcoming in the installation instructions. Of particular note is that there is a presumption that any lack of conformity that becomes apparent within six months of delivery of the goods shall be presumed to have existed at the time of delivery unless this presumption is incompatible with the nature of the goods or the nature of the lack of conformity. Raising this presumption in the consumer's favour marks a step forward in consumer protection.

The most notable changes, however, are in relation to the remedies available to the injured consumer. Under the Sale of Goods Act 1979, the classification of ss 12–15 as implied conditions has meant that breach brings an automatic right of termination where the purchaser is a consumer, different remedies potentially applying by virtue of s 15A where the purchaser is in the course of a business. However, the Directive proposes a variety of remedies that fall short of termination, namely repair, replacement or a price reduction as alternatives to rescission.

The basic remedy, which appears in art 3.2, stipulates that the consumer is entitled to have the goods brought into conformity with the contract free of charge. Thereafter it is a matter of how this is to be achieved. In the first instance, the consumer may require the seller to repair or replace the goods free of charge unless this is either impossible or disproportionate. A remedy is deemed to be dispropor-tionate if it imposes costs on the seller which are unreasonable in comparison with alternative remedies. In assessing whether the costs are unreasonable, account must be taken of the value of the goods if there were no lack of conformity, the significance of the lack of conformity and whether the alternative remedy could be completed without significant inconvenience to the consumer. Any repair or replacement must be completed within a reasonable time and without any significant inconvenience to the consumer, taking account of the nature of the goods and the purpose for which the consumer required the goods. Article 3 marks a significant shift from the existing law under the Sale of Goods Act 1979 as regards remedies for breach of provisions relating to quality and contractual conformity. As implied conditions, the breach of ss 12–15 automatically gives a right of rescission to consumers although the remedies available to business purchasers may be limited under s 15A (see above). However, the breach of the equivalent provisions under the Directive only gives consumers a right to repair or replacement in the first instance. As such, the Directive could be viewed as a diminution of consumer rights.

Article 3.5 provides for the alternative remedies of a reduction in the price of the goods or the ability to have the contract rescinded. These remedies will apply where the consumer is not entitled to either repair or replacement or the seller has not completed the remedy within reasonable time or the seller has not completed the remedy without significant inconvenience to the consumer. However, the consumer is not entitled to have the contract rescinded if the lack of conformity is minor, an approach that is similar to that applied to business purchasers under s 15A of the Sale of Goods Act 1979.

Under art 4, a final seller who has been held liable to a consumer for the lack of conformity of goods caused by the producer, a previous seller in the chain of distribution or any other intermediary, may pursue an action against them in accordance with national law.

As in any legal action, time limits are extremely important and art 5 of the Directive introduces not only time limits for commencing a legal action but also presumptions about the implied durability of the goods. The basic provision is that the seller of goods will be liable for any lack of conformity which becomes apparent within two years from the date of delivery of the goods. Member states whose national legislation will control this limitation period must ensure that the prescribed period is not less than two years, although a period of one year is permissible for second-hand goods. Further, member states may impose an obligation on the consumer to inform the seller of the lack of conformity within two months of the consumer detecting it and thus consumers must act quickly to protect their rights in the event of a breach.

As to the durability of the goods, art 5.3 provides that any lack of conformity which becomes apparent within six months of the delivery of the goods shall be deemed to have existed at the time of delivery unless that is incompatible with the nature of the goods or the type of lack of conformity. Thus, for example, food with a limited shelf-life such as a yoghurt would not attract the six-month presumption as it is not intended to last for six months.

Article 6 is a valuable addition to the law in this area as it specifically addresses the legality and status of manufacturers' guarantees, an area which has always been rather uncertain in English law. Article 6.1 states that a guarantee shall be legally binding on the offeror (the person giving it) under the conditions laid down in the guarantee statement and the associated advertising. This avoids the difficulties under English law of trying to establish a collateral contract. Article 6 continues that the guarantee must clearly state that it does not affect the consumer's legal rights under the relevant national legislation and must set out in plain intelligible language the contents of the guarantee and the particulars for making a claim. The latter must include the duration of the guarantee and where it applies as well as the name and address of the guarantor. On request by the consumer, the guarantee must be made available to him in writing or in another durable medium that is available and accessible to the consumer. The member states in which the goods are to be marketed may stipulate in which language(s), drawn from among the official languages of the Community, the guarantee must be made available. The breach of any of the requirements listed above will not affect the validity of the guarantee and the consumer's right to enforce it.

Question

Jeremy was a sales representative for Carpets Ltd. He visited the premises of Aquarius Ltd, who were interested in refurbishing their reception area. Jeremy spoke to Andrew, the purchasing officer for Aquarius Ltd, and showed him a sample of a royal blue carpet described as being of 'heavy industrial quality'. Andrew decided to purchase the carpet and placed an order. On delivery, Andrew was certain that the carpet was not of the same colour or quality as the sample that he had been shown. However, he could not check this as he no longer had access to the sample.

Two months after the carpet was laid, Andrew noticed that some of the carpet tufts were coming out and that some faded patches were starting to appear.

Advise Andrew.

Answer

This question involves the application of ss 13, 14(2), (3) and 15 of the Sale of Goods Act 1979. Jeremy is a sales representative for Carpets Ltd, which means that the sale is happening 'in the course of a business'. While this does not matter for ss 13 and 15, it is vital for ss 14(2) and (3), which apply only to business sales.

The carpet was described as 'heavy industrial quality'. This does make definite statements about the quality of the goods and its likely durability. If the carpet is not 'heavy industrial quality' as Andrew suspects, there will have been a breach of s 13 entitling Aquarius Ltd to terminate the contract.

There has also been a *prima facie* breach of s 15, sale by sample. The section states that the bulk will correspond with the sample, and that the goods will be free from any defect making their quality unsatisfactory which would not be apparent on reasonable examination. Here there is clear suggestion that the bulk does not correspond with the sample. The quality issue appears in both s 14(2) and s 15. We are told that tufts are coming out of the carpet and that faded patches are appearing. Applying the definition from s 14(2A) and the list of factors from s 14(2B), Andrew would appear to have a very strong case for arguing that the carpet is not of a satisfactory quality. It can be argued that a reasonable person would feel that either or both defects would render the goods unsatisfactory. Both the faded patches and the missing tufts would be classed as affecting the 'appearance and finish' of the carpet and its 'durability', while the missing tufts would be evidence of the fact that the goods are not 'fit for the purpose'. This latter point would mean that Andrew could allege a breach of both s 14(2) 'unsatisfactory quality' and s 14(3) 'fitness for purpose'.

Irrespective of what the court decides on the issue of quality, Andrew has a major problem in that the court may hold that, after two months, he has accepted the goods and that any breach of condition can be treated only as a breach of warranty. Acceptance is covered by s 34 and s 35 as well as by decisions such as **Bernstein** *v* **Pamson Motors** and Andrew is entitled to examine the goods to ensure compliance with the contract and to take the opportunity of comparing the bulk with the sample. Andrew may have made a fatal mistake at the time of delivery by allowing the fitters to lay the carpet despite his certainty that it was the wrong carpet. He should have queried it then. The laying of the carpet could be seen as an act of acceptance such that Aquarius Ltd cannot rescind the contract but merely sue for damages.

Further reading

Atiyah, P S, Adams, J N and Macqueen, H (2001). *The Sale of Goods*, 10th edn (Longman)

Bradgate, R (2000). *Commercial Law*, 3rd edn (Butterworth)

Dobson, P (2000). *Sale of Goods and Consumer Credit*, 6th edn (Sweet & Maxwell)

Furmston, M and Shears, P (1995). *Commercial Law* (Cavendish)

Harvey, B W and Parry, D L (1996). *The Law of Consumer Protection and Fair Trading*, 5th edn (Butterworth)

The supply of goods and services

8.1 Introduction

Prior to 1982, contracts for the supply of services were governed by the common law. In 1982, largely following the recommendations of the report *Service Please – Services and the Law: A Consumer View* published by the National Consumer Council, the supply of Goods and Services Act 1982 was passed with effect from 4 July 1983. This Act has been amended from 3 January 1995 by the Sale and Supply of Goods Act 1994.

Contracts for services may be either those for pure services such as hairdressing or insurance, or those where the transfer of some goods at the end of the contract forms an integral part of the agreement. The latter would include, for example, the repair of a car, installation of central heating or the painting of a portrait.

8.2 Part I – implied conditions

Part I of the 1982 Act deals with the insertion of implied conditions into certain contracts involving the transfer of the property or possession of goods. Thus it goes a long way towards providing protection for people who acquire goods otherwise than by sale.

Sections 2–5 imply conditions of title, compliance with description, satisfactory quality, fitness for purpose and compliance with sample. Section 1 stipulates that these conditions will apply to contracts for the transfer of goods other than contracts of sale, hire-purchase, trading stamp exchange, gratuitous transfers by deed and mortgages, pledges and other securities. Thus they would apply, for example, to contracts of barter. The terms of the conditions are similar but not identical to ss 12–15 of the Sale of Goods Act 1979.

Sections 7–10 of the 1982 Act imply similar conditions into contracts of hire. The notable difference is in relation to s 7, which corresponds to s 12 of the Sale of Goods Act 1979. Obviously, under a contract of hire there is no intention that the property in the goods will ever transfer to the hirer and consequently a provision confirming the owner's right to sell is inappropriate. Instead, s 7 provides that the bailor of the goods has the right to transfer possession of the goods for the period of the hire and, in the case of an agreement to hire in the future, that he will have such a right at that time. Sections 8–10, though worded differently, echo the provisions of ss 13–15 of the Sale of Goods Act 1979. A chart showing the relationship between the various provisions appears in Figure 8.1.

Type of contract	Act of Parliament	Title	Description	Satisfactory Quality	Fitness for Purpose	Sample
Sale of goods	Sale of Goods Act 1979	s 12	s 13	s 14(2)	s 14(3)	s 15
Transfer other than sale or HP	Supply of Goods and Services Act 1982	s 2	s 3	s 4(2)	s 4(3)	s 5
Hire-purchase	Supply of Goods (Implied Terms) Act 1973	s 8	s 9	s 10(2)	s 10(3)	s 11
Hire	Supply of Goods and Services Act 1982	s 7	s 8	s 9(2)	s 9(5)	s 10

Figure 8.1   Relationship between the various statutory provisions

Given the similarity of these Part I provisions to the corresponding provisions of the 1979 Act, much of the case law discussed in the last chapter is equally pertinent here. However, not all of the amendments introduced into ss 12–15 of the Sale of Goods Act 1979 are reproduced in Part I of the Supply of Goods and Services Act 1982. The variations relate to the implied conditions of satisfactory quality and the implied conditions covering sales by sample.

In respect of the implied conditions of satisfactory quality found in s 4 (applicable to transfers other than sale, etc) and s 9 (applicable to contracts of hire), the main provision contained in s 14(2A) of the Sale of Goods Act 1979 is reproduced in s 4(2A) and s 9(2A) respectively. Thus, in both sections, goods are deemed to be of a satisfactory quality if a reasonable person would regard them as satisfactory taking into account any description of the goods, the price (if relevant) and all other relevant circumstances. It is noticeable, however, that the list of factors to be taken into consideration that appears in s 14(2B) of the Sale of Goods Act 1979 has not been incorporated in the Supply of Goods and Services Act 1982. Nonetheless, given that the major definition of 'satisfactory quality' is the same, it is probable that in practice cases decided under the Sale of Goods Act 1979 will continue to be used when interpreting the provisions of the Supply of Goods and Services Act 1982, and hence in time the list will be adopted by stealth.

The implied conditions relating to transfers/bailment by sample appear in their original form rather than in the amended form. Thus, in both s 5 (transfer) and s 10 (hire) there remains an implied condition that the buyer/bailee of the goods will have the opportunity of comparing the bulk with the sample. This provision relates to the acceptance of the goods under the contract. In the Sale of Goods Act 1979 this provision has been deleted from s 15 and moved to a revised s 35 on acceptance. However, there are no separate statutory acceptance provisions in the Supply of Goods and Services Act 1982 and so the original provision has been retained. The modification to remedies for breach of the implied conditions of compliance with description, satisfactory quality and sale by sample has been incorporated in the Supply of Goods and Services Act 1982 by s 5A (transfer other than sale) and s 10A (hire). Thus, where the transferee/bailee deals other than as a consumer and the breach is so slight that it would be unreasonable for him to terminate the contract, the breach of condition will be treated as a breach of warranty with the consequent change of remedy from termination to damages.

Exclusion of the implied conditions is permitted to the extent allowed by the Unfair Contract Terms Act 1977. Section 7 of that Act provides that exclusion is not permitted against anyone 'dealing as a consumer' but is allowed against anyone not dealing as a consumer to the extent that the exclusion is reasonable. Thus, in **Fry** *v* **First National Leasing Ltd** (2000) Fry was a farmer who hired a CCTV security system from First National Leasing, a finance company. The original supplier of the system sold it to FNL as being suitable for recording at night, one of Fry's main requirements. There was an exclusion clause in the contract which read 'FNL gives no condition, warranty or undertaking, express or implied, as to the quality or fitness of the equipment'. It transpired that the CCTV system did not work at night and therefore was not of satisfactory quality or fit for the purpose under s 9 of the Supply of Goods and Services Act 1982. Further, the judge held that Fry was a consumer and, therefore, that FNL could not rely on the clause as the contract fell within s 7 of the Unfair Contract Terms Act 1977, which forbids exclusion clauses in consumer hire contracts.

8.3   Implied terms in services

Part II of the 1982 Act provides three terms that are to be implied into contracts for the supply of a service. Section 12 defines this to include contracts where the supplier agrees to carry out a service other than contracts of employment or apprenticeship. Further, the fact that some goods may be transferred or bailed as part of the contract does not prevent it being a contract for the supply of a service. Thus a contract to repair and maintain a fleet of vehicles is a contract for the supply of a service even though the vehicles will necessarily be fitted with new parts on occasion.

Sections 13–15 contain the three implied terms. Note that they are implied terms and not implied conditions or warranties. They are effectively statutory implied innominate terms. Consequently, there is no certain remedy for any individual breach. The court has the discretion to stipulate the remedy appropriate to the breach in hand.

8.3.1   Care and skill

Section 13 is the basic provision regarding the quality of the service. It states:

> In a contract for the supply of a service where the supplier is acting in the course of a business, there is an implied term that the supplier will carry out the service with reasonable care and skill.

Note that the section applies only where the supplier of the service is acting in the course of a business. The case law discussed in the previous chapter in respect of s 14 of the Sale of Goods Act 1979 applies here. Not all providers of services are covered by s 13. The Secretary of State has the power to make orders exempting specified groups of people from its provisions. This he has done in respect of arbitrators, the directors of building societies, members of the management committees of industrial and provident societies and directors of companies in their capacity as such. In respect of directors, they already owe a duty of care to the company. Section 13 would merely have created an artificial divide between those directors appointed under the articles of a company and those appointed under a contract of service.

Section 13 of the Supply of Goods and Services Act 1982 is the statutory adoption into contract of the tortious concept of care and skill central to negligence. The supplier must act with at least the care and skill to be expected of an ordinary man and, if he claims any particular expertise, then the standard of care and skill expected of him will rise accordingly. (For a full discussion of the standard of care, see later, Chapter 11.)

The section calls for reasonable care and skill. It does not require the supplier to guarantee the result of the service or to guarantee the safety of his customers, although it does seem that if the purpose of the service is to produce an end product that product should be fit for its purpose. To quote Lord Denning in **Greaves & Co Contractors Ltd** v **Baynham, Meikle & Partners** (1975):

> The law does not imply a warranty that he will achieve the desired result, but only a term that he will use reasonable care and skill. The surgeon does not warrant that he will cure the patient. Nor does the solicitor warrant that he will win the case. But, when a dentist agrees to make a set of false teeth for a patient, there is an implied warranty that they will fit his gum.

In the **Greaves** decision, the plaintiff, Greaves, contracted to build a warehouse for a third party for the storage of oil drums. The plaintiff retained the defendants, a firm of structural engineers, to design a warehouse and floor suitable for the purpose. After relatively short use, the floor cracked. It was held that the plaintiff was liable to the third party and the defendants were liable to indemnify the plaintiff as they had breached their duty of care and skill. By contrast, in **Whitehouse** v **Jordan** (1981) a surgeon was held not liable for the brain damage suffered by a baby as a result of a forceps delivery. There had been an error of judgement by the surgeon but not a lack of care and skill sufficient to amount to negligence. Similarly, in **Wilson** v **Best Travel Ltd** (1993) a holiday company did not breach the s 13 duty of care and skill when a customer was seriously injured as a result of falling through a glass patio door at a Greek hotel advertised in the defendant's holiday brochure. Their duty of care was satisfied by them inspecting the premises, ensuring that the glass in the doors complied with Greek safety standards and that there were no obvious dangers that would have dissuaded a normal person from booking.

The final issue is whether the plaintiff can sustain both a contractual action and a claim in tort arising out of the same incident. For many years, the presumption was that the plaintiff could sue only in contract. However, in **Midland Bank Trust Co Ltd** v **Hett, Stubbs and Kemp** (1979), a case involving a solicitor who negligently failed to register an option for the purchase of land, the court held that the plaintiff could sue in both contract and tort. This decision was followed in **Forsikringsaktieselskapet Vesta** v **Butcher** (1986) and **Thake** v **Maurice** (1986) and most recently in **Lancashire & Cheshire Association of Baptist Churches Inc** *v* **Howard & Seddon Partnership** (1993). The ability to sue under both contract and tort is potentially significant for the limitation period for contract begins at the time of breach, but for a claim in tort it does not begin until the damage is sustained. In practice, therefore, the limitation period in tort may continue for some time after the contractual limitation period has expired.

8.3.2 Time

Section 14(1) of the Act provides:

> Where, under a contract for the supply of a service by a supplier acting in the course of a business, the time for the service to be carried out is not fixed by the contract, left to be fixed in a manner agreed by the contract or determined by the course of dealing between the parties, there is an implied term that the supplier will carry out the service within a reasonable time.

Again this provision applies only where the seller is acting in the course of a business. Thus, the time for performance is not of the essence when the supplier is a private individual unless the parties expressly agree in the contract that it should be. Section 14 applies only where no agreement about the time for contractual performance is made expressly, or by a previous course of dealing or by a method determined by the contract. In brief, the section is effective only where there is a vacuum.

What is a reasonable time is a question of fact dependent upon the circumstances of each individual case. Thus, in **Charnock** *v* **Liverpool Corpn** (1968) the plaintiff contracted for the repair of his car. The work should have taken five weeks but, because the repairers gave priority to manufacturer's warranty work, the repairs took eight weeks. The Court of Appeal held that the plaintiff could recover damages being the cost of hiring a replacement car for the extra three weeks. Equally, in **Rickards** *v* **Oppenheim** (1950) the customer was entitled to refuse to take delivery of a car when the supplier failed to deliver at the appropriate time.

8.3.3 Consideration

The last of the three implied terms applies to all contracts for the supply of a service and not merely those where the supplier is in the course of a business. Section 15 relates to the payment of consideration. Section 15(1) reads:

> Where, under a contract for the supply of a service, the consideration is not determined by the contract, left to be determined in a manner agreed by the contract or determined by the course of dealing between the parties, there is an implied term that the party contracting with the supplier will pay a reasonable charge.

As with s 14, this section applies only where the parties have left a vacuum about the price to be paid for the contract. One would expect that the contract price would be agreed between the parties but this is not always so. For example, in an emergency the customer may instruct a supplier without giving any thought to the cost. Similarly, in contracts of repair, it may not be possible to assess the cost of the repair accurately until the repairer has inspected the item to assess both the extent of the work needed and which parts will need to be replaced. In this context, the difference between an estimate and a quotation should be acknowledged. An estimate is just that, with it having no binding effect. By contrast, a quotation is a definite offer of a contract price and is binding. What is a reasonable price is a question of fact in each case. What is clear, though, is that the customer should not pay a price that he believes to be too high but should question it immediately and, if necessary, refuse to pay until a reasonable figure is agreed. If the customer does pay, this will be construed as a contractual agreement and he will not be able to have the contract reopened in the absence of duress.

8.3.4 Exclusion

Section 16 of the 1982 Act allows the parties to a contract for the supply of a service to exclude the implied terms in ss 13–15 of that Act to the extent that this is permissible under the Unfair Contract Terms Act 1977. Under s 2 of the 1977 Act it is impossible to exclude liability for death or personal injury caused by negligence but it is permissible to exclude liability for other damage subject to the exclusion being reasonable. In **Eagle Star Life Assurance Co Ltd** *v* **Griggs** (1997) it was held that where the contract for the supply of services includes an express provision that the quality of the supply was to be judged by the supplier, then the implied terms would be excluded by virtue of s 16. It must be noted, however, that an express provision in a contract will not negate an implied term unless it is inconsistent with it.

Question

Aquarius Ltd, a small company, decided to have their central heating system overhauled and employed Brian to come and service it. Brian arrived and stated that the job would take two days. He refused to give a quotation for the job, stating that apart from the basic charge of £50, the price would depend upon the amount of work to be done and any new parts needed.

Work was started on schedule on Monday morning but it soon became obvious that several new parts were needed. Although the parts were readily available, Brian did not install them and finish the job for five days.

Aquarius Ltd were charged £400 for the service, which they paid. It later transpired that a reasonable price would have been £250.

Three weeks later the system failed.

Advise Aquarius Ltd.

Answer

This problem involves the supply of goods and services and raises three points: the length of time taken to do the job, the price charged and the subsequent fault with the system.

The length of time will depend to some extent on whether the fact that Brian said the job would take two days means that time has become of the essence in this contract. If it has, the failure to complete on time would be a contractual breach giving rise to damages. If it has not, there is the possibility that s 14 of the Supply of Goods and Services Act 1982 would apply, which states that the work must be completed within a reasonable time. It is suggested that a reasonable time here would be two days and that Aquarius Ltd could claim for compensation after this. On the facts, the former of the two seems more likely.

Brian has not quoted a price, merely that it will be more than £50. Therefore, Aquarius Ltd can look to s 15 of the 1982 Act for relief, which states that where no agreement has been made about price a reasonable charge must be paid. Reasonable in this context would be £250. However, as Aquarius Ltd have already paid the £400 Brian requested it is now too late to complain. The act of paying will be seen as contractual acceptance, which will not be overturned unless Aquarius Ltd can show that they paid under duress. Alternatively, the court might hold that the statement about the price depending on any new parts, etc is a mechanism for deciding the price under the terms of the contract. If this is so, s 15 will not apply anyway and Aquarius Ltd will be bound by the contract price. Any complaint about the price should have been settled before payment was made.

The system failed after three weeks. This might be due to a lack of skill and care on Brian's part when doing the job, in which case there is a breach of s 13 of the 1982 Act and Aquarius Ltd will be entitled to a remedy. Remember that ss 13–15 of the 1982 Act are implied terms not implied conditions and thus there is no automatic right to terminate. Alternatively, it may be that one of the replacement parts was either not of satisfactory quality or not fit for the purpose, in which case there has been a breach of the implied conditions in s 4 of the 1982 Act.

Further reading

Adams, A (2000). *Law for Business Students*, 2nd edn (Longman)

Atiyah, P S, Adams, J N and Macqueen, H (2001). *The Sale of Goods*, 10th edn (Longman)

Bradgate, R (2000). *Commercial Law*, 3rd edn (Butterworth)

Dobson, P (1997). *Charlesworth's Business Law*, 16th edn (Sweet & Maxwell)

Dobson, P (2000). *Sale of Goods and Consumer Credit*, 6th edn (Sweet & Maxwell)

Harvey, B W and Parry, D L (1996). *The Law of Consumer Protection and Fair Trading*, 5th edn (Butterworth)

Keenan, D (2000). *Smith and Keenan's Advanced Business Law*, 11th edn (Longman)

Keenan, D and Riches, S (2001). *Business Law*, 6th edn (Longman)

Stone, R (2000). *Principles of Contract Law*, 4th edn (Cavendish)

9 Delivery and payment

9.1 Introduction

When considering the law relating to the delivery of, payment for and passage of title of goods, it is wise first to distinguish between the concepts of transfer of possession and the passage of title or property. There is no requirement that possession and title are vested in the same person.

Possession involves the physical control of the goods by a person who may or may not have any ownership rights. Thus, the hirer in a hire-purchase agreement gains possession of the goods at the outset of the agreement but does not acquire ownership of them until the option to purchase is exercised at the conclusion of the hire period. Similarly, in a hire agreement, even one with the potential to last for several years, the hirer has possession while the owner retains the title. Likewise, the repairer of goods acquires temporary possession of them during the period of the repair but there is no intention that he will ever acquire ownership rights.

The converse is also true. Title or property speaks to the ownership of the goods and thus passage of title deals with the acquisition of property rights. Again, there is no requirement that the owner has physical possession of the goods or has ever sought to have possession. The finance company in a hire-purchase agreement has the title to the goods but no intention of seeking possession unless the hirer defaults on the agreement. The buyer in an export or import contract in which the goods are being shipped will acquire title to them when he receives the bill of lading although he will not acquire possession until the goods are unloaded. Likewise, the purchaser of a three-piece suite identified at the time that the contract is made in the shop will acquire immediate title to the furniture although he will not acquire possession until it is delivered.

9.2 Delivery and payment

9.2.1 Delivery

Delivery is concerned with the transfer of possession. In the commercial context delivery is arguably more significant than title for it is delivery by the seller that gives rise to a right to payment. Section 28 of the Sale of Goods Act 1979 provides that, unless there is an agreement to the contrary, the delivery of the goods and the payment of the price are concurrent conditions. The seller must be ready and willing to give possession of the goods to the buyer in exchange for the price and the buyer must be ready and willing to pay the price in exchange for possession of the goods. Both parties are under a duty to fulfil their respective obligations in accordance with the terms of the contract.

Delivery is defined in s 61 of the 1979 Act as being 'the voluntary transfer of possession from one person to another', except that in relation to ss 20A and 20B it includes such appropriation of goods to the contract as results in property in the goods being transferred to the buyer. Goods are deemed to have been appropriated to the contract when they have been identified as the goods that the buyer will receive under the contract (see Chapter 10). Delivery may be effected in a variety of ways. The seller may physically hand over the goods or he may give the buyer the means of controlling them, for example the keys to a car. If the goods are currently held by a third party, delivery will occur when that person acknowledges that he now holds them on behalf of the buyer as stated in s 29(4).

Delivery may take place via a carrier. Section 32(1) of the 1979 Act provides that where the seller is authorised or required to send the goods to the buyer, delivery to the carrier is *prima facie* delivery to the buyer. The responsibility is on the seller to arrange an appropriate contract of carriage unless otherwise authorised by the buyer. Should the seller fail to do so and as a result the goods are lost or damaged in the course of transit, the buyer may refuse to treat the delivery to the carrier as effective delivery to himself and hold the seller liable in damages. Section 32(3) states that unless otherwise agreed, where the goods are to be sent by sea and it would be usual to insure them, the seller is under an obligation to inform the buyer so as to allow him to arrange insurance. Should the seller fail to do this, the goods will be at his risk during the transit by sea.

Place of delivery

The parties have the right to decide either expressly or impliedly where delivery will occur and whether the obligation is on the buyer to collect the goods or on the seller to send them to the buyer. In the absence of any agreement the place of delivery is deemed to be the seller's place of business if he has one, or otherwise his residence. Alternatively, if the contract is for the sale of specific goods (see Chapter 10 for definition) which to the knowledge of both parties are at some other place at the time that the contract is made, then delivery will occur at that place. Where the goods at the time of sale are in the possession of a third person, there is no delivery by the seller to the buyer unless and until the third person acknowledges to the buyer that he now holds the goods on the buyer's behalf.

Section 33 provides that when the goods are to be delivered by the seller at his risk to a place other than that where they are sold, the buyer must take the risk of any deterioration in the goods incidental to the transit unless there is an agreement to the contrary.

Time of delivery

The time of delivery is usually important to the parties particularly in a commercial transaction, where the buyer may be buying to resell under another contract, either wholesale or retail, or buying materials for a production process. This would be particularly true if the buyer uses 'just-in-time' stock rotation. It is normally assumed therefore that the time of delivery will be of the essence. Where this is so, the buyer would be entitled to terminate the contract and reject the goods if the seller fails to meet the delivery date. Thus, in **Rickards v Oppenheim** (1950) the seller agreed to build a car for the buyer, delivery due on 20 March. The car was not ready on time but the buyer allowed the seller to continue with the project. At the end of June the buyer announced that if the car was not ready in four weeks he would repudiate the contract. It was not ready. The court held that the buyer was under no obligation to accept it after that date as, although he had waived the original delivery date, he had made time of the essence again by stipulating delivery in four weeks. Alternatively, of course, the buyer may elect to affirm the contract and accept late delivery, although he would still have a right to sue for damages.

Where no delivery date has been agreed and the responsibility is on the seller to send the goods to the buyer, s 29(3) stipulates that he must do so within a reasonable period. Delivery must take place at a reasonable time, this being a question of fact.

Delivery of wrong quantity

The seller is under an obligation to deliver the correct quantity of goods ordered although minimal variations in amount will be tolerated as the law is not concerned with trifles. So, for example, in **Shipton, Anderson & Co v Weil Bros & Co** (1912) the seller contracted to deliver 4,950 tons of wheat. He actually delivered 55lb too much, an excess delivery worth 20p in a contract worth £40,000. The court held that the excess, for which the buyer was not being charged, was so slight that it was of no effect.

Commercial contracts are likely to include a clause stipulating an acceptable percentage tolerance in the amount delivered while expecting the price charged for the contract to reflect the amount actually received by the buyer.

Section 30 of the 1979 Act as amended regulates the delivery of an incorrect quantity, be it too much or too little. It provides:

(1) Where the seller delivers to the buyer a quantity of goods less than he contracted to sell, the buyer may reject them, but if the buyer accepts the goods so delivered he must pay for them at the contract rate.

(2) Where the seller delivers to the buyer a quantity of goods larger than he contracted to sell, the buyer may accept the goods included in the contract and reject the rest, or he may reject the whole.

(2A) A buyer who does not deal as a consumer may not—

(a) where the seller delivers a quantity of goods less than he contracted to sell, reject the goods under subsection (1) above, or

(b) where the seller delivers a quantity of goods larger than he contracted to sell, reject the whole under subsection (2) above,

if the shortfall or, as the case may be, excess is so slight that it would be unreasonable for him to do so.

(2B) It is for the seller to show that a shortfall or excess fell within subsection (2A) above.

(2C) Subsection (2A) and (2B) above do not apply to Scotland.

(2D) Where the seller delivers a quantity of goods—

(a) less than he contracted to sell, the buyer shall not be entitled to reject the goods under subsection (1) above,

(b) larger than he contracted to sell, the buyer shall not be entitled to reject the whole under subsection (2) above,

unless the shortfall or excess is material.

(2E) Subsection (2D) above applies to Scotland only.

(3) Where the seller delivers to the buyer a quantity of goods larger than he contracted to sell and the buyer accepts the whole of the goods so delivered [. . .] he must pay for them at the contract rate.

(4) [*Repealed*]

(5) This section is subject to any usage of trade, special arrangement, or course of dealing between the parties.

Sections 30(1), (2) and (3) specify the remedies *prima facie* available where the seller has delivered the wrong quantity of goods, be it too much or too little. The provisions allow a degree of flexibility to the buyer by allowing him a variety of potential options without ever requiring him to accept anything. Thus if too little is delivered, the buyer can either reject the whole consignment or choose to accept the smaller quantity actually delivered. By contrast, if too much is delivered, the buyer has the option of rejecting the whole quantity, accepting the quantity contracted for and rejecting the remainder or accepting the larger quantity actually delivered. If, in either instance, the buyer elects to accept the quantity actually delivered he must pay for it at the contract rate.

Sections 30(2A)–(2E) were added by the Sale and Supply of Goods Act 1994 and came into effect from 3 January 1995. Subsections (2A) and (2B) apply in England and Wales and Northern Ireland, while subss (2D) and (2E) apply in Scotland. Once again, the new provisions are designed to draw a distinction between consumer buyers and non-consumer buyers (cf. s 15A on modification of remedies for a breach of the implied terms). Section 30(2A) places a restriction on the options mentioned above where the buyer does not deal as a consumer. A non-consumer buyer is not allowed to reject the whole consignment delivered, be it too little or too much, in the way described above if the shortfall or excess, as the case may be, is so slight that it would be unreasonable for him so to do. It is a question of fact as to what parameters the court will place on the definition of 'slight', which will have to be assessed by reference to the contract, recognised tolerances within the particular industry, previous dealings between the parties, etc.

It should also be remembered that the delivery of a quantity other than that specified in the contract may also be a breach of s 13 sale by description and an offence against the Trade Descriptions Act 1968 and the Weights and Measures Act 1985.

Delivery in instalments

Whether by accident or design, goods may be delivered in instalments. Section 31 acknowledges three possibilities: the parties did not agree to delivery by instalments, the parties did agree to delivery by instalments of a non-severable contract and the parties agreed to delivery by instalments of a severable contract.

Where there is no agreement between the parties about delivery by instalments the buyer is not under any obligation to accept delivery by that method. Where the contract does allow for delivery by instalments it will be a matter of construction whether the contract is severable or non-severable. An indication can usually be gained from whether each instalment carries with it a right for the seller to be paid in respect of it. If so, the contract is likely to be severable. The distinction is important because the remedies available to both seller and buyer will depend on it. If the seller fails to deliver an instalment, or the buyer refuses to accept delivery or make payment for an instalment of a severable contract, it is likely to give rise to a claim for compensation but not affect the continuance of the contract. If the contract is non-severable a failure would carry a right to repudiate the whole contract.

In **Jackson *v* Rotax Motors** (1910) the seller contracted to sell motor horns to the buyer, delivery to be in instalments. About half of the horns were dented and scratched. The Court of Appeal held that the buyer was entitled to reject the whole consignment. By contrast, in **Maple Flock Co Ltd *v* Universal Furniture Products (Wembley) Ltd** (1934) the buyer was held to have wrongly rejected the whole consignment when one instalment out of 20 (the sixteenth) proved defective. The breach was relatively slight and not likely to recur.

9.2.2 Examination and acceptance

Sections 34 and 35 govern acceptance of the goods. As seen in **Bernstein *v* Pamson Motors (Golders Green) Ltd** (1987) (see Chapter 7) the fact of acceptance can make a vital difference to the remedies open to the buyer in the event of breach. In that case the buyer was entitled to damages only instead of termination in respect of an unmerchantable car because he was deemed to have accepted it.

Section 34 provides the buyer with a statutory right to examine the goods. Thus, unless there is an agreement to the contrary, the seller when tendering delivery to the buyer must, if so requested, give the buyer a reasonable opportunity to examine the goods. The purpose of the examination is to ascertain whether the goods delivered comply with the contract and, in a contract of sale by sample, to compare the bulk with the sample. Note that the examination is not intended to be an opportunity to try out the goods to find any defects, a view that accords with the judicial opinions expressed in **Bernstein *v* Pamson Motors** above.

Issues relating to acceptance are dealt with in a revised and expanded s 35. The main provisions governing acceptance are contained in ss 35(1), (2) and (4), which read:

> (1) The buyer is deemed to have accepted the goods, subject to subsection (2) below—
>   (a) when he intimates to the seller that he has accepted them, or
>   (b) when the goods have been delivered to him and he does any act in relation to them which is inconsistent with the ownership of the seller.
> (2) When goods are delivered to the buyer, and he has not previously examined them, he is not deemed to have accepted them under subsection (1) above until he has had a reasonable opportunity of examining them for the purpose—
>   (a) of ascertaining whether they are in conformity with the contract, and
>   (b) in the case of a contract for sale by sample, of comparing the bulk with the sample.

[. . .]

(4) The buyer is also deemed to have accepted the goods when after the lapse of a reasonable time he retains the goods without intimating to the seller that he has rejected them.

Section 35(1) admits two possibilities. The first is relatively straightforward: that the buyer has told the seller that he has accepted the goods. The words of acceptance must be clear and unequivocal. Normally the signing of a delivery note merely acknowledges receipt of the goods and does not constitute acceptance. However, if the delivery note is phrased in terms of acceptance and the person who signs it has the authority to accept the goods it may be binding.

The second possibility is more demanding, requiring two separate elements to constitute acceptance. First, the goods must have been delivered to the buyer and, second, the buyer must then have done something with them that is inconsistent with the continued ownership of the seller. An obvious example would be where the buyer has altered the goods to make them in some way different from those that the seller provided. Thus, in **Sabir *v* Tiny Computers** (1999) the buyer purchased a computer from Tiny Computers. He experienced problems with the computer and sued. It transpired that the buyer had upgraded the software on the computer from Windows 95 to Windows 98 using the appropriate upgrade software but without the seller's knowledge. The seller confirmed that they would not have recommended the upgrade because of the unreliable nature of the Windows 98 system. The court held that the installation of the upgraded software by the buyer was an act inconsistent with the continued ownership of the seller and that the buyer had lost his right to reject the goods. It found that the fault was 50 per cent due to a faulty component and 50 per cent due to the buyer's intervention. Therefore, his damages would be reduced accordingly.

A second obvious example would be where the buyer has sold the goods or given them to a third party as he is not then in a position to return them to the seller. This may be most pertinent in the commercial context, where it is often understood between the parties that the buyer should have the right to sell the goods before contractually accepting them. Indeed, he may need to do so in order to raise the money to pay for them. A related issue is whether the buyer has accepted the goods by passing them to a sub-buyer if the buyer had not had the opportunity to examine the goods as recognised by s 34. Thus, if a buyer resold goods in a sealed container to a sub-buyer without any opportunity for intermediate examination, would he still be able to reject them if on examination the sub-buyer found the goods to be defective? The matter has been placed beyond dispute by s 35(6), which expressly provides that a buyer will not be deemed to have accepted the goods merely because he has delivered them to another under a sub-sale or other disposition.

The recent case of **Truk (UK) Ltd *v* Tokmakidis GmbH** (2000), in which it was recognised that the intention of the parties had always been that the buyer would resell the goods, also addressed these issues. Tokmakidis, the buyer, entered a contract with Truk, the seller, whereby Truk would supply and fit an underlift to a lorry chassis belonging to Tokmakidis, the intention being that Tokmakidis would then sell it to a sub-buyer as a recovery vehicle. In the event, Tokmakidis was informed by a a potential sub-buyer that the underlift was unsuitable and

Tokmakidis, having removed the underlift from the vehicle, sought to reject it. The court held that the actions of Tokmakidis were consistent with the seller's continued ownership of the goods and that they could reject them.

Section 35(2) reinforces the importance of the examination of the goods prior to acceptance. It echoes the provisions of s 34 by stipulating that where the goods are delivered to the buyer and he has not previously examined them, he is not deemed to have accepted them under the provisions of s 35(1) until he has had a reasonable opportunity of examining them to establish whether they comply with the contract, and, in the case of a sale by sample, to compare the bulk with the sample. It should be noted that, unlike s 34, the buyer cannot lose his right to examine the goods under s 35(2) by agreement or waiver. It is an inalienable right.

The third method of acceptance is stipulated in s 35(4), which provides that acceptance will occur when a reasonable period of time has elapsed and the buyer has retained the goods without intimating to the seller that he has rejected them. It is a question of fact whether a reasonable time has elapsed, which will depend on all the circumstances of the case but will certainly include whether the buyer has had a reasonable opportunity to examine the goods for the purposes stipulated above. The **Tokmakidis** decision is a case in point. In that case, the buyer had not rejected the goods immediately and did not raise the issue of the suitability of the goods for six months after purchase, it being a further three months later before expert opinion about the goods was received by the buyer and the goods were rejected. The court held that when goods are intended for sub-sale, it may be that the defect will not come to light until after the sub-buyer has taken delivery. Where this is so, a reasonable period for rejection by the original buyer would be the time that it takes to resell the goods plus a reasonable period in which the ultimate buyer would have the opportunity to ensure that the goods are satisfactory and in accordance with the contract. In the Tokmakidis case, the rejection of the goods had taken place within a reasonable time.

In addition to the problem of sub-sales and other dispositions mentioned above, the other problem relating to actions by the buyer potentially constituting acceptance related to repairs to the goods. There was a strong case for arguing that if a buyer permitted a seller to repair defective goods he was impliedly accepting those goods. If he was not accepting the defective goods, the buyer would have rejected them rather than agreeing to a repair. This could mean that a buyer who acted reasonably in the circumstances by permitting the seller to attempt a repair could discover that he had accepted the goods and consequently forfeited his right to reject them. However, s 35(6)(a) has addressed this problem by expressly providing that the buyer is not deemed to have accepted the goods merely because he asks for, or agrees to, a repair by or under an arrangement with the seller. Thus, for example, repairs under an after-sales service arrangement would not detract from the buyer's right to reject the goods should the repairs prove unsuccessful.

The last new provision enacted in the revised version of s 35 is to be found in s 35(7), which addresses the acceptance of 'commercial units' of goods, which are defined as being 'a unit, division of which would materially impair the value of the goods or the character of the unit'. The subsection provides that where a contract exists for the sale of one or more commercial units, a buyer accepting any goods included in a unit will be deemed to have accepted all the goods comprising the unit.

Hitherto, rights of rejection have always needed to be exercised against all the goods comprised in the contract. However, situations can arise in which only some of the goods delivered under the contract are defective such as to justify rejection while the remainder conform to the contract and are of appropriate quality, etc, as in **Jackson v Rotax Motors** and **Maple Flock Co Ltd v Universal Furniture Products (Wembley) Ltd** (above). In practice, it may suit the buyer's purposes to accept those goods which are satisfactory while not wishing to be obliged to accept those which are defective. The ability to accept the satisfactory goods would negate the need to wait for alternative supplies, or even to find an alternative supplier. Production can continue unhindered while an alternative to the defective goods is being arranged. Similarly, the seller can salvage some of the contract. Section 35A of the 1979 Act addresses this problem by providing a new right of partial rejection, which applies unless there is an agreement to the contrary which appears in, or is to be implied from, the contract.

Section 35A(1) provides:

(1) If the buyer—

(a) has the right to reject the goods by reason of a breach on the part of the seller that affects some or all of them, but

(b) accepts some of the goods, including, where there are any goods unaffected by the breach, all such goods,

he does not by accepting them lose his right to reject the rest.

This provision permits the buyer to accept some or all of the goods unaffected by the breach without losing the right to reject the remainder. For these purposes, goods are affected by a breach if this means that they are not in conformity with the contract. Further, in respect of a delivery by instalments, s 35A(1) applies as if references to the goods meant references to the instalment.

Lastly, s 36 provides that where a buyer legitimately refuses to accept goods that have been delivered to him, he is not under any obligation to return them to the seller. His responsibility is satisfied if he intimates his refusal to the seller.

9.2.3 Payment

Unlike delivery, s 10 provides that time is not of the essence as regards payment unless a different intention is evinced by the contract. Thus while payment becomes due when delivery is effected or when the contract stipulates that it is due, a failure by the buyer to provide payment is not a breach that would justify repudiation by the seller, although he would have a right to sue for damages for non-payment (see further below).

9.3 Remedies

Both seller and buyer have statutory remedies available to them in respect of breaches arising out of delivery and payment.

9.3.1 Seller's remedies

While the primary duty of the seller is to deliver the goods, the primary duty of the buyer is to make payment. If he fails to do so, the seller can seek two sorts of remedy: personal remedies and those against the goods.

Personal remedies

An action for the price

Under s 49 the seller has a right to sue for the price in appropriate circumstances. The section provides:

> (1) Where, under a contract of sale, the property in the goods has passed to the buyer and he wrongfully neglects or refuses to pay for the goods according to the terms of the contract, the seller may maintain an action against him for the price of the goods.
>
> (2) Where, under a contract of sale, the price is payable on a day certain irrespective of delivery and the buyer wrongfully neglects or refuses to pay such price, the seller may maintain an action for the price, although the property in the goods has not passed and the goods have not been appropriated to the contract.

There are two possibilities for redress: under s 49(1) when the property in the goods has passed to the buyer and under s 49(2) where the price was due to be paid on a 'day certain'. Property in the goods will pass under ss 16–19 of the Act (discussed later), whereas a 'day certain' will have been agreed upon by the parties. To qualify as a 'day certain' it must be either a fixed date or, in limited circumstances, may be decided by reference to the progress of the work, as in **Workman Clark & Co Ltd *v* Lloyd Brazileno** (1908), a shipbuilding case in which the seller was able to sue for instalments on the day they became payable, the relevant dates being established by reference to the stages of construction of the vessel.

Both ss 49(1) and (2) require that the buyer had 'wrongfully' neglected or refused to pay the price. As the obligation to pay arises concurrently with the seller's duty to deliver, it follows that the buyer's refusal to pay will not be wrongful unless the seller is ready and willing to effect delivery. Further, the refusal to pay will not be wrongful if the 'day certain' has not arrived even though the goods have been delivered. Thus if the contract allows the buyer a period of credit after delivery the seller will not be able to sue the buyer until that period has elapsed. Lastly, a refusal to pay will not be wrongful if the buyer is seeking to reject the goods and terminate the contract.

Allied to a claim under s 49 would be a claim under s 37 for any consequential loss that the seller has sustained as a result of the buyer's failure to pay or failure to take delivery. This would include any costs of storage that the seller has incurred.

Damages for non-acceptance

If the seller is unable to sustain an action for the price because, for example, property has not passed or there is no 'day certain', the seller can still maintain an action under s 50 for damages for non-acceptance. The section merely requires that the buyer has wrongfully neglected or refused to accept and pay for the goods. The measure of damages to which the seller is entitled is the loss directly and naturally resulting in the ordinary course of business from the buyer's breach. Section 50(3) provides that where there is an available market for the goods in question the measure of damages is *prima facie* the difference between the contract price and the market or current price at the time when the goods ought to have been accepted, or, if no such time was fixed, at the time of the refusal to accept.

Note that this is a *prima facie* level of damages. If the seller can demonstrate that the actual loss suffered was different, he can maintain an action for his actual losses as long as they were foreseeable within the rules of **Hadley *v* Baxendale** (1854). His actual losses will depend to some extent upon the supply and demand for the goods. If supply exceeds demand so that the seller can legitimately say that he has lost a sale he may be able to sue for his lost profit. If demand exceeds supply, he will not have lost a sale but will sell to an alternative buyer. His actual loss will be less.

Remedies against the goods

When the seller is an 'unpaid seller' under s 38 of the 1979 Act he may be able to exercise three potential actions against the goods: lien, stoppage in transit and resale.

Section 38 defines a seller as an 'unpaid seller':

(a) when the whole of the price has not been paid or tendered;
(b) when a bill of exchange or other negotiable instrument has been received as conditional payment, and the condition on which it was received has not been fulfilled by reason of the dishonour of the instrument or otherwise.

The remedies of lien, stoppage in transit and resale are all granted to the seller under s 39(1) and take effect even if the property in the goods has passed to the buyer. When the property has not passed the seller will have the additional remedy of withholding delivery.

Lien

The seller has a lien over the goods and is entitled to retain possession of them for any part of the outstanding payment in three situations:

(a) where the goods have been sold without any stipulation as to credit;
(b) where the goods have been sold on credit but the term of credit has expired;
(c) where the buyer becomes insolvent.

Where any of these arises the seller can retain possession of the goods as a whole or any part of them still in his possession unless any part delivery that has occurred shows an intention to waive the lien or right of retention. In a severable contract where each instalment carries with it a right to payment he cannot retain one instalment as a lien for the payment of a different instalment. It does not matter whether the seller has possession in his own right or as an agent, bailee or custodian for the buyer.

Being a right in possession, it follows that the right of lien will be lost if the seller loses possession of the goods lawfully. Thus, if the seller gives the goods to the buyer or to a carrier for transmission to the buyer without retaining a right of disposal, or if the buyer or his agent lawfully acquires possession, the lien will cease as it will if the seller chooses to waive it.

Stoppage in transit

If the buyer is insolvent and the goods are in transit, the seller can stop them and reclaim possession of the goods.

Transit starts when the goods are delivered to a carrier or other bailee or custodian for transmission to the buyer and finishes when the buyer or his agent takes delivery from the carrier, bailee or custodian. If the buyer or his agent takes delivery before the goods have reached their appointed destination, the transit will end then. If after arrival the carrier remains in possession of the goods but acknowledges that he is holding them on behalf of the buyer, this will cause the transit to end even if the buyer then instructs that the goods be taken to another place.

Rejection of the goods by the buyer does not cause the transit to end. By contrast, if the carrier wrongfully refuses to make delivery, the transit will end at that time.

Particular arrangements are prescribed for transit involving a sea voyage on a ship chartered by the buyer. Whether the master of the ship accepts the goods as a carrier, meaning that they are still in transit, or as an agent for the buyer, in which case delivery will have taken place and the transit will have ended, is a matter to be determined from the circumstances of the particular case.

The seller effects a stoppage in transit either by taking physical possession of the goods or by giving notice to the carrier or his principal. In the latter instance, the seller must allow reasonable time for the notice to pass from the principal to the person in physical possession of the goods, but once notice has been received by the appropriate person he must re-deliver the goods to the instruction of the seller, who must pay any expenses associated with the re-delivery.

In practice, stoppage in transit is of limited use in the commercial world because of the common practice of including a retention of title clause in the contract retaining the property in the goods to the seller until they have been paid for. Where this is the case, the seller will have a right to recover his goods in the event of non-payment even if they are in the possession of the buyer. Retention of title clauses are considered in the next chapter.

Neither the seller's lien nor the right of stoppage in transit is effected by a sub-sale of the goods by the buyer. However, s 47(2) provides that where the documents of title have been lawfully transferred to the buyer, who has then transferred those same documents to a *bona fide* sub-buyer for value, then the seller's rights will be destroyed if the sub-purchase was by way of a contract of sale. If the last transfer was by way of pledge the seller can only exercise his lien or right of stoppage subject to the rights of the innocent sub-buyer.

Right of resale

Section 48 provides the unpaid seller with limited rights of resale and makes clear that where the seller exercises such rights the new buyer acquires good title as against the original buyer.

Resale is permitted where the goods are of a perishable nature or where the seller informs the buyer of his intention to resell and the buyer does not make payment of the outstanding price within a reasonable time. The seller may resell the goods and recover from the buyer damages for any loss occasioned by the breach.

It is possible for the seller to reserve a right of resale in the contract so that he can resell the goods if the buyer defaults. Where a resale occurs in this way the original contract is rescinded although the seller may still sue for damages for any consequential loss.

9.3.2 Buyer's remedies

The buyer's remedies fall under three headings: an action for specific performance, damages for non-delivery and damages for a breach of warranty.

Specific performance

An order of specific performance has the effect of requiring the seller to comply with the terms of the contract and deliver the goods to the buyer. As explained in Chapter 5 the court will normally grant specific performance in a contract of sale only if the goods are of a unique nature that cannot be purchased elsewhere.

Damages for non-delivery

Section 51 of the 1979 Act provides that where the seller has wrongfully neglected or refused to deliver the goods, the buyer may sue for damages for non-delivery. The measure of damages is the estimated loss directly and naturally arising, in the ordinary course of events, from the seller's breach of contract. As with the seller's claim for non-acceptance, s 51(3) provides that where there is an available market for the goods in question the measure of damages to be awarded to the buyer for non-delivery is *prima facie* the difference between the contract price and the market or current price at the time that the goods were to be delivered or, if no such date exists, the time when the wrongful refusal to deliver occurred. This is to allow the buyer to recover the difference between the price at which he expected to receive the goods and the price that he actually has to pay to acquire replacement goods. Thus, if the buyer was buying goods at a contract price of £2,500 and, at the time of the seller's refusal to deliver, the market had risen to £2,800 the buyer would be able to recover £300 from the seller. If the market price for the goods had fallen to £2,300, however, the buyer would not have suffered any loss as the replacement goods would not have cost as much as the original goods. In this instance only nominal damages would be recoverable from the seller to acknowledge the breach.

A recent application of s 51(3) occurred in the Court of Appeal decision of **Barry v Davies (t/a Heathcote Ball & Co)** (2000). In that case, Heathcote Ball were a firm of auctioneers. Barry bid £200 for each of two engine analysers which had been entered in Heathcote's auction without a reserve price. In fact the analysers were worth £14,000 and Heathcote refused to sell them to Barry on the basis that his bid was too low. The analysers were sold a few days later. The Court of Appeal held that a collateral contract exists between an auctioneer and bidders such that, in the absence of a reserve price, the auctioneer is obliged to sell to the highest bidder. It followed that Heathcote's failure to do so was a breach of contract for which Barry was entitled to recover damages, the level of damages being the difference between the contract price and the market value of the goods.

It is possible that the buyer was buying for the purposes of resale. The losses arising from the loss of resale are not recoverable from the seller unless they were foreseeable within the rules of **Hadley v Baxendale**. For this to be the case the buyer will need to demonstrate that to the knowledge of the seller those particular goods were to be used for a sub-sale, that the contract for the sub-sale was in place before delivery by the seller was due and that the contract of sub-sale was not unusual.

Damages for breach of warranty

Section 53 provides that where the buyer is suing for a breach of warranty he can claim against the seller for either a reduction or extinction of the price of the goods, or may sue for damages, the level of damages being the estimated loss directly and naturally resulting, in the ordinary course of events, from the breach of warranty. Thus, in **Amstrad plc v Seagate Technology Inc** (1998) (see Chapter 7) Amstrad were able to recover damages for the lost and delayed sales of the computers containing the faulty hard drives but not for the lost sales of the successor range of personal computers as they were not within the reasonable contemplation of the parties at the time the contract was made. Section 53(3) provides that where the breach is related to a loss of quality, as, for example, where the goods have been held unsatisfactory under s 14, but the right of rejection has been lost through acceptance by the buyer as in the **Bernstein** decision (see Chapter 7), the damages are *prima facie* the difference in value between the goods at the time of delivery and their value if they had not breached the warranty. However, being a *prima facie* measure of damages the court is free to move away from that rule if the facts of the case so demand, as in **Naughton v O'Callaghan** (1990).

Question

Charisma Ltd is a construction company. It entered into two contracts:

(a) It ordered 20 tonnes of sand from Duggan Ltd. Duggan Ltd actually delivered 20 tonnes and 918kg. Charisma Ltd wants to know whether it is obliged to accept the whole delivery or whether any other options are open to it.

(b) It ordered 5,000 metres of timber to be delivered in five instalments of 1,000 metres, each instalment to be paid for on delivery. The timber delivered in the third instalment was not properly seasoned and Charisma Ltd wants to reject it. It needs to know if this is possible.

Advise Charisma Ltd regarding both contracts.

Answer

(a) The first contract involves a delivery of the wrong amount. Charisma Ltd ordered 20 tonnes of sand and has received 20 tonnes and 918kg. Effectively, Charisma Ltd can do one of three things, all of which are provided for under s 30 of the 1979 Act. Under s 30(2), they have the choice of either rejecting the whole consignment or accepting the amount contracted for (20 tonnes) and rejecting the rest. However, these options must be considered in the light of s 30(2A), which provides that the options are not available to a business purchaser if the excess is so slight that it would be unreasonable for him to reject the goods. The onus is on the seller to show that the excess is slight. In this example, 918kg on 20 tonnes is a significant excess and Charisma Ltd could reasonably expect to be able to reject either the whole consignment or the excess, as appropriate. The third option available to Charisma Ltd, under s 30(3), is to accept the whole of the consignment, but they will then be under an obligation to pay for all the goods at the contract rate.

(b) Charisma Ltd wants to reject the wood from the third instalment. Given that each instalment carries with it a right to payment, it will probably be classed as a severable contract, allowing Charisma Ltd to reject the one instalment without affecting the remainder of the contract. The matter is now beyond dispute because of s 35A which permits a right of partial rejection.

Further reading

Adams, A (2000). *Law for Business Students*, 2nd edn (Longman)

Atiyah, P S, Adams, J N and Macqueen, H (2001). *The Sale of Goods*, 10th edn (Longman)

Bradgate, R (2000). *Commercial Law*, 3rd edn (Butterworth)

Dobson, P (1997). *Charlesworth's Business Law*, 16th edn (Sweet & Maxwell)

Dobson, P (2000). *Sale of Goods and Consumer Credit*, 6th edn (Sweet & Maxwell)

Harvey, B W and Parry, D L (1996). *The Law of Consumer Protection and Fair Trading*, 5th edn (Butterworth)

Keenan, D (2000). *Smith and Keenan's Advanced Business Law*, 11th edn (Longman)

Keenan, D and Riches, S (2001). *Business Law*, 5th edn (Longman)

Stone, R (2000). *Principles of Contract Law*, 4th edn (Cavendish)

10 Passage of title and risk

10.1 Introduction

The passage of title to goods is governed by ss 16–19 of the Sale of Goods Act 1979. Passage of title is significant in establishing who owns the goods and thus who has the risk in them given that s 20 provides that risk passes with title unless there is an agreement to the contrary. Thus it is the owner of goods who should insure them. Further, if the goods are destroyed it is the owner who has the right to sue for damages. Lastly, and particularly pertinent in recessionary times, the ownership of the goods dictates what happens to them if either the buyer or the seller goes into liquidation or is declared bankrupt before contractual performance is complete. Thus, if the buyer goes into liquidation while in possession of the goods the seller will be able to recover the goods if he still has the title in them, but only claim the price through the liquidator if title has already passed to the buyer. In the latter situation he would be unlikely to recover the full price, hence the attraction of retention of title clauses. Conversely, if the seller goes into liquidation while in possession, the buyer can claim the goods from the liquidator if the title has already passed to him but can only claim a refund of any money he has already paid if title was still in the seller. Again, the chances of recovering the full amount are very slim.

10.2 Specific, ascertained and unascertained goods

To interpret and apply the provisions of ss 16–19, it is necessary to distinguish between specific, unascertained and ascertained goods.

All goods are either specific or unascertained at the time that the contract is made. 'Specific' goods are defined in s 61 of the 1979 Act as being 'goods identified and agreed on at the time a contract of sale is made and includes an undivided share, specified as a fraction or percentage, of goods identified and agreed on as aforesaid'. This requires that the actual goods that the buyer is to receive under the contract can be identified at the time that the contract is agreed. Thus, goods taken through the till in a trade warehouse or a supermarket would be specific goods, as would a second-hand car chosen off a garage forecourt and sold by reference to its registration number. In each instance the actual goods can be readily identified.

It follows that any goods incapable of identification at the time that the contract is made cannot be specific and therefore must be unascertained. This would include contracts for the sale of a smaller part out of a larger identified whole, for example

5 tons of sand out of a pile of 20 tons stored in a builder's merchant. The part to be sold can be measured in any way, quantity, height, size, location, etc. For example, in **Re Wait** (1927) the seller agreed to sell 500 tons of wheat from a cargo of 1,000 tons being carried by the ship *Challenger*. The Court of Appeal held that this was a sale of unascertained goods because it was impossible to identify the 500 tons out of the bulk of the cargo. Similarly, in **Kursell *v* Timber Operators & Contractors Ltd** (1927) the buyer agreed to buy timber over a period of 15 years. The contract covered 'all trunks and branches of trees, but not seedlings and young trees of less than six inches in diameter at a height of four feet from the ground'. The timber that could be felled was unascertained as it could not be identified until the time of felling, which could be at any time during the 15-year period.

Another example of unascertained goods would be goods sold by a purely generic description, for example 40 reams of typing paper, with no reference to manufacturer or from where the goods are to be acquired.

Unascertained goods never become specific; they only become ascertained. This normally occurs when the goods are unconditionally appropriated under s 18 of the 1979 Act, which may not happen until the goods are delivered to the buyer.

The descriptions specific, unascertained and ascertained apply equally to future goods as to goods that are already in existence. Section 5 of the 1979 Act defines future goods as those to be manufactured or acquired by the seller after the contract has been made. The decision of **Varley *v* Whipp** (1900) involved the sale of a specified second-hand reaping machine which the seller had not acquired at the time that the contract was made. It was held that the sale was for future specific goods as they were identified at the time of the contract but had yet to be acquired by the seller. Future unascertained goods would include anything yet to be manufactured, for example a made to measure suit, an item of furniture to be made by the seller or manufacturer, and double glazing to be made for a particular building.

10.3 Passage of title

10.3.1 Section 17

The basic provision of the 1979 Act as regards passage of title is found in s 17, which reads:

> (1) Where there is a contract for the sale of specific or unascertained goods the property in them is transferred to the buyer at such time as the parties to the contract intend it to be transferred.
>
> (2) For the purpose of ascertaining the intention of the parties regard shall be had to the terms of the contract, the conduct of the parties and the circumstances of the case.

This makes clear that the passage of property is a matter between the contracting parties in exactly the same way as most other terms of the contract. Thus they have the ability to decide if property will pass at the time that the contract is made, when delivery takes place, when payment takes place or at any other time agreed upon. Indeed, reservation of title clauses expressly authorised by s 19 are themselves an example of such an agreement.

Agreements about the passage of title must be made at the time that the contract is made. It was held in **Dennant *v* Skinner & Collom** (1948) that it is too late for either party to insert a clause about the passage of title after the conclusion of the contract.

10.3.2 Section 18 rules

While the passage of title may be addressed in many commercial contracts, if only by the use of a reservation of title clause, not all contracting parties will make any express agreement. In the average consumer sale the matter is never mentioned and assumes any importance only when things go wrong.

Section 18 is designed to fill this void for it provides five rules that dictate when title will pass in any specified situation. Rules 1 to 3 deal with specific goods, rule 4 with goods on approval and rule 5 with unascertained goods and future goods by description.

Rule 1
Rule 1 provides:

> Where there is an unconditional contract for the sale of specific goods in a deliverable state the property in the goods passes to the buyer when the contract is made, and it is immaterial whether the time of payment or the time of delivery, or both, be postponed.

For rule 1 to apply the contract must be unconditional and the goods must be 'in a deliverable state'. Unconditional in this context means that there are no preconditions that must be satisfied before the contract can take effect or conditions subsequent that must be satisfied afterwards. Thus, for example, a contract for future specific goods could not fall under rule 1 because there is something that remains to be done, for example the seller must acquire the goods.

Goods are in a 'deliverable state' for the purposes of rule 1 when they are in such a state that the buyer would be bound to take delivery of them under the terms of the contract. If something remains to be done to put them into a condition whereby the buyer would be contractually bound to accept them, they are not in a deliverable state and property will not pass under rule 1. Hence, in **Underwood Ltd *v* Burgh Castle & Cement Syndicate** (1922) the seller agreed to sell a 30-ton condensing machine the contract of carriage being f.o.r. (free on rail). At the time of sale the machine was bolted to the floor and the contract required the seller to arrange for its removal from the building and its delivery onto a train. The machine was damaged during the process of freeing it from the floor. It was held that rule 1 did not apply as the goods were not in a deliverable state as something remained to be done to them, and further that the f.o.r. contract implied that the parties had not intended property to pass until the goods were loaded onto the train.

Lastly, note that it is immaterial whether the time of payment or delivery or both is postponed. This underlines the distinction between property and possession and makes clear that the passage of title depends on factors other than delivery. Of course, a delay in delivery may be evidence of some agreement by the parties.

Rule 2

Rule 2 is the counterpart of rule 1 and deals with specific goods that are not in a deliverable state. It reads:

> Where there is a contract for the sale of specific goods and the seller is bound to do something to the goods for the purpose of putting them into a deliverable state, the property does not pass until the thing is done and the buyer has notice that it has been done.

This is relatively straightforward and would cover situations such as the **Underwood** case. Note that the rule requires both that the outstanding thing has been done and that the buyer has had notice of the fact. It must be assumed that notice means actual notice and thus it must come to the buyer's attention.

Rule 3

Rule 3 covers the situation where specific goods are to be sold but where the seller must ascertain the price by specified means. It states:

> Where there is a contract for the sale of specific goods in a deliverable state but the seller is bound to weigh, measure, test, or do some other act or thing with reference to the goods for the purpose of ascertaining the price, the property does not pass until the act or thing is done and the buyer has notice that it has been done.

Note that this rule applies only if the seller has the responsibility for the measuring, etc. If the responsibility is placed on someone else the rule will not apply and property will pass immediately. Thus, in **Nanka-Bruce v Commonwealth Trust** (1926), the seller agreed to sell cocoa to the buyer at a unit price per 60lb. The buyer contracted to resell the cocoa to a sub-buyer who would undertake the weighing of the product to establish the price of the original contract. It was held that rule 3 did not apply and that the property passed to the buyer before the price was agreed.

Rule 4

Rule 4 covers two related yet different scenarios, related in that in both situations the buyer has possession of the goods with the agreement of the seller without there being any firm commitment to purchase. The buyer will have the goods on approval when he wishes to have a period in which to examine and perhaps use the goods in order to establish if they are suitable for his purposes. This is most likely to occur when goods have been purchased through a catalogue with the buyer not having seen the goods prior to ordering them. Sale or return is common in the commercial context. The buyer acquires the goods with the express intention of reselling them but will not be committed to the original purchase until the sub-sale is agreed.

Under rule 4 the title passes to the buyer either:

(a) when he signifies his approval or acceptance to the seller or does any other act adopting the transaction;
(b) if he does not signify his approval or acceptance to the seller but retains the goods without giving notice of rejection, then, if a time has been fixed for the return of the goods, on the expiration of that time, and, if no time has been fixed, on the expiration of a reasonable time.

What constitutes a notice of rejection was considered by the Court of Appeal in the case of **Atari Corpn (UK) Ltd** *v* **Electronics Boutique Stores (UK) Ltd** (1998), in which the seller supplied the buyer with goods under a sale or return contract. The contract required the buyer to pay for the goods in full by 30 November 1995 but permitted the buyer to return the goods until the end of January 1996. In the event, the buyer decided to exercise his right to return the goods in mid-January 1996 and informed the seller. At the time the buyer gave notice to the seller, he was not able to provide a list of all the goods that were to be returned as they had been distributed to retail outlets and needed to be recalled. The seller tried to argue that the failure to provide a comprehensive list meant that the notice of rejection was ineffective as it did not identify which goods were being returned. The Court of Appeal held that, in the absence of any specific contractual requirements, all that is required is that the notice makes clear the intention to reject the goods.

Rule 5

Rule 5 deals with unascertained goods and future goods by description and is the most complex of the s 18 rules. It must be read first in the light of s 16, which provides that the title in unascertained goods cannot pass unless and until the goods are ascertained. Further, it is subsidiary to s 17 in that any express agreement about the passage of unascertained goods will take precedence. Rule 5(1) reads:

Where there is a contract for the sale of unascertained or future goods by description, and goods of that description and in a deliverable state are unconditionally appropriated to the contract, either by the seller with the assent of the buyer or by the buyer with the assent of the seller, the property in the goods then passes to the buyer; and the assent may be express or implied, and may be given either before or after the appropriation is made.

The key factors are that the goods must be both ascertained and unconditionally appropriated. The two concepts do, to some extent, interweave as when goods are ascertained they may be unconditionally appropriated at the same time. Goods are ascertained when they are identified as the goods that the buyer will receive under the contract. Thus when the buyer is to receive a smaller part of a larger whole, as in the **Re Wait** case, they will be ascertained when they are separated out from the remainder of the bulk. This may happen in two ways: either by the goods being separated out from the bulk either prior to delivery or at the latest at the time of delivery, or by exhaustion by virtue of being the only goods left from the bulk capable of fulfilling the contract, the rest having been sold. For example, a seller loads 100 boxes of apples onto his lorry for distribution to three buyers, A who is buying 40 boxes, B who is buying 35 boxes and C who is buying 25 boxes. All the goods are unascertained at that point. A's apples will be ascertained at the time of delivery, when they are separated out from the bulk, as will B's 35 boxes when they are delivered. C's boxes will be ascertained by exhaustion at the time of the delivery to B, for they are the only boxes left on the lorry capable of fulfilling the contract.

A good example of ascertainment by exhaustion occurred in the decision of **The Elafi** (1982), in which the buyer contracted to buy 6,500 tons of a bulk cargo of 22,500 tons being carried on board the *Elafi*. The ship unloaded 16,000 tons in Hamburg, leaving only the buyer's goods, part of which were damaged thereafter. It was held that the buyer's goods had been ascertained by exhaustion and title had passed such as to enable him to claim compensation. Similarly, in **Healy** *v* **Howlett & Sons** (1917) the seller despatched 190 boxes of mackerel, 20 of which were for the buyer. The appropriation was to be done by the carrier. Due to a delay, the mackerel deteriorated before it reached the buyer, who refused to pay for it. It was held that he had no liability as the goods had not been appropriated and hence the property in the goods had not passed.

This approach has been reinforced by the provisions of the Sale of Goods (Amendment) Act 1995, which amended s 18 of the Sale of Goods Act 1979 with effect from 19 September 1995. A newly inserted rule 5(3) provides that:

> Where there is a contract for the sale of a specified quantity of unascertained goods in a deliverable state forming part of a bulk which is identified either in the contract or by subsequent agreement between the parties and the bulk is reduced to (or to less than) that quantity, then, if the buyer under that contract is the only buyer to whom goods are then due out of the bulk—
> (a) the remaining goods are to be taken as appropriated to that contract at the time when the bulk is so reduced; and
> (b) the property in those goods then passes to that buyer.

Thus in a decision like **The Elafi** there was a specifed quantity of goods, namely 6,500 tons, that were in a deliverable state in that the buyer would have been required to take delivery of them under the terms of the contract. They constituted part of a bulk agreed by the parties, if only because of the arrangements for carriage. Thereafter, when the quantity of goods remaining in the ship was only sufficient to satisfy the buyer's contract, rule 5(3) would now take effect to mean both that the goods are to be taken as appropriated to the contract and that the property in them would pass to the buyer. Hence, under the new provisions **The Elafi** would be decided the same way.

A new paragraph (4) to rule 5 covers situations where a buyer has more than one contract relating to goods being delivered out of a bulk. When the bulk is reduced to (or to less than) the total amount of the quantities due to that single buyer from those contracts and he is the only buyer to whom goods are due out of that bulk, rule 5(3) will then take effect to appropriate those goods and pass the property in them to the buyer. A 'bulk' for these purposes, and for the purposes of passage of risk under s 20, is defined as being 'a mass or collection of goods of the same kind which—(a) is contained in a defined space or area; and (b) is such that any goods in the bulk are interchangeable with any other goods therein of the same number or quantity'. Thus, the cargo in **The Elafi** is a prime example of a bulk, as were the boxes of mackerel in **Healy** v **Howlett & Sons**, which could easily have been interchanged between buyers.

The term 'unconditional appropriation' has given rise to much litigation. It occurs when the last act completing the contract has taken place such that the seller is irrevocably committed to using those goods to satisfy the buyer's contract and is incapable of changing his mind. Thus, for example, in **Carlos Federspiel & Co SA** v **Charles Twigg & Co Ltd** (1957) the seller contracted to manufacture and transport f.o.b. (free on board) some bicycles to a buyer in Costa Rica. The bikes were crated up in crates bearing the buyer's name but had not been despatched when the seller went into liquidation. The buyer, who had already paid, sought possession of the goods. The court held that unconditional appropriation had not taken place; this would have occurred at the time of loading the crates onto the ship. By contrast, in **Hardy Lennox (Industrial Engines) Ltd** v **Puttick Ltd** (1984) unconditional appropriation of some generators did take place when the seller set them aside and labelled them with the buyer's name but also sent the buyer a delivery note giving details of the serial numbers of the relevant generators. The goods were identified and irrevocably attached to the contract.

The terms of a delivery note may make a crucial difference. If it identifies the actual goods, as in the **Hardy Lennox** decision, property passes at that time. If, however, it merely informs the buyer that the correct quantity of goods is awaiting collection, appropriation will not take place until the buyer collects the goods even if they have been labelled, as happened in **Wardar's (Import and Export) Co Ltd** v **W Norwood & Sons Ltd** (1968).

Finally, rule 5 requires that the appropriation has been done with the consent of the parties, either express or implied.

10.3.3 Retention of title

It is often in the seller's best interests to retain title to the goods until some condition, usually payment by the buyer, is satisfied. Since the recognition by the Court of Appeal of retention of title clauses in **Aluminium Industrie Vaassen BV** v **Romalpa Aluminium Ltd** (1976) such clauses have become commonplace in commercial contracts as they protect the seller against the liquidation of the buyer and give the seller preferential treatment over other creditors. Section 19 of the Sale of Goods Act 1979 legitimates such clauses for both specific goods and goods appropriated to a contract and provides that where the passage of title depends upon certain conditions being fulfilled, title will not pass until those conditions are fulfilled.

In the **Romalpa** decision the plaintiff, a Dutch company, sold some aluminium foil to an English company. Clause 13 of the contract was a retention of title clause which retained to the seller the ownership of any unmixed foil in the possession of the buyer until the seller had been paid all that was owing to it. Further, if the foil was used to manufacture any other items, the seller's retention of title should transfer to the manufactured items and the buyer should hold them as 'fiduciary' for the seller as he would the proceeds of sale of such manufactured items. The buyer went into liquidation while in possession of some of the unmixed foil. He had also sold some of the unmixed foil to a sub-buyer. The seller sought to enforce the clause. It was held by the Court of Appeal that the plaintiff seller was able to recover the unmixed foil in the buyer's possession and the proceeds of sales by the buyer.

The **Romalpa** decision was the highspot of the judicial approach to retention of title clauses and later decisions have been less favourable to the seller. While many decisions appear contradictory and are to some extent dependent on their individual facts, the approach of the court appears to differ depending on whether the goods are unaltered or have lost their identity through being subsumed in another product and whether the clause is seeking to recover the goods themselves or the proceeds of sale.

The Court of Appeal in **Clough Mill Ltd *v* Martin** (1984) confirmed that there is no difficulty enforcing a properly worded retention of title clause if the goods in their original form are in the possession of the buyer. However, in practice many goods will change their identity through some manufacturing process, this always having been the intention of both buyer and seller. In this situation, the court has construed retention of title clauses as really being a form of security for payment and, as such, should be registered as a charge under s 395 of the Companies Act 1985. In that situation, the assumption is that the property has passed to the buyer despite the retention of title clause. Thus, in **Borden (UK) Ltd *v* Scottish Timber Products Ltd** (1981) the seller supplied resin to the buyer for incorporation into chipboard. It was held that the seller's retention clause under which he tried to claim a portion of the chipboard must fail as the resin had lost its identity. Similarly, in **Re Peachdart** (1983) the buyer had incorporated leather supplied to him by the seller into handbags. The court held that although the individual pieces of leather could be recognised they had lost their identity in that they had become a new product. As such the retention of title clause was of no effect and merely created a registerable charge. As the seller had not registered the charge, it was unenforceable. Title had passed to the buyer. A more recent example of the application of a retention of title clause was the decision of **Chaigley Farms Ltd *v* Crawford Kaye & Grayshire Ltd** (1996), in which the seller had a contract to provide live animals to an abattoir, the contract including a retention of title clause over the 'livestock'. When the abattoir called in the receivers, the seller sought to recover the remaining live animals together with the meat thought to have come from the already slaughtered animals that he had provided. The receiver refused and instructed that the remaining live animals be slaughtered and the meat sold. The court held that the term 'livestock' only applied to the animals still alive at the time that the seller sought to enforce the clause and therefore that he could only recover the proceeds of sale of the meat coming from those animals.

A retention of title clause covering goods would seem to be effective even if it is an 'all monies' clause whereby the seller seeks to retain title to any of his goods still in the buyer's possession until the buyer has settled all the debts that he owes to the seller. This approach, accepted by the House of Lords in **Armour *v* Thyssen Edelstahlwerke AG** (1990), is significantly broader in its effect as it permits goods from one contract to be used as security for debts owing to the seller from other contracts. It further prevents the need for the seller to have to identify which batch of goods was delivered in respect of each contract.

The courts are noticeably less supportive in respect of retention of title clauses that attempt to hold the buyer liable to the seller for the proceeds of any resale to a sub-buyer. While a clause of this nature was successful in the **Romalpa** decision the buyer in that case did acknowledge that he was holding the proceeds as a fiduciary for the seller. In the average seller/buyer relationship it would be very difficult to establish that a fiduciary relationship exists and hence such clauses are unlikely to be upheld.

10.4 The passage of risk

Section 20 of the Sale of Goods Act 1979 raises the presumption that the risk in the goods will pass with the property, although this presumption can be rebutted by an agreement between the parties or by their conduct.

The close relationship between property and risk is significant for it follows that the buyer should arrange for appropriate insurance cover for the goods from the moment that title passes even though the goods may not have been delivered. Indeed, rule 1 of s 18 specifically mentions that where that rule applies property passes, it being irrelevant whether delivery or payment or both are delayed. The converse is also true. If the buyer has possession of the goods in a situation where property has not passed the goods are at the seller's risk. Obvious examples would include goods sent to a buyer on approval, or on a sale or return basis. Equally, this would apply where goods have been supplied to a buyer subject to a retention of title clause, though clearly in this situation one would expect that the contract would stipulate that the buyer must insure the goods while they are in his possession.

This basic rule locating risk with the passage of property is mitigated by s 20(2), which provides that if delivery of the goods has been delayed through the fault of either the seller or the buyer, then that person carries the risk in the goods for any loss which would not have occurred but for their fault. The responsibility for the goods is further reinforced by s 20(3), which stipulates that the normal duties and liabilities of a contractual bailee or custodian will apply to both buyer and seller. Thus, if either is in possession of the goods belonging to the other, they are under a duty to take good care of them and will be responsible for any loss arising out of negligence. A new s 20A, inserted with effect from 19 September 1995 by the Sale of Goods (Amendment) Act 1995, deals with the passage of risk of undivided shares which form part of a bulk. It applies where there is a contract for the sale of a specifed quantity of unascertained goods where those goods, or part of them, form part of a bulk which is identified either by the contract or by a subsequent agreement by the parties and the buyer has paid for some or all of the goods which are the subject of the contract. Thus, for example, a contract for the purchase of 200 tons of grain to be carried on a named ship leaving a given port on a specified date would satisfy the requirements where those goods are to constitute part of a bulk transport of goods of that type and the buyer has paid for them. Where the section applies, then, subject to any agreement to the contrary, the property of the goods in the undivided bulk is transferred to the buyer and he becomes an owner in common of the bulk along with other buyers who have satisfied the condition regarding payment. His share will be such share as the quantity of goods paid for and due to him out of the bulk bears to the quantity of the goods in the bulk at the time. Thus, if he has paid for all the goods under his contract and the bulk quantity is large enough to satisfy all the contracts drawn against it, then the buyer will be an owner in common for the full amount due under his contract. However, if the total of the undivided shares exceeds the quantity actually contained in the bulk, the undivided share of each buyer will be reduced proportionately. Thus, for example, if the total quantity contracted for by a group of buyers was 5,000 tons while the total amount contained in the bulk was only 4,500 tons, each buyer would acquire ownership to only 90 per cent of the amount for which he contracted.

The assumption thus far is that the buyer has paid for all the goods due under his contract. However, in practice he may have paid for only part of them. Where this is so, any delivery to the buyer from the bulk shall relate first to those goods for which he has paid. Similarly, part payment of the price for goods is to be treated as payment for a corresponding part of the goods for which the buyer has contracted. Thus, for example, if the buyer has paid only 40 per cent of the contract price, claims under s 20A will apply to only 40 per cent of the goods for which he has contracted. In situations of common ownership such as are anticipated here, there needs to be clear guidelines as to the rights and obligations of the common owners. Under s 20B the owners in common of a bulk are deemed to have consented to two things. First, they are deemed to have consented to the delivery of goods from the bulk to any other owner in common of that bulk where those goods are due to him under the contract. Thus, each buyer is entitled to receive his goods without interference by any other owner in common. Second, owners in common are deemed to have consented to a co-owner dealing with or removing, delivering or disposing of the goods in the bulk to the extent that those goods fall within the co-owner's undivided share of the bulk at the time of the dealing, removal, delivery or disposal. This would, for example, permit co-owners to contract to sell their share of the goods in the bulk to a sub-buyer.

Sections 20A and 20B create a new relationship between buyers when their goods form part of an undivided bulk. However, it is important to recognise the restrictions placed on this relationship, for the owners in common are unlikely to have had any previous dealings and have certainly not chosen to have a legal relationship. This reality is impliedly recognised by s 20B(3), which provides that neither section imposes any obligation on a buyer of goods to compensate any other co-owner of the goods in that bulk for any shortfall in the goods received by that other co-owner. Similarly, they do not create any contractual relationship between the buyers of goods in a bulk for any adjustments between themselves, or affect the rights of any buyer under his contract. The relationship is one in which all co-owners acquire rights recognised by the other co-owners but falls short of creating any contractual relationship between them. Sections 20A and 20B are clearly of value to buyers of goods for they provide them with rights in property in situations in which they may already have taken the risk. Thus, for example, in contracts for the carriage of goods by sea, it is common for the risk in the goods to be transferred to the buyer when the goods cross the rail on the ship when being loaded. However, where those goods are unascertained, traditional rules would have meant that the property in the goods had not passed as the goods had not been appropriated and thereby ascertained. Thus a buyer could easily be in a situation where he carried the risk in the goods while not having any ownership rights. The new situation is clearly an improvement in the protection afforded to such buyers. The new provisions may also be of real significance should the seller go into liquidation before the undivided shares in the bulk goods have been delivered to the buyers. Under the previous interpretation of rule 5, the seller's liquidator would have been able to claim ownership of the undivided bulk on the basis that it constituted unascertained goods which had not been unconditionally appropriated and therefore no property could have passed to the buyers. However, under the new s 20A, it would seem that as soon as the condition of payment has been met, the property in the goods passes to the owners in common of the bulk, and therefore they would be able jointly to defeat any claim made by the seller's liquidator. The liquidator would have no claim against that portion of the bulk goods for which payment has been made, although, arguably, he would still be able to reclaim any of the bulk goods for which payment had not been received as they would not fall under the provisions of s 20A.

10.5 Sale by a non-owner

In dealing with the passage of title, the assumption has been made that the seller had the right to sell in accordance with the implied condition contained in s 12. Of course, this is not necessarily the case and situations may arise where the seller has no right to sell. The problem then posed to the law is who should be protected – the innocent buyer, who has bought in good faith, or the true owner, who has been deprived of his goods.

The basic presumption is to be found in s 21 of the Sale of Goods Act 1979 and is that a seller cannot pass better title than he has, often expressed in the Latin maxim *nemo dat quod non habet*. However, the law has developed a selection of exceptions to this basic rule, five of which are to be found in the 1979 Act itself.

10.5.1 Estoppel

Section 21 provides the first such exception, namely estoppel. Section 21(1) reads:

> Subject to this Act, where goods are sold by a person who is not their owner, and who does not sell them under the authority or with the consent of the owner, the buyer acquires no better title to the goods than the seller had, unless the owner of the goods is by his conduct precluded from denying the seller's authority to sell.

An estoppel under this section would be effective to protect an innocent purchaser if certain criteria are satisfied:

(a) the owner has by word or conduct made a representation that the seller has his authority to sell;
(b) the representation was made intentionally or negligently; and
(c) the innocent purchaser has relied on that representation.

'Intentionally' in (b) above would also include fraudulently, as in **Eastern Distributors Ltd** *v* **Goldring** (1957), in which the owner of a van wanted to use his van to raise some money. He conspired with a trader to raise the money by deceiving a hire-purchase company. The owner, pretending that the car was owned by the trader and that he was a customer, completed a hire-purchase application form on the vehicle. The trader also completed the requisite form inviting the finance company to buy the car from him and sell it on hire-purchase to the owner. The finance company agreed. They discovered the fraud when the owner/customer defaulted on the loan and sold the car to an innocent third party. The question arose as to whether the finance company owned the car or whether the innocent third party owned it. The answer hinged on whether the original owner still had ownership such as to be able to pass it on to the third party or whether, because of the fraud, the finance company had acquired the title. The court held that by signing the hire-purchase proposal form the owner had represented that the trader had the authority to sell it to the finance company and was estopped from denying the representation. The car belonged to the finance company which could recover it from the third party.

This case should be contrasted with the decision of **Mercantile Credit Co** *v* **Hamblin** (1965), a case with strikingly similar facts to the **Goldring** decision. The significant difference is that the customer was induced to sign the hire-purchase proposal form by a fraudulent trader who led her to believe that it was a loan application form. The court held that she had not made any intentional representation that the trader owned the car; neither had she been negligent in relying on the trader's advice. As such there was no representation and no estoppel. The car was still owned by her.

Merely allowing a person to have possession of the goods is not a representation by the owner, as evidenced by yet another car-related hire-purchase case, **Central Newbury Car Auctions** *v* **Unity Finance** (1956). In that case, a trader allowed a customer to take possession of a car together with the registration document before the finance company had replied to the hire-purchase proposal. The customer sold the car to an innocent third party. It was held that the trader was entitled to recover the car as he had not made any representation and thus could not be estopped from recovering his property. Note that the registration document of a car is not a document of title and thus even the possession of that was not sufficient to raise an estoppel.

It is clear that for an estoppel to be effective it must have misled the innocent third party and that the falsity of the representation was not known to the third party at the time that the property in the goods was due to pass. It follows that if the third party became aware of the falsity before the property passed he cannot rely on the estoppel and the true owner will have the right to sue the third party in conversion with a view to recovering either the goods or monetary compensation.

10.5.2 Market overt

Section 22 of the Sale of Goods Act 1979 previously contained the market overt exception to the *nemo dat* rule. This exception, though historically quaint, was of little real significance in the modern commercial context. However, there was considerable concern over the possibility that the exception permitted markets overt to be used as a means of disposing of stolen goods. The rule, which related to properly constituted markets overt established by royal charter, or statute or long usage (and of which there were none in Wales or Scotland), permitted good title to be created in respect of any goods sold in the market to a *bona fide* purchaser provided that the goods were openly displayed to the public with the sale taking place according to the normal usages of the market and between the hours of sunrise and sunset. The market overt exception was repealed with effect from 3 January 1995 by the Sale of Goods (Amendment) Act 1994. The net effect of this abolition is that innocent purchasers are no longer protected should they buy goods that the market seller does not have the right to sell, with the consequent effect that the innocent buyer would be forced to surrender the goods to the true owner and seek to recover the purchase price from the market trader. This reduction in the rights of the innocent buyer flies in the face of reform expected from the European Commission, which seems likely to issue a Directive aimed at harmonising and protecting the rights of innocent purchasers.

10.5.3 Voidable title

Section 23 provides a specific statutory application of the law of misrepresentation as to identity discussed in Chapter 3. Section 23 provides:

> When the seller of goods has a voidable title to them, but his title has not been avoided at the time of sale, the buyer acquires a good title to the goods, provided that he buys them in good faith and without notice of the seller's defect of title.

While the section is wide enough to cover any situation in which the innocent third party acquires goods from someone with voidable title, the most common example will be where the buyer has misrepresented his identity to the original seller. To recap briefly, a seller is presumed to want to contract with the person with whom he is actually dealing. If that person misrepresents his identity the contract will be voidable, i.e. a perfectly valid contract under which the fraudulent buyer acquires good title to the goods until such time as the contract is avoided. The buyer is capable of passing good title to an innocent third party provided he does so before his own title is avoided. Thereafter the third party would not get good title. If, however, the supposed identity of the fraudulent buyer was crucial to the contract with the seller the contract will be void, the fraudulent buyer will not acquire any title and neither will the third party.

Equally, the situation will arise where the buyer has simply acted frauduently, such as in **Colwyn Bay Motorcycles *v* Poole** (2000), in which Colwyn Bay Motor-cycles sold a motorcycle to a fraudster who paid by telephone with a fraudulent credit card transaction and took possession of the vehicle. Two days later the plaintiff discovered the fraud and avoided the transaction, informing the police and trying (but failing) to contact the fraudster. The fraudster subsequently sold the motorcycle to a dealer who, in turn, sold it to a consumer. It was held that, as the seller had avoided the sale prior to the fraudster reselling the car, the dealer had not gained good title and so could not pass title to the consumer.

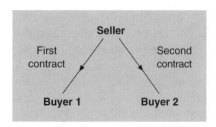

Figure 10.1   Seller in possession

10.5.4   Seller in possession

We have already recognised that there may be situations in which the seller of goods retains possession of them after sale. This might occur, for instance, where the goods are physically too big for the buyer to remove them at the time of sale or, alternatively, where the seller retains them in order to do some necessary repair or alteration to the goods. Section 24 allows for the possibility that when in such possession the seller might resell the goods to an innocent second buyer as in Figure 10.1.

The question arises as to which of the two buyers, both of whom are innocent, should be able to claim ownership of the goods. Section 24 provides:

> Where a person having sold goods continues or is in possession of the goods, or of the documents of title to goods, the delivery or transfer by that person, or by a mercantile agent acting for him, of the goods or documents of title under any sale, pledge, or other disposition thereof, to any person receiving the same in good faith and without notice of the previous sale, has the same effect as if the person making the delivery or transfer were expressly authorised by the owner of the goods to make the same.

This section is markedly similar to s 8 of the Factors Act 1889, which provides essentially the same protection, although s 8 extends to goods under an 'agreement for sale, pledge or other disposition'.

Provided that the provisions of the section can be satisfied the second buyer will acquire good title, leaving the first buyer to sue the seller for conversion. The requisite criteria are manifold. The seller must have continued in physical possession of the goods after the first sale, although it does not matter in what capacity he retained possession, whether as seller, repairer or some other capacity. Thus in **Worcester Works Finance Ltd** *v* **Cooden Engineering Ltd** (1972) the seller wrongfully remained in possession after selling the goods to a finance company as part of a fraudulent hire-purchase application. His subsequent return of the vehicle to the person from whom he had acquired it originally was a disposition within the meaning of s 24 and did attract protection for that person.

It is clear though that once the seller has lost possession the *nemo dat* exception expires and will not be revived by the seller regaining possession at some future point.

The section requires that there must be a delivery or transfer of the goods to the third party. Thus in **Nicholson** *v* **Harper** (1895) it was held that where the seller of the goods remained in possession via a warehouseman with whom the goods were stored he did not transfer or deliver them for the purposes of the section when he pledged them a second time to the warehouseman. It was held, in a questionnable decision, that there was no physical delivery. The issue was revisited by the Court of Appeal in **Michael Gerson (Leasing) Ltd** *v* **Wilkinson** (2001), in which the owner of goods sold them to a finance company under a sale and leaseback agreement. Under this agreement, the seller would retain possession of the goods under a hire agreement from the finance company. The seller subsequently sold part of the goods under a similar agreement to a second finance company. The issue was whether there had been a 'delivery or transfer' of the goods to the second finance company sufficient to satisfy s 24. The Court of Appeal held that although the second finance company had never had physical possession of the goods, the sale and leaseback agreement between the seller and the second finance company did constitute 'a voluntary transfer of possession' such as to give the second company good title.

In these situations where the seller has wrongly resold goods belonging to the buyer, the latter will be able to sue the seller for conversion and recover damages. However, s 24 does not affect the right of the unpaid seller to resell the goods under s 48 of the 1979 Act as discussed in the previous chapter. Where such a resale does occur, the second buyer acquires good title to the goods as against the original buyer but the seller is not liable for a breach of contract.

10.5.5 Buyer in possession

The buyer may acquire possession before property. We have already seen how, in a commercial context, the buyer often acquires the goods with the express purpose of resale with the possibility of the resale happening before property passes. This could occur where the buyer needs to resell the goods to raise the money to pay the seller for them while the goods are subject to a retention of title whereby the buyer does not acquire title until after full payment has been made. Clearly it would be very disruptive to trade if the innocent sub-buyer was not sufficiently certain of acquiring title in this situation such as to give him the confidence to purchase.

Section 25(1) of the 1979 Act provides appropriate protection and reads:

> Where a person having bought or agreed to buy goods obtains, with the consent of the seller, possession of the goods or the documents of title to the goods, the delivery or transfer by that person, or by a mercantile agent acting for him, of the goods or documents of title, under any sale, pledge or other disposition thereof, to any person receiving the same in good faith and without notice of any lien or other right of the original seller in respect of the goods, has the same effect as if the person making the delivery or transfer were a mercantile agent in possession of the goods or documents of title with the consent of the owner.

Again this section is very similar to a section of the Factors Act 1889, s 9, although again that provision is slightly wider than the Sale of Goods Act 1979 as it extends to anyone who receives the goods under any 'agreement for sale, pledge or other disposition'.

The provision takes effect only where the first buyer has 'bought or agreed to buy' the goods. The case of **Helby *v* Matthews** (1895) confirms that the hirer in a hire-purchase contract has not bought or agreed to buy the goods and thus a sub-buyer acquiring goods subject to a hire-purchase contract could not acquire title (but see the section below on the Hire Purchase Act 1964). This approach was followed in the decision of **Close Asset Finance *v* Care Graphics Machinery Ltd** (2000), in which the court held that a hire contract which lasted for seven years, at the end of which the hirer could exercise an option to purchase, was not an agreement to buy for the purposes of s 25. There was no obligation on the hirer to exercise the option even though the commercial reality was that the hirer would almost certainly exercise the option given the minimal cost of so doing relative to the value of the goods. Section 25(2) confirms a similar position in respect of conditional sales.

Possession must have taken place with the consent of the seller. However, the House of Lords in **National Employers Mutual General Insurance Association Ltd *v* Jones** (1990) adopted a restrictive approach to the meaning of the word 'seller'. Rejecting the literal interpretation and seeking one that was more attuned to the problem at hand, the court held that in this context seller should mean owner. Thus if the seller is anyone other than the owner, for example a thief, s 25 will not protect an innocent sub-buyer, who will not get title. Having gained possession with consent, it does not matter if the owner's consent is later withdrawn as long as the sub-buyer is not aware of this as otherwise he would not be acting in good faith.

The court has been more liberal in its interpretation of the requirement that the buyer has possession and has been prepared to accept that constructive possession may occur where the seller delivers the goods direct to a sub-buyer at the request of the original buyer. Such constructive notice does satisfy the requirements of s 25.

A last difficulty posed by the wording of the section was exposed in the decision of **Newtons of Wembley Ltd *v* Williams** (1964). The section states that the disposal by the buyer will have the same effect as if it were made by a mercantile agent. A mercantile agent is in business selling from business premises and thus a private buyer reselling the goods would be unlikely to satisfy this provision. Consequently, it may be that an innocent sub-buyer buying from such a private buyer would not be protected against a claim by the seller.

10.5.6 Mercantile agent

Of real interest to the commercial buyer is the position regarding sales by mercantile agents. A mercantile agent is an independent agent acting in the course of a business who buys and sells goods or raises money on the security of goods on behalf of one or more principals. Under s 2 of the Factors Act 1889 special protection is given to *bona fide* purchasers acquiring goods from mercantile agents on condition that certain criteria are met. Section 2(1) reads:

> Where a mercantile agent is, with the consent of the owner, in possession of goods or of the documents of title to goods, any sale, pledge, or other disposition of the goods, made by him when acting in the ordinary course of business of a mercantile agent, shall, subject to the provisions of this Act, be as valid as if he

were expressly authorised by the owner of the goods to make the same; provided that the person taking under the disposition acts in good faith, and has not at the time of the disposition notice that the person making the disposition has no authority to make the same.

For the disposition in question to be covered, the mercantile agent must have had possession of the goods in his capacity as a mercantile agent as opposed to any other capacity. Further, possession must have been with the consent of the owner, whether obtained legitimately or by deception, and possession must have been for a purpose related to the sale of the item. This would include, for example, displaying the item for sale and receiving offers.

Lastly, the disposition must have been undertaken by the agent when acting in the normal course of his business and in the manner that one would expect an agent to act. This will be a question of fact in each individual instance. Hence, in **Stadium Finance Ltd** *v* **Robbins** (1962) the owner gave a car to a trader to get offers for it prior to sale. While the owner left the registration document in the car, he retained the keys. The trader subsequently obtained a spare key and sold the car to an innocent third party. It was held that this was not a sale in the ordinary course of business as a mercantile agent and title did not pass to the innocent purchaser. The **Colwyn Bay Motorcycles** decision (see above) also considered what constitutes a sale 'in the ordinary course of business'. The point at issue was whether the fraudster acted as a mercantile agent within the meaning of s 25 when he sold the motorcycle he had gained fraudulently to the innocent dealer. The dealer knew that the fraudster had given a false name and that the documents for the motorcycle did not match that name. The court held that this was not a sale in the ordinary course of the business of a mercantile agent, that the dealer did not gain good title and could not pass good title to the ultimate consumer.

10.5.7 Hire Purchase Act 1964

Part III of the Hire Purchase Act 1964 provides one specific exception in respect of certain hire-purchase agreements. As already explained, the hirer in a hire-purchase agreement does not have ownership of the goods during the lifetime of the agreement and has no right to dispose of them. Where such a disposal occurs the finance company still owns the goods and has the right to recover them.

The Hire Purchase Act 1964 provides an exception to this rule for motor vehicles. Section 27 provides that where the hirer of a motor vehicle under a hire-purchase agreement disposes of it before the property is vested in him, the first private purchaser to acquire the vehicle in good faith will acquire good title. This is so whether that private purchaser acquires the car directly from the hirer or obtains it through an intermediate trader or financier.

This provision clearly is of real benefit to the private purchaser, who acquires good title and is able to pass it on to subsequent purchasers. However, the Act is restricted in that it applies only to goods subject to hire-purchase or conditional sale agreements and does not apply, for example, where the car is subject to a lease or is a company car. Further, it applies only to private purchasers and thus business purchasers acting in good faith are not protected.

Question

Farm Supplies Ltd, agricultural merchants, made the following contracts with Angus, a farmer:

(a) To supply Angus with 30 bags of chemical fertiliser. Farm Supplies Ltd had 90 bags of the relevant fertiliser in stock at the time that the contract was made. They put 30 bags to one side and labelled each bag with Angus's name before sending a delivery note to him. The bags were destroyed in a fire at Farm Supplies Ltd's warehouse before Angus had collected them.

(b) To sell Angus a rotovator for £350. The contract was subject to a clause stating that property in the goods would not pass until Angus had paid for it. The rotovator was stolen from Angus's farm before he had paid.

(c) To sell 30 immature trees to Angus for replanting. The trees were to be delivered by Farm Supplies Ltd and were part of a consignment of 100 trees intended for several purchasers. The trees were not labelled. Due to poor care by the carrier, the 65 trees remaining on the lorry at the time it reached Angus's farm had perished and Angus refused to accept delivery.

Advise Farm Supplies Ltd about who must bear the risk in each of the three situations.

Answer

These three contracts with Angus concern the passage of title and therefore the passage of risk, because under s 20 of the Sale of Goods Act 1979 risk passes with property unless there is an agreement to the contrary. Along with risk will go the decision as to whether to cover the risk with insurance.

(a) These are unascertained goods as the contract is to supply 30 bags of fertiliser out of a stock of 90 bags. The issue therefore is whether unconditional appropriation has taken place such as to permit title to pass to Angus under s 18, rule 5. We know that the bags have been put to one side, labelled and a delivery note sent to Angus. Although there are conflicting authorities, this is probably enough to constitute unconditional appropriation, particularly if the delivery note makes reference to specific bags. If this is so, the risk is with Angus, who must bear the loss.

(b) The rotovator was sold subject to a retention of title clause, which is valid under s 19 of the Sale of Goods Act 1979. Therefore, *prima facie*, the risk is with Farm Supplies Ltd, the seller. However, there are two further possibilities. One is that the contract of sale included a term agreeing that the risk would pass to Angus along with possession of the goods. If this is so Angus will have to bear the loss. The other possibility is that the contract included a term requiring Angus to insure the goods while they were in his possession. If this is so, a claim can be made against the insurance company irrespective of who owned the goods at the time. Both Farm Supplies Ltd and Angus would have sufficient insurable interest to permit them to insure the goods.

(c)   Here the 30 trees form a specified quantity of goods in a deliverable state which form part of a bulk, i.e. 30 trees out of a bulk of 100 trees. Under s 18, rule 5(3), if the bulk has been reduced to the specified quantity or less and the buyer is the only person still to be provided with goods out of the bulk, then the property will pass. In this example, however, there are still 65 trees on the lorry at the time that the goods are damaged and so property cannot have passed to Angus under rule 5. However, s 20A of the Sale of Goods Act 1979 provides that where the buyer has paid for all or part of the goods forming part of a bulk, he will become an owner in common of the bulk. As such, the property and risk in the goods will pass to Angus as an owner in common if he has paid for some or all of the 30 trees for which he has contracted. If this is the case, Angus will be able to claim damages from Farm Supplies Ltd for the loss caused by their negligence.

Further reading

Adams, A (2000). *Law for Business Students*, 2nd edn (Longman)

Atiyah, P S, Adams, J N and Macqueen, H (2001). *The Sale of Goods*, 10th edn (Longman)

Bradgate, R (2000). *Commercial Law*, 3rd edn (Butterworth)

Dobson, P (1997). *Charlesworth's Business Law*, 16th edn (Sweet & Maxwell)

Dobson, P (2000). *Sale of Goods and Consumer Credit*, 6th edn (Sweet & Maxwell)

Harvey, B W and Parry, D L (1996). *The Law of Consumer Protection and Fair Trading*, 5th edn (Butterworth)

Keenan, D (2000). *Smith and Keenan's Advanced Business Law*, 11th edn (Longman)

Keenan, D and Riches, S (2001). *Business Law*, 6th edn (Longman)

Stone, R (2000). *Principles of Contract Law*, 4th edn (Cavendish)

Part III The law of tort

11 Negligence

11.1 Introduction

Contract law, as discussed in Parts I and II of this book, is only of any real benefit to those persons who have contractual privity. Legal action is limited to immediate buyers and sellers. This restriction creates two real problems in the present context. First, it denies the purchaser of the product the opportunity to sue anyone other than his immediate supplier, this being so even if his supplier has gone into liquidation or somebody further up the distributive chain may be better able to satisfy his claim. Second, contract ignores the needs of non-purchasers who suffer damage because of faulty goods or services but lack privity totally.

11.2 Duty of care

This void is filled by the law of tort and, in particular, by the tort of negligence. The modern law of negligence is founded on the renowned decision of **Donoghue** *v* **Stevenson** (1932). The plaintiff, Mrs Donoghue, went to a cafe with a friend. While there, the friend bought a bottle of ginger beer for consumption by the plaintiff. The drink was contained in an opaque bottle. After consuming half of it, the remainder of the drink was being poured out of the bottle when the remains of a decomposed snail floated out. Mrs Donoghue suffered from shock and gastro-enteritis as a result of the experience and wished to sue for compensation. She could not sue in contract as she lacked privity and thus tried to sue the manufacturer of the drink for her injuries. The case was remitted to the House of Lords to decide whether, as a matter of law, the manufacturer of a product owed any duty of care to the ultimate user or consumer of his product. Their Lordships held that such a duty does exist.

Lord Atkin in giving judgment spelt out the duty laid upon manufacturers. He stated:

> A manufacturer of products, which he sells in such a form as to show that he intends them to reach the ultimate consumer in the form in which they left him with no reasonable possibility of intermediate examination, and with the knowledge that the absence of reasonable care in the preparation or putting up of the products will result in an injury to the consumer's life or property, owes a duty to that consumer to take reasonable care.

This statement has been analysed and applied in numerous cases over the last 60 years. Consequently, the term 'manufacturer' would now be interpreted to include wholesalers, distributors, repairers, assemblers, indeed anyone who has played a part in the construction or packaging of the final product. The phrase 'ultimate consumer' includes any user of the product as opposed to a contractual purchaser. Reference is made to the potential lack of the opportunity for an intermediate examination, a factor of particular pertinence nowadays given the extent to which products, particularly foodstuffs, are pre-packed and sealed with no opportunity for intermediate examination at any stage of the distribution process. It has been suggested that the manufacturer may remain liable for a defect in an item if the goods are examined but the defect remains undisclosed. Naturally, if an examination reveals the defect but the consumer knowingly continues to use the goods, the manufacturer will be free from liability.

While specifically setting out the liability of manufacturers **Donoghue v Stevenson** also laid the foundations for a much wider use of the concept of duty of care. Consequently, actionable negligence exists if the plaintiff can establish that the defendant owed him a duty of care, that there was a breach of that duty and that the plaintiff suffered damage as a result of the defendant's breach.

The traditional approach to establishing the existence of a duty of care was laid out by Lord Atkin in **Donoghue v Stevenson** in his much-quoted 'neighbour principle':

> The rule that you are to love your neighbour becomes in law, you must not injure your neighbour; and the lawyer's question, Who is my neighbour? receives a restricted reply. You must take reasonable care to avoid acts or omissions which you can reasonably foresee would be likely to injure your neighbour. Who, then, in law is my neighbour? The answer seems to be – persons who are so closely and directly affected by my act that I ought reasonably to have them in contemplation as being so affected when I am directing my mind to the acts or omissions which are called in question.

This quote begs the leading question as to who is reasonably foreseeable as a person likely to be affected by the defendant's actions. Arguably, in the context of faulty goods and services, it is possible to identify certain categories of people who would fall naturally into that grouping. Thus the user or consumer of the product, whether a businessperson or a private individual, is foreseeable as is anyone likely to be in the vicinity when the product is being used. However, the boundaries are not necessarily as clear-cut as that. Supposing the brakes on a car are defective, as a result of which an accident occurs. The driver of the car together with his passengers are clearly foreseeable as, arguably, are other motorists or pedestrians who might become embroiled in the accident. But what of an innocent bystander watching from an office window who happens to witness the accident and suffers nervous shock. He is probably not foreseeable.

The law is littered with cases in which the courts have tried to decide whether an individual plaintiff was foreseeable and to establish a satisfactory test for deciding foreseeability. More recently the courts have shifted the emphasis away from foreseeability and towards an analysis of whether the plaintiff was sufficiently proximate to the defendant for it to be reasonable to impose a duty of care on the defendant.

Potential defendants who might be held to owe a duty of care in the context of the supply of goods and services would naturally include the manufacturer of the product but would also include anyone else involved in the distribution or supply of the product. Thus wholesalers, retailers, etc are under a duty to store goods correctly so as to prevent them becoming damaged and thereby posing a threat to potential plaintiffs. For example, distributors of chilled foodstuffs that need to be stored below a given temperature would be under a duty to ensure the correct storage of the products as a failure to store correctly could result in a deterioration of the product causing food poisoning to the ultimate user. As well as founding an action in negligence, these facts would also constitute a criminal offence contrary to the Food Safety Act 1990.

11.2.1 Standard of care

Having established the existence of a duty of care, the level or standard of that duty must be settled. The basic requirement is that the defendant must exercise the same standard of care when going about his affairs as would be exercised by an ordinary reasonable man, the so-called 'man on the Clapham omnibus'. Thus, he must act in the normal reasonable manner to be expected of any adult in that situation. A recent example of the application of this approach can be seen in the Court of Appeal decision of **Mansfield v Weetabix Ltd** (1998), a case arising out of a road accident. In that case, a lorry driver crashed his vehicle into a shop premise after his ability to drive was impaired due a medical condition of which he did not know. Evidence was adduced to show that he would not have continued to drive had he known of the condition. The Court of Appeal held that he should be judged against the standard to be expected of a reasonably competent driver who was unaware of a medical condition and, by reference to that standard, he was not liable. However, a mere lack of experience or qualification will not lower the standard of care to be expected of an individual. Thus, in **Nettleship v Weston** (1971), the Court of Appeal held that a learner driver would be expected to display the same level of skill and be judged by the same standard of care as a qualified driver.

Naturally, in applying this general approach of requiring people to exercise a reasonable standard of care, particular mention must be made of children. It would be inappropriate to judge their behaviour by reference to that expected of adults. Instead, a child is to be judged by reference to the reasonable standard to be expected from an ordinary child of that age. **Mullin v Richards** (1998) is a case on point. It concerned two 15-year-old schoolgirls who were involved in a mock fight with plastic rulers during a lesson. When one of the rulers snapped, a piece of plastic entered the plaintiff's eye causing serious injury and loss of vision. It transpired that such 'fights' were common practice in the school and had not been banned; nor had the children been warned of the danger. The court held that, by reference to the behaviour of a normal prudent 15-year-old, the defendant had not been careless and therefore was not liable.

Professional standards

While the standard of care to be expected of an adult will never be lower than that expected of an ordinary reasonable man, the actions of a defendant who professes some expertise in the matter complained of will be judged in accordance with the standard to be expected of someone with that level of expertise. The higher the level of professed expertise, the higher the standard of care demanded. This view was expounded in the decision of **Bolam v Friern Hospital Management Committee** (1957), in which the plantiff had been injured during the use of electric shock treatment during psychiatric care. The court held that the defendant would not be liable if 'he has acted in accordance with a practice accepted as proper by a responsible body of medical men skilled in that particular art'. The issue was reconsidered by the House of Lords in the decision of **Bolitho v City and Hackney Health Authority** (1998), when the House held that the view held by the body of practitioners must be one that it reasonably held, but then continued that it would seldom be right for a judge to conclude that views held by a medical expert are unreasonable. While both of these decisions involved the medical profession, it is reasonable to assume that the same approach would apply in relation to any other profession.

It should be noted, though, that even where a higher standard of care exists it does not guarantee results but merely requires that the defendant will exercise the appropriate level of care and skill when attempting to achieve the desired results. Hence, in **Whitehouse v Jordan** (1981) a surgeon was not held liable for the brain damage caused to an infant at birth by a forceps delivery, when the surgeon's decision was held to be an error of judgment rather than negligence.

Naturally, there is a requirement that a professional person will be up to date in his field and employ the skills and knowledge available at the time, as held in the decision of **Roe v Minister of Health** (1954), in which the defendant was found not liable for injury caused to the plaintiff when an adulterated anaesthetic was used during an operation. The adulteration had occurred due to the storage of the ampoules of anaesthetic in disinfectant, a common practice at the time. Of course, once a risk is known then the plaintiff must take appropriate action. Hence, in the decision of **N v United Kingdom Medical Research Council; sub nom Creutzfeld–Jakob Disease Litigation** (1996), one of several cases involving damage caused to recipients of a growth hormone treatment which carried a risk of the users developing CJD, it was held that the United Kingdom Medical Council was under a duty to investigate the risk when it was first identified. Their failure to investigate and suspend use of the treatment was negligent. The issue of prevailing knowledge has assumed a new significance since 1987 with the introduction of the state-of-the-art defence in strict liability. This will be considered in depth in the next chapter.

Of course, if no expertise is professed, the normal standard will apply. Thus, in **Luxmoore-May v Messenger May Baverstock** (1990) a firm of provincial auctioneers were employed to attribute two foxhound paintings and then auction them. They took the paintings to London for examination at Christies, but neither Christies nor the defendants correctly attributed the paintings to Stubbs, a noted eighteenth-century artist. The defendants sold the paintings at auction for £840 but they were subsequently sold at Sothebys for £88,000. The defendants were not liable for negligence as they had acted reasonably and satisfied the standard of care demanded of provincial auctioneers.

11.2.2   Breach of the duty

A breach of the duty occurs when the defendant is shown not to have satisfied the duty placed on him. Where goods and services are concerned, a breach is likely to take one of three forms, either that the manufacturer has produced goods that are defective and his quality control systems are not sufficiently good to have prevented the circulation of the faulty item, or the design of the goods is defective or appropriate instructions for use and warnings were not given such as to allow the plaintiff to use the product safely.

In assessing whether there has been a breach, the defendant has the right to assume that the plaintiff will use the product properly and in accordance with any instructions provided.

11.3   Causation

Liability will arise only if the plaintiff can establish that the defendant's breach of duty caused his injuries. There is no need to show that the defendant's breach was the only cause of the damage, but it must be established that it was one of the causes and that the court should consider it so when deciding liability. The chain of causation between the defendant's breach and the plaintiff's damage must be unbroken and thus the defendant's liability will cease if there has been an intervening act either by the plaintiff or by a third party.

11.4   Defences

When considering causation, the court will assess the extent, if any, to which the plaintiff is responsible for his own injuries. This does not deny the liability of the defendant but permits the court to state that the plaintiff was also culpable and partly responsible for the incident that injured him. While the plaintiff does not owe a duty of care to the defendant, the plaintiff is expected to exercise care and concern for his own safety and it is any lack in this respect that will cause the plaintiff to be held contributorily negligent. The care to be exercised by the plaintiff will be that to be expected of an ordinary reasonable person and thus appropriate allowances will need to be made for children, who can only be expected to act as a reasonable child of their age.

Many of the cases involving contributory negligence will necessarily involve accidents. Thus, for example, a pedestrian who walks into the road without looking and is knocked over will be held partly to blame for his injuries. However, while many cases do arise out of accidents, it is important to note that the defence can be used in respect of claims for economic loss, as shown in the decision of **Cavendish Funding Ltd** *v* **Henry Spencer & Sons Ltd** (1998).

Where contributory negligence has occurred then, by virtue of the Law Reform (Contributory Negligence) Act 1945, it will impact on the amount of damages that the plaintiff will receive. His damages will be reduced by a percentage equivalent to his share of the blame. Thus, if the court finds that the plaintiff was 40 per cent contributorily negligent and that the total value of the claim is £1,000 the plaintiff will receive £1,000 minus 40 per cent, i.e. £600. It may be, of course, that the court will find the plaintiff 100 per cent contributorily negligent, in which case the defendant has a total defence.

In addition to being able to show that the plaintiff was contributorily negligent, the defendant may be able to show that the plaintiff has failed to establish one or more of the essential elements of the tort. Thus, it may be that the plaintiff had failed to show that he was a foreseeable plaintiff to whom there was any duty owed.

The other possible defence lies in the concept *volenti non fit injuria* – the law will not aid a volunteer. This simply means that if the plaintiff has consented to run the risk he cannot complain of any injury that he suffers. Consent is a complete defence. To be valid, the consent must be genuine as opposed to a situation in which the plaintiff really had no choice but to agree to run the risk. For example, in **Smith** *v* **Baker & Sons (1891)**, the plaintiff employee who worked in a quarry complained to his employer on numerous occasions about the danger posed by a crane working overhead. When the plaintiff was injured by a load falling from the crane, the House of Lords held that his decision to continue working despite the risk did not constitute consent.

11.5 Recoverable damage

To be recoverable, the damage suffered must have been of a type that was foreseeable. The leading authority on the point is the Privy Council decision of **Overseas Tankship (UK) Ltd** *v* **Morts Dock and Engineering Co Ltd, The Wagon Mound** (1961). The defendants negligently spilt some oil into the water at a harbour, causing an oil slick. The slick spread to a nearby jetty belonging to the plaintiffs. Some welding work was under way on two ships moored at the jetty and, believing that the oil posed a fire risk, the plaintiffs stopped work. However, work was restarted when an expert confirmed that there was no fire risk from oil on water. Subsequently the two ships and the jetty were damaged when the oil caught fire. The Privy Council held that the defendants were not liable for the damage caused by the fire as damage by fire was unforeseeable. By contrast, damage due to oil pollution would have been foreseeable and provided grounds for recovery.

Once it is established that the type of damage suffered was foreseeable, the defendant is liable for all the damage of that type suffered by the plaintiff even though its extent may be far greater than would have been expected. This is the so-called 'eggshell skull' rule, which says that you must take your plaintiff as you find him and are responsible for whatever level of damage he has actually suffered even though it might be more than would have been suffered by a normal person.

The plaintiff can claim for death and personal injury, together with property damage for personal property and business property. The remaining two heads of damage – nervous shock and economic loss – are both more restrictive and less clear-cut.

11.5.1 Nervous shock

Anybody witnessing an accident may suffer from some degree of shock. In the example of the car accident mentioned earlier there is no doubt that the witness watching from the window did suffer shock. But that alone is not sufficient to found an action in nervous shock. If it were, the defendant in any action would be liable potentially to a very large number of plaintiffs. By the same token, anyone bereaved by an accident is likely to suffer grief, but this is not sufficient to found a nervous shock case. Nervous shock is provable psychiatric damage caused by the defendant's negligence.

Whether the court will hold there to be a duty of care owed to a plaintiff in respect of psychiatric injury was reconsidered by the House of Lords in **White and Others** *v* **Chief Constable of South Yorkshire** (1998), a case arising out of the Hillsborough disaster. Essentially, the extent to which a plaintiff may be able to claim damages for nervous shock will depend on whether he was physically injured in the incident, whether he was put in physical danger but actually suffered only psychiatric damage (a primary victim), whether he was not at physical risk by the incident in question but suffered psychiatric damage as the result of the aftermath or, lastly, was a mere bystander.

When a plaintiff has suffered physical injury in the incident, they will also be able to recover, as a matter of course, for any psychiatric injuries that they suffer. As long as they can establish the normal requirements of the existence of a duty of care, breach, causation and consequent damage, recovery will follow.

Of more interest are the cases involving a 'primary victim' where the victim was put at risk of physical injury but only suffered psychiatric injury. The decision in **White** above confirmed that a primary victim is entitled to recover for psychiatric damage irrespective of whether the threatened physical damage actually occurs. However, the threat of physical injury to the plaintiff and his fear of that possibility must be reasonable in all the circumstances. Thus, in **McFarlane** *v* **Wilkinson** (1997), in which the plaintiff had witnessed the fire on board the oil rig Piper Alpha from a boat 50 yards away, the Court of Appeal held that he could not recover because he was not at risk of injury being a safe distance away from the fire. Any fear of injury was unreasonable. To be a participant in the situation and thereby be able to claim damages, the plaintiff would have needed to show that he was in the actual area of the danger, or that he reasonably thought that he was in danger due to the sudden and unexpected nature of the danger.

However, in the House of Lords' decision of **Page** *v* **Smith** (1995), a case involving a road accident victim, it was shown that where a primary victim can establish a cause of action, the 'eggshell skull' principle will extend to psychiatric damage and the 'eggshell personality'. Thus, if the plaintiff is within the range of persons who are foreseeable as being likely to be injured by the defendant's actions, then the plaintiff is entitled to recover irrespective of whether the damage he actually suffers is physical injury or psychiatric damage. In the **Page** *v* **Smith** decision, the plaintiff was the victim of a road accident caused by the defendant's negligence. Although physically unhurt, the accident caused the onset of myalgic encephalomyelitis (ME), from which the plaintiff already suffered although the condition had been in remission. As a consequence, the plaintiff was forced to give up work. The House of Lords held that he was entitled to recover damages for the nervous shock caused by the accident. As a primary victim of the incident, his right to recover depended on whether the defendant owed him a duty of care, dependent upon whether the defendant could reasonably foresee that the plaintiff could be injured by his actions. As the plaintiff was foreseeable, he was entitled to recover for the psychiatric injury suffered, the absence of a physical injury not being relevant.

The liability of defendants for nervous shock suffered by plaintiffs involved in the immediate aftermath of an accident has caused much judicial discussion, such victims now being termed 'secondary victims' within the classification used in the **White** decision. In another case arising from the Hillsborough case, **Alcock** *v* **Chief Constable of South Yorkshire** (1991), the House of Lords stipulated the three criteria to be used when assessing whether any individual plaintiff could recover for nervous shock as a result of being bereaved in an accident:

1 whether the relationship between the plaintiff and the deceased was sufficiently close for it to be foreseeable that the plaintiff would suffer nervous shock;
2 whether the proximity between the plaintiff and the accident or its immediate aftermath was sufficiently close in both time and space; and
3 whether the plaintiff suffered nervous shock through seeing or hearing the accident or its immediate aftermath.

Clearly, the combination of these factors means that the scope for successful claims in nervous shock is restricted. In practice, the only successful claims are likely to be those from a parent, spouse or fiancé(e) who has witnessed an accident or its immediate aftermath, claims from brothers, brothers-in-law and grandparents having failed in the **Alcock** decision. Similarly, in the **White** decision, claims made by four police officers who were present at the stadium and involved in attempting to revive injured fans and moving the dead failed.

Mere bystanders cannot recover for nervous shock caused by what they have seen in an accident situation, unless it can be shown that there was a sufficient degree of proximity to the accident both in time and place and a close relationship of love and affection between the plaintiff and the deceased.

For many years, the law held that there was a duty of care owed to rescuers, whether the damage they suffered be physical or psychiatric, as held in **Chadwick** *v* **British Railways Board** (1967), in which an amateur rescuer involved in the aftermath of a major rail disaster was held able to recover for the nervous shock that he suffered. This liability was held to exist in recognition of the fact that rescuers will put themselves at risk in order to help others and policy required that such rescuers should be owed a legal duty of care in order to enable them to recover damages for any injury suffered. However, this principle has been completely overturned by the **White** decision, in which the House of Lords ruled that rescuers are not a special case and that they are subject to the normal rules. Thus, if the rescuer is at risk of physical injury, as in the **Chadwick** case, he will be a 'primary victim' and recovery for psychiatric damage will be possible but in the absence of a risk of physical injury rescuers will be deemed 'secondary victims' and not be able to recover.

11.5.2 Economic loss

Of more concern in the commercial context is the limited opportunity to recover for economic loss, i.e. to recover for monetary loss such as profit. The law has always taken a restrictive approach to the recovery of damages for economic loss and recent decisions have confirmed this general position.

One must differentiate between financial loss consequent upon physical injury or property damage and pure economic loss that is not connected to other damage. The distinction is crucial, for the first is recoverable while in most instances the second is not. The decision of **Spartan Steel & Alloys Ltd** *v* **Martin & Co (Contractors) Ltd** (1973) demonstrates the distinction. The defendants cut through a power cable to the plaintiffs' factory, thereby interrupting the electricity supply. The plaintiffs claimed for damage to the metal in their furnace at the time of the power cut and for the lost profit on that metal. They further claimed for the lost profit on another four melts that were planned but could not take place because of the power cut. The court allowed the plaintiffs to recover for the physical damage to the metal in the furnace and the lost profit attached to that damage. However, the plaintiffs could not recover for the lost profit on the other four melts as that was pure economic loss not attributable to any physical damage.

This would mean that, for example, lost earnings due to being hospitalised following injury by a faulty product would be recoverable as being economic loss resultant upon physical injury.

Pure economic loss can seldom be recovered as the rules are very restrictive and firmly applied. Pure economic loss falls basically into three types: that suffered because of an inherent defect in the quality of a product or service, a loss of profit or business of the type seen in **Spartan Steel** caused by the defendant's negligent act and, lastly, that suffered through reliance on negligent advice.

It is clear from the decisions of **D & F Estates Ltd** *v* **Church Commissioners for England** (1988) and **Department of the Environment** *v* **Thomas Bates & Sons** (1990) that the court will not allow a negligence action to recover the cost of repairing a defect in an item. Such a claim should really be made in contract under s 14 of the Sale of Goods Act 1979 (or other equivalent relevant section) by the purchaser of the defective item. As a claim in tort, it would be for pure economic loss and is not permissible. In the **D & F Estates** decision the plaintiff was the lessee and occupier of a flat. The defendant was the builder of the premises, who had employed a sub-contractor to do the plastering in the building. The claim arose because the plastering was sub-standard and the plaster was coming off the walls. The House of Lords held that the defendant builder was not liable because the cost of repairing a defect in a chattel or structure before it had caused any personal injury or physical damage was pure economic loss and not recoverable in tort.

A similar approach was adopted in the **Department of the Environment** case when the House of Lords refused to allow a claim for the cost of remedial work to a building necessary to render the building safe for its design purpose when the defect had not caused any damage to person or property. The House of Lords adopted that approach again in the leading decision of **Murphy** *v* **Brentwood DC** (1990) when holding that a local authority was not liable for the cost of remedying a defect in a property caused by the authority's negligent failure to ensure that the property was designed and built in accordance with building regulations. However, the court did express the opinion that while a complex structure such as a building manufactured and equipped by one contractor must be treated as a single unit for this purpose, ordinary liability in negligence would arise in respect of damage done to the structure by defective ancillary equipment such as central heating or electrical installations.

Pure economic loss such as lost business or loss of profit caused by the negligent act of the defendant is not recoverable, as evidenced in **Spartan Steel**.

The third cause of pure economic loss is likely to be reliance upon negligent advice. The extent to which damage can be recovered in this situation will be considered in the next section.

11.6 Negligent misstatement

Prior to 1963, the law of tort did not recognise any liability for negligent misstatements, only for the fraud-based tort of deceit. However, a new avenue of liability was opened up that year by the unanimous decision of the House of Lords in the case of **Hedley Byrne & Co Ltd** *v* **Heller & Partners Ltd** (1964). Their Lordships decided that liability would arise in respect of a statement made by a defendant to someone with whom he had a special relationship if he had not validly disclaimed his liability. Hedley Byrne were a firm of advertising agents retained to do some work for Easipower Ltd. Wanting to ensure that Easipower were creditworthy, Hedley Byrne asked their bankers to make some inquiries. Heller & Partners, Easipower's bankers, confirmed in a statement headed 'without responsibility' that Easipower were good for their normal business commitments. Relying on this, Hedley Byrne did business with Easipower and lost £17,000 when Easipower went into liquidation. The House of Lords held that there was a duty owed in this situation and that the defendants (Heller & Partners) could be liable for their negligent misstatement. However, on the facts they escaped liability because of the exclusion clause.

Certain factors are relevant when analysing the **Hedley Byrne** decision. It is clear that there must be a relationship between the person making the statement and the person receiving it. This is necessary to set reasonable boundaries to the potential liability of the makers of statements, who might otherwise face an open-ended liability to an infinite number of people. The relationship is the means of establishing to whom a duty is owed. Further, the maker of the statement should know the purpose for which it is to be used and that the recipient will rely on the statement and act upon it without making any other inquiries. The importance attached to the purpose for which the statement was made is evident from two recent decisions, **Smith** *v* **Eric S Bush** (1990) and **Caparo Industries plc** *v* **Dickman** (1990).

Smith *v* **Eric S Bush** investigated the liability of a surveyor for a valuation carried out on a house. While it was undertaken on behalf of a building society, the surveyor knew that it would be shown to the customer, who would rely on it when considering whether to purchase the property. It was held that the surveyor owed a duty of care to the purchaser.

In **Caparo Industries plc** *v* **Dickman** the duties of auditors were analysed. The auditors in auditing the accounts of a company called Fidelity plc for the year ended 31 March 1984 negligently concluded that the company had made a pre-tax profit of £1.3 million whereas in fact it had made a loss of £400,000. In reliance on these accounts, Caparo Industries bought shares in the company and mounted a successful takeover bid. On discovering the real state of the company, Caparo Industries sued the auditors. The House of Lords held that the auditors did not owe any duty of care to potential investors in general or to individual shareholders who might rely on the accounts when considering further share purchases. The purpose of accounts is to allow the shareholders of a company as a body to exercise informed control over the company and not to provide information for potential investors. The duties of an auditor were revisited by the Court of Appeal in the decision of **Galoo Ltd** *v* **Bright Grahame Murray** (1995). In that case it was held that, while there is no duty owed to potential bidders in general, if an auditor is aware that a particular identified bidder or lender will rely on the audited accounts and the auditor intends that he should so rely, a duty of care then exists and the auditor will be liable for any loss caused through the negligent compilation of the accounts.

A commercial situation of particular note exists where the plaintiff has relied upon a negligent piece of advice from the defendant when deciding whether to enter into business with the defendant. While a contract action may exist in misrepresentation, the related issue is whether there is a tortious duty of care such as to give rise to liability under the principles of **Hedley Byrne**. This issue has been explored in two cases, **Esso Petroleum Co Ltd** *v* **Mardon** (1976) and **Williams and Reid** *v* **Natural Life Health Foods Ltd and Mistlin** (1998), which considered whether there was a special relationship between the parties. In the **Esso** case, the plaintiff was the lessee of a petrol station from Esso Petroleum Ltd. During the negotiations, Esso had provided advice about the expected turnover of the site, indicating that Mardon would sell approximately 200,000 gallons of petrol per year. Relying on the statement, Mardon agreed to lease the garage. In the event, he sold only 78,000 gallons and sued. The Court of Appeal held that a special relationship did exist between Esso and Mr Mardon and that he could recover damages for their negligent misstatement. By contrast, in **Williams and Reid** *v* **Natural Life Health Foods Ltd and Mistlin** it was held that no special relationship existed. The plaintiff had acquired a franchise for a health food shop from the defendants, relying upon statements about projected profits included in literature supplied by the defendants. The literature proved to be wrong and the plaintiff was eventually forced to close his business. When Natural Life Health Foods went into liquidation, the plaintiff tried to pursue an action against Mr Mistlin, who had been the managing director of the company. It was held that he was not liable as no special relationship existed between Mistlin personally and the plaintiff, a relationship between the company and the plaintiff not being sufficient to give effect to personal liability on the directors. There was no evidence to suggest that Mistlin had taken on any personal liability over and above his normal liabilities as a director and, hence, he was not liable.

The provision of references for employees is a normal part of business life and can have a significant effect on a prospective new employer. The House of Lords in **Spring** *v* **Guardian Assurance plc** (1995) held that an employer, when providing a reference for an employee, whether present or past, owes a duty of care to the employee and will be liable to him in damages for any economic loss suffered by the employee as the result of a reference being prepared negligently. This duty exists in tort, although it may, in appropriate circumstances, also be held to arise as the result of an implied term in the contract of employment.

11.6.1 Liability for services

In practice, the majority of advice received by any business will be from paid advisers such as solicitors, accountants, marketing agencies, etc. In these situations, there will be a contract for the provision of the advisory service governed by the Supply of Goods and Services Act 1982. As s 13 of the Act requires that the provider of a service acts with appropriate skill and care, an action for breach of contract would exist if the advice were negligent. This would permit the recovery by a contracting party of all direct consequential loss, including economic loss, under the normal rules of contract. Of course, this remedy would not normally extend to anyone suffering damage who was not a party to the contract.

However, as regards tortious liability, the House of Lords made clear in the decision of **Henderson** *v* **Merrett Syndicates Ltd** (1995) that the rules of **Hedley Bryne** *v* **Heller** do apply to the negligent provision of services if a special relationship exists between the plaintiff and the defendant. In that case, 'Lloyds Names' (people who invest in syndicates in the insurance market and have an unlimited liability in the event of a claim but for whom the market typically provides a sound investment with good financial returns) were liable to pay vast sums in respect of insurance claims arising out of a series of major incidents, both natural and man-made. As a consequence, many faced financial ruin and sought compensation from the managers of the syndicates who were responsible for running them and for looking after the Names' financial interests. The House of Lords held that duty of care existed and recovery was possible.

This approach to services was re-examined in **White** *v* **Jones** (1995) and **Goodwill** *v* **British Pregnancy Advisory Service** (1996) when the courts looked again at the scope and boundaries of the special relationship. In the **White** decision, a solicitor was held liable for his failure to amend the terms of a will within a reasonable time. The testator died and the beneficiary of the intended amendments to the will was not able to receive the bequest. It was held that the solicitor did owe a duty of care to the intended beneficiary in that situation. By contrast, in the **Goodwill** decision, there was no special relationship and hence no duty of care owed to the plaintiff in respect of an unwanted pregnancy some three years after her partner had had a vasectomy provided by the defendants. It transpired that the plaintiff did not have a relationship with the man at the time of the vasectomy and, thus, the court held that no duty of care existed and she could not recover.

11.7 Vicarious liability

Any business acts through its personnel, from the managing director at the top to the newest junior clerk at the bottom. Vicarious liability addresses the extent to which a business may be held liable for the negligent acts of its employees while they are working for the business.

Two criteria must be satisfied if the employer is to be held liable: first, it must be shown that the person committing the tortious act is an employee and not an independent contractor and, second, the tortious incident must have occurred during the course of the person's employment.

The distinction between employees and independent contractors is vital as the employer will have vicarious liability for his employees but not his contractors. The original test was the so-called 'control' test whereby if the employer had the power to dictate both what the worker did and how he did it, the worker would be an employee. However, with increasingly sophisticated machinery and skills, this test has proved too simplistic and has been replaced with a multiple test involving factors such as who pays the worker's wages, who provides any necessary equipment and whether the worker must undertake the work personally or can delegate it to another person. In practice, an independent contractor is likely to be in business for himself.

Liability attaches only in respect of tasks done by the employee in the course of his employment. Anything falling outside the course of his employment remains the personal liability of the individual employee. Thus, if he undertakes an activity for which he was not employed, the employer may reject liability for his actions. Similarly, no vicarious liability arises in respect of acts that the employer has expressly forbidden, although liability will arise if the employee does an authorised act in an unauthorised manner. Thus in **Limpus** *v* **London General Omnibus** (1862) the defendant bus company were held liable for an accident caused by one of their drivers while he was 'racing' in the bus. While the defendant had forbidden drivers to race, they had employed the individual employee to drive buses, which is what he was doing. It was an authorised act carried out in an unauthorised manner.

An employer may even be liable for the fraudulent acts of his employees if they were committed in the course of the employment. Thus in **Lloyd** *v* **Grace Smith & Co** (1912) a firm of solicitors were held liable for the fraudulent act of their managing clerk when he defrauded a client.

Under vicarious liability the employer can be held liable to any foreseeable plaintiff under the normal rules of negligence. In particular, this includes other employees who may be affected by the tortious act.

Vicarious liability has the effect of providing the plaintiff with an additional defendant for, naturally, the employee remains liable for his own tortious actions as well. In practice, one would expect most plaintiffs to opt to sue the employer on the basis that he is more likely to be in a financial position to satisfy the claim. If the employer is sued, he assumes the rights and liabilities of the employee and thus would be able to claim the benefit of any defences that would have been open to the employee.

Question

Yazoo Ltd is a wholesaler storing large quantities of goods in a warehouse. Bill was an employee employed to drive a fork-lift truck. He received appropriate training and the company had stressed to him the importance of driving the truck carefully and safely with due regard for other people on the premises. One afternoon, Bill was hurrying to finish a job and backed the truck too quickly through a plastic dividing screen without checking whether anyone was standing on the other side. He knocked over Fred, the stores manager, and David, a visiting surveyor who had come to inspect the premises. Both were injured.

Advise Yazoo Ltd and Bill about their potential liability, if any, as a result of this incident.

Answer

This question involves the vicarious liability of Yazoo Ltd for the actions of its employee, Bill, and the type of person who can make a claim in a work-based accident.

Employers are vicariously liable for the actions of their employees while those employees are acting in the course of their employment. This is so even if the employee is doing his appointed task in a manner specifically forbidden by the employer, as in **Limpus** v **London General Omnibus** (1862). The employer ceases to be liable only if the employee is on a frolic of his own, i.e. doing something other than his appointed job.

Bill is employed to drive a fork-lift truck and was doing so when the accident occurred. Therefore, Yazoo Ltd is vicariously liable for his actions despite its instructions and despite providing him with appropriate training. Naturally, Bill is also liable for his actions.

Clearly, there is a duty of care owed to other people on the premises as it is foreseeable that such people could be hurt if Bill performed his job negligently. This duty has been breached with the result that Fred and David have been hurt. Both of them are entitled to claim for their injuries. Under common law there was no duty owed to fellow employees, with the result that Fred would have been unable to claim. However, this position no longer exists and a duty of care is owed to fellow employees. Fred has a valid claim.

Therefore, both Yazoo Ltd and Bill will be liable in negligence.

Further reading

Elliott, C and Quinn, F (1999). *Tort Law*, 2nd edn (Longman)

Harvey, B W and Parry, D L (1996). *The Law of Consumer Protection and Fair Trading*, 5th edn (Butterworth)

Lunney, M and Oliphant, K (2000). *Tort Law: Text and Materials* (Oxford University Press)

Markesinis, B S and Deakin, S F (1999). *Tort Law*, 4th edn (Oxford University Press)

12 Product liability

12.1 Introduction

There has been increasing concern over the ability of the law of negligence to cope with liability for injuries caused by defective products since the late 1960s and early 1970s, a concern made more real by the apparent inability of the negligence system to provide a remedy for the victims of the thalidomide tragedy. In 1973 a Royal Commission was set up under the chairmanship of Lord Pearson to consider and make proposals on civil liability and compensation for personal injury. This Commission, which reported in 1978 (Cmnd 7054 (1978)), came out strongly in favour of the adoption of a system of strict liability for the producers of defective products. This accorded with the conclusions of the joint Law Commission and Scottish Law Commission report *Liability for Defective Products* (Law Commission No 82, Scot Law Commission No 45, Cmnd 6831 (1977)) published in 1977, which likewise wished to see the implementation of a system of strict liability in Britain.

Strict liability negates the need for the plaintiff to show that anyone is to blame for his injuries. The emphasis is switched away from the blameworthiness of the tortfeasor, as occurs in negligence, and concentrates instead on the defective condition of the product. To found a claim, therefore, the plaintiff must demonstrate that the product in question was faulty and that there was a causal link between the defect and the injuries suffered. Whether the defect arose through negligence is not relevant.

12.2 The American experience

Strict liability for defective products was not a totally new concept; it was already in place in America, where it had been expounded in 1963 by Justice Trayner in the decision of **Greenman *v* Yuba Power Products** (1963), who declared on behalf of a unanimous court:

> A manufacturer is strictly liable in tort when an article he places on the market knowing that it is to be used without inspection for defects, proves to have a defect which causes injury to a human being . . .

This strict liability duty is intended to protect the same people to whom a duty of negligence would be owed in Britain by virtue of **Donoghue *v* Stevenson**. The

Greenman case was followed only two years later by the statutory Restatement of Torts, 2d, s 402A of which stipulates that 'one who sells any product in a defective condition unreasonably dangerous . . . is subject to liability for physical harm caused to the ultimate user or consumer'. This statutory statement of strict liability for products has now been adopted in the vast majority of states.

Unfortunately, the American experience of strict product liability has been far from happy, although the difficulties are more to do with the American legal system than with the concept of strict liability. The problems are threefold: pro-plaintiff juries, punitive damages and the contingency fee system.

America, unlike Britain, uses juries to decide liability in product liability cases and it is suggested that juries tend to be pro-plaintiff in that they are biased in favour of the injured plaintiff rather than the defendant producer and that this may influence their decision in the case. This would certainly explain some of the more extreme decisions such as **Luque v McLean** (1972), a Californian decision, which effectively required manufacturers to make their products idiotproof. In that case the plaintiff had put his hand through an unguarded hole in the cover of a rotary lawn mower when the machine was switched on. The second problem is the use of punitive damages, the purpose of which is to punish the defendant producer rather than compensate the injured plaintiff. These punitive damages come to the plaintiff as a windfall in addition to any award of compensatory damages. The example quoted most often is the case of **Grimshaw v Ford Motor Co** (1981), in which the plaintiff received 90 per cent burns when his Ford Pinto car burst into flames after being hit from the rear. The plaintiff received $2,842,000 in compensatory damages and a further $125,000,000 in punitive damages. While the punitive damages were reduced to $3,500,000 on appeal, the case still demonstrates the willingness of American courts to award significant sums in damages.

The third recognised issue is the existence of the contingency fee system. Under this system, the advocate receives as his fee a percentage of the damages awarded to the plaintiff with the obvious risk that if the case is lost he does not earn anything. The effect of this system has been twofold. First, plaintiffs have become more litigious for they have nothing at risk; if they win they get the damages, if they lose they owe nothing to their lawyer. Second, where the plaintiff wins his action, it may lead to an award of artificially inflated damages by the jury to allow for the lawyer claiming his percentage.

In addition to these three acknowledged features of the American legal system, other developments have put further strain on the American system and consequently on people producing for the American market. The decision of the Californian Supreme Court in **Sindell v Abbott Laboratories** (1980) developed the concept of 'market share liability', under which liability was imposed upon the producers of a defective drug without proof of causation, their individual liability being for a percentage of the damages equivalent to their percentage share of the market for the drug at the time of distribution. The **Sindell** case revolved around the so-called 'DES Daughters', who developed vaginal and cervical cancers as a result of being exposed to the drug diethylstilbestrol (DES) while *in utero*. These side effects did not become apparent until approximately 10 to 12 years after birth and sometimes not until the plaintiff was in her twenties. After that period it was impossible to prove which company (of approximately 200–300 producers) had manufactured the particular pill that had caused the damage to any individual plaintiff. The court apportioned the liability between the five defendant companies to the action who, together, accounted for approximately 90 per cent of production. The application of strict product liability in America caused a crisis within the production sector as producers found it increasingly difficult to obtain insurance to cover their potential liability. Producers in some industries, notably the high-risk industries such as drug production, found it impossible to get insurance cover and were forced to 'go bare' and run the risk of liquidation if faced with a successful product liability action. Producers from other countries likewise found it difficult to get insurance cover for products being exported to America because of the potential legal exposure in that jurisdiction.

12.3 Consumer Protection Act 1987

Reform in Britain arose out of the implementation of Directive 85/374/EEC on product liability. This Directive was first proposed in 1976 with the intention of harmonising European law on product liability and increasing protection for users of defective products. However, because of deep-rooted divisions of opinion among the member states, the Directive in its final form contained three derogations which allow member states to assert their own preferences. Two of these derogations, which relate to global financial limits for liability under the Directive and the inclusion of a development risk defence, are still in force and seriously undermine the concept of harmonisation. The third derogation created an exception for certain primary agricultural products. However, by virtue of Directive 99/34/EC, this derogation was withdrawn and the 1985 Directive now applies to unprocessed primary agricultural products. The derogations have the combined effect of encouraging 'forum shopping', where the plaintiff in an action, if faced with the possibility of suing in more than one jurisdiction, will opt for that most beneficial to his claim. Given the movement of components and finished products between member states and the increased mobility of purchasers within the Community, it is entirely feasible that a British tourist on holiday in France might purchase a product manufactured in Germany containing a defective component manufactured in Italy. The scope for forum shopping is obvious. Directive 85/374/EEC was given force in Britain by Part I of the Consumer Protection Act 1987, which came into effect on 1 March 1988.

12.3.1 'Producer' and 'product'

Section 1 of the Consumer Protection Act 1987 defines some of the key terms used in the Act. Thus, a 'producer' in relation to a product means:

(a) the person who manufactured it;
(b) in the case of a substance which has not been manufactured but has been won or abstracted, the person who won or abstracted it;
(c) in the case of a product which has not been manufactured, won or abstracted but essential characteristics of which are attributable to an industrial or other process having been carried out (for example, in relation to agricultural produce), the person who carried out that process.

This definition recognises that there is a variety of ways in which a person may be responsible for the production of a product. Apart from the manufacture of a product, it acknowledges that some products (such as coal) exist already but need to be abstracted from the earth before they are in a usable form. Further, it acknowledges the potential significance of other processes that may be needed to bring the product to fruition. Thus a firm involved in assembling products from components bought in for that purpose would be classed as a producer with the consequent liability as such. Likewise, in respect of agricultural produce, some processes sufficiently change the character of the goods to mean that production of a new product has taken place. For example, the production of apple juice by squeezing apples would fall into this category and the person producing the juice would be a 'producer'.

'Product' for the purposes of Part I of the 1987 Act means any goods or electricity, including any component part or raw material comprised in another product. The previous exclusion in respect of 'any game or agricultural produce . . . at a time when it had not undergone an industrial process' has now been overruled by the Consumer Protection Act 1987 (Product Liability) (Modification) Order 2000, which has implemented Directive 99/34/EC. The net effect is that the Act now applies to primary agricultural products and game. Thus, in respect of food, product liability now extends from farm to fork, an important addition to consumer protection given recent food scares (see Chapter 15 for more information about food safety law).

An unresolved issue is whether computer software is classed as a product for this purpose. Clearly, computer hardware is a product and poses no difficulty of interpretation, but computer software is a different proposition. The true value of a piece of software is not the actual disk (which may be worth only a few pounds) but the intellectual property stored on it. The loss of this could have far-reaching consequences within any business, as could the introduction of a computer virus via a piece of software. This issue has been addressed in respect of sale of goods legislation by the decision of **St Albans City and District Council** v **International Computers Ltd** (see Chapter 7), which held that, in some circumstances, software could be classed as goods. We will have to wait to see whether the courts follow the same approach in respect of product liability.

12.3.2 Who is liable

One advantage to an injured user of a defective product is that the Act has broadened the range and number of potential defendants, all of whom are jointly and severally liable. The plaintiff can decide which defendant he wishes to sue and is most unlikely ever to face the situation where there is no accessible defendant, as can happen under both contract and negligence. Under contract the plaintiff is limited by privity (with the exception of third party rights) and may discover that his supplier has either ceased to exist or, in a non-consumer sale, has validly excluded his liability. Similarly in negligence, he can sue only the negligent defendant, the identity of any other party involved in the production or distribution process being irrelevant. Section 2(2) places liability for any damage caused wholly or partly by any defect in a product upon:

(a) the producer of the product;

(b) any person who, by putting his name on the product or using a trade mark or other distinguishing mark in relation to the product, has held himself out to be the producer of the product;

(c) any person who has imported the product into a Member State from a place outside the Member States in order, in the course of any business of his, to supply it to another.

The first and third are straightforward, for the first includes anyone who falls within the definition of 'producer' while the third places liability on the initial importer into the Community. The latter means that, with at least one identifiable defendant within the Community subject to Community legislation, the injured defendant is not faced with enforcing unknown product liability laws in a foreign jurisdiction. The second relates to the use of 'own-branding' whereby one person passes off goods manufactured by another person as his own. It is most common at retail level with department stores and, more latterly, supermarkets indulging in the practice. Clearly it has marketing advantages because it develops and emphasises a store's identity in the public mind, but it does leave the own-brander exposed to legal liability. The wording used on the packaging will be crucial in deciding whether the own-brander has 'held himself out to be the producer of the product'. If the only name that appears on the product is that of the own-brander, then he has done so. If however, the packaging reads to the effect 'specially prepared for X' there is a clear implication that another person actually produced the product and the own-brander may be nothing more than a supplier able to evade liability by revealing the name of his supplier. Lastly, if the producer's name appears on the pack along with the own-brander's, the own-brander will be merely a supplier.

Section 2(3) fixes secondary liability on anyone who supplied the defective product, whether to the injured person or to someone else. Such a supplier will be liable, however, only if he fails to identify his own supplier (whether still in existence or not) within a reasonable period of being so requested by the injured person.

12.3.3 Defective

Defects fall into three main categories: manufacturing defects, design defects and 'duty to warn' defects. The first, manufacturing defects, occur when the product deviates from the manufacturer's specification. It is a rogue product and, however good a manufacturing system the producer may employ, it is a statistical certainty that rogue products will occur. If the producer's quality control system fails to recognise the rogue item, a defective product will reach the market. The cost of damage done by such products can be covered by insurance with the risk spread among purchasers of the item through a few extra pence on the price. The second type of defect, design defects, has a far greater potential for harm. In this situation the product accords with the specification but the specification itself is defective and poses a risk. This has very serious economic ramifications for a business as it means that whole production runs, as opposed to isolated items, will be faulty. This may involve scrapping whole batches prior to distribution or removing them from sale, or even mounting a product recall with the attendant publicity that causes. At its most extreme a design defect may cause catastrophic damage such as occurred with thalidomide with consequent heavy liability. The final type of defect is the 'duty to warn' defect, where the accident has occurred because the producer failed to warn the user about dangers posed by the product and how to use the product safely. The meaning of defective within Part I of the 1987 Act is crucial to establishing liability, for liability arises only in respect of defective products. The term is considered in s 3(1), which states that a product is defective for the purposes of Part I if:

> the safety of the product is not such as persons generally are entitled to expect; and for those purposes 'safety' in relation to a product, shall include safety with respect to products comprised in that product and safety in the context of risks of damage to property, as well as in the context of risks of death or personal injury.

The test is an objective one, being based on the expectations of consumers generally rather than the plaintiff in particular. In applying the test the court must consider all the circumstances, including three factors specifically mentioned in s 3(2). The first is 'the manner in which, and purposes for which, the product has been marketed, its get-up, the use of any mark in relation to the product and any instructions for, or warnings with respect to, doing or refraining from doing anything with or in relation to the product'. This covers a variety of factors such as whether the product was aimed at children or adults, whether appropriate safety features were included to take account of the likely product users, the quality and relevance of instructions for use and, of course, whether appropriate warnings of potential dangers were provided. As we have already seen, a failure to provide appropriate warnings is considered to be a defect.

In assessing defectiveness the utility of the product can be crucial. For example, it is widely accepted that many drugs have side effects but the risk posed by them is tolerated as long as they are less serious than the illness being treated. In a risk–benefit analysis, the product is not defective.

The second specific factor drawn to the court's attention is 'what might reasonably be expected to be done with or in relation to the product'. It is reasonable to impose liability for defects that occur while the product is being used for one of its usual purposes, but it would be unreasonable to expect producers to be liable for injuries caused through product misuse if that use was not reasonably foreseeable. However, it may be reasonable to expect producers to issue appropriate warnings in respect of foreseeable misuse.

The last of the three specific factors mentioned in s 3(2) is 'the time when the product was supplied by its producer to another'. The section also states that a product shall not be deemed defective merely because a later product is safer. This requires the court to consider the safety of the product and therefore its defectiveness in the context of the time when it was produced. Products move on with newer, safer versions being developed, and it would be unrealistic to judge one product by comparison with a later version. This idea of judging situations in their own context was overtly considered as far back as 1954 in the decision of **Roe v Minister of**

Health (1954) when the court ruled in a medical negligence case that 'we must not look at the 1947 accident with 1954 spectacles'. Further, this protection must be afforded to producers if we are to encourage product development, for if producers were to be penalised for improving their products, improvements would never take place and innovation would be non-existent.

In practice, there have been only a handful of court cases relating to claims under the Consumer Protection Act 1987, two of which related to whether or not the goods were defective under s 3. These were the decisions of **Worsley _v_ Tambrands Ltd** (2000) and **Richardson _v_ LRC Products Ltd** (2000), with the claim failing in both instances. The **Tambrands** case concerned an alleged duty to warn defect. The plaintiff suffered toxic shock syndrome from the use of a tampon and alleged that the product was defective because of a failure to warn of the risk on the outside of the box rather than on a leaflet contained in the box, which might not be read or kept. The court ruled that the warnings were sufficient and therefore that the product was not defective. Equally, the court held that there was no liability in the **Richardson** case, in which the plaintiff was claiming damages for becoming pregnant when the condom that her husband was using burst during intercourse. It was accepted by both parties that the condom had ozone damage but the preferred opinion was that this had occurred when the used condom was being stored prior to the legal hearing. Scientific evidence was that condoms did burst sometimes for no apparent reason and the court held that the claim had not been proved.

12.3.4 Defences

The 1987 Act imposes strict liability, not absolute liability. Consequently s 4 provides six defences that are open to anyone sued under Part I of the Act. The first is that the defect is attributable to compliance with any requirement imposed by or under any enactment or with any Community obligation. Note that the defence applies only if compliance with the requirement is mandatory and the compliance is the cause of the defect. Even though standards agreed by a group of people with vested interests often reflect the lowest common denominator rather than the highest common factor, it still seems unlikely that compliance with a regulation would itself be the cause of a defect.

Section 4(1)(b) provides a defence if the defendant did not at any time supply the product to another. This will provide protection in two possible situations where the defendant has acted innocently. The first is where the product has been stolen from him and put into circulation by the thief. The producer may be able to show that the product had failed his own quality control systems and was due to be discarded or destroyed at the time that it was stolen. Clearly accurate production and quality control records would be helpful in establishing this. The second situation is where the goods were not even manufactured by the producer but are counterfeit. Given the quality of some of the counterfeit goods currently in the market it may be virtually impossible for the purchaser to recognise that they are imitation. For the producer, however, it is the perfect defence. Further, while the supply of counterfeit goods may no longer be a criminal offence under s 1 of the Trade Descriptions Act 1968 as long as the supplier makes clear that the goods are not genuine, as held in **Kent County**

Council *v* **Price** (1993), such a supply would still constitute an offence under the Trade Marks Act 1994 and/or the tort of 'passing off'.

The defence contained in s 4(1)(c) is designed to protect private sellers. It requires both that the supply by the defendant was not in the course of a business and that the defendant is either not a producer within the meaning of s 2(2) or that while they are a producer they acted otherwise than with a view to a profit. This defence will protect voluntary organisations such as the Guide movement or the Boys Brigade who produce and supply goods for sale to raise funds. The fourth defence is that the defect did not exist at the relevant time. The relevant time for a defendant under s 2(2) (i.e. producer, own-brander or importer) is the time at which they supplied the product to another person. For any other defendant (i.e. a supplier under s 2(3)) the relevant time is the last occasion on which a producer, own-brander or importer supplied the product. Thus no liability under the 1987 Act exists in respect of any defect that was introduced to the product after it last left the control of a s 2(2) defendant. Damages in respect of defects introduced later remain recoverable under the law of negligence.

The fifth and most controversial of the defences is the so-called 'development risk' defence found in s 4(1)(e). This states that it is a defence to show:

> that the state of scientific and technical knowledge at the relevant time was not such that a producer of products of the same description as the product in question might be expected to have discovered the defect if it had existed in his products while they were under his control.

This defence is one of the optional derogations included in Directive 85/374/EEC on product liability, disagreement about the inclusion of such a defence being one of the major causes of the delay in its implementation. Approximately half of the member states have opted to include the defence to some extent in their national legislation. Britain opted to include the defence, as producers argued that it would be unfair to hold them responsible for unknowable defects and that to expose them to such liability would affect, adversely, future developments in industries at the forefront of scientific and technical knowledge. By contrast, the consumer lobby argued that it is not unreasonable to expect producers to accept such liability as they both take the profit from the resultant goods and are in the best position to spread the risk through insurance. The defence seeks to protect producers against damage caused by defects that were unknowable at the time that the product was put into circulation. The acid test is whether the producer might be expected to have discovered the defect. This places a burden on the producer to be up to date with developments in his field and to implement new knowledge as it becomes available. Of particular concern is the extent to which knowledge may be transferable within industries such as to mean that it is available to a producer in a different industry from that in which the research and development has been made. The Directive takes a hard line, limiting the defence to situations where:

> the state of scientific and technical knowledge at the time when [the producer] put the product into circulation was not such as to enable the existence of the defect to be discovered. . . .

There is no mention in the Directive of there being any limitation based on individual industries. By contrast, s 4(1)(e) of the 1987 Act seeks to extend the defence to a producer unless the scientific and technical knowledge was available to other producers of the same product. This is a far more liberal defence and places a less onerous burden on the producer. The validity of this version of the defence was challenged in the decision of **Commission of the European Communities v United Kingdom (C300/95)** but the European Court of Justice held that there was no obvious conflict between s 4(1)(e) of the Act and art 7 of the Directive and, therefore, that the UK version of the defence is valid.

The relevant time for assessing whether the risk was unknowable is the time at which the product was put into circulation, for that is the moment that it passes beyond the control of the producer. Therefore, it is incumbent upon the producer to ensure that there have not been any developments between the date of manufacture of the goods and the time that they leave his control. Clearly, the stockpiling of products by a producer presents a potential risk of liability. Further, any producer would be wise to keep good stock control records so as to establish beyond doubt when any individual item passed out of his control. This could be crucial given that products cannot be declared unsafe and therefore defective purely because a later product is safer.

The practical application of the defence was considered by the Court of Appeal in the decision of **Abouzaid v Mothercare (UK) Ltd (2001)**. In that case, the plaintiff, then aged 12, had lost the sight in one eye when trying to affix a Mothercare product to a pushchair. Mothercare contended that they had a defence under s 4(1)(e) as there were no scientific or technical reports available at the time relating to any other accidents caused by the product. The court held that there was an identifiable defect and that liability under the Act depended upon the public's expectations as to safety. Further, the defendant could have discovered the risk before the plaintiff's accident and that accident reports were not 'technical knowledge' for the purposes of the case. The defendant was liable.

The final defence, which has two potential strands, is aimed at the producers of component parts. The first strand is that the defect in the component is wholly attributable to the design of the product in which it was subsequently used. It may be, for example, that the component was expected to withstand far greater stresses than those for which it was designed. Products such as screws, which may be used for everything from car manufacture to kitchen shelves, are particularly susceptible to this problem. The second strand is that the component producer can demonstrate that he manufactured the component in accordance with a specification provided by the producer of the finished product and that the defect is in the specification rather than in the physical production of the item. Component producers would be well advised to keep copies of all such specifications for future reference.

12.3.5 Recoverable damage

Section 5 prescribes the heads of damage for which compensation can be claimed under Part I of the 1987 Act. Recovery is permitted in respect of death, personal injury and certain property damage. Economic loss is not recoverable.

There are three restrictions on the plaintiff's ability to recover for property damage. First, only damage to private property can be recovered. The property concerned must be of a type ordinarily intended for private use, occupation or consumption and, further, the plaintiff must have intended to use it mainly for his own private use, occupation or consumption. Note that there is no need for it to have been exclusively for the plaintiff's private use. Thus, for example, a private car that is occasionally used for business would be covered. Second, a claim for property damage must exceed £275. The intention of this provision is to prevent a multiplicity of very small claims by restricting such claims to a negligence action. Such an arbitrary rule may, of course, create some apparent unfairness in that a claim for £276 is subject to strict liability while a claim for £274 must be founded in negligence. Lastly, no claim can be made for damage to the defective item itself. As the decision in **Murphy _v_ Brentwood DC** (1990) prevents such recovery in negligence as well (see Chapter 11), the onus is on the purchaser of the item to make a contractual claim under s 14 of the Sale of Goods Act 1979 (or other equivalent relevant section).

In assessing damages the court must consider the extent, if any, to which the plaintiff was responsible for his own injuries as the statutory provisions relating to the reduction of damages for contributory negligence apply to claims under Part I.

12.3.6 Time limits

Two time limits are of interest here. The Limitation Act 1980 as amended by s 6(6) of and Schedule 1 to the Consumer Protection Act 1987 provides that claims for personal injury or property damage must be commenced within three years of the date on which the cause of action accrued or the date of knowledge of the injured party, whichever is the later. In respect of property damage the date of knowledge of the plaintiff includes, if earlier, the date of knowledge of any person in whom the claim was vested previously.

Under s 14(1A) of the Limitation Act the plaintiff's date of knowledge is determined by when he first had knowledge of the following:

(a) such facts about the damage caused by the defect as would lead a reasonable person who had suffered such damage to consider it sufficiently serious to justify his instituting proceedings for damages against a defendant who did not dispute liability and was able to satisfy a judgment; and

(b) that the damage was wholly or partly attributable to the facts and circumstances alleged to constitute the defect; and

(c) the identity of the defendant.

More controversial is the ten-year cut-off period found in s 11A of the Limitation Act 1980, which provides that a claim under Part I of the 1987 Act cannot be brought after the expiration of ten years from the relevant time, i.e. the time when the product last left the control of a producer, own-brander or importer. This cut-off period applies even though the cause of action may not yet have accrued. This is most likely to be of import in cases for drug-related injuries, where the damage may not become obvious for 15 or 12 years after the relevant time. **Sindell** *v* **Abbott Laboratories**, discussed earlier, is a prime example of where the plaintiffs would have been deprived of their right of action under Part I before they were even aware of their injuries. Clearly, this is contrary to the individual consumer's best interests. However, the rationale behind the adoption of such a cut-off period is that it permits a definite end to a producer's liability in respect of any individual product and this eases both the availability of insurance cover and general corporate planning.

The application of this provision was considered in the decision of **H (A Child)** *v* **Merck & Co Inc** (2001), a case brought on behalf of a child who had been injured by a rubella and measles vaccine. An action had been started against Merck as the producer of the vaccine but it had been discovered after the expiration of the ten-year period that the real producer of the vaccine had been S. H's representatives applied to have S substituted as the defendant in the action, the substitution being allowed on the basis that the representatives had been genuinely mistaken within the meaning of the Limitation Act 1980 and the Civil Procedure Rules 1998 when thinking that Merck was the producer.

12.3.7 Global limits

The other derogation still permitted under Directive 85/374/EEC relates to the imposition of global financial limits. Article 16 of the Directive provides that member states may restrict the total liability of any producer to not more than 70 million ECU (approximately £40 million) in respect of death or personal injury caused by identical items with the same defect. The potential problem with such global limits is to find an equitable scheme of payment. One method is to pay compensation to plaintiffs on a first-come first-served basis, in which case those who claim towards the end of the ten-year cut-off period may find that there is no money left to satisfy their claim. An alternative method is that no claims are paid until the expiration of the ten-year period and then all plaintiffs are paid on the same *pro rata* basis. This is fairer but involves making all plaintiffs wait ten years. In the event, Britain has not adopted this derogation, with the result that producers subject to English law have unlimited liability.

12.3.8 Exclusion

Section 7 of the 1987 Act prohibits the limitation or exclusion of Part I liability, whether by contract term, notice or any other provision.

12.3.9 Reform

The European Commission reviews the working of Directive 85/374/EEC every five years. The second report, COM (2000) 893 final, was published on 31 January 2001. It concludes that, at present, there is insufficient evidence to justify any amendments to the Directive. However, the Commission has decided to set up an expert group to look at product liability issues, the legal application of the Directive, recent case law and changes in national law. The Commission also proposes to undertake two studies, one related to the economic impact of introducing producer liability for development risks and abolishing the maximum financial limits for serial incidents while the other will look at the practicalities of the different systems in different member states and whether it is viable to introduce a genuinely uniform product liability system throughout the Community.

Question

Screen Ltd is a manufacturer of television sets which include component parts manufactured by Components Unlimited. While in use, one of these sets caught fire because of a faulty component produced and supplied by Components Unlimited. In the ensuing blaze, a video costing £300 was damaged and the nearby curtains valued at £175 caught alight. Elsie, who was watching the television at the time, burnt her hand while fighting the blaze. Advise Elsie about any claim she may have under Part I of the Consumer Protection Act 1987.

Answer

Elsie is interested in what claim, if any, she has under Part I of the Consumer Protection Act 1987 for the injuries and damage she has suffered as a result of the faulty television.

Product liability under Part I of the 1987 Act is strict and hence Elsie will need to demonstrate only that the set was faulty and that she suffered loss as a result. Given the facts it should not be difficult to prove this. She can sue either Screen Ltd, the producer of the item, or Components Unlimited because it was their defective item that caused the problem. She has suffered personal injury and property damage. The claim for personal injury is straightforward. However, the claim for property damage is slightly more complicated. Under s 5 of the Act the property must be of a type ordinarily intended for private use or consumption and so intended by the actual user. Again, Elsie should have no difficulty with this. The issue is over the value of the damaged property. Section 5(4) states that you cannot claim unless the value of property exceeds £275. Applying this, the cost of the video (£300) can be claimed but the curtains (£175) fall below this threshold. However, the section seems to allow for the total property damage to be added together in which case Elsie's loss is £475 and can be claimed.

Lastly, she cannot claim the cost of the defective item under the 1987 Act. The original purchaser of the item will have to make a claim against the seller under s 14 of the Sale of Goods Act 1979.

Further reading

Atiyah, P S, Adams, J N and MacQueen, H (2001). *The Sale of Goods*, 10th edn (Longman)

Clark, A M (1989). *Product Liability* (Sweet & Maxwell)

Dobson, P (2000). *Sale of Goods and Consumer Credit*, 6th edn (Sweet & Maxwell)

Geddes, A (1992). *Product and Service Liability in the EEC* (Sweet & Maxwell)

Harvey, B W and Parry, D L (1996). *The Law of Consumer Protection and Fair Trading*, 5th edn (Butterworth)

Stapleton, J (1994). *Product Liability* (Butterworth)

Part IV   Consumer protection

13 Criminal liability for false statements

13.1 Introduction

Parts I to III of this book have dealt exclusively with the civil law governing the rights and liabilities between individuals arising out of contract or tort. Such rights are enforced by the two parties to the action with no involvement by the State. The only way that a central government department or local authority would be involved in such an action is as a plaintiff or defendant enforcing its own contractual and tortious rights and obligations.

This Part of the book turns to the criminal law aspect of consumer protection. In this context, criminal law comprises those statutes establishing the basic standards of trading to be enforced by the State. It stipulates the level of behaviour to be expected from traders and the basic level of protection afforded to consumers generally. In most instances enforcement of consumer protection law is the responsibility of local authorities, primarily consumer protection departments, although government departments and the Office of Fair Trading also play a part. Ultimately, enforcement is by means of criminal prosecution.

13.2 Trade Descriptions Act 1968

The Trade Descriptions Act 1968 controls the application of false trade descriptions to goods and services. While the primary purpose of criminal prosecution under this Act is to punish the offender, typically by means of a fine or custodial sentence, it is possible for the victim of the crime to receive compensation as well. Section 130 of the Powers of Criminal Courts (Sentencing) Act 2000 provides that the court has the power to make a compensation order against anyone convicted of an offence up to a maximum of £5,000 per offence. The compensation is to compensate the victim of the crime for any personal injury, loss or damage resulting from the offence.

13.2.1 Goods

Section 1(1) of the Trade Descriptions Act 1968 provides the basic offence prohibiting the application of false trade descriptions to goods. It reads:

> Any person who, in the course of a trade or business,—
> (a) applies a false trade description to any goods; or
> (b) supplies or offers to supply any goods to which a false trade description is applied:
> shall, subject to the provisions of this Act, be guilty of an offence.

The section creates two distinct offences, the first ('applies') being aimed at the primary offender responsible for the creation of the false trade description, while the second ('supplies or offers to supply') is aimed primarily at traders further down the distributive chain who, while not responsible for the creation of the false trade description, have nonetheless supplied goods to which the description is attached. For example, a manufacturer of an electrical item who includes a false trade description on the outer packaging would be guilty of the 'applying' offence, while a retailer who merely bought in the item and resold it would be guilty of the 'supplying' offence.

Note that s 1 does not include any words such as knowingly, intentionally or recklessly and thus creates strict liability offences. There is no need to prove *mens rea* (a guilty mind) as the state of mind of the defendant is irrelevant. 'Goods' are defined for this purpose in s 39 as including ships and aircraft, things attached to land and growing crops. It follows that land and houses are not covered by the Act. However, after much criticism of that fact, misdescriptions of new property are now governed by the Property Misdescriptions Act 1991.

13.2.2 In the course of a trade or business

The Act is aimed at preventing false statements by traders. Hence, ss 1 and 14 apply only if the offence has occurred 'in the course of a trade or business'. This concept is central to criminal liability under this statute and thus its meaning and ambit are crucial. Until 1999, there was a common interpretation applied both to criminal liability under trading legislation including the Trade Descriptions Act 1968 and to civil law liability under, for example, s 14 of the Sale of Goods Act 1979. However, the decision of **Stevenson *v* Rogers** (1999) has altered that situation (see Chapter 7) and thus the interpretation to be applied in criminal law must be considered separately here. The key decisions are **Havering London Borough Council *v* Stevenson** (1970) and **Davies *v* Sumner** (1984), with the bottom line appearing to be that if the supply of the goods could be classed as an integral part of the supplier's business then the supply will be held to be 'in the course of a trade or business'. By contrast, if the supply is ancillary to the supplier's main business, then the supply will not be classed as being 'in the course of a trade or business' and will fall outside the strictures of the Act.

In **Havering London Borough Council *v* Stevenson** a car hire company regularly sold off their hire cars after a period of two years. The court held that this was an integral part of the company's business. By contrast, in **Davies *v* Sumner** the House of Lords decided that the sale by a self-employed courier of the car that he used for his business purposes was not a sale in the course of a trade or business. The car was ancillary to his business rather than part of his stock-in-trade. He could just as easily have used a hire car.

While the prosecution will need to show that the application of the false trade description, or the supply or offer to supply the relevant goods, occurred as an integral part of the defendant's business, the decision in **Kirwin** *v* **Anderson** (1991) makes it clear that there is no need for a profit or commission to have been made. The decision of **Roberts** *v* **Leonard** (1995) confirmed that the Act extends to professional people. In that case, veterinary surgeons were convicted of offences under s 1(1)(b) when they falsely stated on an export health certificate that they had inspected 557 calves instead of the 207 calves that they had actually inspected.

A particular problem is posed where the supply in question is viewed as the first in a series of such sales. In **Abernethie** *v* **A M & J Kleinman Ltd** (1969) it was suggested that such a sale can be in the course of a trade or business. By contrast, the Divisional Court in the later decision of **Devlin** *v* **Hall** (1990), involving the first sale of a taxi by a taxi proprietor, held that the first sale could not establish a normal practice and that there was no liability. The more recent Scottish decision of **Elder** *v* **Crowe** (1996) has one again suggested that the first sale is capable of being in the course of a trade or business. A related issue is that of the hobbyist and the point at which a hobby becomes a trade or business, as in **Blakemore** *v* **Bellamy** (1982).

There is no requirement that the person applying the false trade description is the seller or supplier of the goods. It is clear from the decision of **Fletcher** *v* **Budgen** (1974) that an offence can be committed by a trader buying goods in the course of a business. In that case, a car trader told a customer that his car was irreparable and had only scrap value. Having bought the car for £2, the dealer spent some money repairing it before offering it for sale for £135. The trader was convicted of an offence against the Trade Descriptions Act 1968.

13.2.3 Trade description

Consideration of the meaning of the phrase 'trade description' is central to the provisions and enforcement of the Act. Section 2 provides that a trade description is an indication, direct or indirect, and by whatever means given, with respect to the goods or parts of them or any of a variety of factors. The factors are listed in s 2(1) and are:

(a) *quantity, size or gauge*: this would include length, width, height, area, capacity, volume, for example 2 litres, 4 tonnes, 72 centimetres wide, 20 denier;
(b) *method of manufacture, production, processing or reconditioning*: for example hand-made, organically grown;
(c) *composition*: for example plastic, stainless steel, oak, Harris tweed;
(d) *fitness for purpose, strength, performance, behaviour or accuracy*: for example child-resistant, rustproof;
(e) *any physical characteristics not included in the preceding paragraphs*: colour and shape would be included here;
(f) *testing by any person and results thereof*: for example MOT;
(g) *approval by any person or conformity with a type approved by any person*: for example the use of the BSI Kitemark. Note that there is a specific offence under s 12 of falsely claiming approval by a member of the Royal Family or using

without authority any device or emblem signifying the Queen's Award to Industry;

(h) *place or date of manufacture, production, processing or reconditioning*: for example made in England, 1999 car, locally grown;

(i) *person by whom manufactured, produced, processed or reconditioned*: for example Rolls Royce;

(j) *other history, including previous ownership or use*: the most common example here is that applied by the mileometer on a car, for example 39,000 miles. Other examples would include 'one owner'.

Any description that does not fit into one of the categories listed is not a trade description for the purposes of the Act. Thus in **Cadbury Ltd** *v* **Halliday** (1975) a bar of chocolate bore the legend 'Extra Value' on the outer wrapper. The Divisional Court held that this did not constitute a trade description. All the factors in s 2 are for definite identifiable characteristics of the item, whereas 'value' is an imprecise term and 'extra' merely added further uncertainty.

13.2.4 False trade description

To be actionable the trade description complained of must be 'false' within the meaning given to that term by the Act. Section 3(1) stipulates the basic requirement that a trade description is false for the purposes of the Act if it is false to a material degree. This confirms that the falsity must be substantial and that the law is not concerned with trivialities. Each case will be dependent on its facts, but it would be reasonable to assume that the section is concerned with criminal liability arising from descriptions that would mislead a potential purchaser rather than with advertising puffs that an average person would not treat seriously. In **R** *v* **Ford Motor Company** (1974) a car was described as a 'new Ford Cortina'. In fact, the car had received slight damage while in a compound and had been repaired at a cost of £50 to be as good as new. The Court of Appeal held that the car had not been misdescribed.

Section 3(2) further states that where a trade description, though not false, is misleading to a material degree, it shall be deemed to be a false trade description. This covers both those statements which though strictly true are nonetheless misleading and those where only half the truth has been told. Thus, in **R** *v* **Inner London Justices,** *ex parte* **Another** (1983) a car was described as having had one previous owner. This was strictly true but the one owner had been a car leasing company and the car had been used by five different clients.

Section 3(3) provides that anything which, though not a trade description, is likely to be taken for an indication of any of those matters and, as such an indication, would be false to a material degree, shall be deemed to be a false trade description. This catchall provision would have the effect of covering an indication given by some means other than those expected. A prime example would be where the goods have effectively lied about themselves. Two cases illustrate this.

In **Cottee** *v* **Douglas Seaton (Used Cars) Ltd** (1972) the owner of a rusty car had repaired it with plastic filler without seeking to disguise the fact. He sold it to the defendant garage, who smoothed down the filler and painted over it to disguise its existence. The defendant then sold it to another garage, who, in turn, sold it to a customer, who was involved in an accident. While the defendant escaped liability on a technicality, the court was satisfied that the deliberate concealment of the repair constituted a false trade description.

The size of a container may also be a false trade description. Thus, in the decision of **R v A F Pears Ltd** (1982) the company packed moisturising cream in double-skinned containers which had false bottoms. While the correct weight of the cream was shown on the container, the volume of the container was approximately 30 per cent larger than the volume of the cream it contained. The court held that the container was capable of being construed as a description within s 3(3) as to the volume of the product, one of the factors listed in s 2.

Section 3(4) makes it an offence to suggest approval by a non-existent person or compliance with a non-existent standard.

13.2.5 Applying

The offence under s 1(1)(a) requires that the defendant applied the false trade description. Section 4(1) states that a person applies a trade description to goods if he:

(a) affixes or annexes it to or in a manner marks it on or incorporates it with—
   (i) the goods themselves, or
   (ii) anything in, on or with which the goods are supplied; or
(b) places the goods in, on or with anything which the trade description has been affixed or annexed to, marked on or incorporated with, or places any such thing with the goods; or
(c) uses the trade description in any manner likely to be taken as referring to the goods.

This subsection covers a wide range of methods by which a trade description may be applied. Clearly it includes labels on the goods or on packaging, but it has a much greater impact than that. Shelf edge tickets such as appear in most trade warehouses and self-service retail premises would be covered, as would posters in shops or warehouses and point-of-sale literature placed near the goods. Hence, in **Roberts v Severn Petroleum & Trading Co Ltd** (1981) the defendants were found guilty of an offence of applying a false trade description contrary to s 1(1)(a) when a petrol station displayed Esso signs on the premises when not supplying Esso petrol.

Application of a false trade description may also occur by omission of relevant information. For example, in **R v Haesler** (1973) a car which had been registered first in the Channel Islands was re-registered when it was brought to England. The registration book was stamped with the words 'Ex Channel Islands' to indicate that the car was re-registered and thus older than its registration number suggested. The defendant car dealer erased the words 'Ex Channel Islands' from the registration document. It was held that this amounted to the application of a false trade description and an offence against s 1(1) had been committed.

Further, the case of **Cavendish Woodhouse Ltd** *v* **Wright** (1985) held that it is possible to use a comparison with other goods as a means of description. In that decision the defendant was found guilty of an offence for failing to supply goods identical with those on display, having promised to do so.

Application not only relates to documentary or written descriptions but by virtue of s 4(2) expressly includes oral descriptions. The difficulty of oral descriptions is the same as that with oral contracts, namely proof. Evidence of oral descriptions may be difficult to establish unless a witness was present, particularly given that the burden of proof is higher for a criminal prosecution than for a civil law claim. In criminal cases, it is 'beyond reasonable doubt' instead of 'on the balance of probabilities' as is the case in civil law actions.

It is not always the case that the supplier applies the description but rather that he responds to a description applied by the recipient of the goods. Section 4(3) provides that where goods are supplied in pursuance of a request in which a trade description was applied and it is reasonable to assume that the goods supplied corresponded to the description, the supplier will be deemed to have applied the trade description to the goods. As the s 1 offences are strict liability offences there is no need to prove that the defendant knew that the description was false although he will need to be aware that there was a description. Equally, there must be goods to which the description can apply. In **Robins & Day Ltd** *v* **Kent CC Trading Standards Department** (1996) the defendant placed an advert in the window of his premises indicating that he had for sale a 1992 Peugeot 402 with air conditioning at £9,995. None of the remaining cars had air conditioning. The court held, quashing the conviction, that there was no evidence identifying any particular vehicle to which the advertisement related.

There is no requirement that the description actually misled anyone. Thus descriptions that are obviously false are capable of giving rise to liability under s 1(1) if they are applied deliberately. A particular example of the problem relates to the one-time practice of zeroising the mileometers on cars, a practice that had received judicial approval in the case of **K Lill (Holdings) Ltd** *v* **White** (1979) on the basis that a mileage reading of zero on a second-hand car would not mislead anyone. However, in **R** *v* **Southwood** (1987) the Court of Appeal held that the practice was illegal as it is as much the application of a false description to zeroise the mileometer as it is merely to reduce the mileage reading. Either practice results in an inaccurate reading.

While the actual supply of the misdescribed item is not essential to create an offence of application under s 1(1)(a) there must be an ability to supply the goods at some point. Traditionally, it has been assumed that goods could not be supplied to a person who was already their owner. Thus, in **Wycombe Marsh Garages Ltd** *v* **Fowler** (1972) the defendant garage wrongly refused an MOT certificate stating that the tyres on the car were faulty. In fact, they were all right. It was held that the garage had not committed an offence against s 1 as there was no intention to supply the goods at any stage. The garage was undertaking the MOT on behalf of the owner. By contrast however, it was held that a supply had taken place in the decision of **Formula One Autocentres Ltd** *v* **Birmingham City Council** (1999), in which a garage gave a car back to its owner having undertaken repair work on the vehicle for payment. It was held that when the repair work had not been carried out in the way stated, an offence of applying a false trade description had occurred.

13.2.6 Supplies or offers to supply

The s 1(1)(b) offence relates to the supply or offer to supply goods to which a false trade description has been applied. Thus there is the potential for any subsequent supplier to be charged under this subsection. It should be noted that there is no requirement that the goods have been sold, merely offered for supply. This broadens the ambit of the offence considerably for it would cover goods supplied on hire-purchase, barter, promotional free gifts, hire, etc under which the possession of goods changes hands by means other than a contract of sale. The decision of **Wadham Kenning Motor Group Ltd** *v* **Brighton and Hove Council** (1997) confirmed that it applies to conditional sales.

Section 6 stipulates that a person shall be deemed to 'offer to supply' goods when he is 'exposing goods for supply or having goods in his possession for supply'. This section has two interesting phrases. The first 'exposing for supply' means that any goods displayed in a business premises on shelves, or in bins, or in the window would be classed as being offered for supply even though no subsequent supply takes place. There is a presumption that they are intended for supply. Similarly goods on display at an auction would be deemed to be offered for supply. This differs significantly from the contractual position, where goods on display would merely constitute an invitation to treat and not create any civil liability or any obligation to sell, as was held in **Fisher** *v* **Bell** (1961). The second phrase is 'having goods in his possession for supply'. This does not require that the goods are visible. Thus goods stored in a back room or a warehouse would be caught by this provision. This is reasonable given the modern trading practice, notably with larger items, whereby a demonstration model is on display in the seller's premises but the buyer actually receives an item from the stores. Further, there is no requirement that the goods in the seller's possession must necessarily be held at his business premises. In the case of **Stainethorpe** *v* **Bailey** (1980) the defendant car dealer advertised a car with a false mileage reading. The car was parked at his private address rather than at his business premises. The Divisional Court held that the car was in his possession for supply.

13.2.7 Disclaimers

The innocent businessman involved in the supply of goods will wish to protect himself against criminal liability in respect of goods to which someone else has affixed a false trade description. To deal with this situation the courts have re-cognised the validity of disclaimers. A disclaimer is very different in effect from a defence. A defence is an acceptable reason why a defendant should be excused from liability for an offence that has occurred. By contrast, the purpose of a disclaimer is to avoid liability arising by preventing the offence from ever taking place. Thus a disclaimer is preventive rather than curative.

It has always been thought that disclaimers are relevant only to charges under s 1(1)(b), those of supplying or offering to supply, and that they cannot be used by a defendant charged with an offence of 'applying' under s 1(1)(a) as held in the Court of Appeal decision of **R** *v* **Southwood** (above). The logic is straightforward. It would be contrary to public policy to allow a person wilfully to apply a description and then escape liability for his criminal act by disclaiming it. This would place a premium on criminal actions. However, this traditional approach has been challenged by the Court of Appeal decision in **R v Carl Bull** (1996). The defendant had sold a car with a false mileage reading. The reading was written on the sales invoice along with a qualifying statement to the effect that the defendant had been unable to confirm the mileage and thus that customers should treat the mileage reading as being inaccurate. The Court of Appeal held that the prosecution had failed to show that there was a case to answer as the qualified mileage reading did not amount to a false trade description. Whether this case constitutes a significant change to the law on disclaimers or is merely an example of a poorly prepared case remains to be seen.

The validity of disclaimers was acknowledged by the Divisional Court in the decision of **Tarleton Engineering Co Ltd v Nattrass** (1973). However, two basic requirements must be satisfied if the disclaimer is to be effective, these being the prominence of the disclaimer and the time at which it is drawn to the customer's attention. In the decision of **Norman v Bennett** (1974), a car clocking case in which the mileage of the vehicle had been reduced from 68,000 miles to 23,000 miles, the court held that for a disclaimer to be effective it:

> must be as *bold, precise and compelling* as the trade description itself and must effectively be brought to the attention of any person to whom the goods may be supplied. In other words the disclaimer must equal the trade description in the extent to which it is likely to get home to anyone interested in receiving the goods. [emphasis added]

The requirement of prominence means that, in practice, the disclaimer will need to be closely associated physically with the description, hence the practice in the car trade of affixing disclaimers over the mileage reading on the mileometer. Subsequent cases have established that notices on office walls or desks will not be effective if they are not proximate to the description. Similarly documentary disclaimers may not be effective, as held in **R v Hammerton Cars Ltd** (1976) and in the decision of **May v Vincent** (1990), in which it was held that a disclaimer in an auctioneer's catalogue was not effective.

As well as the prominence of the description, the time of its application is also crucial. The cases of **Doble v David Greig** (1972) (a case under the now defunct s 11 of the Trade Descriptions Act 1968), **Zawadski v Sleigh** (1975) and **Norman v Bennett** itself all confirm that the disclaimer must be given no later than the time at which the description is applied. Once the description has taken effect, it is too late to disclaim it. In recent years, there has been increasing concern over the use of disclaimers as a means of attempting to evade the controls of the Trade Descriptions Act 1968 as regards counterfeit goods. The issue was addressed in the decision of **Lewin v Fuell** (1990) but major concern has arisen because of the decision in **Kent County Council v Price** (1993). In **Lewin v Fuell** the defendant sold watches from the boot of his car, the watches bearing well-known names such as 'Rolex' and 'Cartier'. The watches were replicas, a fact known to the defendant. There were no written disclaimers accompanying the goods. A trading standards officer approached the car and on inquiring about the goods was told that they were replicas. The defendant was charged with offences contrary to s 1(1)(b) of the Trade Descriptions Act 1968.

The magistrates acquitted the defendant on the basis that he had intended to sell replica watches and that, given the price of approximately £20 to £30, customers were aware that they were replicas and would not be misled. However, on appeal the defendant was convicted, it being held that the goods bore a false trade description which had not been validly disclaimed.

The decision of **Kent County Council** *v* **Price** has caused much concern to the trading standards service with the fear that it may amount to a 'counterfeiters' charter'. The defendant was a market trader who had a large number of children's T-shirts for sale. They had brand names on the front including 'Adidas', 'Puma' and 'Reebok'. The defendant knew that the T-shirts were not genuine and put a sign adjacent to the T-shirts which read 'Brand copy' and the price. At the time of sale, the defendant also told customers that the goods were copies but very good value for money. On appeal to the Crown Court, the defendant was found not guilty of offences against s 1(1)(b) of the Trade Descriptions Act 1968, the court being of the opinion that the description of the goods, the notice stating 'Brand copy' and the oral disclaimer at the time of sale did not amount to a trade description. If the effect of **Kent County Council** *v* **Price** is as serious as the trading standards service believes, matters relating to counterfeit goods will be better dealt with in the future by s 92 of the Trade Marks Act 1994, which seeks to control the unauthorised use of trade marks (see Chapter 19).

13.2.8 Services

Section 14(1) provides that it shall be an offence for any person in the course of a trade or business

(a) to make a statement which he knows to be false; or
(b) recklessly to make a statement which is false;
as to any of the following
   (i) the provision in the course of a trade or business of any services, accommodation or facilities;
   (ii) the nature of any services, accommodation or facilities provided in the course of a trade or business;
   (iii) the time at which, manner in which or persons by whom any services, accommodation or facilities are so provided;
   (iv) the examination, approval or evaluation by any person of any of the services, accommodation or facilities so provided; or
   (v) the location or amenities of any accommodation so provided.

As with s 1 offences, 'false' means false to a material degree. Many of the cases relating to s 14 involve package holidays. However, the law is equally applicable to other services such as building, repair work and insurance. Thus it essentially covers the same area as the Supply of Goods and Services Act 1982. A major difference between the s 1 and s 14 offences is that s 14 requires *mens rea* as actual knowledge is required for the s 14(1)(a) offence and a degree of recklessness is needed for the s 14(1)(b) offence. However, in respect of the requirement for recklessness it is perhaps fairer to say that it is a half *mens rea* offence, for the court in **MFI Warehouses Ltd *v* Nattrass** (1973) held that 'recklessly' in this context does not imply dishonesty, merely that the defendant did not pay due regard to whether the statement was true or false. Further, a statement will not be reckless if it was true at the time that it was made but was rendered untrue subsequently by something beyond the defendant's control, as long as the defendant was unaware of its falsity. Thus, in **Sunair Holidays Ltd *v* Dodd** (1970) the defendant company advertised holiday accommodation as 'all rooms with terrace overlooking the harbour'. Such accommodation had always been provided previously. However, on the occasion in question, the hotel allocated different accommodation to the defendant's clients. It was held that the defendant had not been reckless.

Of course, if the defendant knew that the statement had become false, it would be reckless not to correct it. Further, the decision of **Best Travel Co *v* Patterson** (1986) held that an advertiser was reckless when he failed to check the truth of a statement when he had cause to doubt its accuracy.

The leading decision of **Wings Ltd *v* Ellis** (1984) considered the time at which the defendant must know of the falsity of a statement if he is to be convicted of making a statement which he knows to be false' contrary to s 14(1)(a). Again it is a holiday case, but the decision would be equally relevant to any situation in which services are described in a brochure or leaflet. In **Wings Ltd** the defendant company advertised a holiday in a hotel in Sri Lanka stating that the hotel had air conditioning. This was not so, a fact which was brought to the defendant's attention. Despite the company's attempts to remedy the situation, a customer subsequently booked a holiday relying on an unamended brochure. The House of Lords held the company liable on the basis that the statement was false and the company knew of its falsity at the time that the client relied upon it. The company's belief in its truth at the time of publication of the brochure was irrelevant. Thus there is an obligation on those supplying services to ensure that any brochure, leaflet or other advertising material is accurate at all times for liability will arise as soon as the defendant is aware of any falsity. Further, the decision of **R *v* Thomson Holidays Ltd** (1974) confirms that a new offence occurs every time the brochure is read and thus one misdescription may give rise to many offences.

The need to demonstrate *mens rea* in s 14 cases has always made those offences more difficult to prove. However, it is possible that the *mens rea* requirement may be removed as suggested in the 1999 DTI white paper *Modern Markets: Confident Consumers*, which would render such offences subject to strict liability instead.

In determining what is covered by s 14, it is important to examine what constitutes a 'service, accommodation or facility'. In **R *v* Breeze** (1973) it was held to be an offence falsely to describe one's qualifications, as this relates to the provision of professional services. 'Facility' has posed greater difficulty. Thus the provision of a 'closing down sale' was held not to be a facility in **Westminster City Council *v* Ray Allan (Manshops) Ltd** (1982). In **Newell *v* Hicks** (1983) the promise of a free video cassette recorder with every X-registered Renault bought at a specific time was not a facility as it related to the acquisition of goods. By contrast, in **Kinchin *v* Ashton Park Scooters Ltd** (1984) the offer of free insurance with the purchase of a motorcycle was the provision of a facility. A more recent discussion as to the nature of a service took place with the decision of **Ashley *v* Sutton London Borough Council** (1995) when it was held that a money-back guarantee is a statement as to the nature or provision of a service. The defendant had produced a book containing a betting strategy inviting customers to try out the strategy for 90 days and offering a money-back guarantee if the customer was dissatisfied. Ten clients tried to recover their money but were unsuccessful. The defendant argued that s 14 did not apply because the case related to the sale of a book, i.e. goods not services. However, the court held that the real supply related to the betting strategy, which was a service to which s 14 applied and therefore that the false money-back guarantee was in breach of s 14.

Section 14 is limited further by the fact that it relates only to statements about present or past facts and does not cover promises as to the future. Thus in **Beckett** *v* **Cohen** (1973) the defendant builder contracted to build a garage in ten days identical to one on adjacent premises. The garage was not completed within the ten-day period and differed from the neighbouring garage. The court held that the defendant was not liable under s 14 as it does not extend to future promises, only statements about past or existing facts. The breach was a breach of contract not a breach of the criminal law.

However, if the promise as to the future also contains some element of present fact, liability will arise. Thus, in **British Airways Board** *v* **Taylor** (1975) the defendants practised a policy of overbooking on planes to take account of 'no-shows'. As a result of this policy there was no seat available for a customer on his flight. The court held that liability was possible as a letter confirming that a seat had been reserved for the customer made a statement about the present availability of his seat as well as its future availability. On the facts, the defendants escaped liability on the basis that the statement had been made by their predecessor BOAC, for which they could not be held liable. A similar approach was taken in the Court of Appeal decision of **R** *v* **Avro** (1993). The defendant company issued a return flight ticket between Alicante and Gatwick. The return flight was stated as being at 12.55 pm, with Dan Air as the carrier. On the outward flight, a customer was given another ticket for the return journey indicating that the flight would be at 12 noon with another carrier. It later transpired that the 12.55 pm flight had never existed. The Court of Appeal held that the statement on the original ticket was a statement of existing fact, namely that the 12.55 pm return flight existed. The statement was false to Avro's knowledge and an offence had been committed. However, the law on promises to the future must now be viewed in the light of the decision of **Lewin** *v* **Barratt Homes Ltd** (2000), a case under the Property Misdescriptions Act (1991), in which it was held that pictures and a show home which incorrectly depicted the houses that were to be built were statements of existing fact and not promises to the future.

Lastly, it should be noted that s 14 does not cover statements about price, as held in **Dixons Ltd** *v* **Roberts** (1984). The defendant company issued an advertisement promising to 'refund the difference if you buy Dixon's Deal products cheaper locally at the time of purchase and call within seven days'. The defendant intended that the offer would apply only to selected goods but the advertisement was ambiguous. A refund was refused to two customers who had bought goods to which the advertisement was not intended to apply. The defendant was acquitted as the court held that a statement relating to a refund of part of the price was not a service within s 14 of the Trade Descriptions Act 1968.

Misleading price indications are now covered by Part III of the Consumer Protection Act 1987, to which reference will be made later in this chapter.

13.2.9 Defences

Section 24 provides the main statutory defences in the Trade Descriptions Act 1968. It provides that it shall be a defence for the person charged to prove:

(a) that the commission of the offence was due to a mistake or to reliance on information supplied to him or to the act or default of another person, an accident or some other cause beyond his control; and

(b) that he took all reasonable precautions and exercised all due diligence to avoid the commission of such an offence by himself or any person under his control.

For the defence to succeed the defendant must be able to satisfy both strands of the defence. Part (a) of the defence recognises five different options. Case law has established that the mistake must have been that of the person charged, as held in **Birkenhead & District Cooperative Society** *v* **Roberts** (1970). By contrast, reliance on information supplied or the act or default of another necessarily implies the presence of a third party. It was held in **Tesco Supermarkets Ltd** *v* **Nattrass** (1972) that in a corporate structure an employee or manager can be 'another person' for this purpose and that a company may escape liability by alleging an employee's act or default. Only those persons, typically the directors and company secretary, who constitute the alter ego of the company would not be classed as another person in this context. Indeed, s 20 of the 1968 Act impliedly recognises that the directors, managers, secretary and other similar corporate officers control the company's actions in that s 20 provides that those persons, or anyone purporting to act in any of those capacities, can be charged with an offence under s 20 if the company has committed an offence with their consent, connivance or neglect. The reference to anyone purporting to act in those capacities takes account of persons who are acting as *de facto* directors, managers, etc but who have not been appointed formally to such a position.

In the **Tesco** decision, the supermarket company were running a 'flash' offer on washing powder whereby customers obtained the product at a specially reduced price. An advertising poster to this effect appeared in the store. The store in question ran out of the special packs of washing powder and a shop assistant put ordinary packets on the shelf without removing the advertising poster. The manager of the store who was responsible for checking that everything was in order did not notice this. A customer was charged the full price for a packet of washing powder. The House of Lords held that the offence had been committed by the shop manager, who was another person for the purposes of the s 24 defence.

If the defendant wishes to plead reliance on information or the act or default of another he must give the prosecutor seven days clear notice of this fact and provide the prosecutor with information identifying or assisting with the identification of that other person.

The second strand of the defence requires that the defendant show that he took all reasonable precautions and exercised all due diligence. In the **Tesco** decision the court held that all reasonable precautions involved the establishment of a suitable system and due diligence involved ensuring that it worked. Indeed, it was accepted in **Newcastle-upon-Tyne City Council** *v* **Safeway plc** (1994), a case involving a pricing issue, that a company which has adopted a quality control system can still maintain that it has exercised all reasonable precautions and all due diligence where the offence has resulted from an individual employee's failure rather than a systems failure. It has yet to be seen whether the setting up and operation of an approved quality control system will *prima facie* constitute due diligence, although certainly it would appear to be good evidence of such. The parameters of the due diligence defence are extremely important as it appears regularly in consumer protection legislation, including weights and measures and food safety, both of which are discussed later.

One aspect of reasonable precautions and due diligence involves the question of sampling and the extent to which the supplier of goods should sample them to ensure compliance with any description. This question was addressed in **Garrett** *v* **Boots Chemists Ltd** (1980) in which the defendant company was found guilty of an offence against the Pencils and Graphic Instruments (Safety) Regulations 1974 for having for sale pencils that exceeded the permitted levels of lead and/or chromium. The Divisional Court held, overruling the magistrates' court, that the defendant had not exercised reasonable precautions as, even though it was a condition in the contract with their supplier that all goods must conform to regulatory standards, they had not taken any random samples to ensure compliance. The court acknowledged that the level of sampling to be required will depend to some extent upon the nature of the defendant. Thus it would be unreasonable to expect a small corner shop to undertake the same level of testing as a major national retailer, particularly if the tests are of a technical nature or very expensive.

However, simple tests can be undertaken by anybody, as seen in **Sherratt** *v* **Gerald's The American Jewellers Ltd** (1970), in which the defendant was charged under s 1(1)(b) with supplying a diver's watch which was falsely described as 'waterproof' when, in fact, the watch stopped after being submerged in water for one hour. The Divisional Court held that the retailer had not exercised all reasonable precautions and due diligence in relying on a manufacturer's statement. It would have been a simple matter to test a watch by placing it in water. The defendant was convicted. Section 24(3) provides a further defence to those charged with offences of supplying or offering to supply contrary to s 1(1)(b). It provides that it shall be a defence for the person charged to show that he did not know, and could not with reasonable diligence have ascertained, that the goods did not conform to the description or that the description had been applied to the goods.

Section 25 provides a separate defence for the innocent publisher of an advertisement containing a false trade description. It is a defence for him to show that he is a person whose business is to publish or arrange for the publication of advertisements, that he received the offending advertisement in the ordinary course of his business and that he did not know and had no reason to suspect that the advertisement would amount to an offence under the Act.

Section 23, while not strictly a defence, dovetails with s 24. It provides that where an offence committed by one person is due to the act or default of another, that other person shall be guilty of an offence and can be proceeded against irrespective of whether proceedings are taken against the first person. Thus, in the situations discussed above where a company claims that the offence was due to the act or default of an employee, the enforcement authorities could charge the employee irrespective of whether they prosecute the company. The only requirement for the section, confirmed in the case of **Coupe v Guyett** (1973), is that a *prima facie* case can be made against the main offender. If no case could be made because, for example, the main offender is not in the course of a business, no action under s 23 is permitted. The fact that the main offender would be able to make out a s 24 defence is not relevant. The second, and rather surprising, point is that s 23 can be used to prosecute a private individual as the section does not contain a requirement that the defendant be in the course of a trade or business. This was confirmed in the decision of **Olgeirsson v Kitching** (1986). However, this decision has been much criticised and it seems likely that the law will be changed at some point.

13.2.10 Enforcement

Enforcement is undertaken by local authority authorised officers, the main enforcement issues being the general approach that should be taken to enforcement matters and the problem of persistent offenders. The Act provides the usual enforcement powers of entry, search and seizure and creates an offence of obstructing an officer.

The Cabinet Office Enforcement Concordat of March 1998 has seen the promotion of a voluntary alternative approach to enforcement which seeks to promote principles of good enforcement for both policies and procedures. This includes matters such as the maintenance of standards, openness and helpfulness, a consistent approach to enforcement, the provision of advice before formal action, discussing and resolving points of difference unless immediate action is called for, and explaining and confirming any proposed action in writing. This voluntary concordat seems likely to be given force as a mandatory code of practice if the present Labour government is returned to power in the General Election of 7 June 2001.

A different approach to enforcement practices should not be viewed, however, as a dilution of intent, as evidenced by recent strategies. While the decision of **Walker v Simon Dudley Ltd** *sub nom* **Shropshire CC v Simon Dudley Ltd** (1997) confirmed that, as a matter of public policy, enforcement authorities should exercise a discretion in deciding whether any given case warrants the use of the criminal law, the courts are still willing to impose a custodial penalty where appropriate, as evidenced in the decision of **R v Richards** (1999), in which the defendant was given a 21-month term of imprisonment for clocking cars. That case also saw the suggestion that for intricate and complicated trade description cases, it may be more appropriate to bring a common law count of conspiracy to defraud.

The issue of persistent offenders was addressed by the Court of Appeal in **London Borough of Barking & Dagenham v Jones** (1999), when it was held that if a trader persistently breaches the criminal law, it is appropriate to obtain an injunction under s 222 of the Local Government Act 1972 to restrain them from further breaches.

13.3 Prices

Misleading price indications are controlled by Part III of the Consumer Protection Act 1987, s 20(1) of which provides that:

> a person shall be guilty of an offence if, in the course of any business of his, he gives (by any means whatever) to any consumers an indication which is misleading as to the price at which any goods, services, accommodation or facilities are available (whether generally or from particular persons).

Further, s 20(2) provides that if a price indication becomes misleading after it was given to any consumers and that some or all of those consumers were likely to rely on it after it became misleading, the defendant will be guilty of an offence if he fails to take all such steps as are reasonable to prevent the consumers from relying on it. This might be true if, for example, a trader published a brochure or other advertising material which became inaccurate after publication because of a change in the rate of VAT increasing prices. The s 20 offence is broader than the now defunct s 11 of the Trade Descriptions Act 1968 which it replaced in that the new offence covers both goods and services while the old provision covered only goods. Services are defined as including the provision of credit, insurance and banking services together with ancillary services, the purchase or sale of foreign currency, the supply of electricity, the provision of a place (other than on a highway) for the parking of a motor vehicle and the making of arrangements for a person to site a caravan other than for use as his main residence. It expressly does not include the carrying on of an investment business or any services provided to an employer under a contract of employment. The 'price' is the aggregate of the sums payable by the consumer for the supply of goods or the provision of services, accommodation or facilities.

In construing the s 20 offence it is important to note that it applies only where the person making the indication was acting in the course of any business of his. The House of Lords in **Warwickshire County Council** *v* **Johnson** (1993) held that the section applies only where the defendant is the owner of the business or has a controlling interest in it. Thus, where the offending statement had been made by a branch manager, a mere employee of the company, there was no liability.

The meaning of the phrase was revisited in the decision of **Denard** *v* **Burton Retail Ltd** (1997) when the defendant, Burton Retail Ltd, was convicted of a pricing offence. Burton had granted a concession to another company, B, for that company to run its business in Burton's premises. The goods on display in the concession area belonged to B, although some of them carried Burton's price labels. The prices were set by B with Burton having no opportunity to monitor or control prices. Goods were paid for through Burton's tills. The court held that sales did take place in the course of Burton's business such as to render them liable under s 20.

A further restriction on the impact of s 20 is that it applies only where the indication is given to consumers, who are defined in s 20(6) as being:

> (a) in relation to any goods, . . . any person who might wish to be supplied with the goods for his own private use or consumption;

    (b) in relation to any services or facilities, . . . any person who might wish to be provided with the services or facilities otherwise than for the purposes of any business of his; and

    (c) in relation to any accommodation, . . . any person who might wish to occupy the accommodation otherwise than for the purposes of any business of his.

Thus these provisions do not apply in business to business sales, and companies compiling brochures for use by business purchasers or, for example, by the supply departments of local authorities would not be governed by the Act. Nonetheless, great care should be taken for if it is possible that personnel within such a business or local authority might buy an item from the catalogue in their personal capacity, s 20 would apply in relation to that purchase. Thus, for example, suppose an office equipment catalogue is available in the offices of a company or local authority and that a member of staff ordered a word processor for his private use at home, the purchase would be subject to s 20 and if the price indication was misleading an offence would have occurred. Further, note that the s 20(6) definition does not require that the item purchased was of a type ordinarily acquired for private use or consumption, merely that that particular consumer was buying it for his private use or consumption. The test is subjective.

For the purposes of the Act a price indication is misleading if it would imply any of the following, namely;

1   that the price is lower than it is;
2   that the price does not depend on facts on which it does depend, for example cash sales only;
3   that the price includes matters for which an additional charge will be made, for example service extra;
4   that the person expects the price to be increased, reduced or maintained when this is not the case;
5   that a price comparison is accurate when it is not so.

Again, this approach is more comprehensive that that which previously pertained under s 11 of the Trade Descriptions Act 1968. Thus, while such cases as **Doble** *v* **David Greig Ltd** (1972) would still be good law, s 20 of the 1987 Act goes well beyond this decision. The defendant displayed bottles of fruit cordial some distance from the checkout in the shop. The labels on the bottles read 'the deposit on this bottle is 4d refundable on return'. Each bottle also bore a price label stating '5s 9d'. At the cash desk was a notice stating 'In the interests of hygiene we do not accept the return of any empty bottles. No deposit is charged by us at the time of purchase'. A customer was charged 5s 9d. On appeal, the defendant was convicted of an offence of indicating that the price was lower than it was in fact.

The ambit of the offences has been examined recently in the decisions of **Toyota (GB) Ltd** *v* **North Yorkshire CC** (1998) and **MGN Ltd** *v* **Ritters** (1997). In the Toyota case, it was held that an advertisement for a car quoting a price of £11,655 was misleading in that it did not include the delivery charge of £455, which was referred to in the small print. The fact that the car could actually be purchased and delivered for less than £11,655 because of various discounts was irrelevant and did not prevent the advertisement from being misleading. Meanwhile, in the MGN Ltd case, in which there was an advertisement offering a £50 watch for £4.99, the court held that it was necessary to show that goods at the higher price were available in the market if conviction for a false price indication was to be avoided.

The use of computer pricing and price scanning has increased the potential for difficulties to arise in relation to the prices quoted and charged for goods and services. It follows that traders need to be diligent in the use of computer pricing systems. For example, in **Toys 'R' Us** *v* **Gloucestershire County Council** (1994) the defendant company was found regularly to have goods on display in the store for which a price ticket attached to the goods indicated one price while the price scanning of the bar code on the goods caused a different price to be displayed on the till. The company adopted a policy whereby cashiers were required to check that the price displayed for the goods on the till corresponded with that on the price ticket. Where there was a discrepancy, the lower ticket price was charged. On appeal, the defendant was acquitted of charges against s 20(1) of the Consumer Protection Act 1987 on the basis that the price indication was that displayed on the price ticket, which was the price actually charged and hence not misleading.

In **Berkshire County Council** *v* **Olympic Holidays Ltd** (1994) a computer used for booking holidays malfunctioned and quoted a price £182 higher than that detailed in the brochure. The computer screen carried the message 'confirm booking' and 'confirm costing' and produced a print-out detailing the price. The company was charged with an offence against s 20(1) of the Consumer Protection Act 1987. On appeal, it was held that in view of the testing of the computer software, the use of an on-screen disclaimer and the fact that the software was correct (this being an isolated incident of the computer malfunctioning), the defendant had taken all reasonable precautions and exercised all due diligence to avoid committing the offence and should be acquitted.

The due diligence defence relevant to pricing offences contrary to s 20 of the Consumer Protection Act 1987 is to be found in s 39 of the Act. Unlike s 24 of the Trade Descriptions Act 1968, the version of the defence contained in the 1987 Act is the so-called single strand defence, in which the defendant must demonstrate that he took all reasonable precautions and exercised all due diligence, but there is no need for him to establish a mistake, reliance on information, etc as required by the first strand of the Trade Descriptions Act defence.

Two recent cases have considered the use of the due diligence defence in the context of pricing offences. In **Berkshire County Council** *v* **Olympic Holidays Ltd** (1994) the testing of the software and the use of the on-screen disclaimer constituted reasonable precautions and due diligence in the circumstances. By contrast, in **Newcastle-upon-Tyne City Council** *v* **Safeway plc** (1994), in which the defendant company sold ten grocery items which were the subject of 'special offer' promotions, the price charged for nine of the items was higher than that shown on an adjacent shelf ticket. The tenth item, a pack of jam doughnuts, had been repriced although the price ticket showing the lower price had become detached from the product. The doughnuts were advertised by means of a tannoy announcement in the store. On appeal, the defendant was acquitted in respect of the nine items because the company did have a policy and system to control pricing and the incident occurred due to the individual actions of a junior employee. However, it was convicted in respect of the doughnuts as the system covered only planned price promotions and not *ad hoc* price reductions announced in the store.

In addition to the due diligence defence, specific defences relating to pricing offences are contained in s 24 of the Consumer Protection Act 1987. This includes the defence that the act or omission was authorised under regulations made under s 26, that the indication was not contained in an advertisement, that an advertisement was published innocently by a professional publisher, that the price indication did not apply to the availability of the goods or services from the defendant, that it was reasonable for the defendant to assume that the price recommendation was being followed and that the offence arose because of the failure of any person to follow the recommendation.

The understanding of the pricing provisions of the Act has been assisted by the publication of the Code of Practice for Traders on Price Indications by the Department of Trade in November 1988 under powers contained in s 25 of the Act, although there have been calls by enforcement officers for the code to be updated. The code of practice seeks to explain the provisions clearly and provides many examples of how they would apply in practice. Thus, for example, it provides guidance about making price comparisons, price reductions, compliance with preprinted prices, the quoting of VAT, the amendment of price indications which have become misleading after they have been given and selling through agents. Compliance with the code can be used as defence evidence in a prosecution, but it is not an absolute defence and, naturally, can only be of use if the trader has complied with its requirements. Thus, in the decision of **AG Stanley Ltd *v* Surrey County Council Trading Standards Office** (1995), the trader argued that they had a defence because they had complied with the code. However, the court held that a breach of the code had occurred and that the defendant was liable for an offence. The trader had advertised the normal price of £4.99 for an occasional table comparing it with the original price of £7.99, a normal practice in sales. However, this comparative pricing in which the trader quoted the previous price alongside the current price continued for three months, being used in a 'Style and Value' promotion, a 13-day sale, the Style and Value promotion again and a Christmas sale without the price being raised to the original price at any time between the various promotions/sales. The court held that this was misleading in that a quoted price reduction implies that the goods have been for sale at the higher price immediately beforehand and this was not the case here.

In addition to the publishing of the code of practice, the Secretary of State has power, under s 26 of the Act, to make regulations controlling the circumstances and manner in which any person gives an indication as to the price at which goods, services, accommodation or facilities will be, or are being or have been supplied or provided; or the manner in which any person indicates any other matter in respect of which any such indication may be misleading. To date, three sets of regulations have been made under this section: the Price Indications (Method of Payment) Regulations 1991, the Price Indications (Bureaux de Change) (No 2) Regulations 1992 and the Price Indications (Resale of Tickets) Regulations 1994. Apart from the provisions of the Consumer Protection Act 1987, other controls relating to pricing are to be found in the Prices Acts 1974–75 and the regulations made thereunder. The main section of interest is s 4 of the Prices Act 1974, which is concerned with the way that prices are marked or otherwise indicated. Under this section, the Secretary of State can make orders to ensure that prices are indicated on or near goods that are intended for sale by retail, that charges for services are indicated and that in respect of either the price indication is given in an appropriate manner, for example by reference to a unit of measurement and inclusive or exclusive of VAT.

There are two orders currently in force: the Price Marking (Food and Drink on Premises) Order 1979 and the Price Marking Order 1999. The latter Order, which is arguably the more important, came into force on 18 March 2000 and includes provisions requiring that where goods are for retail sale the price must be indicated in writing. Regulation 7 stipulates that any selling price, unit price, commission, conversion rate or change on the rate of VAT must be:

1 unambiguous, easily identifiable and clearly legible;
2 placed in proximity to the products to which it relates; and
3 so placed as to be available to consumers without the need for them to seek assistance from the trader or someone else on his behalf in order to ascertain it.

This has overcome the problems posed by the decision of **Allen *v* Redbridge Borough Council** (1994), decided under the now repealed Price Marking Order 1991, in which it was held that it was sufficient for the price label to be on the goods, there being no requirement that the consumer could see the label without assistance.

It should be noted, however, that the Price Marking Order 1999 does not apply to products which are supplied in the course of the provision of a service or to sales by auction or sales of works of art or antiques.

One final piece of legislation that impacts on pricing, but was made under s 18 of the Development of Tourism Act 1969, is the Tourism (Sleeping Accommodation Price Display) Order 1977.

13.4 Property misdescriptions

As stated earlier, the Trade Descriptions Act 1968 does not cover land or buildings. Most specifically, therefore, it does not cover the supply of houses or commercial buildings. This omission, at least with regard to new property, has been addressed by the passage of the Property Misdescriptions Act 1991. Section 1 of the Act provides the main offence, which is that:

> where a false or misleading statement about a prescribed matter is made in the course of an estate agency business or a property development business, otherwise than in providing conveyancing services, the person by whom the business is carried on shall be guilty of an offence under this section.

A property development business for this purpose means a business wholly or substantially concerned with the development of land. A statement is made in the course of such a business if it is made for the purpose of, or with a view to, disposing of an interest in land consisting of or including a building, or part of a building, constructed or renovated in the course of the business.

To be an offence under s 1 the statement must relate to a 'prescribed matter', it being the function of the Secretary of State to stipulate by Order which matters are to be covered. The Order currently in force is the Property Misdescriptions (Specified Matters) Order 1992, which came into force on 4 April 1993. The Order stipulates 33 things that are specified matters for the purpose of the Act and hence are subject to control. They include *inter alia* the location or address, the aspect, view, outlook or environment, fixtures and fittings, price, tenure or estate, physical or structural characteristics, form of construction or condition, and the existence and extent of any public or private right of way.

Section 2(1) of the Act provides a statutory due diligence defence available to the defendant if he can show that he 'took all reasonable steps and exercised all due diligence to avoid committing the offence'. However, it is qualified by s 2(2), which provides that if the defendant wishes to rely on information provided to him as part of his defence, he must demonstrate that it was reasonable for him to have relied on the information, particularly having regard to what steps he took to verify it and whether he had any reason to disbelieve it.

Question

Downshire County Council ordered some outdoor jackets from Clothes Ltd, a clothing wholesaler, for use by employees in the authority's direct labour organisation. The jackets were described as 'waterproof' and bought on that basis. In fact, they were only showerproof and not suitable for their intended usage. Clothes Ltd had relied for the description on information supplied to them by Koats Ltd, the manufacturer. The jackets were packed in sealed boxes which Clothes Ltd had not opened but merely passed on to Downshire County Council.

Consider whether any offences have been committed contrary to the Trade Descriptions Act 1968.

Answer

The jackets ordered by Downshire County Council have been ordered by reference to a description. The description 'waterproof' has been applied to them and Clothes Ltd have sold them as complying with that description. In fact, the jackets are only showerproof and therefore the description is false. The first issue is whether the description is false to a material degree as required by s 3 of the Trade Descriptions Act 1968 and whether the description is of a type controlled by the Act. It is a controlled description for it would fall within the category of 'fitness for purpose' specified in s 2. It also appears to be false to a material degree for its falsity affects the suitability of the item.

There are two potential defendants: the manufacturer who applied the original description and has committed an offence against s 1(1)(a) of the Act, and Clothes Ltd, who may have committed offences of offering to supply and supplying under s 1(1)(b). Clothes Ltd may be able to claim a defence under s 24 in that they relied on information supplied to them by the manufacturer. However, they will still need to prove reasonable precautions and due diligence, which is more difficult after the decisions of **Garrett *v* Boots Chemists Ltd** (1980) and **Sherratt *v* Gerald's The American Jewellers Ltd** (1970), as the court may hold that a simple test would have proved the falsity of the statement.

Downshire County Council might receive compensation under s 130 of the Powers of Criminal Courts (sentencing) Act 2000 if Clothes Ltd are convicted. Alternatively, the county council could sue for compensation under ss 13 and 14 of the Sale of Goods Act 1979.

Further reading

Dobson, P (2000). *Sale of Goods and Consumer Credit*, 6th edn (Sweet & Maxwell)

Harvey, B W and Parry, D L (1996). *The Law of Consumer Protection and Fair Trading*, 5th edn (Butterworth)

Miller, C J and Harvey, B W (1985). *Consumer and Trading Law – Cases and Materials*, (Butterworth)

Parry, D L, Rowell, R and Harvey, B (eds) (1997). *Butterworth's Trading and Consumer Law* (Butterworth)

14 Product safety

14.1 Introduction

The safety of products is extremely important in both civil and criminal law. As we have already seen, defectiveness in Part I of the Consumer Protection Act 1987 is determined by whether the product provides the safety that persons generally are entitled to expect.

The criminal controls over unsafe products, which have as their underlying rationale to prevent unsafe goods from reaching the market and injuring consumers, are to be found currently in the General Product Safety Regulations 1994 and Part II of the Consumer Protection Act 1987. This dual approach has arisen from the fact that when the UK promulgated the General Product Safety Regulations 1994 in order to comply with the obligation to adopt Directive 92/59/EEC on general product safety, s 10 of the Consumer Protection Act 1987 was not repealed. Instead, it was merely disapplied in situations falling within the ambit of the General Product Safety Regulations. Hence, when considering criminal controls over unsafe products the General Product Safety Regulations 1994 must be applied first, with s 10 filling in any gaps thereafter to the extent that it is applicable.

14.2 General Product Safety Regulations

The General Product Safety Regulations came into effect on 3 October 1994 and exercise controls over producers and distributors in order to prevent their placing a product on the market unless the product is safe. For these purposes, a producer includes the manufacturer of the product, any person presenting himself as the manufacturer by affixing his name, trade mark or other distinctive mark to the product and any person who reconditions the goods. If the manufacturer is based outside the Community, then the manufacturer's representative is classed as the producer for the purposes of the Regulations. In the absence of a manufacturer's representative, the importer of the product is liable. Lastly, any professional in the supply chain whose activities affect the safety properties of the product is classed as a producer. Hence, for example, a retail shopkeeper who fails to store refrigerated food at the correct temperature would be classed as a producer for this purpose if the effect of his actions is to render the food unsafe. A 'distributor' is defined as any professional in the supply chain whose activities do not affect the safety properties of the product.

The basic aim of the Regulations is found in reg 7, which provides a general safety requirement that no producer shall place a product on the market unless the product is a safe product. By virtue of reg 9, distributors are similarly required to act with due care in order to ensure compliance with the general safety requirement.

14.2.1 'Product' and 'safe product'

Given the requirements of regs 7 and 9, it is vital that producers and distributors understand the definitions of 'product' and 'safe product' for the purposes of the Regulations.

A 'product' is defined as being one intended for consumers or which is likely to be used by consumers, supplied, whether for consideration or not, in the course of a commercial activity and whether new, used or reconditioned. This definition limits the impact of the Regulations for it seeks to provide protection only in respect of products intended for consumers, a 'consumer' being classed as someone not acting for the purposes of a trade or business. Thus, there is clearly no protection offered in respect of products used for commercial activities. This latter point is reinforced by the fact that the Regulations expressly provide that where a product is used exclusively for commercial activities it is not covered by the Regulations even if the user is a consumer.

The second strand of the definition is that the product must have been supplied in the course of commercial activity. Hence the producer or distributor of the product must have been acting for the purposes of a trade or business. There is no requirement that this commercial supply was done for profit, however, the Regulations making clear that it is irrelevant whether any consideration was paid. Thus, products supplied by commercial concerns as gifts or for marketing purposes, etc would fall within the ambit of the Regulations. The Regulations are not limited to new products but control the supply of used and reconditioned products as well. However, the Regulations do not apply to second-hand antiques; products supplied for repair or reconditioning before use, provided that the supplier has informed the person to whom he supplies the product; or any product which is subject to specific provisions in rules of Community law governing all aspects of the safety of the product.

Having examined the parameters of the definition of 'product' and thereby determined which products are subject to the control of the Regulations, it is vital to understand the concept of 'safe products' in this context, for the essential requirement is that only safe products will be placed on the market. A product is deemed to be 'safe' when it does not present any risk, or only the minimum risks compatible with its use when used for normal or reasonably foreseeable conditions of use. Note that there is no requirement that the product be safe for other purposes not reasonably foreseeable. Any risk posed must be acceptable and consistent with a high level of protection for the safety and health of persons. In assessing this, four particular factors must be considered, namely:

(a) the characteristics of the product, including its composition, packaging, instructions for assembly and maintenance;

(b) the effect on other products, where it is reasonably foreseeable that it will be used with other products;

(c) the presentation of the product, the labelling, any instructions for its use and disposal and any other indication or information provided by the producer; and

(d) the categories of consumers at serious risk when using the product, in particular children.

Further, no product is to be considered unsafe merely because higher levels of safety are possible or products posing a lesser risk are available. There is a rebuttable presumption that products are safe if they conform to specific UK laws governing the health and safety requirements applicable to those products. Where no specific rules exist, factors such as voluntary national standards, Community technical specifications, codes of practice and the state of the art and technology can be taken into account when deciding whether a product conforms with the general safety requirement.

14.2.2 Obligations of 'producers' and 'distributors'

Regulations 7–9 are the crux of the Regulations, for it is there that the statutory obligations of the producers and distributors are to be found. As explained above, the central requirement is contained in reg 7 and states that no producer shall place a product on the market unless it is safe.

In addition to this basic requirement, other obligations are placed on producers by reg 8. The producer must, within the limits of his activity, provide consumers of his products with sufficient information to allow them to assess the inherent risks posed by a product during normal or foreseeable use where those risks are not immediately obvious. The provision of this information then permits consumers to take appropriate precautions in respect of those risks.

An ongoing obligation placed on producers is to keep themselves informed of the risks posed by their products and they are obliged to adopt whatever measures are necessary to achieve that aim. A non-exhaustive indication of what measures might be deemed appropriate is given in reg 8(2) and includes:

1 the marking of products or product batches in such a way that they can be identified;
2 sample testing of marketed products;
3 investigating complaints; and
4 keeping distributors informed of such monitoring.

Presumably, in assessing whether a producer has adopted appropriate measures, regard will be had to factors such as the size of the producer's business. This was held in **Garrett v Boots Chemists Ltd** (1980) to be a relevant factor in determining whether an appropriate level of sampling had taken place. It would be unrealistic to expect a small producer to undertake the same volume or standard of sampling as a large multi-national commercial company. Armed with the information gleaned by these various measures, a producer must take appropriate action including, if necessary, the withdrawal of the product from the market. By implication, it would also include other measures such as the issuing of product recall notices.

The obligations placed on distributors are laid out in reg 9 and reflect the secondary nature of the distributor and of his likely impact on the safety features of the product. Thus, he is required to act with due care and to help ensure compliance with the primary requirements laid on the producer by reg 7. In particular, the distributor must not supply to any person products which he knows, or should have presumed, are dangerous products on the basis of the information in his possession and as a professional. Further, within the limits of his activities, a distributor must participate in the monitoring of the safety of products placed on the market. In particular, a distributor should be involved in passing on information on the risks in products and cooperating in any action taken to avoid such risks.

14.2.3 Offences and defences

The contravention of regs 7 and 9(a) is made criminal offences by virtue of reg 12. Thus, the producer will be criminally liable if he places any product on the market which is not a safe product, while the distributor will be criminally liable in respect of products which he has supplied to any person when he knew or should have presumed that they were dangerous. Regulation 13 creates two other offences which extend to both producers and distributors. They are, first, that it is an offence to offer or agree to place on the market any dangerous product, or expose or possess any such product for placing on the market; and, second, that it is an offence to supply or agree to supply any dangerous product, or expose or possess any such product for supply. Offences against regs 12 and 13 are punishable on summary conviction by a term of imprisonment not exceeding three months, or a fine not exceeding level 5 (currently £5,000) or both.

As is typical of consumer legislation, liability for offences can be placed upon any person by whose act or default the offence has been committed. This provision, found in reg 15(1), is similar in effect to s 23 of the Trade Descriptions Act 1968 except for one key requirement, namely that the person must have been acting in the course of commercial activity. As such the decision of **Olgeirsson** *v* **Kitching**, noted in Chapter 13, in which it was held that a private individual could be held liable under the s 23 provision, would not be applicable here. Regulation 15(1) firmly requires that the person charged must have been involved in a commercial activity as defined within the Regulations, and further that it was *his* commercial activity. Thus it seems he must be the owner or proprietor rather than a mere employee.

Directors, managers and secretaries of companies can be held liable for offences committed by those companies against the Regulations if the offences were committed with the consent or connivance of such people or were due to their negligence. This recognises the reality of corporate structures and that companies act through their human alter egos and are effectively at their whim.

The due diligence defence appears at reg 14 and is in the single-strand form favoured in recent legislation as opposed to the two-strand defence that appears in s 24 of the Trade Descriptions Act 1968. Thus, reg 14(1) provides that it is a defence for the person charged to show that he took all reasonable steps and exercised all due diligence to avoid committing the offence. The cases discussed in Chapter 13 in relation to s 24(1) are equally applicable in this context. However, by contrast with s 24(1) there is no need to prove any of the five specified matters that appear there such as mistake, reliance on information, etc. To that extent, this version of the defence is easier for the defendant to prove, but potentially provides a fairer and more reasonable test for the reasonable, innocent defendant. For the purposes of enforcement of the Regulations, ss 13–18 of the Consumer Protection Act 1987 apply. These provisons are considered later in this chapter.

14.3 Consumer Protection Act 1987

14.3.1 The general safety requirement

Section 10 of the Consumer Protection Act 1987, which creates a general safety requirement, remains effective in those situations that fall within its ambit and are not covered by the General Product Safety Regulations. Section 10 reads:

> A person shall be guilty of an offence if he—
> (a) supplies any consumer goods which fail to comply with the general safety requirement;
> (b) offers or agrees to supply any such goods; or
> (c) exposes or possesses any such goods for supply.

Three points are immediately obvious from this subsection. First, it refers only to the supply of goods, not to their sale. Thus the Act applies to goods supplied by any means including hire-purchase, barter, hire, promotional offers, etc.

Second, its application is limited to 'consumer goods', which are defined in s 10(7) as being:

> any goods which are ordinarily intended for private use or consumption, not being—
> (a) growing crops or things comprised in land by virtue of being attached to it;
> (b) water, food, feeding stuff or fertiliser;
> (c) gas which is, is to be or has been supplied by a person authorised to supply it by or under section 6, 7 or 8 of the Gas Act 1986 (authorisation of supply of gas through pipes);
> (d) aircraft (other than hang-gliders) or motor vehicles;
> (e) controlled drugs or licensed medicinal products;
> (f) tobacco.

In practice, (b) to (e) are controlled through other Acts and regulations such as the Food Safety Act 1990 and the Agriculture Act 1970 as amended. Thus local authority supplies departments negotiating contracts for the supply of food for school canteens or fertilisers for use in public parks would be more concerned with the protection offered by those other Acts. What is equally clear from s 10(1) is that goods intended for business or industrial use are not included in Part II of the 1987 Act, although in practice they will be covered by the Health and Safety at Work, etc Act 1974 instead.

Third, s 10(1) reads such that liability is placed on 'any person' who undertakes the prohibited acts. Therefore, liability is not limited to producers, importers and own-branders but can be imposed on anyone involved in the production, importation or distribution process right down to retailers. As such, it has greater impact than Part I, where suppliers can evade civil liability through identifying their own supplier (see Chapter 12). In Part II criminal liability is imposed on all parties involved, subject, of course, to the statutory defences.

In deciding whether consumer goods conform to the general safety requirement, consideration must be given first to the definition of 'safe' contained in s 19 and then the provisions contained in s 10(2).

Section 19 states that goods are safe for this purpose when there is no risk, or no risk apart from one reduced to a minimum, that the goods will cause death or personal injury. Note that it refers only to death and personal injury and does not include property damage. Thus in this respect, it is narrower in effect than Part I and any goods that are likely to cause only property damage will not offend against the general safety requirement.

Section 10(2) stipulates the factors that the court must consider when deciding whether the goods are reasonably safe. They are:

(a) the manner in which, and purposes for which, the goods are being or would have been marketed, the get-up of the goods, the use of any mark in relation to the goods and any instructions or warnings which are given or would be given with respect to the keeping, use or consumption of the goods;

(b) any standards of safety published by any person either for goods of a description which applies to the goods in question or for matters relating to goods of that description; and

(c) the existence of any means by which it would have been reasonable (taking into account the cost, likelihood and extent of any improvement) for the goods to have been made safer.

Paragraph (a) is very similar to the matters to be considered in deciding whether a product is defective under Part I and thus goods that fail the general safety requirement are likely to be defective for the purposes of civil action under Part I. However, one distinction is crucial. Civil liability under Part I arises only if someone has been injured or suffered recoverable loss caused by a defective product, whereas Part II, being regulatory in nature, is enforced regardless of whether anyone has been injured. Indeed, one of the main effects of good enforcement is that with a reduced number of unsafe products on the market, the likelihood of injuries to product users should be reduced together with the resultant civil claims for compensation.

Section 10(3) provides that goods will not fail the general safety requirement in respect of any aspect attributable to compliance with any regulation imposed by or under any enactment or Community obligation. This echoes one of the Part I defences. Further, a failure to do more than is required by any safety regulations, approved standards of safety or the provisions of any enactment or subordinate legislation will not cause the goods to fail the general safety requirement. This means that the minimum standard required by such regulations or standards has effectively become the maximum to be demanded when applying the general safety requirement. This is a lower standard than under Part I, where it would be reasonable to expect a producer to incorporate the latest safety features in his product even though they exceed any regulatory requirement.

Section 10(4) provides the statutory defences to anyone charged with a s 10(1) offence. The first defence is that the defendant reasonably believed that the goods would not be used or consumed in the UK. This acknowledges the realities of manufacturing in that manufacturers may be producing goods for export and, as such, producing them in conformity with regulatory standards applicable in the recipient country. The defendant would need to demonstrate that none of the goods were intended to reach the UK market and have done so by methods beyond his control, for example theft.

The second defence is available only to retailers and applies if the retailer can show that at the time that he supplied the goods, or offered or agreed to supply them or exposed or possessed them for supply, he neither knew nor had reasonable grounds for believing that the goods failed to comply with the general safety requirement. This defence is very similar to that provided in s 24(3) of the Trade Descriptions Act 1968.

The third defence is that the goods supplied were second-hand goods for sale. Note that it does not cover goods on hire, so companies involved in the hire of second-hand goods cannot claim protection from the defence.

Section 39 provides a due diligence defence applicable to specified offences including s 10. It provides, in terms very similar to those found in the defence under the Trade Descriptions Act 1968, that it shall be a defence for the defendant to show that he took all reasonable steps and exercised all due diligence to avoid the commission of the offence. Unlike the Trade Descriptions Act defence, the due diligence defence contained in the 1987 Act is a single-strand defence.

14.3.2 Safety regulations

Section 11(1) provides the Secretary of State with the authority to make regulations to ensure that goods are safe, or that their availability is restricted to particular groups of people or that appropriate information is provided and inappropriate information not provided in relation to goods. Section 11(2) provides a comprehensive list of those factors that the Secretary of State may seek to control through the use of such regulations. It includes, among other things, composition, design, packaging, the granting of approvals, the testing or inspection of goods and the requirement that marks, warnings or instructions be included with the goods.

The section applies to goods other than growing crops and things comprised in land by virtue of being attached to it, water, food, feeding stuffs and fertilisers, gas, and controlled drugs and licensed medicinal products. Note, first, that tobacco is not excluded and thus is subject to control under this section and that, second, the section is not restricted to consumer goods and thus is applicable to industrial goods.

When drafting safety regulations, the Secretary of State must consult such organisations as appear to him to be representative of interests substantially affected by the proposals, such other persons as he considers appropriate and, lastly, in respect of goods suitable for use at work, the Health and Safety Commission. The duty to consult was confirmed in the decision of **R *v* Secretary of State for Health, *ex parte* US Tobacco International Inc** (1992), in which the plaintiff sought judicial review of a decision by the Secretary of State to introduce the Oral Snuff (Safety) Regulations 1989 without undertaking appropriate consultation with the plaintiff, who was the only manufacturer of oral snuff in the UK and had been encouraged by the government to establish a factory in Scotland. The decision to ban oral snuff was based on a report and recommendation to which the plaintiff was denied access. The plaintiff sought to have the Regulations quashed on the basis that due consultation had not occurred. The Court of Appeal found in favour of the plaintiff and granted an order to quash the Regulations. A side issue in the case was whether, as the plaintiff suggested, the Secretary of State's power to make regulations under s 11 is limited to matters governing consumer protection and safety and that the regulations in question were *ultra vires* as they purported to deal with health. The court held that regulations to protect the health of the consumer do fall within the general aim of consumer protection.

Several safety regulations have been made under this section, including the Furniture and Furnishings (Fire) (Safety) Regulations 1988 as amended, the Low Voltage Electrical Equipment (Safety) Regulations 1989, the Toys (Safety) Regulations 1989, the All-Terrain Motor Vehicles (Safety) Regulations 1989, the Gas Cooking Appliances (Safety) Regulations 1989, the Heating Appliances (Fireguards) (Safety) Regulations 1991, the Dangerous Substances and Preparations (Safety) (Consolidation) Regulations 1994 as amended, the Motor Vehicle Tyres (Safety) Regulations 1994 as amended, the Cosmetic Products (Safety) Regulations 1996 as amended, the Fireworks (Safety) Regulations 1997, the Pencils and Graphic Instruments (Safety) Regulations 1998, the Cigarette Lighter Refill (Safety) Regulations 1999 and the Dangerous Substances and Preparations (Nickel) (Safety) Regulations 2000. In addition, the Act has adopted the numerous safety regulations formulated under the Consumer Protection Act 1961 and the Consumer Safety Act 1978.

Section 12 creates a number of offences dependent upon the terms of individual safety regulations. Thus s 12(1) makes it an offence to supply or offer or agree to supply, or expose or possess any goods for supply where any safety regulations prohibit such action. Further, s 12(2) provides that where a safety regulation requires that a particular test or process is to be adopted in connection with goods, or where the goods must be dealt with in a particular way when the whole or part of them does not satisfy a test, it is an offence not to act in the correct way. Section 12(3) and (4) creates offences relating to the non-compliance with any requirement imposed by safety regulations with regard to use of marks or the provision of information. Offences against s 12 are punishable on summary conviction by up to six months imprisonment, or a fine not exceeding level 5 (currently £5,000) or both.

It is recognised that someone may be injured by a product which does not comply with an appropriate safety regulation. Where that is so, s 41 of the Act permits the injured user to sue for compensation for breach of statutory duty.

14.3.3 Enforcement

Sections 13–18 of the Consumer Protection Act 1987, which provide the essential enforcement strategy for Part II of that Act, are equally applicable to the enforcement of the General Product Safety Regulations 1994. Thus, irrespective of which of the statutory controls is relevant in any given situation, the enforcement mechanism is the same. The strategy is one that seeks to control dangerous products through the use of prohibition notices and suspension notices, the rationale for which is to attempt to prevent unsafe goods from reaching the market.

Prohibition notices

Section 13 re-enacts provisions first introduced by the Consumer Safety Act 1978. Section 13(1)(a) permits the Secretary of State to serve a prohibition notice on any person prohibiting that person, except with the consent of the Secretary of State, from supplying, or from offering to supply, agreeing to supply, exposing for supply or possessing for supply, any relevant goods which the Secretary of State considers are unsafe and which are described in the notice.

A prohibition notice may be made against any individual involved in the manufacture or supply of the unsafe goods. Thus it would include manufacturers, wholesalers, retailers, etc. It relates to the prohibition of relevant goods, which are defined as being goods to which s 11 applies. The object of such notices is to prevent any individual from introducing unsafe goods into the market or selling them to vulnerable groups, for example small toys to children aged under three. A prohibition notice must state that the Secretary of State considers the goods to be unsafe together with the reasons for that decision, the date on which the prohibition notice is to come into effect and the ability of the trader to make representations in writing to the Secretary of State to establish that the goods are safe. If the trader wishes to challenge the prohibition notice, he should compile a full written report with all the relevant details, expert opinions, etc to establish the safety of the product. The Secretary of State must either revoke the notice or appoint somebody to consider further representations from the trader and to examine any relevant witnesses according to the procedure laid down in Schedule 2 to the Act. Ultimately, the Secretary of State can confirm the order, or revoke or vary it, although it cannot be varied to be more restrictive on the trader.

Section 13(1)(b) permits the Secretary of State to serve a notice on any person requiring him to publish at his own expense, in a form and manner and on occasions specified in the notice, a warning about any relevant goods which the Secretary of State considers are unsafe, which that person supplies or has supplied and which are described in the notice. Relevant goods mean any goods to which s 11 applies together with growing crops or things comprised in the land by virtue of being attached to it. To date, this provision has never been used.

Offences against s 13 are punishable in the same way as those under s 12.

Suspension notices

Speed is of the essence when seeking to prevent dangerous goods from being sold in the market. Therefore, s 14 provides the enforcement authority, i.e. trading standards departments, with the ability to act quickly to remove unsafe goods from supply. It provides that where the authority has reasonable grounds for believing that any safety provision has been contravened in relation to any goods, it can serve a suspension notice on any person prohibiting him from supplying, offering to supply, agreeing to supply or exposing for supply the goods for a period not exceeding six months. Note that it requires only 'reasonable grounds' for belief and not absolute proof of the contravention of a safety provision. This approach is necessary to encourage effective enforcement. The suspension notice must describe the goods sufficiently, set out the reasons for believing that a safety provision has been contravened and explain the person's right of appeal under s 15. Breach of a safety provision in this context includes breach of the general safety requirement, a safety regulation, a prohibition notice or a suspension notice. A suspension notice can be served only once, unless either criminal proceedings are pending against the person for breach of a safety provision or the goods are in the process of being forfeited under s 16 or 17. During the period of the suspension notice the enforcement authority has the right to be kept informed about the whereabouts of the goods. If it is established that there had not been any contravention of a safety provision in respect of those goods and that the notice was not served as a result of the neglect or default of the person, then the person upon whom the notice was served is entitled to compensation.

The limitations on s 14 were considered recently in the decision of **R *v* Liverpool City Council, *ex parte* Baby Products Association** (1999). In that case, the local authority issued a press release informing the public that babywalkers manufactured by BPA did not meet the relevant safety requirements, which resulted in a product recall. It was held that the press release was *ultra vires* the statutory code contained in s 14 and the General Product Safety Regulations in that it was not accompanied by the issue of a prohibition notice. To issue a press notice in the absence of a prohibition notice was outside the remit of the section.

Appeals against a suspension notice must be taken under s 15, decisions not being subject to judicial review, as established in **R *v* Birmingham City Council, *ex parte* Ferrero Ltd** (1993), in which the plaintiffs were the manufacturers of a chocolate novelty called a 'Kinder Surprise Egg'. It comprised a small chocolate egg in which was placed a plastic capsule containing the pieces to construct a child's toy, some of which were a model of the Pink Panther. A three-year-old child died after swallowing a foot from one of these toys. Birmingham City Council issued a suspension notice which, despite offers of undertakings from the plaintiffs, they refused to withdraw. Ferrero Ltd sought judicial review to have the council's decision quashed. The Court of Appeal refused the application, judging that the purpose of the suspension notice as issued was to remove dangerous goods from the market as envisaged by the Act and that the statutory appeal procedure under s 15 was adequate to allow the plaintiffs to put their case.

It was made clear in the **Ferrero** case that an enforcement authority is not under any duty to consult a trader either before or after the service of a suspension notice as that would frustrate the purpose of permitting the immediate withdrawal of unsafe goods. The statutory appeal system, combined with the right to compensation if a suspension notice has been served wrongly, is adequate to achieve justice.

Forfeiture

Under s 16 (s 17 in Scotland) an enforcement authority may apply to the court for an order for the forfeiture of any goods if there has been a breach of a safety provision in respect of those goods. This will also apply if goods from the same consignment or batch, or goods of the same design have been the subject of a contravention. The court has the authority to order that the goods be destroyed, or that they be given to a specified person for repair or reconditioning or for use as scrap. Under s 16(5) anybody aggrieved by such a decision may appeal to the Crown Court, with the order for destruction or disposition of the goods being suspended until after the decision of the appeal.

14.3.4 Enforcement powers

Part IV of the 1987 Act (ss 27–35) contains details of the enforcement powers given to local authority enforcement officers enforcing Parts II and III of the Act (no enforcement powers are needed in respect of Part I as it relates only to civil law rights and compensation). The powers contained in ss 27–35 are typical of those contained in most criminal consumer legislation, including the Trade Descriptions Act 1968, the Food Safety Act 1990 and the Weights and Measures Act 1985. Indeed, standard wording is often used.

The powers given under the Consumer Protection Act 1987 include the power to make test purchases, to search premises and to seize goods and records. The obstruction of an authorised officer acting in pursuance of the Act is an offence punishable by a fine not exceeding level 5 on the standard scale. Naturally, the Act provides an appeal procedure against the detention of goods together with provisions for compensation if there has not been any contravention of any safety provision in relation to the seized goods.

14.4 Health and Safety at Work etc Act 1974

Businesses and public authorities are equally, if not more, concerned about the safety of goods intended for use in business or public service. This issue is addressed by the Health and Safety at Work etc Act 1974, s 6(1) of which, as amended by Schedule 3 to the Consumer Protection Act 1987, provides:

> (1) It shall be the duty of any person who designs, manufactures, imports or supplies any article for use at work or any article of fairground equipment—
> (a) to ensure, so far as is reasonably practicable, that the article is so designed and constructed that it will be safe and without risks to health at all times when it is being set, used, cleaned or maintained by a person at work;
> (b) to carry out or arrange for the carrying out of such testing and examination as may be necessary for the performance of the duty imposed upon him by the preceding paragraph;

    (c) to take such steps as are necessary to secure that persons supplied by that person with the article are provided with adequate information about the use for which the article is designed or has been tested and about any conditions necessary to ensure that it will be safe and without risks to health at all such times as are mentioned in paragraph (a) above and when it is being dismantled and disposed of; and

    (d) to take such steps as are necessary to secure, so far as is reasonably practicable, that persons so supplied are provided with all such revisions of information provided to them by virtue of the preceding paragraph as are necessary by reason of its becoming known that anything gives rise to a serious risk to health or safety.

Section 6(1A) provides for similar duties in respect of the design, etc of fairground equipment.

Section 6(1) is far-reaching in that it applies to importers, manufacturers and anyone involved in the supply of the goods, 'supply' in this context meaning 'sale, lease, hire or hire-purchase, whether as principal or as agent for another',

The essential weakness of s 6(1), however, is the level of the duty that it imposes. In this subsection (and indeed throughout other parts of the section) the phrase 'as far as is reasonably practicable' is used. This means that many of the offences created by the section are not absolute, or even strict in nature, but are similar to the civil law duties in negligence. Thus if a defendant can prove that further safety features were not practical, no offence will be committed. This duty is lower than that commonly found in consumer safety legislation, which tends to impose strict liability for offences, subject to statutory defences.

Not all the duties imposed by s 6(1) carry this relatively light burden. Section 6(1)(b) provides an absolute duty to ensure that the appropriate testing has been carried out by either the person or another. Similarly, s 6(1)(c) contains an absolute duty to ensure that adequate information and warnings are provided to ensure that the article can be used safely and without risks to health both when it is being set, used, cleaned or maintained and when it is being disposed of or dismantled. Section 6(1)(d) emphasises that the defendant's responsibility for the product does not end when he supplies it. There is a continuing duty to provide further information about serious risks to health or safety, so far as is reasonably practicable, to people to whom goods have been supplied.

Section 6(2) places an absolute duty on the designers and manufacturers of articles for use at work to ensure that all necessary research is done to eliminate or minimise, as far as is reasonably practical, any risk to health or safety posed by the article.

Section 6(3) turns to the installation or erection of articles for use at work by placing a duty on installers and erectors to ensure, as far as is reasonably practical, that nothing about the way an article is installed or erected will make it unsafe or a risk to health when it is being set, used, cleaned or maintained.

Thus far, the section has dealt with articles for use at work, but ss 6(4) and (5) move on to impose similar duties in respect of substances, defined as including 'any natural or artificial substance, whether in solid or liquid form or in the form of a gas or vapour'. This would include, for example, chemicals for use in school laboratories and substances used by local authority officers for the control of vermin. Section 6(4) provides that manufacturers, importers and suppliers must ensure, as far as is reasonably practical, that such substances are safe when being used, handled, processed, stored or transported. The remainder of the subsection echoes the s 6(1) duties of arranging for testing and the provision of information. Section 6(5) requires the carrying out of necessary research.

14.4.1 Defences

Section 6(6)–(8) provides some defences to persons to whom s 6 applies. First, s 6(6) makes clear that there is no need for a potential defendant to repeat any testing that has previously been carried out by someone else if it is reasonable for him to rely on such tests. Thus, for example, it would be reasonable for a defendant supplier to rely on the fact that an article carries the BSI Kitemark in respect of those factors to which the Kitemark applies. This is particularly pertinent to alleged offences against ss 6(2) and (5).

Section 6(7) makes clear that the duty imposed by s 6 is restricted to a supplier who supplies 'in the course of a trade, business or other undertaking carried on by him (whether for profit or not) and to matters within his control'. However, the breadth of this phrase is far wider than under other Acts such as the Trade Descriptions Act 1968 where the course of a trade or business has been relevant. Here the duty extends beyond trade or business and into other undertakings under the defendant's control. Of particular note is the fact that the undertaking need not be profit making. It is difficult to envisage how someone supplying articles for use in work would be able to use this defence.

Lastly, s 6(8) provides a defence if the designer, manufacturer, importer or supplier of an article (note substances are not included) has supplied the article to another person on the basis of a written undertaking that the other person will undertake the necessary steps to ensure that the article is safe. Note that it must be a written undertaking; an oral one will not suffice.

14.4.2 Enforcement

Sections 20–26 of the 1974 Act stipulate the enforcement powers available to the inspectors responsible for enforcing s 6. They include, as one would expect, powers of entry, examination and seizure. As under the Food Safety Act 1990 (see next chapter), enforcement officers can issue improvement notices requiring the remedying of contraventions of the Act and prohibition notices prohibiting the recipient from carrying on specified activities which breach the Act.

14.4.3 Civil liability

Section 47 of the Act makes clear that a breach of s 6 does not give a civil law right of action to anyone who has been injured as a result of the breach. In practice, however, it is likely that such an incident would give rise to action in negligence.

14.4.4 Recent regulations

Health and safety at work are further promoted by the use of regulations which address a variety of specific issues. Regulations passed since 1992 have related to *inter alia* goods used in the workplace, the management of the work environment and the control of hazardous substances. They include, among others, the Health and Safety (Display Screen Equipment) Regulations 1992, the Provision and Use of Work Equipment Regulations 1992, the Personal Protective Equipment at Work (PPE) Regulations 1992, the Management of Health and Safety at Work Regulations 1992, the Workplace (Health, Safety and Welfare) Regulations 1992, the Manual Handling Operations Regulations 1992, the Control of Substances Hazardous to Health Regulations 1994 and the Chemical (Hazard Information and Packaging for Supply) Regulations 1994.

Question

Good-Toy Ltd is an importer of toys. They supplied Fred, a retailer, with some long-haired dolls which had been manufactured outside the European Union. There was no recommended minimum age at which children should have access to one of these dolls. Mary bought one from Fred and gave it to her daughter, Jessica, aged two. A few hours later Mary discovered Jessica chewing a large piece of the doll's hair which had become detached from the doll's scalp. She reported the incident to the authorities.

Advise the authorities about any possible offences contrary to product safety legislation.

Answer

The enforcement authority will want to consider whether any offences have been committed against the General Product Safety Regulations 1994, which seek to prevent unsafe goods from reaching the market. The doll in question would fall within the control of the Regulations as it is a product intended for use by a consumer, has been bought by a consumer and sold by someone in the course of his business. Good-Toy Ltd, as the importer of the goods, will be responsible for the doll as they will be classed as a producer for these purposes. As such, they must comply with the general safety requirement under reg 7. Fred, the retailer, is likely to be classed as a distributor for these purposes and will be subject to reg 9 unless it can be shown that he is a supplier who could have affected the safety of the goods by, for example, giving a warning of the defect, in which case he too would be classed as a producer and governed by s 7. As the product was clearly unsafe given the ease with which the hair became detached, both Good-Toy Ltd and Fred may be criminally liable. Consideration would also have to be given to possible offences against the Toys (Safety) Regulations 1989, although, in practice, a choking hazard of this type is not included in these Regulations.

Further reading

Harvey, B W and Parry, D L (1996). *The Law of Consumer Protection and Fair Trading*, 5th edn (Butterworth)

Howells, G (1998). *Consumer Product Safety* (Ashgate)

Keenan, D and Riches, S (2001). *Business Law*, 6th edn (Longman)

Whincup, M (1999). *Sales Law and Product Liability – A Business Guide* (Gower)

15 Food safety

15.1 Introduction

Food and water are unique in that, unlike any other products, they alone are both intended for internal consumption and are essential to the health and well-being of a normal healthy person. Given this unique status, the quality of food and water is an issue of particular importance to the community as a whole and must be both promoted and preserved.

Food quality has been subject to some measure of quality control since the passage of the Assize of Bread and Ale in 1266. Modern food law, however, dates from the mid-nineteenth century, with the latest statute in a long line being the Food Safety Act 1990 together with a vast array of statutory regulations. The Food Safety Act itself provides more extensive control than was the case previously and adopts a rationale of firm quality control 'from farm to fork'.

Food safety has undoubtedly attained a much higher profile in recent years given public concern over food safety scares such as salmonella in chickens, listeria in soft cheese and, more recently, *E. coli* 0157 and BSE. At the date of writing (7 May 2001), we are in the middle of a foot and mouth epidemic with 1,563 reported cases affecting 7,132 premises and with 2,560,000 animals either slaughtered or awaiting slaughter. In addition, many more animals are subject to movement restrictions as part of the strategy to prevent the spread of the disease. This outbreak, while posing no risk to human health, has once again raised food safety issues in the public's mind.

15.2 Food

Section 1 identifies food for the purposes of the Act as including:

(a) drink;
(b) articles and substances of no nutritional value which are used for human consumption;
(c) chewing gum and other products of a like nature and use; and
(d) articles and substances used as ingredients in the preparation of food or anything falling within this subsection.

Food does not include live animals or birds, or live fish which are not used for human consumption while they are alive; fodder or feeding stuffs for animals, birds or fish; controlled drugs; and licensed medicinal products.

The word 'substances' as used in s 1 is defined in s 53 to include 'any natural or artificial substance or other matter whether it is in solid or liquid form or in the form of a gas or vapour'. This acknowledges the trend in modern food production that a large percentage of foodstuffs supplied commercially will include an artificial substance of some sort, be it colourant, preservative, anti-oxidant, emulsifier, etc. Many of these have no real nutritional value but are used for purposes such as to make the food last longer, spread more easily or be more appealing to the eye or palate.

Section 3 addresses the issue of when food shall be presumed to have been intended for human consumption. Subsections (2)–(4) provide:

> (2) Any food commonly used for human consumption shall, if sold or offered, exposed or kept for sale, be presumed, until the contrary is proved, to have been sold, or, as the case may be, to have been or to be intended for sale for human consumption.
>
> (3) The following, namely—
>
> (a) any food commonly used for human consumption which is found on premises used for the preparation, storage, or sale of that food; and
>
> (b) any article or substance commonly used in the manufacture of food for human consumption which is found on premises used for the preparation, storage or sale of that food,
>
> shall be presumed, until the contrary is proved, to be intended for sale, or for manufacturing food for sale, for human consumption.
>
> (4) Any article or substance capable of being used in the composition or preparation of any food commonly used for human consumption which is found on premises on which that food is prepared shall, until the contrary is proved, be presumed to be intended for such use.

The rebuttable presumptions effectively reverse the burden of proof, leaving it to the defendant to establish that the food was not so intended rather than requiring the prosecution to show that it was.

15.3 Sale and commercial operations

The Food Safety Act 1990 seeks to exert increased control both by the extension of the Act to persons not previously covered by food safety legislation and by an extension to the meaning of the word 'sale' and thereby to the number and types of situations covered.

A 'business' is defined in s 1 to include 'the undertaking of a canteen, club, school, hospital or institution, whether carried on for profit or not, and any undertaking or activity carried out by a public or local authority'. Thus, premises such as those used by local authorities are subject to prosecution under food safety legislation, a significant burden given the volume and variety of food that may be purchased, stored and supplied by a local authority through its schools, etc. Indeed, depending upon the contracting arrangements within any particular authority, individual schools may be classed as businesses and prosecuted for offences against the Act. Similarly, colleges and universities will be liable for the supply of food in their refectories, and hospitals for the food they supply to their patients. A business becomes a 'food business' when commercial operations with respect to food or food sources are carried out. 'Food sources' are defined as growing crops, live animals, birds or fish from which food is to be derived by harvesting, slaughtering, milking, collecting eggs or otherwise. All premises used for the sale of cooked and raw meat must be licensed.

In considering the breadth of 'commercial operations' we must first address the definition of 'sale', which underlies both the meaning of commercial operations and the main offences under the Act. The meaning of 'sale' under the Food Safety Act 1990 is far wider than that considered previously under the Sale of Goods Act 1979. In addition to the accepted meaning of 'sale', it includes for the purpose of the 1990 Act:

(a) the supply of food, otherwise than on sale, in the course of a business; and
(b) any other thing which is done with respect to food and is specified in an order by the Ministers,

with references to purchasers and purchasing being construed accordingly. Further, the Act extends to any food offered as a prize or reward, or given away in connection with any entertainment to which the public are admitted, whether on payment of money or not (including social gatherings, amusement, exhibition, performance, game, sport or trial of skill), any food offered as a prize, reward or gift for the purposes of an advertisement or in furtherance of a trade or business, and any food exposed or deposited in any premises for the purposes described above. Given the breadth of this definition, it seems likely that virtually any supply of food, other than in a purely private or domestic situation, is likely to fall within the definition of 'sale' and thus be subject to the provisions of the Act.

'Commercial operations' are defined as being any of the following, namely:

(a) selling, possessing for sale and offering, exposing or advertising for sale;
(b) consigning, delivering or serving by way of sale;
(c) preparing for sale or presenting, labelling or wrapping for the purpose of sale;
(d) storing or transporting for the purpose of sale;
(e) importing and exporting.

Again, this is a very wide definition and would include virtually any activity in relation to food or contact materials carried out by a food business.

15.4 Food safety offences

Food safety standards are promoted within the Act through two criminal offences and use of notices and orders that can be used to support and encourage food safety and which, if not complied with, can lead to criminal sanctions.

15.4.1 Rendering food injurious

Section 7(1) of the Food Safety Act 1990 makes it an offence to render any food injurious to health by any of the following means:

(a) adding any article or substance to the food;
(b) using any article or substance as an ingredient in the preparation of the food;
(c) abstracting any constituent from the food;
(d) subjecting the food to any other process or treatment;
with the intent that it shall be sold for human consumption.

In establishing whether food is injurious to health, regard must be had not only to the probable effect of the food on the health of the person consuming it but also to the probable cumulative effect of the food on the health of a person consuming it in ordinary quantities. Injury means any impairment whether temporary or permanent.

It seems unlikely that any food producer would wilfully render his food injurious because of the obvious resultant effects on publicity and future sales. However, it is quite feasible that normal production processes may render the food injurious nonetheless. For example, a normal part of food production is the addition of additives. Suspicions have been raised about the long-term effect of some additives and the possibility that they may cause a variety of disorders such as hyperactivity in children or even cancer. Given the increasing sophistication of analytical techniques and advances in medical science it seems feasible that ultimately such a link will be established beyond doubt and that someone will be held criminally liable in respect of the addition of a normal additive. It must be remembered, of course, that a prosecution under s 7 will only succeed if it can be proved that the person rendering the food injurious to health *intended* that the food was for sale for human consumption in that state.

Of course, any food business, including local authorities, may be the victim of sabotage either by a disgruntled employee or by a blackmailer making criminal demands against the threat of introducing injurious articles into the food, thereby affecting both production and sales. Clearly, such persons would be liable under s 7 although, in practice, they are likely to face far more serious criminal charges.

Food can be rendered injurious to health only by one of the methods specified in s 7. However, this does not include all the foreseeable methods. As Howells, Bradgate and Griffiths (1990) point out, the section does not include rendering food injurious by failing to subject it to some process or treatment. Thus no liability under s 7 would arise in respect of such food.

15.4.2 The food safety requirement

Section 8 provides the more general offence of food not satisfying the food safety requirement. It reads:

Any person who—
(a) sells for human consumption, or offers, exposes or advertises for sale for such consumption, or has in his possession for the purpose of such sale or of preparation for such sale; or

(b) deposits with, or consigns to, any other person for the purpose of such sale, any food which fails to comply with the food safety requirement shall be guilty of an offence.

Again, this is a wide-reaching provision that is likely to cover all situations in which someone deals with food. There is no requirement that a sale has actually occurred for paragraph (a) extends to mere offers to sell or exposures or advertisements for sale, while paragraph (b) goes even further by including the mere deposit or consignment of food. Thus, the delivery of unsafe food to a school for preparation for supply would be an offence. In practice, local authorities are likely to be the recipients rather than the creators of food that fails the safety requirement and, if in doubt about the quality of the food, should inform the duly authorised enforcement officers. If a school or other local authority institution were to serve it to diners, the authority would commit an offence itself.

Section 8 does not provide a general safety requirement in the way that s 10 of the Consumer Protection Act 1987 does. Instead it defines what constitutes unsafe food in this context. Section 8(2) stipulates the three ways in which food may be deemed to fail the food safety requirement, namely:

1 it has been rendered injurious to health by one of the means mentioned in s 7(1);
2 it is unfit for human consumption;
3 it is so contaminated (whether by extraneous matter or otherwise) that it would not be reasonable to expect it to be used for human consumption in that state.

The first two appear clear-cut, while the third is worthy of comment. Food is likely to become contaminated by the growth of a mould or the development of an infestation such as, for example, maggots, or by the presence of a foreign object. With respect to the existence of a contaminant the section requires that the contamination means that it is not reasonable for the food to be used for human consumption. In respect of a mould growth this may be so even though the mould does not present a health risk to a human being, as in **David Greig Ltd v Goldfinch** (1961). With regard to an extraneous object, there is an implication that it must affect the food microbiologically such as to render it unfit for human consumption. An object such as, for example, a milk bottle top in a loaf of bread, which would not have a microbiological effect on the food, may not create an offence under this section. In practice, it would be prosecuted under s 14 as being food not of the nature or substance or quality demanded by the purchaser. Naturally, anyone storing food for sale must be careful to ensure that it does not become unfit through poor storage, a problem particularly pertinent to perishable food. Further, care must be taken to ensure that foodstuffs do not become contaminated by mould, infestation or through contact with extraneous objects.

As with s 7 matters, if purchasers (be it local authority or otherwise) are of the belief that food with which they have been supplied does not meet the food safety requirement, they should inform the duly authorised enforcement officers.

15.4.3   Enforcement of s 8

Enforcement of s 8 is normally carried out by authorised officers from food authorities. Following local government reorganisation, the enforcement of food law is in the hands of the new single-tier unitary authorities, which have seen a coming together of the enforcement functions previously divided between trading standards departments and environmental health departments. This should facilitate a more coherent and harmonised approach to issues of food safety enforcement.

Enforcement of food safety law emanates from two sources: regular routine inspection of both food and food premises by authorised officers and also as a result of complaints received from members of the public. Section 9 provides authorised officers with specific powers to inspect all food intended for human consumption which has been sold or offered or exposed for sale or is in possession of or has been deposited with or consigned to any person for the purposes of sale or of preparation for sale at all reasonable hours. In practice, this probably means during normal business hours, making allowance for the fact that business hours may vary between different businesses. The power is to inspect the food, not the premises, and thus would seem to extend to any location where the food is sold, stored, etc.

Under s 9(2) there is also a right to act where the officer believes, otherwise than on inspection, that any foods are likely to cause food poisoning or any disease communicable to human beings.

In either of these situations the officer has the power to issue a notice to the person in charge of the food stipulating that the food is not to be used for human consumption and is either not to be moved or alternatively is to be moved to a place specified in the notice. The officer has 21 days in which to decide whether the food does comply with the food safety requirement and either withdraw the notice or have it dealt with by a magistrate. Alternatively, the officer may seize the food and seek an order from a magistrate for the food to be condemned and destroyed. In this instance, the owner of the food has a right to be heard in the hearing before the magistrate.

If the notice is withdrawn or the magistrate refuses to condemn the food, the owner will be entitled to compensation.

15.5   Notices and orders

Time is often of the essence in the enforcement of food safety legislation. The preparation of criminal prosecutions takes time, while more immediate action is necessary to control imminent health risks. Sections 10–13 of the Food Safety Act 1990 provide for a range of notices and orders, some of which are exercisable by authorised officers and some of which need court involvement or ministerial action. These provisions are given weight by the fact that a failure to comply is an offence. Section 10(2) creates an offence of failing to comply with an improvement notice. Sections 11(5), 12(5), (6) and 13(2) make it an offence for any person knowingly to contravene a prohibition order, an emergency prohibition notice, an emergency prohibition order or an emergency control order respectively.

15.5.1 Improvement notice

Section 10 applies to any regulations which make provision:

(a) for requiring, prohibiting or regulating the use of any process or treatment in the preparation of food; or

(b) for securing the observance of hygienic conditions and practices in connection with the carrying out of commercial operations with respect to food or food sources.

This would include regulations governing the cleanliness of kitchens and food preparation areas and the maintenance of machinery and utensils to be used in the preparation of food. Thus, the kitchens of restaurants, hospitals and school canteens are equally eligible for inspection and subject to improvement notices if found wanting. Where an authorised officer from an enforcement authority has reasonable grounds for believing that the proprietor of a food business is failing to comply with regulations he may serve a notice stating the grounds for his belief that there is a failure to comply, the matters that constitute the failure, the measures which in the officer's opinion must be taken to secure compliance and the period, being not less than 14 days, within which the measures (or their equivalent) must be undertaken. A failure to comply is an offence.

15.5.2 Prohibition orders

Section 11 deals with prohibition orders, which potentially have a far greater impact than improvement notices. If the proprietor of a food business is convicted of breaching a regulation to which the section applies and the court is of the opinion that a health risk is posed by:

(a) the use for the purposes of the business of any process or treatment;

(b) the construction of any premises used for the purposes of the business, or the use for those purposes of any equipment; and

(c) the state or condition of any premises or equipment used for the purposes of the business,

the court may issue an order prohibiting the use of the process, treatment, premises or equipment for the purposes of the business or any other food business of the same class or description as appropriate. Further, the court can prohibit the proprietor from participating in the management of any food business or any food business of a class or description specified in the order.

When an order is made, the enforcement authority is under a duty to serve a copy of the order on the proprietor of the business and, where appropriate, affix a copy to the premises. An order relating to processes, treatments, premises or equipment continues in force until the enforcement authority certifies that it is satisfied that the risk no longer exists. An order relating to the proprietor of a business is terminated when the court gives a direction to that effect. After a period of six months, the proprietor may apply for such a direction, although it is at the court's discretion whether to grant one.

15.5.3 Emergency prohibition notices and orders

Recent outbreaks of food poisoning including salmonella and listeria have proved the need for officers to be able to take immediate action to put an end to a health risk posed by food. Where an authorised officer is of the opinion that the health risk condition discussed above is fulfilled in respect of any food business, he can serve an emergency prohibition notice under s 12(1) on the proprietor of the food business. A magistrates' court if similarly satisfied can issue an emergency prohibition order under s 12(2). Before applying for an order, an officer must give one day's notice to the proprietor of the business. When a notice or an order has been made, a copy must be affixed to the premises and a copy of any order must be served on the proprietor of the business. A notice is effective for only three days unless an application for an emergency prohibition order has been made, in which case it remains effective until the application for the order is decided. It is an offence knowingly to fail to comply with either a notice or an order.

Both emergency prohibition notices and orders cease to have effect when the enforcement authority issues a certificate confirming that it is satisfied that the health risk condition no longer exists. The certificate must be issued within three days of the authority being so satisfied. Alternatively, the proprietor of the business can apply for such a certificate, the authority then having 14 days in which to make its decision and give its reasons for any refusal.

The proprietor of the business is entitled to compensation in respect of the service of the notice if either the enforcement authority fails to apply for an emergency prohibition order within three days or the court is not satisfied that a health risk condition existed at the time that the notice was issued.

15.5.4 Emergency control orders

It is in the nature of modern trading with widespread distribution of foodstuffs that a health risk may be posed across a wide geographic area, well beyond the jurisdiction of any individual enforcement authority. Section 13(1) provides a solution in the ability of the Secretary of State to issue an emergency control order. This system has been supplemented recently by s 17 of the Food Standards Act 1999, which allows arrangements to be agreed between the Secretary of State and the Food Standards Agency authorising the Agency to make emergency control orders on behalf of the Secretary of State. An emergency control order is made when the Secretary of State or the Food Standards Agency as relevant is satisfied that the carrying out of commercial operations with respect to food, food sources or contact materials involves or may involve imminent risk of injury to health. They have the power to give such directions and do such other things as appear to them to be necessary or expedient to prevent any commercial operations involving food, food sources or contact materials which they reasonably believe are subject to the emergency control order. However, they also have the power to consent, either unconditionally or conditionally, to allow prohibited activities to be undertaken by particular individuals. Such a consent is a defence to any charge of knowingly contravening an emergency control order, which normally is an offence.

15.6 Consumer protection

The other major offences contained in the Act have as their rationale the protection of the purchaser rather than the general maintenance of food safety standards. They seek to protect the purchaser in relation to quality, description, presentation, etc. These provisions are of particular concern to anyone regularly involved in the purchasing of food as they deal with offences relating to specific purchases as opposed to general standards.

15.6.1 Food not of the nature or substance or quality demanded

Section 14 reproduces a provision that has appeared in food safety legislation since 1875 and thus is a well-established part of food safety law in this country. Section 14(1) reads:

> Any person who sells to the purchaser's prejudice any food which is not of the nature or substance or quality demanded by the purchaser shall be guilty of an offence.

In this context 'a person' includes both individuals and bodies corporate and unincorporated businesses. Thus any business, be it a partnership or a limited company, can commit this offence, as can any individual. Employers will be liable for the acts of their employees, as will principals for the acts of their agents.

The sale must be to the prejudice of the purchaser, which will occur if the purchaser does not receive goods of the quality that he ordered and for which he has paid. Thus it follows that prejudice must be considered by reference to what the purchaser thought he was buying, i.e. the contract description. It effectively makes a criminal offence out of a breach of description. It is possible to prevent liability arising if the purchaser is aware of the deficiency in the goods. Thus in the Scottish case of **Brander v Kinnear** (1923) it was held that a notice disclaiming the purity of the food will be effective if it is brought sufficiently to the attention of the purchaser and it makes clear the nature of the food that he is being asked to accept.

Section 14(2) provides that it is no defence to argue that the purchaser was not prejudiced because he bought for analysis or examination. This is a very important provision given that much of the routine enforcement of s 14 involves the purchase of foodstuffs by enforcement staff for analysis by a public analyst. This is crucial to the enforcement of regulations relating to the constituent elements of products such as meat and spreadable fish products, milk and milk products and soft drinks, all of which are subject to control as regards their percentage constituents but which can be checked only via analysis. Many of these regulations are being reviewed.

While s 14 ostensibly governs the sale of food, the decision of **Meah v Roberts** (1978) makes clear that it covers anything that is sold as food. In that case liability existed when caustic soda instead of lemonade was supplied to a child.

The section creates three distinct offences, as held in **Bastin v Davies** (1950). Thus the prosecution must decide which of the three – nature, substance or quality – it wishes to pursue. The terms do overlap to some extent and it is feasible for a prosecution to be brought equally successfully under more than one heading.

Food will not be of the nature demanded if it is different from that ordered even though the product supplied is pure. Thus, caustic soda is not lemonade, jam is not honey and milk is not cream.

It is not of the substance demanded if it fails to satisfy any regulations controlling its constituent elements as described above or if it fails to satisfy a generic description applicable to those goods. Thus in **Anderson v Britcher** (1913) no offence was committed when sugar originating from Mauritius was described as 'Demerara sugar', it being held that 'Demerara sugar' had become a generic term with which the sugar complied. Naturally, it would be an offence against s 1 of the Trade Descriptions Act 1968 to state that a foodstuff had been manufactured in a particular place if this was not true.

Milk is of the substance demanded even if the fat content is below that demanded by the agreement between the parties as long as the milk is as it came from the cow. Such was held in **Few v Robinson** (1921).

Anness v Grivell (1915) held that 'quality' relates not merely to the description of the foodstuff but also to its commercial quality. Thus if the quality is inferior to that reasonably expected by the purchaser given the description, price, etc, an offence will be committed.

Naturally, food will not be of the quality demanded if it is adulterated. Thus foodstuffs that contain extraneous objects, such as string in a loaf of bread, glass in babyfood or a straw in a bottle of milk, would all create offences under this section. There is some overlap with the food safety requirement in s 8 as discussed earlier.

15.6.2 Falsely describing or presenting food

Section 15 creates three offences relating to the false or misleading description, advertising or presentation of food. The offences are all linked to the nature or substance or quality of the food. Thus it is an offence to provide a label (whether or not attached to or printed on the wrapper or container) or to publish an advertisement which either falsely describes the goods or is likely to mislead as to the nature or substance or quality of the food. Further, s 15(3) creates a new offence of selling, offering or exposing food 'the presentation of which is likely to mislead as to the nature or substance or quality of the food'.

An offence relating to a label or advertisement can be committed even though the offending description contained an accurate statement of the composition of the food.

Section 15 is supplemented by the Food Labelling Regulations 1996, which are probably the most important set of regulations relating to food. These require most prepackaged foods to be marked with the name of the food, a list of ingredients in weight-descending order, an indication of appropriate durability, any special storage instructions or conditions of use, the name or address of the manufacturer, packer or seller and instructions for use if necessary.

The likely duration of foodstuffs in good condition is of importance particularly for perishable products. These must be marked with a 'use by' date, it being an offence to sell foodstuffs after the date specified. By contrast, 'best before' dates, found on a variety of foodstuffs, guide the purchaser as to the likely storage period of the goods, no offence being committed by selling goods after that date unless they fail to comply with the food safety requirement. 'Sell by' dates are no longer legal.

15.7 Regulations

Regulations continue to play a central part in the control of food safety. Section 16 of the Food Safety Act 1990 gives power to Ministers to make regulations governing every aspect of food production and sale including, *inter alia*, the composition of food, microbiological standards, processes and treatments, hygienic conditions, labelling, marking and securing compliance with the food safety requirements. Regulations enacted under previous statutes have been adopted by the 1990 Act. Sections 17–19 provide Ministers with other regulatory powers to regulate compliance with Community obligations, matters relating to novel foods and the registration and licensing of food premises.

Naturally, such regulations are continually under review. In recent times, there has been a marked shift away from very specific compositional standards for specified foodstuffs towards the adoption of more general regulations based upon quantitative indications of ingredients (QUID). This approach, which seeks to give more information to consumers about the percentage of any ingredient in a given product, encourages the making of informed choices by consumers. Naturally, some prescriptive regulations will remain. Most of the new regulations are the result of European initiatives.

15.8 Codes of practice

There is an increasing use of statutory and non-statutory codes of practice as a mechanism for encouraging uniformity among food producers. The content of codes of practice is typically agreed upon by experts and enforcement bodies. Food authorities are required to have regard to the provisions of the codes made under s 40 of the Food Safety Act 1990 when exercising their functions under that Act. Failure to do so may affect the admissibility of evidence in subsequent enforcement proceedings. The format of the codes means that they are easier to amend than statutory material and thus are more responsive to the changing needs of the food industry and the encouragement of good practice in food safety.

15.9 Defences

Section 21 provides for a 'due diligence' defence, bringing defences for food safety legislation into line with those contained in other criminal regulatory legislation, including the Trade Descriptions Act 1968 and the Weights and Measures Act 1985.

Section 21(1) creates a single-strand defence requiring the defendant to show that he took all reasonable precautions and exercised all due diligence to avoid the commission of the offence either by himself or by someone under his control. However, he is not required to establish the act or default of another, reliance on information, mistake, etc stipulated in the version of the defence found in the Trade Descriptions Act 1968 (see Chapter 13). In practice, of course, it may be necessary to establish one of these as a means of demonstrating due diligence. A defendant cannot, without the leave of the court, plead the act or default of another or reliance on information provided by another unless he has served a notice to that effect on the prosecution at least seven days before the hearing and provided such information as he can to assist in identifying that other person. If the defendant has already appeared in court in connection with the offence, the notice must also be within one month of the first such appearance.

As under the Trade Descriptions Act 1968, reasonable precautions and due diligence would be established by showing that an effective quality control system had been set up and was functioning correctly in respects of all aspects of the business. This would include, among other things, the hygiene and safety of premises and equipment, the quality, composition and safety of the food, labelling and advertising, compliance with improvement notices, ensuring that the due diligence system is written down, the adequate instruction and training of staff, ensuring that the system will identify faults and correcting them and ensuring that customer complaints are both recorded and dealt with effectively. It would also include ensuring that an appropriate level of product sampling and testing has been undertaken by the defendant.

In addition to the general defence, s 21(2) provides a specific defence for persons charged with offences contrary to s 8 (food safety requirement), s 14 (selling food not of the nature or substance or quality demanded) and s 15 (falsely describing or presenting food). If such a person has neither prepared the offending food himself nor imported it into Britain, under s 21(4) he will be presumed to have satisfied the due diligence defence provided he can establish three things, namely:

(a) that the commission of the offence was due to an act or default of another person who was not under his control, or to reliance on information supplied by such a person;

(b) that the sale or intended sale of which the alleged offence consisted was not a sale or intended sale under his mark; and

(c) that he did not know, and could not reasonably have been expected to know, at the time of the commission of the alleged offence that his act or omission would amount to an offence under the relevant provision.

Own-branders would not be able to satisfy paragraph (b) of this defence. However, by s 21(3) a similar but stricter defence applies to them if in addition to (a) above an own-brander can also establish:

(b) that he carried out all such checks of the food in question as were reasonable in all the circumstances, or that it was reasonable in all the circumstances for him to rely on checks carried out by the person who supplied the food to him; and

(c) that he did not know and had no reason to suspect at the time of the commission of the alleged offence that his act or omission would amount to an offence under the relevant provision.

As with Part I of the Consumer Protection Act 1987, own-branding exposes the trader to a more stringent legal liability and must be balanced against the potential marketing advantages that it offers.

Section 20 of the Act provides a bypass procedure the same as that discussed previously in relation to s 23 of the Trade Descriptions Act 1968 (see Chapter 13). It permits the prosecution to proceed directly against the person by whose act or default the offence was committed irrespective of whether proceedings are taken against the primary offender. As with the Trade Descriptions Act, the prosecution will need to establish the existence of a *prima facie* offence by the primary offender, it being irrelevant whether he would have a valid defence.

Lastly, s 22 provides the standard defence for a person publishing misleading advertisements who can show that it is his business to publish or arrange for the publication of advertisements and also that he received the advertisement in the ordinary course of business and did not know and had no reason to suspect that its publication would constitute an offence.

15.10 Enforcement

As discussed earlier, enforcement of the 1990 Act is usually undertaken by the designated food authorities although some areas such as licensed meat premises are enforced by the Meat Hygiene Service. In addition to the specific powers given by ss 9–12 to authorised officers from those authorities, more general enforcement powers are contained in Part III of the Act. These give an authorised officer the power to take samples, powers of entry, access to records and the right to seize and detain any records which he has reason to believe may be required as evidence of an offence against the Act, or any regulations or orders made thereunder.

15.11 Food Standards Agency

As a response to growing public concern over food safety, the government passed the Food Standards Act 1999, which received Royal Assent on 11 November 1999. The main purpose of the Act, as explained in the official Explanatory Notes, is to establish the Food Standards Agency, set out its main function of protecting public health in relation to food, outline the functions that it will assume in pursuit of that aim and give the Agency the powers necessary to enable it to act in the consumer's interest at every stage in the food production and supply chain.

The Food Standards Agency came into being on 1 April 2000 and comprises a chairman, a deputy chairman and not less that eight or more than 12 other members, who must include one member appointed by the National Assembly for Wales, two members appointed by Scottish Ministers and one member appointed by the Department of Health and Social Services for Northern Ireland. As such, the constitution of the Agency ensures that appropriate regional issues will be taken into account. The 1999 Act also requires the establishment of an advisory committee for Wales, an advisory committee for Scotland and an advisory committee for Northern Ireland while reserving to the Secretary of State the opportunity to set up an advisory committee for England, or any region of England, after consultation with the Agency. The role of the advisory committees is defined in s 5(1) of the Act as being the giving of 'advice or information to the Agency about matters connected with its functions'. The officers of the Agency are headed by the chief executive with directors for Wales, Scotland and Northern Ireland who are responsible under the chief executive for ensuring that the Agency's functions in Wales, Scotland or Northern Ireland are carried out efficiently and effectively.

15.11.1 The functions of the Agency

While the Agency has a variety of functions including some related to animal foodstuffs and food-borne diseases, the major ones relating to food safety are to be found in ss 6–8 and include:

1 developing policies (or assisting in the development by any public authority of policies) relating to matters connected with food safety or other interests of consumers in relation to food;
2 providing advice, information or assistance in respect of such matters to any public authority;
3 providing advice and information to the general public (or any section of the public) in respect of matters connected with food safety or other interests of consumers in relation to food;
4 providing advice, information or assistance in respect of such matters to any person who is not a public authority;
5 obtaining, compiling and keeping under review information about matters connected with food safety and other interests of consumers in relation to food, including (among other things) monitoring developments in science, technology and other fields of knowledge relating to such matters and carrying out, commissioning or coordinating research on those matters.

Naturally, the Act provides the Agency with appropriate powers under ss 10–11 to allow members of Agency staff or other individuals to carry out these functions efficiently and effectively. Further, the Agency has the power under s 19 of the Act to publish in such manner as it thinks fit all or any of the advice or guidance referred to above, information obtained through observations under s 10 or information obtained through the monitoring of enforcement (see below). This power of publication is subject to the Data Protection Act 1998 and cannot be exercised if the publication would be prohibited by an enactment, is incompatible with a Community obligation or would be in contempt of court. Before exercising the power to publish, the Agency must consider whether the public interest in the publication of the advice or information in question is outweighed by any consideration of confidentiality attached to it.

15.11.2 Enforcement

As detailed above, the enforcement of food safety legislation is the responsibility of local authority enforcement officers. However, the Food Standards Agency has a role to play under ss 12–17 of the 1999 Act in the monitoring of such enforcement action.

The essential obligation is contained in s 12, which provides that the Agency has a function of monitoring the performance of enforcement authorities in enforcing the Food Safety Act 1990, the Food Safety (Northern Ireland) Order 1991 and Part IV of the Agriculture Act 1970, together with regulations and orders made under those provisions. This function includes the setting of enforcement standards whether for enforcement authorities generally or any particular authority, making reports to enforcement authorities about their performance and including guidance as to actions which the Agency considers would improve that performance. Further, where a report has been made, the Agency may direct an authority to arrange for the publication of specified information from the report and may require the authority to notify the Agency of what action they have taken or propose to take in response to the report. Naturally, as is common with legislation of this sort, ss 13–14 provide the usual enforcement powers:

1 to require the production of relevant information from appropriate people;
2 to enter premises at a reasonable hour to inspect the premises or anything that may be found on them;
3 to take samples of any articles or substances found on such premises;
4 to inspect and copy any records found on such premises, requiring a legible copy to be provided if the records are kept on computer; and
5 to require any person on the premises to provide such facilities, records, information or other assistance as may reasonably be requested.

Criminal sanctions are in place should an authorised officer wrongfully disclose any information relating to a trade secret that he has acquired after entering a premise in performance of his duty or if a person wilfully obstructs an officer in the performance of his duty or fails without reasonable excuse to comply with a requirement made of him by an authorised officer. In both situations a defendant would be liable on summary conviction to a fine not exceeding level 5 on the standard scale (currently £5,000).

Question

Jenny runs a catering business. She has a contract to supply the catering facilities in the factory canteen of H Ltd, a local manufacturer, and uses the factory kitchens to prepare hot snacks. One lunchtime, she served a hot sausage roll infested with maggots to Joe. The enforcement officer visiting the premises in response to a complaint from Joe noticed that the 'use by' dates on some of the yogurts on display had expired.

Discuss Jenny's criminal liabilities under the Food Safety Act 1990.

Answer

Jenny is a food business for the purposes of the Food Safety Act 1990 and therefore is subject to the controls contained both in the Act and in any regulations made under the Act or adopted by it.

She has sold a sausage roll infested with maggots. This will constitute an offence against the food safety requirement contained in s 8 of the Act. This section makes it an offence to sell for human consumption any food which is so contaminated (whether by extraneous matter or otherwise) that it would not be reasonable to expect it to be used for human consumption in that state. Jenny may be able to claim a due diligence defence if she can show that she took all reasonable precautions and exercised all due diligence to avoid the commission of the offence. Whether she did will depend on all the facts of the case.

She has also committed an offence by offering to sell yogurts on which the 'use by' date has expired. This may have arisen because of poor stock rotation on her behalf or because of an oversight. Either way she will find it very difficult to establish any defence.

Further reading

Attwood, B (2000). *Food Law*, 2nd edn (Butterworth)

Butterworth's Law of Food and Drugs (1996)

Harvey, B W and Parry, D L (1996). *The Law of Consumer Protection and Fair Trading*, 5th edn (Butterworth)

Howells, G, Bradgate, R and Griffiths, M (1990). *Blackstone's Guide to the Food Safety Act 1990* (Blackstone Press)

16 Weights and measures

16.1 Introduction

Large purchases of goods are typically sold either by reference to a unit of length, area, volume, capacity or weight, or by a specified number of prepacks of goods each of a given amount. In either instance, purchasers will want to ensure that they have received the full quantity of goods for which they have paid under the terms of the contract of sale. The Weights and Measures Act 1985 is the statute which currently provides the framework for ensuring that purchasers do not receive short quantity when buying goods.

Goods bought by reference to a unit of size may be sold by length, area, volume, capacity or weight, Parts I–V of Schedule 1 to the 1985 Act stipulating the units of measurement that are legal for use for trade in the UK. The move towards metrication is now virtually complete with very limited derogations remaining.

16.2 Offences of short weight or measure

The 1985 Act provides for various offences relating to the giving of short weight or measure when selling goods, although which Part of the Act applies depends on whether goods are sold by reference to quantity or whether they are sold in 'regulated packages', i.e. made up according to the average quantity principle. Where they are sold by weight, measurement or number Part IV of the Act will apply, while Part V applies to goods sold in regulated packages. Hence Part IV offences relate to items such as bulk deliveries of coal and fuel oil, delivery of prepacked goods in excess of the normal 10kg/10 litres upper limit for goods being controlled by the Part V average quantity requirements.

16.2.1 Goods sold by weight, measurement or number

Section 28(1) provides the general offence relating to short quantity goods and applies to the sale of goods sold by quantity. It reads:

> Subject to sections 33 to 37 below [the statutory defences], any person who, in selling or purporting to sell any goods by weight or other measurement or by number, delivers or causes to be delivered to the buyer—

(a) a lesser quantity than that purported to be sold; or

(b) a lesser quantity than corresponds with the price charged,

shall be guilty of an offence.

The section can apply both at wholesale and retail level but is restricted to incidents when the defendant is selling or purporting to sell the goods. In practice, local authorities are likely to be buying for use rather than resale and thus are unlikely to commit an offence under this section. By contrast, companies may be buying goods for the purposes of resale, in which case an offence may be committed if short quantity were given at that time. As the section states, it is an offence to provide a quantity less than that purported to be sold. For example, in **Frank H Mann (Torquay) Ltd** *v* **Womersley** (1972) (unreported, but quoted by *O'Keefe: Law of Weights and Measures*) an offence was committed when a trader sold a box of apples accompanied by an invoice which stated '1 case of 30lbs of Bramleys' but which actually weighed 25lb 11oz. The matter was complicated further by the fact that the purchaser, the Corporation of Torquay, had ordered 28lb of apples.

By the same token a deficiency in the amount of any of the following delivered pursuant to a contract would create an offence, for example heating oil by volume for use in schools, ballast sold by weight for use by a highways department, potatoes bought by weight for use in canteens or crayons sold by number for use in nursery schools. If a purchaser believes that he has received short weight goods he can, of course, ask a duly authorised inspector of weights and measures to weigh the goods for him to establish the actual weight. Of course, the practical limitation to this power is that the goods delivered must be capable of identification and not have become mixed in any way with any other goods. Thus, for example, coal cannot be re-weighed if it has been deposited into a bunker in which some coal remains from a previous delivery. In addition, coal poses particular problems in that its weight will vary depending on how wet it is.

The purchaser has another line of action in very particular circumstances. Under s 41, where any road vehicle is loaded with goods for sale by weight to a single buyer, or for delivery to the buyer after they have been so sold, the buyer or seller of the goods can demand that the driver of the road vehicle gets the vehicle check-weighed to confirm the weight of the goods. Thus, for example, if a lorryload of topsoil sold by weight is being delivered to a local authority leisure services department, the authority can demand that it be check-weighed. It is an offence to refuse to have a vehicle check-weighed if so requested by the seller or buyer of the goods.

An offence under s 28(1) is also committed if the goods supplied do not correspond to the price charged. Thus, for example, if a contract was for '£33 worth of meat at £3.30 per kilo' an offence would be committed if less than 10 kilos were delivered, subject to the *de minimis* principle. This principle, that the law is not concerned with trifles, would mean that no prosecution would be taken in respect of any trifling, insignificant short weight.

It must be remembered that the purpose of s 28 is to attach criminal liability for the delivery of a short quantity of goods. It does not provide the purchaser with compensation. The civil law remedies of the buyer are set out in s 30(1) of the Sale of Goods Act 1979 as discussed in Chapter 9. It provides that where the seller of goods delivers a quantity less than that he contracted to sell, the buyer may reject the goods, or alternatively may accept them and pay for them at the contract rate. Thus the contract price would be reduced to reflect accurately the quantity of goods actually delivered.

Sections 29–31 of the 1985 Act create other offences that are connected with the sale of short quantity. Section 29 makes it an offence in the sale or purchase of any goods, or when offering goods for sale or purchase, to make any representation, whether oral or otherwise, calculated to mislead anyone buying or selling the goods as to the quantity of the goods. In this context 'calculated to mislead' means 'likely to mislead' rather than 'intended to mislead'. Such a misdescription could also constitute an offence against s 1 of the Trade Descriptions Act 1968 and could give rise to civil liability under s 13 of the Sale of Goods Act 1979 and the laws governing misrepresentation.

Section 30(1) deals with statements made when goods covered by this Part of the Act are prepacked in or on containers marked with a written statement as to the weight of the goods. An example would be where apples are prepacked in a plastic sealed bag and labelled with the statement '2kg net'. If the goods weigh less than the declared weight, an offence will be committed by any person who has them in his possession for sale, subject, naturally, to the statutory defences not being available. Further, if the deficiency cannot be accounted for by anything that has happened to the goods after they had been sold by retail sale to the buyer or his representative, an offence will have been committed by anyone who sold or agreed to sell the goods in their prepacked state. Section 30(2) provides a similar offence for non-prepacked goods. In line with accepted tolerances under average weight principles, it would seem unlikely that a prosecution would ensue for deficiencies of less than about 4 per cent.

Section 31(1), which provides the last offence in this group, states that, in relation to goods which are required by Part IV of the Act to be accompanied by a document containing particular statements, it shall be an offence to make materially incorrect statements.

16.2.2 Defences

The two major defences in Part IV are to be found in ss 33 and 34 and relate to written warranties and due diligence.

Section 33 provides a written warranty defence similar to that provided previously under food safety legislation. The defendant can employ the defence if he bought the goods from some other person as being of the quantity represented and was provided with a written warranty that the quantity was correct. Further, the defendant must show that he believed that the statement in the warranty was accurate and had no reason to doubt its accuracy. If the warranty was provided by a person outside Great Britain, the defendant must also have taken reasonable steps to check its accuracy. If he wishes to rely on a warranty defence, the defendant must send a copy of the written warranty, together with the name and address of the person who provided it, to the prosecutor at least three days before the date of the hearing.

Section 34 contains the due diligence defence similar to that already discussed in relation to both the Trade Descriptions Act 1968 and the Food Safety Act 1990. In this Act it is a single-strand defence requiring that the defendant took all reasonable precautions and exercised all due diligence to avoid the commission of the offence. The test promulgated by Fisher J in **Tesco Supermarkets Ltd** *v* **Nattrass** (1972) requiring the defendant to demonstrate that he had established an efficient quality control system and then ensured that it functioned correctly would be equally applicable here. This would include such factors as appropriate sampling of the product to ensure compliance, as in **Garrett** *v* **Boots Cash Chemists Ltd** (1980) and **Sherratt** *v* **Gerald's The American Jewellers Ltd** (1970) discussed earlier. A case decided under the Weights and Measures Act 1979 is **Bibby-Cheshire** *v* **Golden Wonder Ltd** (1972) in which the defendant, a manufacturer of potato crisps, produced approximately 20 million packets per week. The case related to an individual packet which was weight marked 15 grams but weighed only 9 grams. The packets were filled by machine, it being shown that the defendant used the best machines available, that it was statistically impossible not to produce any under-weight packets and that none of the machines in use consistently produced deficient packets. Further, an efficient system for the check-weighing of packets randomly was in use. It was held that the defendant had established the due diligence defence.

As with the Food Safety Act 1990, there is no need to demonstrate that the offence was due to the act or default of another or that the defendant had relied on information supplied by another. However, if the defendant wishes to adduce such evidence as part of his defence, appropriate notice must be given to the prosecutor. Sections 35 and 36 provide additional, more limited, defences. Section 35(2) provides for a defence to be available in respect of a deficiency in the quantity of goods as compared with a weight marking on a container or a statement in a document accompanying the goods. In either situation it is a defence to show that the deficiency arose after the marking of the container or statement in the document, and further that it was attributable wholly to factors for which reasonable allowance was made when marking the container or making the statement. Section 35(3) provides a further defence if the deficiency is in non-prepacked food if it can be shown that the deficiency arose through unavoidable evaporation or drainage.

Section 36 provides an unusual defence in that it covers the situation where the inaccuracy in the weight of goods provided is due to an excess of the goods. The defence exists when the defendant can demonstrate that the excess was attributable to the taking of reasonable measures to avoid a deficiency. The civil law position regarding an excess delivery is covered in s 30(2) of the Sale of Goods Act 1979, which provides that where the seller delivers a quantity of goods larger than the buyer had contracted to purchase, the buyer can (a) reject the whole consignment, (b) accept only the amount for which he contracted and reject the remainder or (c) accept the whole consignment and pay for it at the contract rate.

16.3 Regulated packages

Part V of the Weights and Measures Act 1985 as supplemented by the Weights and Measures (Packaged Goods) Regulations 1986 gives effect to Directives 75/106/EEC and 76/211/EEC, which introduced the average quantity system into the UK in respect of certain prepacked goods. Packaged goods must conform to the Packers' Rules.

The average quantity system considers the quantity of goods in a batch rather than individually and dictates that the average quantity of items in the batch as a whole will not be less than the quantity marked on the individual item. The system permits the quantity of some items in the batch to be greater than the nominal quantity while others are less than the nominal quantity. Provision is made for a 'tolerable negative error' (TNE) of approximately $2^{1}/_{2}$ per cent in individual items as long as the batch as a whole complies. While this ensures a consistent standard across a batch, there is no guarantee that any individual item will not be deficient. An individual item becomes an 'inadequate' (a crucial concept in the system) only when its deficiency exceeds twice the TNE (approximately 5 per cent). The production of an inadequate is illegal. Similarly, the possession of an inadequate package can lead to an offence by the packer. However, it is an accepted statistical principle that even a packing system totally in control will occasionally, i.e. one package in 10,000, produce an inadequate package. It would seem unlikely that the authorities would prosecute for the single inadequate which will inevitably be produced. Goods packaged anywhere in the European Union that conform to the average weight system will be 'e' marked.

Enforcement of the average quantity system by inspectors qualified under the Weights and Measures Act and employed by local authorities occurs primarily at packer level, where complete batches are available. A batch for this purpose consists of an identifiable collection of items produced by the same process from the same constituent parts. Alternatively, where goods are produced on a continuous production line, a batch can consist of one hour's production. It is impractical to undertake enforcement at retail or purchaser level unless the retailer/purchaser has taken delivery of an identifiable batch. This is unlikely, though not unknown. This Part of the Act places purchasers in both a weak and strong position. The weakness is that they have no comeback if they receive deficient prepacked items covered by Part V unless they have purchased the whole identifiable batch and can arrange for it to be tested, an unlikely scenario, or if an item is inadequate. Thus, for example, if a local authority takes delivery of 1,000 tins of baked beans, some of which are deficient, nothing can be done unless some of the cans are inadequates. The strength of the purchaser's position is that as the strict controls in Part V of the Act are aimed at packers, it is unlikely that a purchaser would be guilty of an offence.

The offences in Part V are contained in s 50 and are aimed at the packer or importer of a product. However, s 50(5) does provide one offence which could be committed by someone who has purchased with the intention of resale, though not by an ultimate purchaser. It states:

> If a person has in his possession for sale, agrees to sell or sells a regulated package which is inadequate and either—
>   (a) he is the packer or importer of the package; or
>   (b) he knows that the package is inadequate,
> he shall be guilty of an offence.

Note that there are three restrictions on liability, namely, that it is related to sale, that the item must be 'inadequate', i.e. deficient by more than twice the TNE, and that the defendant (if not the packer or importer) must know that it is inadequate.

Given these strictures, the ultimate purchaser buying the goods for use cannot be guilty. Packers and importers charged under s 50(5) can use the due diligence defence provided by s 51. The defence is not open to other defendants as the s 50(5) offence requires that the defendant knew that the item was inadequate, such knowledge being inconsistent with reasonable precautions and due diligence.

Question

The Supplies Department of Westshire County Council ordered 2,000 tins of sliced carrots from Vegetables Ltd. The carrots were for use in school canteens, to which the county council distributed them. Doris, a school cook, opened one of the tins in the presence of Lisa, one of her assistants. The tin was less than half full. There was a weight statement on the side of the tin which read '2kg e'. Doris put the tin to one side to prevent it being disturbed and reported the matter to the Supplies Department. They, in turn, reported it to the Trading Standards Department. Discuss whether any offences against the Weights and Measures Act 1985 have been committed.

Answer

Section 50(5) of the 1985 Act makes it an offence to have in possession for sale, to agree to sell or sell a regulated package that is inadequate if the defendant is either the packer or importer of the package or, alternatively, knows that the package is inadequate. An inadequate package is one that is deficient by over 2TNE (approximately 10 per cent deficiency).

The tin of carrots is a regulated package subject to the average quantity system as it is 'e' marked. As it was less than half full, it is a reasonable assumption that it is an inadequate and therefore illegal.

The school will not have committed an offence as they have not sold it and did not know that it was inadequate. The same is true of the Supplies Department of Westshire County Council. The first possible offence may have been committed by the wholesaler who sold it to the county council, although they will be liable only if they knew that the tin was inadequate. As it is a sealed product, this is highly unlikely. The primary offence will have been committed by the packer or importer at the place that the product was first sold. It will be the responsibility of the Trading Standards Department in that area to decide whether to prosecute.

Further reading

Harvey, B W and Parry, D L (2000). *The Law of Consumer Protection and Fair Trading*, 6th edn (Butterworth)

Painter, A (ed.) (1996). *O'Keefe: Law of Weights and Measures* (Butterworth)

Part V Related legislation

17 Legal aspects of outsourcing

17.1 Introduction

Very few businesses are capable, or indeed would wish, to provide for themselves all the goods and services that they need in order to run their business efficiently and effectively. The buying-in of goods and services is thus a normal part of modern commercial practice and this chapter seeks to investigate this practice of outsourcing for both goods and services, whether the purchaser is a private business or a public body, be it a government department, a local authority or other body supported by public money.

In seeking to outsource for goods and services, good practice and business efficacy demand that the purchaser wants to find a supplier who will be both reliable and will provide products or services that are good value for money. Good value for money does not, of course, simply mean the cheapest but will include a variety of other factors such as quality, compliance with tender criteria, after-sales service, etc. In practice, suppliers are most likely to be identified by a process of tendering which will, in appropriate situations, be governed by the EU Public Procurement Directives and the requirements of compulsory competitive tendering.

17.2 Tenders

The role of tenders in traditional contract law was considered in Chapter 1 but nonetheless will bear repeating here because of the central role that tenders play in the process of outsourcing. As explained previously, a tender is, at law, a contractual offer which can be accepted or rejected by the person to whom the tenders are provided. The issues raised by the use of tenders are:

1 whether there is an obligation on the person inviting the tenders to consider all the tenders submitted providing they have complied with the terms of the tendering process; and
2 whether the person who invited the tenders is obliged to accept the lowest/highest tender (depending on the circumstances) or indeed any tender of those submitted.

The answers would appear to be 'yes' to the first and 'no' to the second. In respect of the first, the case of **Blackpool & Fylde Aero Club Ltd** *v* **Blackpool BC** (1990) is instructive. It confirms that there is a contractual obligation to consider all tenders that are received by any deadline set and which comply with all the requirements of the invitation to submit such tenders. In that case, Blackpool Borough Council invited tenders for a concession to run pleasure flights from Blackpool airport. The terms of the invitation were that tenders were to be submitted sealed in the envelope provided before 12 noon on a date specified. The plaintiff's tender, which complied with the prescribed form, was placed in the council's letterbox at 11 am on the relevant day. However, council staff failed to clear the letterbox at noon, resulting in the plaintiff's tender being deemed late and not considered. The court held the council liable for breach of contract, holding that the plaintiff had a contractual right to have its tender considered as it had complied in every respect with the terms of the invitation.

In respect of the second issue the decision of **Spencer *v* Harding** (1870) suggests that there is no obligation to accept the highest bid or indeed any bid at all. There may be good reasons for deciding not to proceed with the contract or alternatively to accept a bid which, though not the highest, may offer other attractions. It is clear that the wording of the circular may be crucial. In **Spencer *v* Harding**, the defendants issued a circular stating that they had been instructed to offer for sale by tender to the wholesale trade, the stock-in-trade of Messrs G Eilbeck & Co. The plaintiffs submitted the highest tender, which the defendants refused to accept. The plaintiffs alleged that the circular constituted a contractual offer, with the implication that the highest tender would be accepted. The plaintiffs had lodged the highest tender. The Court of Common Pleas held that the defendants were not liable to the plaintiffs and that the circular merely constituted an invitation to treat with no implication that they would necessarily accept any tender. However, the court considered that the position would have been different if the circular had continued by making a statement that the highest tender would be accepted. In that situation, the circular would have constituted a unilateral contractual offer capable of acceptance by the highest bidder. The key issue appears to be whether the circular is merely seeking information or whether it evinces a definite intention to contract on specified terms with an appropriate bidder.

The distinction is illustrated in the decision of **Harvela Investments Ltd *v* Royal Trust Co of Canada Ltd** (1986), which dealt with the issue of competitive tendering. In that case, the defendants wanted to sell some shares, the two obvious prospective purchasers being the plaintiffs and the second defendants. Both were invited to tender for the shares by a sealed competitive tender, the defendants confirming that 'if the offer made by you is the highest offer received by us, we bind ourselves to accept such offer providing that such offer complies with the terms of this telex'. In the event, the plaintiffs bid $2,175,000 while the second defendants bid $2,100,000 or $100,000 more than any other higher bid, a 'referential bid'. The defendants sold the shares to the second defendants. The House of Lords held that the defendants were obliged to sell the shares to the plaintiffs as their statement amounted to a contractual offer to accept the highest bid, i.e. that of the plaintiffs. To accept the 'referential bid' of the second defendants was contrary to the offer to accept the highest of the sealed competitive bids.

Tenders may be seeking to establish two differing types of contract between the person inviting the offer and the person submitting the successful tender and thereby entering a contract. It might be that the purchaser is seeking the definite supply of identified goods or services either immediately or at recognised dates or periods in the future. Alternatively, it may be that the prospective purchaser is seeking to appoint a supplier who will provide a 'standing offer' whereby the purchaser will not necessarily purchase any goods from the supplier at all but has the opportunity to purchase goods at an agreed contract price up to the maximum agreed in the contract for the duration of the contract. Thus, to quote the example used earlier, in a contract to supply a local authority with 1,000 tons of rock salt to be spread on the roads in winter, the successful supplier would be obliged to provide 1,000 tons of rock salt on the due delivery date. By contrast, if the contract was a 'standing offer' to supply up to 1,000 tons as and when ordered by the local authority during a period of 12 months, there would be no guarantee that any order would actually be placed. Nonetheless, there would be a contractual obligation to satisfy any order placed up to a total of 1,000 tons during the agreed period, as indicated in the case of **Great Northern Rly Co *v* Witham** (1873).

Traditionally, the acceptance of a tender has not necessarily been the end of negotiation about the terms upon which the parties will contract. There has always been scope for 'post-tender negotiations' whereby the matters and criteria agreed in the tendering process can be fleshed out into the final detailed contractual agreement. However, it should be noted that such post-tender negotiations are not permitted when the tender process has been conducted under the requirements of the EU Public Procurement Directives.

17.3 Letters of intent and letters of comfort

Following the submission of a tender, the prospective purchaser may choose to issue a 'letter of intent' to the chosen supplier indicating their intention to enter a contract with them. Equally, a supplier bidding for a major contract may issue letters of intent to sub-contractors that he would use if he was successful in the main bid. Thus, for example, a building company tendering to a local authority for a contract to build a new school might issue letters of intent to sub-contractors that they would wish to employ if they gained the contract. In that situation, there is no intention to be bound contractually at that stage and no contractual agreement reached and yet it is possible for work to begin on the strength of a letter of intent. The leading case is **British Steel Corpn *v* Cleveland Bridge and Engineering Co Ltd** (1984), in which the defendants negotiated with the plaintiffs for the latter to manufacture some specialist steel nodes to be used in the construction of a bridge. During negotiations, the defendants sent a letter of intent to the plaintiffs proposing that any contract would be on the defendants' standard terms. The plaintiffs were not prepared to contract on those terms. Work was completed and the plaintiffs sued for the price, the defendants counterclaiming for damages for late delivery. The court held that there was no contract, merely a letter of intent, final terms not having been agreed. Nonetheless, the plaintiffs were entitled to claim a *quantum meruit* for the goods supplied.

A further type of letter which may 'oil the wheels' of a commercial venture are 'letters of comfort', as recognised in the leading case of **Kleinwort Benson Ltd *v***

Malaysian Mining Corporation Bhd (1989) and discussed in Chapter 1. However, it must be recognised that such letters are not necessarily legally enforceable. Their enforceability will depend on the facts of the individual case as to whether the person issuing the letter intended to be contractually bound by it and it is incumbent upon the person issuing the letter to make their intentions clear. For example, in the **Kleinwort Benson** case the person did not intend to create a legally binding contract. In that decision, the plaintiff bank agreed to provide a loan to the defendants' wholly owned subsidiary, MMC Metals Ltd, who traded in tin on the London Metal Exchange. The defendants refused to provide a guarantee for the loan but did provide two 'letters of comfort', each of which read 'It is our policy to ensure that the business of MMC Metals Ltd is at all times in a position to meet its liabilities to you under the (loan facility) arrangements'. Due to the collapse of the tin market, MMC Metals Ltd went into liquidation while still owing the plaintiff the whole of the sum borrowed and the plaintiff sued the defendants for the amount owing relying on the 'letters of comfort'. However, the Court of Appeal held that the defendants were not liable, the 'letters of comfort' merely being statements of fact about the defendants' present intentions and not contractual promises as to their future conduct. There was no intention to create a legal relationship, as evidenced by the defendants' refusal to provide a guarantee.

17.4 EU Public Procurement Directives

The Treaty establishing the European Community enshrined four 'freedoms', namely freedom of movement of goods, persons, services and capital. These freedoms remain underpinned by the existence of the single market in which there are no internal frontiers that could pose a barrier to free trade and competition within the external boundaries of what is now the European Union. An integral part of promoting such free trade is the existence of the EU Public Procurement Directives. These Directives, of which there are six, apply to 'contracting authorities' defined as being 'the State, regional or local authorities, bodies covered by public law (and) associations formed by one or several such bodies governed by public law' and impose a system for the tendering and allocation of contracts that exceed the relevant financial thresholds. Such bodies, having some degree of State control and being providers of major public services, are major users of goods and services and regularly award contracts worth millions of pounds, the processing of which must now comply with the relevant Public Procurement Directive.

The six Directives which together constitute the 'Public Procurement Directives' are listed in chronological order. Being Directives, they require the making of national legislation to bring them into effect in the UK. The relevant statutory instruments effective in the UK are given for each Directive.

1 Council Directive 89/665/EEC of 21 December 1989 on coordination of the laws, regulations and administrative provisions relating to the application of review procedures to the award of public supply and public works contracts (the 'Compliance Directive'). Implemented in the UK by the Public Works Contracts

Regulations 1991 (works), the Public Services Contracts Regulations 1993 (services) and the Public Supply Contracts Regulations 1995 (supplies).

2 Council Directive 92/13/EEC of 25 February 1992 coordinating the laws, regulations and administrative provisions relating to the application of Community rules on the procurement procedures of entities operating in the water, energy, transport and telecommunications sectors (the 'Utilities Remedies Directive'). Re-implemented in the UK by the Utilities Contracts Regulations 1996.

3 Council Directive 92/50/EEC relating to the coordination of procedures for the award of public service contracts (the 'Services Directive'). Implemented in the UK by the Public Services Contracts Regulations 1993.

4 Council Directive 93/36/EEC coordinating procedures for the award of public supply contracts (the 'Supplies Directive'). Implemented in the UK by the Public Supply Contracts Regulations 1995.

5 Council Directive 93/37/EEC of 14 June 1993 concerning the coordination of procedures for the award of public works contracts (the 'Works Directive'). Implemented in the UK by the Public Works Contracts Regulations 1991.

6 Council Directive 93/38/EEC of 14 June 1993 coordinating the procurement procedures of entities operating in the water, energy, transport and telecommunications sectors (the 'Utilities Directive'). Implemented in the UK by the Utilities Contracts Regulations 1996.

The last four of these Directives lay down the procedures to be followed in the tendering and awarding of relevant contracts, while the first two provide for remedies for non-compliance with those set procedures. The regulations giving effect to the Supplies Directive, the Services Directive and the Works Directive have all been amended recently as a result of seeking compatibility with the World Trade Organisation Government Procurement Agreement (GPA) agreed in 1994 so that EU suppliers would not be at a disadvantage in the world market. The amendments have been given force in the UK by the Public Contracts (Works, Services and Supply) (Amendment) Regulations 2000, which came into force on 16 August 2000.

The financial thresholds at which the Directives take effect are reviewed regularly with the limits current at the time of writing (May 2001) due to expire on 31 December 2001. Thereafter, of course, they are likely to change and be increased. Nonetheless, the current thresholds will give a feel for the size of contracts that the Directives seek to control. The threshold levels set under the World Trade Organisation GPA are higher than the corresponding EU levels, with the latter being given priority in the European Union. The current threshold levels for the Supplies Directive, the Services Directive and the Works Directive are shown in Figure 17.1.

Different figures apply in relation to utilities provided under Directive 93/38/EEC, the Utilities Directive, and are given in Figure 17.2.

In the tables in Figures 17.1 and 17.2, the term 'indicative notice' refers to the notice that must be published annually by purchasing entities indicating their purchasing needs for the following year, while the term 'small lots' means certain specified small contracts which form part of a group of contracts which combine together to carry out an identifiable piece of work.

The procedures specified in the Directives permit of three different types of procedure; open procedures, restricted procedures and negotiated procedures. The

	Supplies	Services	Works
Central government bodies subject to the WTO Government Procurement Agreement	£93,896	£93,896	£3,611,395
Other public sector contracting authorities	£144,456	£144,456	£3,611,395
Indicative notices	£505,500	£505,500	£3,611,395
Small lots	£134,800	£53,920	£674,000

Figure 17.1 Threshold levels under the Supplies Directive, the Services Directive and the Works Directive

	Supplies	Services	Works
Energy, water and transport sectors	£269,600	£269,600	£3,370,000
Telecommunications sector	£404,400	£404,400	£3,370,000
Indicative notices	£505,500	£505,500	£3,370,000
Small lots			£674,000

Figure 17.2 Threshold values under the Utilities Directive

'open procedure' allows all interested suppliers to tender for the contract, while the 'restricted procedure' is limited to suppliers who are invited by the contracting entity to submit a tender. The 'negotiated procedure' is even more limited as it allows the contracting authority to identify a prospective supplier or suppliers and negotiate the terms of the contract directly with them.

The procedures under the four Directives stipulate the way that tenders for relevant contracts must be handled both in terms of the publication of relevant notices, etc and in terms of a very strict timetable for the various stages of the process. The procedure and the deadlines also vary depending upon whether the bid is subject to the open procedure, the restricted procedure or the negotiated procedure. The publication of the various stages is done via use of the *Official Journal of the European Communities* with simultaneous publication in the *Tenders Electronic Daily (TED)* database. While slightly different procedures apply to the three systems the net effect should be the same, i.e. to gain the best value for money in the award of public contracts. However, the procedures do contain the same inherent weakness, namely that as each contract is dealt with as a separate matter and subject to individual tenders, there is no real opportunity for a good working relationship to be built up between any contracting authority and any given supplier.

17.4.1 Open procedure

The process begins with the publication of the indicative notice (sometimes termed the 'prior information notice') in the *Official Journal of* the *European Communities*, which will be done as soon as possible after the commencement of the financial year. Thereafter, the contracting authority must publish the notice seeking tenders as soon as possible after the decision has been made to offer a contract. Following publication, the contract documents must be supplied within six days of the receipt of a request provided that they have been requested within the given period and any fee has been paid. A prospective tenderer who wants additional information may ask for it with an obligation existing that the information must be sent no less than six days before the final date for submission of the tender. Generally the last date for the receipt of the tender must be not less than 52 days from the date of despatch of the Notice. However, under the Public Contracts (Works, Services and Supply) (Amendment) Regulations 2000, the 52-day period may be reduced to a shorter period of generally no less than 36 days and in any event not less than 22 days providing that in each case the period is sufficient for effective tendering. This applies to relevant contracts provided that a prior information notice has been published at least 52 days and no more than 12 months before the date on which the contract notice is despatched.

Naturally, the contract documents sent to prospective tenderers must make abundantly clear the details of the contract including the criteria upon which it will be judged. Such criteria might include factors such as price, reliability, technical factors, appearance and service maintenance although, as mentioned above, a person considering making a tender can ask for additional information, which must be supplied. However, it is crucial that the person making the tender has all the information because any resulting contract will be made on the basis of the terms included in the tender document and only those. The practice of post-tender negotiations, whereby fundamental aspects of the tender are discussed in the period between the submission of the tender and the award of the contract, are not permitted under the Directives. The only permitted discussions would be to seek clarification of something in the tender document, not to renegotiate it.

The notice announcing the award of the contract must be published within 48 days (two months for the Utilities Directive) of the award being made.

17.4.2 Restricted procedure

The process for a 'restricted procedure' application, whereby the ability to tender is restricted to people whom the contracting authority has invited to tender, is essentially the same as for the open procedure. The notice must be published as soon as possible after the decision to offer a contract has been made, the last date for receipt of requests to tender being received no later than 37 days after the despatch of the notice or 15 days if the matter is urgent. Thereafter, the contracting authority will issue invitations to tender with the consequent tender documents being received no more than 40 days after the issue of the invitation. As with the open procedure, prospective tenderers can seek additional information, which must be despatched no later than six days before the last date for submission of the tenders, and post-tender negotiations are forbidden.

It should be noted that different processes and time limits apply for the Utilities Directive. A notice is only published if needed and is not necessary if an indicative notice has been published. Thereafter, requests to tender must be received generally within five weeks of the issue of the notice but in any event in no less than 22 days. The date for the receipt of the tender itself is open to negotiation between the parties but must be at least three weeks and certainly no less than ten days from the despatch of the invitation.

Notification of the award of the contract must be published in the same way as for the open procedure.

17.4.3 Negotiated procedure

The process for the negotiated procedure is essentially different from that for either the open procedure or the restricted procedure. There are really only two stages, the first being the publication of the notice and the second being the receipt of the requests to negotiate within 37 days from the publication of the notice. This period may be reduced to 15 days if the matter is urgent. In respect of the Utilities Directive, the process is the same as that used in the restricted procedure under that Directive, namely that the notice need only be published if needed and is not necessary if an indicative notice has been published and that requests to negotiate must be received generally within five weeks of the notice but definitely in no less than 22 days.

17.5 Compulsory competitive tendering

For many years, local authorities and others were subjected to the requirements of compulsory competitive tendering (CCT). This process, the primary aim of which was to ensure that value for money was achieved for those services for which a local authority employed its direct labour organisation (DLO) or direct service organisation (DSO), was laid out in the Local Government, Planning and Land Act 1980, the Local Government Act 1988 and the Local Government Act 1992. However this system was swept away by the Local Government Act 1999 in favour of a new regime of 'best value authorities'.

Section 1 of the 1999 Act defines 'best value authorities' as including, amongst others, local authorities, National Park authorities, police authorities, fire authorities, metropolitan county fire and civil defence authorities, waste disposal authorities and metropolitan county passenger transport authorities. Section 2 gives the Secretary of State (the National Assembly in Wales) the power to extend the ambit of best value authorities to include some other bodies while also having the power to disapply some of the provisions to certain authorities specified by him.

The basic duty placed on best value authorities is to be found in section 3 of the 1999 Act which stipulates

> A best value authority must make arrangements to secure continuous improvement in the way in which its functions are exercised, having regard to a combination of economy, efficiency and effectiveness.

The duty is thus premised on a combination of three factors; economy, efficiency and effectiveness. In deciding how to achieve and fulfil this duty, best value authorities are required to consult with representatives of the following groups (it should be noted that the consultation requirements are obligatory and not optional):

1   persons liable to pay any tax, precept or levy to or in respect of the authority;
2   persons liable to pay non-domestic rates in respect of any area within which the authority carries out functions;
3   persons who use or are likely to use services provided by the authority; and
4   persons appearing to the authority to have an interest in any area within which the authority carries out functions.

To be effective and accountable, a duty must, naturally, be subject to performance indicators and standards against which performance can be assessed. Section 4, therefore, empowers the Secretary of State to specify 'performance indicators' by reference to which the performance of a best value authority can be assessed and 'performance standards' that must be met in relation to those indicators. The Secretary of State can provide for different indicators or standards to apply for different functions, for different authorities or to apply at different times. The purpose of introducing performance indicators and standards is to promote improvements of the way in which best value authorities perform their functions.

It is equally important for a best value authority to review and reflect upon its own performance, a practice required of it by the provisions of section 5 which specifies that an authority must conduct best value reviews of its performance with the aim of improving the way in which it carries out its functions having regard to economy, efficiency and effectiveness. The Secretary of State may specify that a review will apply to one authority or more, may make different provisions in relation to different authorities and can require specified functions to be reviewed in specified financial years. Similarly, he can require an authority to specify performance indicators for functions, set performance targets and construct a plan of action in order to ensure that the targets are met while providing guidance about the timetable, procedure and content of the review together with the form in which it should be recorded.

In addition to conducting best value reviews, best value authorities are also obliged, under section 6(1) to prepare best value performance plans for each financial year. Plans must be published no later than 31 March in any year, that date having been selected to tie in with the democratic process. Local elections are always scheduled in May and so statutory publication of plans by 31 March means that the up-to-date plans are always available to the electorate for scrutiny several weeks prior to voting. Section 6(2) gives the Secretary of State the power to stipulate what must be included in a plan and the form and manner in which they must be published. Among the factors that the Secretary of State may require an authority to address in their plans are:

1 The authority's objective in relation to the exercise of its functions and any assessment made by the authority of the level at which and the way in which it exercises those functions.
2 Any period within which the authority is required to review its functions under section 5 and the timetable the authority proposes to follow in conducting the review.
3 Any performance indicators, standards and targets specified or set in relation to the authority's functions and its progress towards meeting those standards and targets together with a plan of action for future progress.
4 The authority's assessment of its performance in the previous financial year with regard to performance indicators and to compare that performance both with the authority's performance in previous years and the performance of other best value authorities.

An authority's performance plan is subject to audit by the authority's auditor who can make recommendations about any amendments needed to bring the plan into compliance with the requirements of section 6. Further, the auditor can, if necessary, forward the plan to the Secretary of State who has the power under section 15 to require an authority to prepare or amend the plan so as to ensure compliance with the requirements of the Act. The Secretary of State may also require the authority to follow specified procedures in relation to the performance plan and to carry out a review of its exercise of specified functions.

17.6 Transfer of undertakings

As a result of outsourcing, but most particularly as a result of CCT whereby it is possible that a local authority may transfer some of its business to a DLO or DSO, the issue of a transfer of undertakings may come into play. Such a transfer occurs where an economic entity, such as a freestanding department of a business or corporation, is transferred to a new employer. This would involve the transfer of the business and the assets, often but not always including a transfer of the employees. The law relating to the transfer of undertakings is that part of the law that seeks to protect those employees and stipulate their employment rights.

17.6.1 Transfer of Undertakings (Protection of Employment) Regulations 1981

The protection of the rights of employees upon a transfer of undertaking was addressed by the European Union in the passage of the Acquired Rights Directive

(Directive 77/187/EEC) as amended in 1998 by Directive 98/50/EEC. In the UK, the Acquired Rights Directive has been given force by the Transfer of Undertakings (Protection of Employment) Regulations 1981 as amended by the Transfer of Undertakings (Protection of Employment) (Amendment) Regulations 1987, the Trade Union Reform and Employment Rights Act 1993 and the Collective Redundancies and Transfer of Undertakings (Protection of Employment) (Amendment) Regulations 1995. A new set of regulations are due to give effect to the provisions of Directive 98/50/EEC and must be in force by July 2001. At the date of writing (6 May 2001) these regulations were not available.

For an employee to gain the protection of the 1981 Regulations, various criteria must be satisfied:

1   there must have been the transfer of an economic entity;
2   the employee(s) concerned must have been employed by the old employer immediately before the transfer of the economic unit;
3   the employment must have been in the economic entity that is being transferred rather than in some other part of the business;
4   the employee must have been in a situation where their contract of employment would otherwise have been terminated by the transfer.

Various issues flow out of this. For example, generally the tribunals have been prepared to accept that an employee is employed in an economic entity if he spends the majority of his working hours in that entity. The requirement for employment immediately before the transfer has been held to mean at the moment of transfer, as in **Secretary of State for Employment** *v* **Spence** (1986).

The new employer does not have the right to pick and choose which employees he wishes to take on as part of the new enterprise. A few possibilities arise as to what may happen to the employees:

1   The new employer employs all of the employed attached to the entity with their rights being protected under the Regulations.
2   Some of the employees lose their jobs as a direct result solely of the transfer, such employees being able to claim compensation for unfair dismissal under the Employment Rights Act 1996.
3   The new employer decides that he needs fewer employees because of 'an economic, technical or organisational reason entailing changes in the workforce'. An economic, technical or organisational (ETO) reason is a legally acceptable reason for not taking the whole of the workforce, with those employees who are not needed being made redundant. Redundancy rights are discussed later. Any employee who has been identified for dismissal in contravention of the redundancy rules would be able to claim for unfair dismissal.
4   An individual employee may exercise their right under reg 5 of the 1981 Regulations to decide that they do not wish to be transferred to the new undertaking, in which case their contract will terminate automatically without any right to compensation.

When the employees have been transferred, their period of service transfers automatically with them so that it is deemed to be continuous service, an important factor as regards statutory employment rights. Thereafter, under the provisions of the Regulations, the new employer will take over the rights and liabilities of the old employer regarding the rights of the employees, reg 5(2) providing that

(a) all the transferor's rights, powers, duties and liabilities under or in connection with any such contract, shall be transferred by virtue of this Regulation to the transferee; and

(b) anything done before the transfer is completed by or in relation to the transferor in respect of that contract or a person employed in that undertaking or part shall be deemed to have been done by or in relation to the transferee.

This will mean that the terms and conditions upon which the employees are employed will remain unaltered and continue as previously. The new employer cannot unilaterally alter terms and conditions for the worse; will take over all the rights and liabilities except criminal liabilities and those arising from an occupational pension scheme; and will take over any collective agreements made on behalf of the employees and in force immediately before the transfer. It follows that there is also a transfer of trade union recognition. Any attempt by the new employer fundamentally to alter for the worse the terms and conditions upon which the employees are employed will give those employees the right to terminate their contracts and claim damages for unfair dismissal.

When there is a proposal to transfer an undertaking, reg 10 provides for consultation with representatives of the employees. This may be the officials of a recognised trade union or, alternatively, representatives appointed or elected by the relevant employees either generally or specifically for the purposes of the transfer. Both the old employer and the new employer are under a duty to consult and must provide the employees' representatives with all the appropriate information to allow them to consult effectively and keep the workforce informed of the situation and of any matters that will affect them. The employers are under an obligation to consider and reply to any representations made to them by the employees' representatives. Should the employer reject those representations, he must give reasons. Should an employer fail to consult with the employees' representatives, a complaint may be lodged with an employment tribunal.

17.6.2 Unfair dismissal

Mention has been made earlier that employees who are dismissed as a direct result of the transfer of undertaking and where there is no legitimate ETO reason for the dismissal can claim damages for unfair dismissal. A claim for unfair dismissal arising from a transfer of undertaking must be lodged with the tribunal within three months of that dismissal. The remedies for unfair dismissal are monetary compensation and a claim for reinstatement or re-engagement. Naturally, reinstatement involves the employee being returned to his previous work on the same conditions, while re-engagement is an appointment on different terms. In practice, many employees would not wish to return to a post from which they have been unfairly dismissed, working for the employer who dismissed them. Hence, such claims are relatively few.

Generally, the employee's claim will be for monetary compensation. The award may be in two parts: the basic award, which is calculated in the same way as a redundancy payment, and an additional award where the employer fails to comply with an order for reinstatement or re-engagement. This may equal the arrears of pay due and any other benefits even though this may exceed the normal level of awards. Further, a special award may be made where the dismissal was automatically unfair and the employee sought reinstatement or re-engagement. This special award will be increased if the employer was ordered to reinstate or re-engage the employee and unreasonably refused to do so. The contributory negligence of the employee will be taken into account and may result in a reduction in the award.

17.6.3 Redundancy

Where employees have been dismissed as the result of a legitimate ETO reason at the time of a transfer of undertaking, the employees are said to be redundant. Under the Employment Rights Act 1996 redundant employees are entitled to compensation although certain employees may not be eligible. Thus, for example, a redundant employee will lose his right to redundancy pay if he has been offered suitable alternative work by his employer and has refused it, or alternatively, has accepted an alternative job.

Any agreed formula for selecting employees must be followed, for example last in, first out. If the procedure is not followed, those employees who have been wrongly selected for redundancy can sue for unfair dismissal. Section 188 of the Trade Union and Labour Relations (Consolidation) Act 1992, as amended by the Collective Redundancies and Transfer of Undertakings (Protection of Employment) (Amendment) Regulations 1995, requires that when an employer is proposing to make redundant 20 or more employees at one time within a period of 90 days or less, the employer must consult all the appropriate representatives of any of the employees. This must be a minimum of at least 30 days before the first redundancy if the proposal is to dismiss between 20 and 99 employees, and at least 90 days before if the proposal is to dismiss 100 or more employees.

Redundancy pay is calculated by reference to the age of the claimant and the period of continuous service. Those aged 18–21 receive half a week's pay for every year of service, those aged 22–40 receive one week's pay for every year and those aged 41–65 receive one and a half week's pay for every year of service. The claimant will receive a maximum of 20 years subject to a specified maximum weekly rate.

Question

East Blankshire local authority decides to offer for tender a contract for the provision of sports and leisure services and the maintenance of sports grounds within their local authority area. The service is currently provided by their direct labour organisation (DLO). The contract falls within the ambit of compulsory competitive tendering (CCT).

(a) Outline the process that must be taken to invite bids and process them before the contract can be awarded.

(b) The DLO currently employs 569 employees to provide the service. The successful contractor under the CCT process needs only 542 employees. Explain the position and rights of the 27 current employees who will lose their jobs.

Answer

(a) The legal requirements for CCT are contained in the Local Government Planning and Land Act 1980 and the Local Government Acts 1988 and 1992. In this scenario, East Blankshire will need to comply with the requirements of the Local Government Act 1988, which demand that certain procedures must be followed before a defined authority (the DLO) can bid for a contract. East Blankshire must have invited tenders from at least three other bidders who are not 'defined authorities' within the meaning of the Act or, alternatively, published a notice inviting offers in at least one local newspaper and one newspaper that circulates among people involved in that type of work. Further, East Blankshire must not do anything that would restrict, distort or prevent competition, a particularly important requirement given that their own DLO is likely to bid. Naturally, the local authority must state clearly the criteria upon which the bids will be judged and are under an obligation to consider all the bids that satisfy all of the criteria. However, East Blankshire is not obliged to accept any of the bids unless they have committed themselves to do so during the process.

(b) The rights of employees at the time of a transfer of undertaking are governed by the Transfer of Undertakings (Protection of Employees) Regulations 1981 as amended. For the employees to gain protection under these Regulations, there must have been the transfer of an economic entity, the employees must have been employed in that economic entity immediately before the transfer and their contract would be terminated at the time of transfer if they were not transferred. In respect of the 27 employees, it must be established whether there is an 'economic, technical or organisational reason' (an ETO) for them not being needed. If there is, then they will be deemed to have been made redundant and can claim normal redundancy rights. If there is no ETO and they are losing their jobs purely because of the transfer of undertakings, they can claim for unfair dismissal.

Further reading

Keenan, D (2000). *Smith and Keenan's Advanced Business Law*, 11th edn (Longman)

Bowers, J (2000). *Bowers on Employment Law*, 5th edn (Blackstone Press)

Bowers, J and Honeyball, S (2000). *Textbook on Labour Law*, 6th edn (Blackstone Press)

Fernandez Martin, J M (1996). *The EC Public Procurement Rules* (Clarendon Press)

Medhurst, D (1997). *EU Public Procurement Law* (Blackwell Science)

Richards, P (2001). *Law of Contract*, 5th edn (Longman)

Stone, R (2000). *Principles of Contract Law*, 4th edn (Cavendish)

Tenders on the Web http:/www.tenders.co.uk/about.htm

18 Competition law

18.1 Introduction

The rationale behind competition law is a determination to ensure fair competition between the providers of goods and services in any given sector and thereby protect users and consumers. This is achieved by controlling various aspects of the market to prevent practices designed to or likely to distort competition and which are held to be contrary to the public interest. Thus monopolies, mergers, restrictive trade practices, resale price maintenance and other anti-competitive practices are all subject to some degree of control.

Competition law in the UK underwent a major overhaul in 1998 with the passage of the Competition Act 1998, which swept aside the previous legal controls. Thus the Restrictive Practices Court Act 1976, the Restrictive Trade Practices Act 1976, the Resale Prices Act 1976 and the Restrictive Trade Practices Act 1977 have all been repealed, together with ss 2–10 of the Competition Act 1980. A further 23 Acts including the Fair Trading Act 1973 have been either partially repealed or amended.

The *raison d'être* of the Act is to introduce into the UK a system of competition law controls that closely echoes the regime under arts 81 and 82 EC (previously arts 85 and 86 of the EC Treaty). Thus, there are two parallel systems, one running at a national level and one at the EU level. The close liaison between the two and the intention for the UK system to be implemented in a manner consistent with the EU approach is evident from the provisions of s 60(1), which states:

> The purpose of this section is to ensure that so far as is possible (having regard to any relevant differences between the provisions concerned), questions arising under this Part in relation to competition within the United Kingdom are dealt with in a manner which is consistent with the treatment of corresponding questions arising in Community law in relation to competition within the Community.

Whilst it is evident from the wording of the section that it only applies to Part I of the Act, in practice it is Part I which includes the major anti-competitive controls, most particularly the Chapter I prohibition (agreements between undertakings) and the Chapter II prohibition (abuse of a dominant position). The section continues by stipulating that when the court decides an issue under Part I, it must ensure (as far as possible given the other requirements of Part I and whether or not it would otherwise have been required to do so) that the principles applied in deciding the question and the decision reached are consistent with corresponding principles laid down by the Treaty and the European Court and decisions of the European Court. Similar obligations are placed on the Director General of Fair Trading and any person acting on his behalf for the purposes of Part I of the Act.

Enforcement of the Act is undertaken partly by the Director General of Fair Trading and partly by the Competition Commission established under s 45 of the Act to replace the Monopolies and Mergers Commission (MMC). All the powers of the MMC have been transferred to the Competition Commission and all legislation referring to the MMC is to be construed as if it referred to the Commission.

18.2 Competition Act 1998

The Competition Act 1998 is divided into four Parts:

- Part I – Competition.
- Part II – Investigations in relation to Articles 85 and 86 (now Articles 81 and 82 EC).
- Part III – Monopolies.
- Part IV – Supplemental and Transitional.

In addition to these Parts, there are 14 Schedules that expand upon various provisions of the Act such as the constitution of the Competition Commission; notifications under Chapters I and II: procedure; appeals; and exclusions.

Part I is the Part of most concern here as it contains the main prohibitions and controls and, hence, will receive most attention in the following text.

18.3 Part I of the 1998 Act

Part I is divided into five Chapters, of which Chapters I and II contain the main controls over agreements between undertakings and abuse of a dominant position. The remaining three Chapters in Part I address investigation and enforcement, the Competition Commission and appeals, and miscellaneous provisions.

18.4 Chapter I

18.4.1 The prohibition

The Chapter I prohibition is to be found in s 2 of the 1998 Act:

> Subject to section 3, agreements between undertakings, decisions by associations of undertakings or concerted practices which—
>
> (a) may affect trade within the United Kingdom, and

(b) have as their object or effect the prevention, restriction or distortion of competition within the United Kingdom,

are prohibited unless they are exempt in accordance with the provisions of this Part.

Three factors become obvious from a close reading of this section:

1   There is no requirement that the parties have entered a binding contract, either written or oral. Section 2 refers to agreements and thus informal arrangements would suffice.
2   There is no requirement that the agreements were made in the UK or indeed that the parties to the agreements are based in the UK.
3   The agreements must seek to affect trade in the UK or prevent, distort or restrict competition in the UK. This would include trade in any part of the country and thus can control agreements that are essentially local in effect. The effect of the agreements outside the UK is irrelevant and would be covered by other legislation. Thus, for example, effects in the remainder of the European Union would be governed by arts 81 and 82 EC.

This far-ranging prohibition is intended to control a wide variety of potentially anti-competitive practices that were governed previously by a selection of legislation. Thus, it seeks to simplify and consolidate control over anti-competitive practices. The practices to which the Chapter I prohibition relates are agreements which seek to:

(a)   directly or indirectly fix purchase or selling prices or any other trading conditions;
(b)   limit or control production, markets, technical development or investment;
(c)   share markets or sources of supply;
(d)   apply dissimilar conditions to equivalent transactions with other trading parties, thereby placing them at a competitive disadvantage;
(e)   make the conclusion of contracts subject to acceptance by the other parties of supplementary obligations which, by their nature or according to commercial usage, have no connection with the subject of such contracts.

This list closely echoes the provisions of art 81 EC, which operate at the EU level. Thus, it seeks to control price fixing (resale price maintenance), restricting output to keep prices artificially high, market sharing, using discriminatory practices against some but not all people in the market and tying (requiring a party to purchase other unrelated goods as a condition for providing the goods that they really want).

To be actionable, the anti-competitive practice complained of must have an appreciable effect on the market. The Director General of Fair Trading, who is responsible for the enforcement of these provisions under s 25 of the 1998 Act, will generally assume that the effect is not appreciable unless the combined market share of the parties concerned exceeds 25 per cent in the area affected by the agreement. However, this is a rebuttable presumption for the Director General may find an appreciable effect where the offending parties control less than 25 per cent and, equally, may find that an agreement involving more than 25 per cent does not have an appreciable anti-competitive effect on trade because of other relevant factors.

Where a breach of the Chapter I prohibition is found to exist, the offending provision will be held to be void, i.e. of no effect at any time. However, it is only the offending aspect of the agreement that will fall in this way with the remainder of the agreement remaining valid. With respect to a legally binding contract, this would of course require that the remainder of the contract satisfied all the requirements of a contractual agreement supported by valid consideration and an intention to be legally bound.

18.4.2 Exclusions

Not all agreements are covered by the Chapter I prohibition. Section 3 of the 1998 Act provides for four statutory exclusions, the fine detail of which are to be found in Schedules 1–4. The exclusions are:

- Schedule 1 (mergers and concentrations).
- Schedule 2 (competition scrutiny under other enactments).
- Schedule 3 (planning obligations and other general exclusions).
- Schedule 4 (professional rules).

The Secretary of State has the power to amend Schedules 1 and 3 in order to add one or more additional exclusions or to amend or remove any provision although his ability to add additional exclusions to Schedule 3 may only be exercised where he is satisfied that agreements which fall within the additional exclusion either do not in general have an adverse effect on competition or are, in general, best considered under Chapter II of the Fair Trading Act 1973.

Briefly, Schedule 1 allows an exemption in respect of mergers, i.e. situations in which two or more enterprises join together and cease to be distinct entities. In the UK, these are still subject to control by the Director General of Fair Trading under the provisions of the Fair Trading Act 1973 (see below). Schedule 1 also provides a specific exclusion for newspaper mergers, which are dealt with under the 1973 Act. Schedule 2 excludes agreements in four specified situations where such agreements are already subject to industry-specific controls, i.e. financial services, companies, broadcasting and environmental protection. Schedule 3 allows for general exclusions on the basis of planning obligations, existing control under s 21(2) of the Restrictive Trade Practices Act 1976, EEA-regulated markets, services of general economic interest, compliance with legal requirements, avoidance of conflict with international obligations, public policy and coal and steel and agricultural products. Finally, Schedule 4 provides for exemptions for professional rules, which are defined as being rules designated by the Secretary of State and which regulate a professional service or persons providing, or wishing to provide, that service. Thus, such rules impose obligations on persons exercising that profession and constitute an agreement by them to comply with the rules. The professional services covered are detailed in Part II of Schedule 4 as being legal, medical, dental, ophthalmic, veterinary, nursing, midwifery, physiotherapy, chiropody, architectural, accounting and audit-ing, insolvency, patent agents, parliamentary agents, surveying, engineering and technology etc, educational and religious.

In addition to the exclusions under s 3, the Secretary of State has the power under s 50(2) to make an order providing for an exclusion or an exemption in respect of vertical agreements and land agreements. A vertical agreement is one in which the two parties to the agreement are drawn from different sectors of the distributive chain and the agreement relates to the sale and/or purchase of goods and services for commercial purposes.

18.4.3 Exemptions

Exemptions, be they individual, block or parallel, are dealt with under ss 4–11 of the 1998 Act. Whichever type of exemption is applicable in any individual case, the net effect is that the Chapter I prohibition will not apply.

Individual exemption

An individual exemption, as the name suggests, is granted for an individual agree-ment whereas a block agreement applies to all agreements of that type. Both types of exemption must be applied for in the prescribed manner. By contrast, a parallel exemption arises automatically and does not require any application to be made to claim its protection.

The same criteria apply for both individual exemptions and block exemptions and are laid down in s 9 of the Act, which states that the section applies to any agreement which balances the positive gains to be achieved by allowing the exemption and off-setting them against any potential disadvantages. To attract an exemption, the agreement must contribute to improving production or distribution, or alternatively, promoting technical or economic progress while allowing consumers a fair share of the resulting benefit. Further, it must neither impose on the undertakings concerned restrictions which are not indispensable to the attainment of those objectives nor provide the undertakings concerned with the possibility of eliminating competition in respect of a substantial part of the products in question.

An individual exemption, which is granted by the Director General of Fair Trading and may be retrospective in effect, can be made subject to such conditions or obligations as may be considered appropriate by the Director General. The exemp-tion will be effective for whatever period the Director General deems appropriate with the period being specified in the grant and subject to renewal. In addition to having the right to grant the exemption, the Director General may also, by notice in writing, cancel the exemption, vary or remove any condition or obligation or impose one or more additional conditions or obligations. This situation arises under s 5 where the Director General has reasonable grounds for believing that there has been a material change of circumstances since he granted the exemption. Equally, it is open to him to take similar action if he has a reasonable suspicion that the information on which he based his original decision to grant an exemption was incomplete, false or misleading in a material way. Further, he may take similar action if there is a failure to comply with an obligation, while the breach of a condition will cancel the exemption.

Block exemption

Where the Director General is satisfied that a particular category of agreements satisfies the s 9 criteria, he can recommend to the Secretary if State that he grant a block exemption order in respect of that category of agreements. The Secretary of State has the authority to grant the order in the form recommended or with such modifications as he thinks appropriate and can impose obligations and conditions to the exemption in the order. Under s 6(6) a block exemption order may provide:

(a) that breach of a condition imposed by the order has the effect of cancelling the block exemption in respect of an agreement;

(b) that if there is a failure to comply with an obligation imposed by the order, the Director may, by notice in writing, cancel the block exemption in respect of the agreement;

(c) that if the Director considers that a particular agreement is not one to which s 9 applies, he may cancel the block exemption in respect of that agreement.

Under s 7 a block exemption order may provide that a party to an agreement that does not qualify for the block exemption but which does satisfy specified criteria may notify the Director General of the agreement and claim the benefit of s 7(2). This allows it to be treated as being included in the block exemption from the end of the period of notice unless the Director General objects to it being included and notifies the party in writing before the end of the notice period.

The procedures applicable for the grant, variation or revocation of a block exemption order are to be found in s 8.

Parallel exemption

A parallel exemption, which takes effect automatically, occurs where the agreement is exempt from a Community prohibition by virtue of a Regulation adopted by the European Commission or Council, or because it has been given exemption by the Commission, or, because it has been notified to the Commission under the appropriate opposition or objection procedure and the relevant time limit for opposition or objection has elapsed.

The parallel exemption regime is intended to promote consistency between the EU and the UK systems. Hence, a parallel exemption will apply in the UK from the date that it was granted in the European Union and will remain effective as long as it remains in force in the European Union. In addition, the exemption will apply to any agreement which does not affect trade between member states but would attract EU exemption if it did. Under s 10(5) the Director General may:

(a) impose conditions or obligations subject to which a parallel exemption is to have effect;

(b) vary or remove any such condition or obligation;

(c) impose one or more additional conditions or obligations;

(d) cancel the exemption.

When exercising his powers under the section, the Director General can require any person who is a party to an agreement to provide him with such information as he needs. The breach of any condition imposed by the Director General cancels the exemption.

18.4.4 Notification

It is clearly of enormous benefit to any party to an agreement to know for certain whether or not the agreement will infringe the Chapter I prohibition. Sections 12–16 of the 1998 Act provide for a notification system whereby a party to an agreement may seek a notification for guidance or a notification for a decision.

Under s 13, the Director General may give guidance as to whether or not the agreement is likely to contravene the Chapter I prohibition and whether it would be likely to be exempt under a block exemption, a parallel exemption or a s 11 exemption and whether he would be likely to grant an individual exemption if asked to do so. No penalty can be imposed if the agreement does infringe the Chapter I prohibition without attracting an exemption from the date of the notification until a date to be specified in writing by the Director General. Section 15(2) provides that the Director General will not take any further action in respect of an agreement unless:

(a) he has reasonable grounds for believing that there has been a material change of circumstances since he gave his guidance;

(b) he has a reasonable suspicion that the information on which he based his guidance was incomplete, false or misleading in a material particular;

(c) one of the parties to the agreement applies to him for a decision under s 14 with respect to the agreement; or

(d) a complaint about the agreement has been made to him by a person who is not a party to the agreement.

Under s 14, a party to an agreement can seek a decision (not merely guidance) from the Director General as to whether an agreement breaches the Chapter I prohibition and include a request that if the agreement does infringe the prohibition, an individual exemption will be granted. In making his decision, the Director General will confirm whether the Chapter I prohibition has been infringed and, if not, whether that is due to the effect of an exclusion or because the agreement is exempt. As with a notice for guidance, no penalty can be imposed in respect of any infringement from the date of notification until a date specified in writing by the Director General. Where the Director General has decided that the agreement does not infringe the Chapter I prohibition, he will not take any further action in respect of the agreement unless either he has reasonable grounds for believing that there has been a material change of circumstances since he made his decision or he has a reasonable suspicion that the information on which he based his decision was incomplete, false or misleading in a material particular.

18.5 Chapter II

18.5.1 The prohibition

Chapter II deals with controls to prevent the abuse of a dominant position. Section 18, which contains the Chapter II prohibition, states:

Subject to section 19, any conduct on the part of one or more undertakings which amounts to the abuse of a dominant position in a market is prohibited if it may affect trade within the United Kingdom.

For these purposes, 'dominant position' means a dominant position within the UK or any part of it. Various factors will play a part in deciding whether an undertaking is in a dominant position. This would include the market share held by the undertaking given that a dominant position is unlikely to occur if an undertaking controls less than approximately 40 per cent of the market. Certainly, the Office of Fair Trading suggests that a dominant position would only occur in exceptional circumstances if the undertaking has less than 20–25 per cent of the market. This emphasis on market share necessarily requires consideration of what factors will contribute to defining the market share in any given situation. In practice, they would include, among other things, the geographic area concerned, the product range and the ease with which other products could be substituted and the temporal limits to the dominance. The bottom line is that an undertaking will be dominant if it can act independently of its suppliers, its competitors and its customers.

It is not illegal to be in a dominant position, the infringement occurs where that position has been abused and it may affect trade in the UK. This follows the approach in the Chapter I prohibition as it is only conduct affecting trade in the UK, or any part of it, that falls within the remit of the Chapter II prohibition. Conduct that would constitute an abuse of the dominant position and thus would infringe the Chapter II prohibition would include:

1 directly or indirectly imposing unfair purchase or selling prices or other unfair trading conditions, i.e. price fixing, which could set prices artificially high or might involve fixing unduly low predatory prices in an attempt to force competitors out of the market;
2 limiting production, markets or technical developments to the prejudice of consumers;
3 applying dissimilar conditions to equivalent transactions with other trading parties thereby placing them at a competitive disadvantage, i.e. discriminatory trading;
4 making the conclusion of contracts subject to acceptance by the other parties of supplementary obligations which, by their nature or commercial usage, have no connection with the subject of the contracts, i.e. a tying arrangement compelling a party to agree to an obligation which is not connected to the main agreement.

18.5.2 Exclusions

In accordance with s 19 of the 1998 Act the Chapter II prohibition will not apply if it is excluded by the provisions of either Schedule 1 (mergers and concentrations) or Schedule 3 (general exclusions). The Secretary of State may amend the application of Schedule 1 with respect to the Chapter II exemption by either providing for one or more additional exclusions or by amending or removing any provision. Schedule 3 provides the Secretary of State with the power to provide that the Chapter II prohibition may not apply in some situations and that he can amend the paragraph of Schedule 3 dealing with the coal and steel industries.

18.5.3 Notification

A person can apply under s 22 for a decision from the Director General as to whether the Chapter II prohibition has been infringed and, if not, whether that is because of the effect of an exclusion. Where, as a result of an application, the Director General either gives guidance that the conduct is unlikely to infringe the Chapter II prohibition or makes a decision that the conduct does not infringe the prohibition, he will not take any further action in respect of the conduct either if he has reasonable grounds for believing that there has been a material change of circumstances since he issued the guidance or decision or if he has a reasonable suspicion that the information on which the guidance or decision was based was incomplete, false or misleading in a material particular.

18.5.4 Investigation and enforcement

Responsibility for investigating alleged infringements of both the Chapter I prohibition and the Chapter II prohibition rests with the Director General. Both he and his duly appointed 'investigating officers' have the usual statutory enforcement powers under ss 26–30 permitting them to require the production of specified documents or information, the power to enter premises with or without a warrant and to search the premises and copy and seize documents. It is an offence under ss 42–44 to fail to comply with a requirement or to obstruct an officer. A person found guilty of an offence on summary conviction will be liable to a fine not exceeding the statutory maximum (currently £5,000), while more serious offences tried on indictment may result in a term of imprisonment not exceeding two years or a fine or both.

Where an investigation is taking place and the Director General has a reasonable suspicion that an infringement of the Chapter I prohibition or the Chapter II prohibition has occurred and he feels that he needs to act as a matter of urgency either to prevent serious or irreparable damage to a particular person or category of people or to protect the public interest, he can give in writing such directions as he thinks appropriate.

On making a decision that an agreement infringes the Chapter I prohibition or that conduct infringes the Chapter II prohibition, the Director General may impose a penalty if he is satisfied that the infringement was committed either intentionally or negligently. The penalty must be notified in writing and must not exceed 10 per cent of the turnover of the undertaking concerned. Appeals against any decision of the Director General or on a point of law can be made to the Competition Commission.

18.6 Fair Trading Act 1973

Many of the provisions of the Fair Trading Act 1973 which provide for the control of monopolies and mergers have been retained although some amendments have been made, which deal largely with the Director General's powers of investigation under ss 44 and 46. It is clear, however, that the Director General's powers in relation to the control of scale monopolies (those dependent upon control of a given percentage of the market) will only be used where there has been an infringement of the provisions of the Competition Act 1998 and where the use of enforcement provisions under that Act has not resulted in the termination of the abuse. Hence, the powers under the Fair Trading Act 1973 will really be used as a second line of enforcement. By contrast, the Director General's powers in relation to complex monopolies (those where a group of companies act in a similar manner but in the absence of a provable agreement, so there is no infringement) allow him to make a reference to the Competition Commission.

18.6.1   Monopolies

A scale monopoly is defined in s 6 of the Fair Trading Act 1973 as occurring when:

(a) at least one-quarter of all the goods of that description which are supplied in the United Kingdom are supplied by one and the same person, or are supplied to one and the same person, or

(b) at least one-quarter of the goods of that description which are supplied in the United Kingdom are supplied by members of one and the same group of interconnected bodies corporate, or are supplied to members of one and the same group of interconnected bodies corporate, or

(c) at least one-quarter of all the goods of that description which are supplied in the United Kingdom are supplied by members of one and the same group consisting of two or more persons as are mentioned in subsection (2) of this section, or are supplied to members of one and the same group consisting of two or more such persons, or

(d) one or more collective agreements are in operation, the result or collective result of which is that goods of that description are not supplied in the United Kingdom at all.

A monopoly may relate equally to the person supplying the goods and the person receiving them, for a buyer may be in a monopoly situation and, as such, be able to dictate the price, quality, etc of the goods. The first two situations adopt a purely numerical approach to the existence of a monopoly, while the last two take account of the behaviour of the person either in addition to or instead of his percentage control. A corresponding provision identifying a monopoly in the provision of services appears in s 7, while s 8 identifies monopoly situations as pertaining to exports. Lastly, s 9 makes clear that a monopoly may be limited in effect to part of the UK and investigated as such.

It is not an offence to be a monopoly but the legislation recognises the ability of a monopoly to distort competition. Thus under s 2 of the 1973 Act the Director General of Fair Trading is required to collate evidence and information regarding commercial activities with a view to identifying monopoly situations. Having identified the possible existence of a monopoly the Director General can refer it to the Competition Commission for investigation to determine whether the monopoly exists and, if so, whether it is operating contrary to the public interest. Again, there is no assumption that it will be. When considering the 'public interest' element of the reference, the Commission must take into account all matters which appear to it to be relevant, with guidance about factors being offered by s 84(1). Further, under s 81 the Commission must take account of any representation made to it by persons appearing to have a substantial interest in the subject matter of the reference.

On conclusion of its investigations, the Commission must prepare a report of its findings including its conclusions on the questions posed to it together with the reasons for those conclusions. Where the Commission finds the existence of a monopoly which may be expected to operate against the public interest the report should specify the expected adverse results and, if the Commission thinks fit, recommendations of such action as should be taken to remedy the situation. Under s 56 an order may be made by the appropriate Minister to exercise powers as a means of remedying the situation including outlawing the withholding of goods or services, making of payments for services other than those received and charging prices different from those included in published lists. Further, the appropriate Minister may order the publication of price lists, regulate prices and prohibit the acquisition of another person's business.

An alternative to making a monopoly reference is for the Director General to propose that the Secretary of State accept an undertaking under s 56A. This option exists where the Director General is satisfied that a monopoly situation either exists or may exist in the future which operates against the public interest, that he intends to make a monopoly reference (except in the presence of a satisfactory undertaking) and that he considers that the undertakings offered by particular persons would be sufficient to deal with the expected adverse effects of the monopoly. The Director General's proposal must contain the terms of the proposed undertaking, the details of the person giving the undertaking and a statement of fact relating to the monopoly and the effects to be avoided. Before this can be done, the Director General must have published a notice with all the details of the proposal inviting a response from relevant people, and must have considered any representations made to him as a result of the notice and the invitation. Where the Secretary of State accepts a proposal, no further monopoly reference can be made in respect of that matter for a period of 12 months following the date of the acceptance of the undertakings unless the Director General considers that the undertaking has been breached, or needs to be varied or superseded and notice of this fact has been given to the person who gave the undertaking.

18.6.2 Mergers

Monopolies often result from mergers and thus the control of mergers itself militates against the creation of monopolies. A merger situation exists when two or more distinct enterprises unite thereby ceasing to be distinct entities. A merger will be subject to possible reference to the Competition Commission if the merged enterprise would have 25 per cent or more of the market or where the value of the assets taken over exceeds £30 million. As with monopolies, a merger may effect only part of the UK and yet be an appropriate merger for consideration. In **South Yorkshire Transport Ltd v Monopolies and Mergers Commission** (1993) the House of Lords held that 'a substantial part of the UK' in this context should be decided by reference to whether the 'area was of such a size, character and importance as to make it worthy of consideration'. In the South Yorkshire Transport case, the merger of a number of bus companies to create a monopoly in an area that was 1.65 per cent of the total UK area and catered for 3.2 per cent of the population was still substantial for this purpose.

There is no presumption that a merger is necessarily contrary to the public interest and no requirement that a reference takes place. Enterprises intending to merge can notify this fact to the Director General, who then has a period of 20 days to decide whether to make a reference. This period may be extended by a total of 25 days, during the last five of which the Secretary of State may institute a reference irrespective of the advice of the Director General. Once the period has expired, no reference can be made, provided that the merger takes place within six months of the expiration of the period.

As with monopoly references, the Competition Commission has investigatory powers and must decide whether a qualifying merger exists and whether it is contrary to the public interest. The report of their findings must be presented within a specified period not exceeding six months. Where the merger is shown to be contrary to the public interest, the Secretary of State may use the same powers as are available to him in a monopoly situation to enable him to remedy the adverse effects of the merger.

As an alternative to a merger reference, the Director General may accept undertakings from the enterprises involved. These undertakings must address and remedy the potentially adverse effects which the proposed merger might have.

18.7 Articles 81 and 82 EC

Anti-competitive practices in the European Union, upon which the provisions of the Competition Act 1998 are closely modelled, are controlled under art 81(1) EC (previously art 85 of the EC Treaty), which provides:

> (1) The following shall be prohibited as incompatible with the common market: all agreements between undertakings, decisions by associations of undertakings and concerted practices which may affect trade between Member States and which have as their object to effect the prevention, restriction or distortion of competition within the common market, and in particular those which:
> (a) directly or indirectly fix purchase or selling prices or any other trading conditions;
> (b) limit or control production, markets, technical development, or investment;
> (c) share markets or sources of supply;
> (d) apply dissimilar conditions to equivalent transactions with other trading parties, thereby placing them at a competitive disadvantage;
> (e) make the conclusion of contracts subject to acceptance by the other parties of supplementary obligations which, by their nature or according to commercial usage, have no connection with the subject of such contracts.

Any agreement or decision which is contrary to this provision is prohibited and automatically void.

The scope of art 81 is broad, covering all agreements between undertakings, decisions by associations of undertakings and concerted practices. There is no requirement that these undertakings are in competition with each other. Thus while art 81 would clearly cover horizontal agreements (those between two or more competitors operating at the same level in the distributive process) it would also include vertical agreements (those between a supplier and a dealer).

Article 81 is concerned with the effect of the offending agreements. This highlights two aspects. First, the agreement must have as its object or effect the prevention, restriction or distortion of competition within the common market. This allows the European Union to be proactive in the enforcement of art 81 by considering the likely effect of the agreement rather than waiting until the distortion occurs. The requirement is that competition is distorted, not that it is adversely affected. Thus it may be that competition is increased as a result of the agreement.

Second, the agreement must affect trade between member states. Thus an agreement which affects trade within one domestic market only will not come within the ambit of art 81. It is possible, of course, that what is ostensibly a domestic agreement may have an effect beyond the national boundaries as it may attract trade into the member state or dissuade it depending on the circumstances.

While the breadth of art 81 potentially encompasses virtually any agreement, it will apply only where the effect on competition is sufficiently serious. Exemptions are available for agreements that are not of sufficient significance, while the European Union can also grant block exemptions by which exemptions covering categories of goods can be introduced, thus negating the need for individual agreements to be cleared.

There is no requirement for any registration of agreements under art 81 but there is a notification system similar to that under Chapters I and II of the Competition Act 1998 discussed above to allow undertakings to gain a ruling on whether an agreement infringes the controls. As with the Competition Act provisions, no penalty can be imposed in respect of an offending agreement from the date of the notification until the date of the decision.

Limitations to the scope of art 81(1) are to be found in art 81(3). This provides that if an agreement can satisfy four criteria art 81(1) will not apply. The criteria are that the restrictions contribute to improving the production or distribution of goods, or to promoting technical or economic progress; that consumers receive a fair share of the resulting benefits; that the restrictions imposed are indispensable to achieving these objectives; and that the agreement does not afford undertakings the possibility of eliminating competition in respect of a substantial part of the products in question. The balance to be achieved is that the agreement must offer substantial benefits justifying overriding its anti-competitive tendencies.

Ultimately, if an agreement is found to offend art 81, the European Commission can impose financial penalties and require the undertakings to desist from enforcing the void agreement.

The EU approach to monopolies is found in art 82 EC (previously art 86 of the EC Treaty), which seeks to prevent abuses of a 'dominant position' which may distort trade between member states. The abuses, upon which the Chapter II prohibition of the Competition Act 1998 is based, include:

(a) directly or indirectly imposing unfair purchase or selling prices or other unfair trading conditions;

(b) limiting production, markets or technical development to the prejudice of consumers;

(c) applying dissimilar conditions to equivalent transactions with other trading parties, thereby placing them at a competitive disadvantage;

(d) making the conclusion of contracts subject to acceptance by the other parties of supplementary obligations which, by their nature or according to commercial usage, have no connection with the subject of such contracts.

These features would clearly have a serious impact upon competition but art 82 will not apply unless an undertaking is shown to be in a dominant position, as in the Chapter II scenario, with similar factors being taken into account.

The European Commission has wide powers to investigate suspected breaches of art 82 and, if proved, has the authority to impose fines on the offending undertaking and to take such other actions as are necessary to prevent the continuation of the abuse.

Where European law applies, the Commission has the power to require any infringement to be remedied and to impose financial penalties. The remedy may involve separating the constituent enterprises of the merger.

Part II of the Competition Act 1998 provides the requisite enforcement powers for officers of the Director General of Fair Trading to whom authorisation has been given to allow them to investigate suspected infringements of arts 81 and 82.

Question

A Ltd, a coach company with 13 per cent of the trade in South Wales, and B Ltd, another coach company with 14 per cent of the trade in the same area, decide to unite so as to render their operations more efficient and potentially more profitable.

Discuss whether this decision is subject to review by the Competition Commission and what actions the Commission may want to take.

Answer

The union of A Ltd and B Ltd will result in a new company which will have 27 per cent of the coach trade in the South Wales area. Because of the percentage of the trade under their control, this merger is subject to review by the Competition Commission to consider whether it is contrary to the public interest. There is no presumption that it is.

Although the merger affects only one area in the UK rather than the whole country, this is sufficient to justify a reference to the Commission if it will create a monopoly in the area. This was held in the decision of **South Yorkshire Transport Ltd *v* Monopolies and Mergers Commission** (1993).

Instead of referring the matter to the Commission, the Director General of Fair Trading can accept undertakings from A Ltd and B Ltd that they will address any presumed risks posed by the merger. However, if the merger is referred to the Commission, it can require a variety of possible solutions as listed in Schedule 8 to the Fair Trading Act 1973.

Further reading

Flynn, J and Stratford, J (1999). *Competition: Understanding the 1998 Act* (Palladian Law Publishing)

Green, N and Robertson, A (1999). *The Europeanisation of UK Competition Law* (Hart Publishing)

Singleton, S (1999) *Blackstone's Guide to the Competition Act 1998* (Blackstone Press)

19 Intellectual property

19.1 Introduction

It is hard to imagine a business that does not have some commercially valuable intellectual property, even if it is only the name that the business trades under or a list of loyal customers. Intellectual property is vital to success in obtaining and maintaining a competitive advantage in any industrial and commercial activity. A company has a vested interest in protecting the ideas, designs and processes that it creates and preventing exploitation of them by competitors.

The subject matter of intellectual property is very wide and includes literary and artistic works, films, computer programs, inventions, designs and marks used by traders for their goods and services. The often monopolistic protection afforded under intellectual property law does not sit easily with the controls on anti-competitive practices discussed in the previous chapter. This chapter examines important areas of intellectual property law relating to breach of confidence and passing off, patents, copyright, designs and trade marks.

19.2 Breach of confidence and passing off

Although breach of confidence and passing off provide very different remedies with entirely distinct historical backgrounds, they are considered together here for the following reasons. Both provide relief against business practices which amount to 'unfair competition'. They are each of uncertain extent and application because of their case by case evolution and therefore continue to be comparatively flexible and evolving. Both constitute 'adjuncts' of statutory rights since breach of confidence law preserves the subject matter of, for example, a patent, before publication of an invention's specification puts it into the 'state of the art', while passing off protects the 'get-up' of a business even if it falls short of copyright or registrable trade mark protection. Each remedy also preserves both individual and commercial interests. Other jurisdictions, notably the USA, have, in contrast with the UK, tended towards combining their laws into broad principles.

19.2.1 Breach of confidence

In the 'Spycatcher' case, **Atttorney-General _v_ Guardian Newspapers** (1999), Sir John Donaldson MR said:

There is inherent public interest in individual citizens and the state having an enforceable right to the maintenance of confidence. Life would be intolerable in personal and commercial terms, if information could not be given or received in confidence and the right to have that information respected supported by the force of law.

The most obvious link with other facets of intellectual property law lies in the area which can loosely be described as trade secrets. A trade secret, whether it be a method of manufacture, design, product ingredients, marketing strategy, names of customers, etc, may be little protected by mainstream intellectual property law but is of great commercial value to a company and its competitors. Companies guard their secrets jealously and take steps to ensure that their employees (and particularly ex-employees) and other companies, suppliers and contractors with whom some secrets may be shared do not compromise their secrecy. It can happen that confidential information is also the subject of copyright and s 171(1)(e) of the Copyright, Designs and Patents Act 1988 states that copyright provisions do not affect the operation of any rule of equity relating to breach of confidence. Despite a recent Law Commission consultation paper, *Legislating the Criminal Code: Misuse of Trade Secrets* (Law Commission CP No 150, 1997), recommending that the unauthorised use or disclosure of trade secrets be a criminal offence, the basis for such action for breach of confidence, save for official secrets, remains in contract or equity.

A company has a legitimate interest in seeking to protect such trade secrets from disclosure, deliberately or inadvertently, by employees or ex-employees who have knowledge of them. This may be achieved expressly through the use of a restraint of trade clause in the recipient's contract of employment. Such clauses are, of course, void at common law (see Chapter 3) unless they are reasonable as regards the geographic area covered, the scope of the restriction and its duration. The protection of trade secrets by this method extends for the period for which it is reasonable to expect the information to remain secret. Thus, for example, in respect of a manufacturing process the information would be protected until the point where it would be reasonable to assume that any competitor would have developed the process independently.

Irrespective of any contractual term protecting trade secrets, a common law duty of confidentiality exists, the breach of which would give rise to an action for breach of confidence, in which a claim for an injunction to prevent further disclosure, damages, etc could be pursued. The three elements normally required for a breach of confidence action to succeed were set out by Megarry J in **Coco** *v* **AN Clark (Engineers) Ltd** (1969):

(a) the information must have the 'necessary quality of confidence about it';
(b) the information was given to the defendant in a situation suggesting confidentiality; and
(c) there has been unauthorised use or disclosure of that information to the detriment of the party communicating it.

Central to the enforcement of this concept is the meaning of 'confidential' and where the dividing line must be drawn between confidential information deserving protection and non-confidential general knowledge and skills that the recipient is entitled to use freely both during and after his employment with the owner of the information. The test for assessing confidentiality was considered in **Thomas Marshall (Exports) Ltd *v* Guinle** (1978), in which it was held that the owner of the information must reasonably believe that the information is not public knowledge and that its release would be harmful to him or advantageous to his competitors. Lastly, the information must be judged by the standards and practices appropriate within the relevant industry.

This distinction between confidential and non-confidential information and the duties that arise from it was discussed further in **Faccenda Chicken *v* Fowler** (1986), in which the following factors were considered relevant:

1 the nature of the employment, i.e. whether the defendant regularly had access to confidential information such as to mean that he should have been aware of its confidential nature;
2 the nature of the information, i.e. was it sufficiently confidential to justify being treated as a trade secret;
3 whether the confidential nature of the information was brought sufficiently to the attention of the employee.

In **Faccenda** the court held that there were two categories of information: trade secrets, which would be protected post-employment either by an express or implied contractual term; and the rest, including information which may have the necessary quality of confidence while the employee was employed, but such 'mere confidences' ceased to be protected impliedly once he had left.

19.2.2 The tort of passing off

In **Reckitt & Colman Products *v* Borden Inc** (1990), the 'Jif Lemon' case, Lord Oliver said that:

> . . . the law of passing off could be summarised in one short general proposition: no man might pass off his goods as those of another.

Passing off serves two functions, the protection of a trader against the unfair competition of his rivals, and the protection of consumers who would otherwise be confused as to the origins or nature of the goods or services which they are offered. In this second function passing off is a necessary ingredient of the ideal hypothetical perfect free market economy allowing consumers to distinguish clearly the goods or services of market rivals on value judgements like price and quality, not on confusion.

The characteristics of the tort according to Lord Diplock in **A G Spalding & Bros *v* A W Gamage Ltd** (1915) are:

(a) a misrepresentation
(b) made by a trader in the course of trade
(c) to prospective customers or ultimate consumers

(d) which is calculated to injure the goodwill or business of another, and

(e) which causes actual damage to that other.

A number of cases including **Consorzio de Prosciutto Di Parma _v_ Marks and Spencer plc** (1991) simplified this as:

(a) the goodwill of the plaintiff
(b) the misrepresentation made by the defendant, and
(c) consequential damage.

'Damage' in this context may result in a number of ways and the diminution in the claimant's goodwill may be caused by lost sales because of confusion, an inferior product being confused with the claimant's, erosion or debasement of an exclusive or unique name or even lost opportunity to license the manufacture or use of a mark or name.

Passing off is closely linked to trade mark law and in many cases the claimant pleads both trade mark infringement and passing off, the latter as a fall-back position if the superior trade mark protection point does not succeed. Indeed, with the relaxation of marks that can be registered and the possibility of protecting similar marks under the Trade Marks Act 1994, it was thought once again that passing off might slip into legal obscurity. However, in **Re Elvis Presley Trade Mark** (1999) the court denied the estate of Elvis Presley a registered trade mark for the singer's name in relation to memorabilia, illustrating the continuing importance of the law of passing off in the UK, particularly in relation to commercially valuable character merchandising. Similarly, in **United Biscuits UK Ltd _v_ Asda Stores Ltd** (1997), the 'Penguin/Puffin' case where Asda marketed a biscuit with similar packaging to 'Penguins', the claimant failed to succeed in an action for trade mark infringement because the marks, a puffin and a penguin, were considered insufficiently similar, but an injunction for passing off succeeded. Passing off is also related to the criminal provisions found in the Trade Descriptions Act 1968 (see Chapter 13).

As in other actions involving intellectual property, a claimant is primarily interested in stopping offending activity, damages being a secondary consideration. If an interim injunction is successful it is unlikely that the case would continue to full trial, but if it does the usual remedies of damages, account of profit, delivery up, etc are available.

19.3 Patents

The patent system in the UK is governed by the Patents Act 1977 as amended by the Copyright, Designs and Patents Act 1988. The Patents Act 1977 was intended to harmonise UK law with that of the European Patent Convention (EPC), the Community Patent Convention (CPC) and the Patent Cooperation Treaty (PCT). The protection afforded by a patent is generally territorial. It is limited to the country in which it is granted, but it is possible to obtain protection in more than one country through a single application under convention or treaty provisions, including the above.

A patent is granted on application by the inventor of a new invention enabling him to control the usage of his invention for a period of up to 20 years. Grant of patent effectively allows the inventor a monopoly of up to 20 years in which to recoup his development costs and make a profit from his invention before it enters the public domain in which anyone can use it freely.

19.3.1   A patentable invention

The Patents Act 1977 identifies four attributes of a patentable invention:

(a)   it must be new;
(b)   it must involve an inventive step;
(c)   it must be capable of industrial application;
(d)   it must not fall within an excluded category.

To attract a patent, the inventor or someone acting on his behalf must demonstrate that the invention, be it a product, component or process, for which the patent is sought represents a new addition to the previous state of the art and further that it is not something that would be obvious to a large number of people. The decision as to whether it is novel is decided by searches and examinations undertaken by the Patent Office. If it is held to be novel, a patent will be granted, while if it is not, the application will be refused. Whether the invention would be obvious to a lot of other people is more difficult to decide and is ultimately a matter for the court to decide, taking into account the prevailing state of the art as applied by a person skilled in the art. This approach has attracted some criticism and is not universally adopted. Lastly, the invention must be capable of being made or used in industry. Patents are granted for four years in the first instance and are renewable for up to 20 years subject to the payment of an annual fee. In the event of two similar applications being made, priority is given in date order of the application dates. Thus the first application lodged will be granted the patent assuming that it satisfies the criteria, while any later applications will be refused.

The granting of the patent does not guarantee that the inventor will be able to produce or profit from the invention. It may be that, in practice, it is not viable to produce the item at a competitive price, or there may be legislation in force at the time the patent is granted or introduced subsequently that renders illegal its manufacture, sale or usage. The only thing that a patent guarantees to the inventor is that he will have control over who, if anyone, is to be allowed to use or produce the invention during the 20-year period. Thus, in a business context, its real value lies in the inventor's ability to prevent competitors using the invention. In practice, of course, competitors will invent alternative systems or products, although clearly this will involve the expenditure of both time and money.

However, there is a fundamental belief underpinning the patent system that it is in the public interest for patented inventions to be worked, a reason specifically referred to in the Patents Act 1977. A patentee may voluntarily make his patent available for licensing to anyone who applies. These are called 'licences of right' and the fact they are available will be endorsed on the register, useful if a small inventor lacks the resources to exploit his own invention. Under certain circumstances, the licence of right may be compulsory. Very few applications for compulsory licences are ever made but in deciding whether to grant a compulsory licence the Comptroller must, under s 50(2)(a)–(c) of the Patents Act 1977, take into account a variety of circumstances, which include measures already taken by the patentee to exploit it and the ability of any future licensee to do so.

Three issues are of interest to businesses in the usage of patents: their enforcement, the position regarding employee inventions and the protection of patents overseas, particularly in the EU, given the increased movement of goods and the removal of trade barriers.

Enforcement of a patent to prevent its abuse is by civil action, with the owner of the patent seeking an injunction to prevent further abuse, an account of profits and/or damages. An actionable infringement arises under s 60(1)of the Patents Act 1977 if a person does any of the following without the consent of the patent owner at a time when the patent is still in force:

(a) where the invention is a product, he makes, disposes of, uses or imports the product or keeps it for disposal or otherwise;
(b) where the invention is a process, he uses the process or he offers it for use in the UK when he knows, or it is obvious to a reasonable person in the circumstances, that its use would be an infringement;
(c) where the invention is a process, he disposes of, offers to dispose of, uses or imports any product obtained directly by means of that process or keeps any such product whether for disposal or otherwise.

In addition to these primary infringements, it is also an infringement for a person to provide another person with the means to work a patent when the first person knows, or it would be obvious to a reasonable person, that the item can be used to put the invention into use in the UK.

Section 60(5) contains statutory defences which permit the use of a patented invention in six situations which would otherwise constitute a patent infringement. They are:

(a) if it is done privately and for purposes which are not commercial;
(b) if it is done for experimental purposes relating to the subject matter of the invention;
(c) if it consists of the extemporaneous preparation in a pharmacy of a medicine for an individual in accordance with a prescription given by a registered medical or dental practitioner or consists of dealing with a medicine so prepared;
(d) it consists of the use, exclusively for the needs of a relevant ship, of a product or process in the body of such a ship or in its machinery, tackle, apparatus or other accessories, in a case where the ship has temporarily or accidentally entered the internal or territorial waters of the United Kingdom;
(e) it consists of the use of a product or process in the body or operation of a relevant aircraft, hovercraft or vehicle which has temporarily or accidentally

entered or is crossing the United Kingdom or the use of accessories for such a relevant aircraft, hovercraft or vehicle;

(f) it consists of the use of an exempted aircraft which has lawfully entered or is lawfully crossing the United Kingdom as aforesaid or of the importation into the United Kingdom, or the use or storage there of any part or accessory for such an aircraft.

Many inventions are made by employees during the course of their employment. The obvious issue is whether the patent belongs to the employee or to his employer. Section 39 of the Patents Act 1977 provides that where an employee makes an invention in the course of his employment or while he is undertaking duties specifically allocated to him although not in his normal course of employment, any resultant invention is the property of the employer. The invention will belong to the employee only if he developed it in his own time. However, the Act seeks to be equitable between the legal rights of the employer and the reasonable expectations of the employee inventor. Section 40 of the Patents Act 1977 provides that where an employer gains outstanding benefits from patenting an employee invention, the employee is entitled to receive fair compensation. The difficulty, of course, is in establishing what constitutes an outstanding benefit. Any attempt to use the employee's contract of employment to limit his rights under s 40 is unenforceable.

In the European Union it is of fundamental concern to ensure free circulation of goods. Article 28 EC (previously art 30 of the EC Treaty) prohibits 'quantitative restrictions on imports and all measures having equivalent effect' between member states. Monopolistic patent protection may conflict with this prohibition, but art 28 recognises that there can be public interest in the monopoly right and that prohibitions or restrictions on imports or exports are justified on the grounds of the protection of commercial property. The European Court of Justice has built up a body of case law which seeks to balance the conflicting imperatives of promoting free competition and protecting patentees' rights. In doing so, it has enunciated the principle of 'exhaustion of rights'. The general principle was summarised in **Zino Davidoff SA** _v_ **A & G Imports** (2000):

> It is well established that a principle of exhaustion applies to all intellectual property rights. So if an article made in accordance with a patent is put into the market in one Member State by or with the consent of the owner of the patent rights, that owner cannot use those rights to prevent or hinder the importation of goods into a second Member State or to prevent their sale there. The expression 'exhaustion of rights' accurately encapsulates the principle involved. The proprietary rights have been used up. The owner of them has nothing left to deploy against further exploitation of the goods.

Many of the cases relating to exhaustion of rights involve pharmaceuticals as government price controls on them mean considerable price differences between member states, making the 'parallel importation' of such products attractive.

The case of **Centrafarm BV** _v_ **Sterling Drug Inc** (1975) established the principle of exhaustion of rights. Sterling owned patents relating to the drug 'Negram' in both the UK and the Netherlands. Centrafarm acquired supplies of the drug which had been marketed in the UK and exported them to the Netherlands, where they could be sold at a higher price. Centrafarm was the 'parallel importer' of the drugs. Sterling sued for patent infringement in the Netherlands. The European Court of Justice stated that it would not allow a derogation from the free market provision in art 36 of the EC Treaty (now art 30 EC) where goods had been put on the market legally by the patentee as to do otherwise would 'partition off national markets' and thereby restrict trade between member states in a situation where no such restraint is necessary to safeguard the subject matter of the patent.

Approving **Centrafarm**, the ECJ in **Merck & Co Inc** *v* **Stephar BV** (1981) succinctly confirmed that the substance of a patent is essentially the exclusive right to first placing of the product on the market. This enables the inventor to obtain a reward for his creative effort 'without however guaranteeing that he will obtain such a reward in all circumstances'. In **Merck** it was a case of 'the proprietor beware' when the patentee decided to market in a member state where there was no patent protection and had to take the consequences, including the possibility that it would be imported into other member states. The key to both **Contrafarm** and **Merck** was *consent*. In both cases the patentee had consented to the first sale in a member state.

In relation to patent rights in the rest of the world the case of **Betts** *v* **Wilmott** (1871) confirmed the principle that where a patentee sells his goods abroad without reservation or condition, he cannot then prevent the importation of those goods into the UK. In **Roussel Uclaf SA** *v* **Hockley International Ltd** (1996), which involved the sale of insecticide in the UK which the defendant had obtained in China, the issue was whether a restrictive statement 'Re-export forbidden' on the original drums supplied to China brought the restriction home 'to every person down the supply chain' so as to avoid exhaustion of rights. It was held that the claimant had failed to establish that the restriction was brought home to the Chinese company that there should be no re-export and the defendants were free to sell in the UK without infringing patent rights.

19.4 Copyright

Copyright law in the UK is governed by the Copyright, Designs and Patents Act 1988. By virtue of s 1 of the Copyright, Designs and Patents Act 1988, original literary, dramatic, musical or artistic works, sound recordings, films, etc invest automatic copyright in the UK creator without the need to register the item or take any other positive actions. Importantly, s 3(1)(b) includes computer programs as literary work. Not all copyright works will be protected in the UK. They must be *qualifying* works, with the author being a British citizen, or a subject or individual domiciled or resident in the UK, or a citizen or a person domiciled or resident in any extension country (a country party to the Berne or Universal Copyright Conventions) or by reference to first publication in a qualifying country.

There is however an important international dimension to copyright law. The Berne Convention for the Protection of Literary and Artistic Works 1886 (as revised) sets minimum standards for protection internationally among participating countries (consisting of most of the industrialised countries in the world, either by virtue of being signatories to the Convention or signatories to the General Agreement on Tariffs and Trade (GATT) and the agreement on Trade Related Aspects of Intellectual Property Rights (TRIPS), which requires adoption of the Berne Convention, etc). The Berne Convention gives authors of works exploited in any participating country other than their own the same rights as are afforded to nationals of those countries. Further international regulation was achieved through later Acts and Conventions such as the Rome Convention 1960 for neighbouring, secondary rights (for example sound recordings, films and broadcasts derived from the original copyright works; in the UK see ss 5–7 of the 1988 Act) and the Act of Paris 1971, which increased uniformity of protection between participating states and the range of copyright works offered protection.

Under the 1988 Act, copyright in the UK lasts, as a basic rule of thumb, for the author's life plus 70 years from the end of the calendar year in which the author died for literary, dramatic, musical and artistic works (the 'original' or primary works) and films, at least 50 years for sound recordings, broadcasts and cable programmes (the secondary or derived works) and 25 years for typographical arrangements of published editions. The periods of protection are aligned in the EU as a result of Council Directive 93/98/EC. Internationally, by virtue of GATT and TRIPS, most industrialised countries in the world are required to conform with minimum periods of copyright protection as outlined in art 7 of the Berne Convention, which generally require protection for the life of an author and 50 years after the author's death. Hence countries that adopt the Berne minimum, for example the USA, afford protection for the 'original' work for the author's life plus 50 years and not life plus 70 years as adopted in the European Union.

Protection spreads further than might first appear, for literary work is defined in s 3(1) of the 1988 Act to include any work, other than a dramatic or musical work, which is written, spoken or sung, and accordingly includes a table or compilation and a computer program and preparatory design material for a computer program. By s 4(1) artistic work includes graphic work, photographs, sculpture or collage, irrespective of its artistic quality, with graphic work including painting, drawings, maps, charts and plans.

Thus, in a normal business using everyday business techniques and mediums, office manuals, product catalogues, advertising literature, computer programs, etc would all attract copyright protection. If the company produces any promotional videos they too would attract copyright.

Copyright is vested in the owner, who is the person who created the work, though where the article is computer-generated the author is the person who made, the arrangements necessary for its creation. Where a literary, dramatic, musical or artistic work is made by an employee in the course of his employment, his employer is the first owner of the copyright subject to any agreement to the contrary.

Section 16 of the 1988 Act stipulates the rights of the copyright owner as being to have the exclusive right to do the following in the UK:

(a) to copy the work . . . ;
(b) to issue copies of the work to the public . . . ;
(c) to perform, show or play the work in public . . . ;

(d) to broadcast the work or include it in a cable programme service . . . ;
(e) to make an adaptation of the work or do any of the above in relation to an adaptation.

These rights are infringed by anyone doing or authorising another to do any of the above restricted acts, directly or indirectly, in relation to the whole work or a substantial part of it without the licence of the copyright owner. There are two elements to primary infringement, outlined in **Francis Day & Hunter v Bron** (1963) as a causal connection between the copyright work and the alleged infringing copy and substantial copying. Substantial is defined qualitatively not quantitatively. Infringement may occur even if a very small but qualitatively important highly recognisable part of a work is copied, as in the case of **Hawkes & Son (London) Ltd v Paramount Film Services Ltd** (1934), where a 50-second extract (only 28 bars) was filmed of the 'Colonel Bogey' march played during the opening of a school.

Importantly, it is not a breach of copyright: by s 50A of the 1988 Act for a lawful user of a computer program to make any back-up copy; by s 50B for a lawful user of a computer program to decompile the program (as long as listed conditions are met); or by s 50C for a lawful user to adapt a computer program (again if listed conditions are met).

Secondary infringements occur when a person 'knowing or having reason to believe' that he is dealing with an infringing copy without the consent of the copyright owner imports an infringing copy into the UK otherwise than for his private or domestic use. This is an objective test. 'Reason to believe', as held in **LA Gear Inc v Hi-Tec Sports Ltd** (1992), means a knowledge of the facts from which a reasonable man would arrive at the relevant belief.

Of equal concern to a business is the s 24 offence of facilitating a breach of copyright by a third party. This occurs where a person makes or imports into the UK or possesses in the course of a business, or sells or lets for hire, or offers or exposes for sale or hire an article specifically designed or adapted for making copies of the work, knowing or having reason to believe that it is to be used to make infringing copies.

In **CBS Songs Ltd v Amstrad Consumer Electronics Ltd** (1988) the House of Lords found Amstrad not liable under s 21 of the Copyright Act 1956 (a provision having similar effect to s 24 of the 1988 Act). The case related to a tape-to-tape facility on twin-deck tape recorders, which were advertised in a way likely to encourage home taping of copyright material, although Amstrad did warn that copyright permission might be needed that they were not authorised to give. Their Lordships held that Amstrad had warned customers of the copyright permission requirement and that they were helpless to control that use of the machines after sale.

Infringement of copyright is enforced by actions for an injunction to prevent further abuse and a claim for damages or an account of the profits made through the breach. The decision of the Chancery Division of the High Court in **Island Records Ltd v Tring International plc** (1995) has overruled previous practice by holding that the plaintiff has a right to be provided with appropriate information about the assessment of damages and the profits made by the defendant from the infringement, so as to allow the plaintiff to make an informed choice about which remedy he should choose after the issue of fact has been determined. In determining whether to apply for an account or damages and to preserve evidence, the usual orders are available to a claimant including search and freezing orders.

Section 28 of the 1988 Act sets out a number of 'permitted acts' in relation to copyright works where, in the public interest, it is possible to make use of copyright material without infringing copyright. The most important permitted acts are fair dealing, use for research and private study and for the purposes of criticism, review and news reporting.

In addition to the exclusive use of the material, the owner of a copyright acquires, under ss 77–89 of the Act, four moral rights in relation to his work. These are the right to be identified as author or director of a film (the paternity right), the right to object to derogatory treatment that distorts or mutilates the work (right of integrity), the right to protection from false attribution and the right of privacy of photographs and films commissioned for private or domestic purposes. The right of paternity under ss 77–79 gives the author the right to be identified whenever the work is published commercially, performed in public, broadcast or included in a cable programme service, or where the copies of a film or sound recording including the work are issued to the public. This right does not extend to computer programs, the design of typefaces or any computer-generated work. The right not to have the work treated in a derogatory manner prevents the distortion or mutilation of the work or its treatment in any other way prejudicial to the honour or reputation of the author or director. The right not to have literary, dramatic, musical or artistic work falsely attributed to him as author is found in s 84. This is a matter of protecting reputation. These moral rights have been bundled into the Act in tardy recognition of Berne Convention obligations and have been much criticised as favouring economic rights. Against Berne principles, all rights may be waived by consent, the paternity right must be specifically asserted and the 1988 Act sets out numerous and important exceptions where the rights do not apply.

In addition to civil liability, criminal offences also arise from a breach of copyright. Under s 107 an offence is committed by any person who, without the licence of the copyright owner:

(a) makes for sale or hire, or
(b) imports into the United Kingdom otherwise than for his private or domestic use, or
(c) possesses in the course of a business with a view to committing any act infringing the copyright, or
(d) in the course of a business—
    (i) sells or lets for hire, or
    (ii) offers or exposes for sale or hire, or
    (iii) exhibits in public, or
    (iv) distributes, or
(e) distributes otherwise than in the course of a business to such an extent as to affect prejudicially the owner of the copyright,

an article which is, and which he knows or has reason to believe is, an infringing copy of a copyright work.

Offences under (a), (b) and (d) (iv) and (e) above are punishable on summary conviction by imprisonment not exceeding six months or by a fine not exceeding level 5 (currently £5,000) on the standard scale or both and on indictment to a fine or imprisonment for a term not exceeding two years or both. For all other offences above on summary conviction a person is liable to imprisonment for a term not exceeding six months or a fine not exceeding level 5 or both. Where the offence is committed by a body corporate, directors, managers, company secretaries or other similar officers are liable as well.

Under s 107A it is the duty of a local weights and measures authority (usually trading standards/consumer protection officers) to enforce s 107 provisions using their powers under ss 27–29 and 33 of the Trade Descriptions Act 1968. Being a 'common informer' statute, private prosecutions by the copyright owner are possible. There is also provision in s 111 of the 1988 Act for the Commissioners of Customs and Excise to seize allegedly infringing goods upon entry into the UK.

19.5 Designs

Protection for designs exists by two methods. One is the registered design right provided for by the Registered Designs Act 1949 as amended, and the other is the design right provided for and along principles broadly similar to copyright law by the Copyright, Designs and Patents Act 1988, Part III.

19.5.1 Design right

The design right regime embodies a modified copyright approach. Like copyright, the right arises automatically without the need for registration but requires some form of tangible expression. There are qualification requirements and the design must be 'original' (not commonplace) for the right to subsist. The right gives the holder limited protection against copying. Section 213(2) of the 1988 Act defines a 'design' as 'the design of any aspect of the shape or configuration (whether interior or exterior) of the whole or part of an article'. Note that the right applies to any aspect of the shape or configuration of the whole or part of an article; it does not apply to the article itself. Unlike registered designs, there is no requirement that an unregistered design appeals to the eye and thus it may be purely functional. Notably design does not extend to a method or principle of construction, or to a surface design or to any other features of shape or configuration which:

(i)   enable the article to be connected to, or placed in, around or against, another article so that either article may perform its function, or

(ii) are dependent upon the appearance of another article of which the article is intended by the designer to form an integral part.

These are the so-called 'must fit' and 'must match' exceptions whereby no infringement occurs if an item is designed deliberately to fit or match with an existing product. This is of most concern in industries producing spare parts for machinery, cars, etc, where the design of the spare part is predetermined by the product onto or into which it must fit.

A design is not original for these purposes if it is commonplace in the design field in question at the time of its creation (s 213(4)).

To create a design right, the design must either have been recorded in a design document or an article must have been made conforming to the design. A design right creates an automatic right of ownership in the same way as a copyright and subsists for a period of 15 years from the end of the calendar year in which it was designed or ten years from the end of the calendar year in which articles made to the design were first available on sale or hire anywhere in the world by or with the licence of the owner. However, under s 237 of the 1988 Act any person has a right to a licence during the last five years permitting him to do anything that would otherwise be an infringement.

As with copyright, the rights are vested in the designer, i.e. the person who created it or in the case of a computer-generated design, the person who undertook the arrangements for the creation of the design. A design created in the course of employment belongs to the employer. To attract protection the designer must be a person, body corporate or other body having a legal personality resident in the UK or formed under the laws of or having substantial business in the UK, European Union or other approved country. Alternatively, rights may be claimed by the first person exclusively authorised to put the product onto the market.

The designer has the exclusive right to reproduce the design for commercial purposes either by making articles to the design or by making a design document. An infringement occurs if anyone breaches these rights without the licence of the designer. A secondary infringement occurs under s 227 where a person without licence imports into the UK for commercial purposes, or has in his possession for commercial purposes or sells, lets for hire, or offers or exposes for sale or hire, in the course of a business, any article which is, and which he knows or has reason to believe is, an infringing copy.

The breach of an unregistered design right gives the designer the right to sue for an injunction and damages or an account for profits. Further, the designer can ask the court for an order instructing the offender to deliver up any infringing articles.

There are proposals for a Community design to apply throughout the European Community and the rights will be of a unitary nature. A two-tier system is under consideration, registered design (not dissimilar to the present UK system) and a shorter-term unregistered design right. The unregistered right will be particularly useful for those designs that have a relatively short exploitation period, for example fashion clothing. The basic requirements for the rights, registered or unregistered, are the same, with 'design' being defined as 'the appearance of the whole or any part of a product resulting from the specific features of the lines, contours, colours, shape and/or materials of the product itself and/or its ornamentation' and 'product' as any 'industrial or handicraft item, including parts intended to be assembled into a complex item, sets or composition of items, packaging, get-ups, graphic symbols and typographic typefaces, but excluding a computer program'.

19.5.2 Registered designs

Registered designs are covered by the Registered Designs Act 1949 as amended. 'Design' means features of shape, configuration, pattern or ornament applied to an article by an industrial process, being features which in the finished article appeal to and are judged by the eye. For this purpose an industrially produced pattern means one that is applied to 50 items not constituting a single set. Design does not extend to features of shape or configuration dictated by function or by the appearance of another article.

The registered proprietor of the design is its author or the person who commissioned it, or an employer if the design was created in the course of employment. Computer-generated designs where there is no human designer belong to the person by whom the arrangements for the design were made. The proprietor acquires rights similar to the designer of an unregistered design, namely the exclusive right to make or import for sale or hire, or expose for sale or hire any article conforming to the registered design or any design not substantially different. This prevents a person making minimal alterations to the design in an attempt to circumvent the proprietor's rights. The prohibition also extends to kits which if assembled would infringe the registered design. The rights last initially for five years, which can be extended under s 8(2) in five-year periods up to a total of 25 years. The normal remedies of an injunction and damages or an account for profit follow an infringement unless the defendant can show that he did not know of the registration.

A Regulation which will create a Community-registered design right and a Community-registered design is currently under consideration. Directive 98/71/EC on the legal protection of designs is due to be incorporated into national law. The Directive proposes a harmonised registered design right regime in the European Union. It is envisaged that there will be a registered design regime based on the Directive, which will be implemented in the UK by regulations similar to those which now exist for protecting trade marks. There will be significant changes in the law in the next few years.

19.6 Trade marks

Words and symbols associated with particular producers or suppliers are currently protected from abuse by the Trade Marks Act 1994 and also by the tort of passing off.

19.6.1 Trade Marks Act 1938

The Trade Marks Act 1938 was repealed with effect from 30 October 1994 by the Trade Marks Act 1994. Some knowledge of the 1938 Act remains important in the process of explaining and comprehending the 1994 Act.

Under the 1938 Act, trade marks could be registered under either Part A or Part B of the register. Part A was more prescriptive but offered greater protection to the proprietor of the trade mark. To obtain Part A registration, the applicant had to show under s 9 that the trade mark contained one of the following:

(a) the name of a company, individual or firm, represented in a special or particular manner; or
(b) the signature of the applicant for registration or some predecessor of his in the business; or
(c) an invented word or words; or
(d) a word or words having no direct reference to the character or quality of the goods, and not being according to its ordinary meaning, a geographical name or surname; or
(e) any other distinctive mark, but a name, signature or word other than those covered by (a) to (d) above, was not registrable except on evidence of distinctiveness.

This list achieved the balance between allowing registration for words or symbols that were inextricably linked with one person's products while not preventing other persons from using other words or marks appropriate to their own products. Any person was entitled to use his own name or that of his place of business, or any *bona fide* description of the quality or character of his goods.

By contrast to that detailed above, Part B registration was far less prescriptive. The crucial difference between the two was that Part A marks had to have been 'adapted to distinguish' goods, while Part B registration merely required that the marks be 'capable of distinguishing' the goods. In practice, the dividing line between the two was very difficult to draw. This problem ceases to exist with the demise of the 1938 Act as the register has been unified under the Trade Marks Act 1994. The registration of a trade mark gave the proprietor the exclusive right to use the mark and thereby distinguish his goods from those of another person. An infringement occurred if someone else used the mark or one that was so similar that it was likely to cause confusion. The usual remedies of an injunction to prevent further abuse and an account for profits could be claimed by the proprietor in the event of an infringement.

19.6.2 Trade Marks Act 1994

The Trade Marks Act 1994, which repeals all previous Trade Marks Acts, represents the first major overhaul of trade mark law in almost 50 years. The Act implements Council Directive 89/104/EEC, which seeks to approximate trade marks legislation in the Community and thereby encourage trade. It is organised into four Parts. Part I covers substantive trade mark law and much of its wording is taken verbatim from the Directive. Part II deals with international matters, including the Community Trade Mark (CTM), the Madrid Protocol and the Paris Convention for the Protection of Industrial Property. Parts III and IV include administrative provisions, etc.

Because the Trade Marks Act 1994 implements the Trade Marks Directive, protection of trade marks is the most uniform of all intellectual property rights in the

European Union (and EEA). In both the case of the CTM and national laws implementing the Trade Marks Directive, the final word in interpretation lies with the European Court of Justice. Despite this, trade mark protection remains essentially territorial in extent. UK trade mark law applies almost exclusively to trade marks registered in the UK and the UK courts have at times followed a markedly different approach to interpreting the Trade Marks Act 1994 than their European counterparts have taken with similar legislation.

Registration

The Trade Marks Act 1994 defines a trade mark in s 1(1) as:

> any sign capable of being represented graphically which is capable of distinguishing goods or services of one undertaking from those of other undertakings. A trade mark may, in particular, consist of words (including personal names), designs, letters, numerals or the shape of goods or their packaging.

It is noticeable that this definition is broader than that contained in the Trade Marks Act 1938 and expressly includes the shape of the article or its packaging. Thus, the proprietor of a distinctively shaped container such as a Coca-Cola bottle or a Jif lemon should be able to register it and not be forced to resort to the tort of passing off as a means of restricting its usage. This reverses the previous position in which the distinctive Coca-Cola bottle was denied registration in **Re Coca-Cola Trade Marks** (1986) and the manufacturers of Jif lemons had to resort to an action in passing off in **Reckitt & Colman Products Ltd *v* Borden Inc** (1990) in order to get an injunction to prevent the defendant using a similar lemon-shaped container for the sale of lemon juice. The list in s 1(1) is not exhaustive and thus would permit the registration of other distinctive features of products or services. The crucial factors are that the trade mark must be capable of being represented graphically, so that the Registrar can easily record and search for them, and must be capable of distinguishing the goods or services of one undertaking from those of another. In **Swizzels Matlow Ltd's Three Dimensional Trade Mark Application** (1999) the applicant sought to register a trade mark consisting of a 'chewy sweet on a stick'. That application did not comply with acceptable forms of graphical representation as it did not define with sufficient precision what was distinctive about the mark.

There is a presumption that a mark will be registered as long as it complies with the requirements of s 1, registration being onto a single register. Typically, registration will continue to involve one individual proprietor, be it a person or a company, but a collective mark is permitted by virtue of s 49. A collective mark occurs where the mark is registered by an association which comprises a number of individuals, each of whom is involved in the business of supplying the goods or services that are the subject of the trade mark. Registration, if granted, lasts for a renewable period of ten years.

Grounds for non-registration

While there is a presumption that registration will be granted there are specified grounds upon which registration may be refused. These grounds are to be found in ss 3–5 of the 1994 Act, which have implemented the relevant articles of the Trade Marks Directive. It is notable that the Directive has limited the grounds for refusal to those stipulated in it and forbids member states from adding additional grounds. The four main grounds, contained in s 3, which provide for an absolute prohibition are:

(a) signs which do not satisfy the requirements of s 1(1),
(b) trade marks which are devoid of any distinctive character,
(c) trade marks which consist exclusively of signs or indications which may serve, in trade, to designate the kind, quality, quantity, intended purpose, value, geographical origin, the time of production of goods or of rendering services, or other characteristics of goods or services,
(d) trade marks which consist exclusively of signs or indications which have become customary in the current language or in the *bona fide* and established practices of the trade.

Further, a trade mark will not be registered if it comprises a shape which results from the nature of the goods themselves, or which is necessary to obtain a technical result or which gives substantial value to the goods. Also, registration will be refused if the trade mark is contrary to public policy or accepted principles of morality, or is of such a nature as to deceive the public. Particular protection exists for royal coats of arms and flags of the UK and its constituent countries.

Section 5 deals with relative grounds for refusal of registration, situations in which a trade mark will be refused registration because of conflict with an earlier trade mark or right. As one of the major reasons for using a trade mark is to distinguish one person's products from those of another person, it would be counterproductive to permit the registration of a trade mark that is identical to or could be easily confused with an existing trade mark. The system aims to prevent confusion, not cause it. Consequently s 5(1) states that a trade mark will not be registered if it is identical to an earlier trade mark and the goods or services for which the trade mark is applied for are identical to the goods or services for which the earlier trade mark is protected. This subsection is very clear: both the proposed trade mark and the goods or services protected by it are identical to an existing registered mark. However, it is clear from the remaining provisions of s 5 that protection will be granted even though the proposal is not identical to an existing mark, merely similar in some respect. Section 5(2) provides two restrictions on registration, namely, that a trade mark will not be registered if it is identical to an earlier trade mark and is to be registered for goods or services which are similar to those for which an earlier trade mark exists, or that the trade mark is similar to an earlier trade mark and is to be registered for goods or services identical to or similar to those for which the earlier trade mark is protected; and, in either instance, there is a likelihood of confusion on the part of the public which includes the possibility of association with the earlier trade mark. Protection may even be afforded in some circumstances to goods which are not similar to those previously protected. Thus, s 5(3) provides that a trade mark which is identical to or similar to an earlier trade mark and is to be registered for goods or services which are not similar to those for which an earlier trade mark is protected shall not be registered if, or to the extent that, the earlier trade mark has a reputation in the UK and the later mark would take unfair advantage of or be detrimental to the distinctive character or the repute of the earlier trade mark.

Infringement and offences

Registering a trade mark provides the proprietor with certain exclusive rights in the UK which will be infringed by anyone using the trade mark without his agreement, the prohibited acts being specified in s 10. Thus s 10(1) stipulates that a person infringes a trade mark if he uses, in the course of a trade, a sign which is identical to the registered trade mark in relation to goods or services identical to those for to it is registered. This is the most straightforward infringement and the one most likely to cause damage to the proprietor of the registered mark. A person is deemed to use a sign for these purposes if he fixes it to the goods or packaging, puts the goods on the market or stocks them for the purposes of offering or exposing them for sale under the sign, offers or supplies services under the sign, imports or exports goods under the sign, or uses the sign on business papers or in advertising. This encompasses a very broad range of activities and includes all the likely uses of a sign that would occur in the course of a trade.

Section 10(2) and (3) provides further examples of infringements and the subsections have the underlying rationale of preventing confusion and preventing the proprietor of the mark from suffering loss through another person taking unfair advantage of the mark or damaging its reputation. Thus, under s 10(2) an infringement occurs if a person, in the course of a trade, uses a sign identical to the trade mark in relation to goods or services similar to those for which the trade mark is registered, or uses a sign which is similar to the trade mark in relation to goods or services which are identical to or similar to those for which the trade mark is registered, if in either instance there is the likelihood of confusion among the public, which would include the likelihood of association with the trade mark. Section 10(3) provides that an infringement occurs if the defendant uses a sign in the course of a trade which is identical to or similar to the trade mark in relation to goods or services which are not similar to those for which the trade mark is registered, where the trade mark has a reputation in the UK and the sign takes unfair advantage of or is detrimental to the distinctive character or reputation of the trade mark. It should be noted that in all of these sections, there is a requirement that the infringement has occurred in the course of a trade.

Where an infringement has occurred, the proprietor of the sign has the right to take action to seek a remedy for the breach and to seek to prevent further infringements. As such, the proprietor may seek various remedies including an injunction, claiming damages and requiring the defendant to account for profits made through the infringement. Further, the court may order the defendant to cause the offending sign to be obliterated from any goods or other articles in his possession or custody, or under his control. If it is not possible for the offending sign to be obliterated, the court can order the destruction of the offending goods and other articles. The proprietor of the trade mark can apply to the court for the offending items to be delivered up, either to him or to such other person as the court may direct. Such an order will not be made, however, unless the court is satisfied that there are grounds to order the destruction of the goods.

In addition to the civil law remedies available for the infringement of a trade mark, the 1994 Act has also introduced criminal controls over the wrongful use of a registered trade mark. These seem likely to replace the Trade Descriptions Act 1968 as the most effective way of controlling such offences. Under s 93 of the 1994 Act the duty of enforcement is placed upon weights and measures authorities (trading standards/consumer protection officers) using enforcement powers contained in ss 27–29 and 33 of the Trade Descriptions Act 1968. The primary offence under s 92(1) is committed where a person, with a view to gain for himself or another, or with intent to cause loss to another, and without the consent of the proprietor:

(a) applies to goods or their packaging a sign identical to, or likely to be mistaken for, a registered trade mark, or
(b) sells or lets for hire, offers or exposes for sale or hire or distributes goods which bear, or the packaging of which bears, such a sign, or
(c) has in his possession, custody or control in the course of a business any such goods with a view to the doing of anything, by himself or another, which would be an offence under paragraph (b).

It is noteworthy that this is a *mens rea* offence in that the defendant must have intended to make a profit for himself or another, or intended to cause loss to another. This indicates a degree of premeditation about his actions and their fraudulent effect upon another's trade. Further, the act must have been done without the agreement of the proprietor, no offence having been committed therefore if the proprietor has given his consent to the use of the mark. Offences against paragraphs (a) and (b) can be committed by anybody, there being no requirement that these were done in the course of a business. By contrast, a paragraph (c) offence can be committed only by a person acting in the course of a business and its effect is consequently more limited. It must be presumed that the phrase 'in the course of a business' will be interpreted in the same way as in s 1 of the Trade Descriptions Act 1968. While s 92(1) deals with the unlawful use of a sign on the goods themselves, s 92(2) addresses the issue of using the unlawful sign in relation to packaging, labelling and advertising. Thus s 92(2) makes it an offence if any person, with a view to a gain for himself or another, or with the intent to cause loss to another, and without the consent of the proprietor:

(a) applies a sign identical to, or likely to be mistaken for, a registered trade mark to material intended to be used—
  (i) for labelling or packaging goods,
  (ii) as a business paper in relation to goods, or
  (iii) for advertising goods, or
(b) uses in the course of a business material bearing such a sign for labelling or packaging goods, as a business paper in relation to goods, or for advertising goods, or
(c) has in his possession, custody or control in the course of a business any such material with a view to doing anything, by himself or another, which would be an offence under paragraph (b).

Again an element of *mens rea* is required for the commission of these offences, and again an offence against paragraph (a) can be committed by any person. Paragraphs (b) and (c), however, are restricted to actions occurring in the course of a business.

Section 92(3) deals with the issue of the manufacture of the articles used for making copies of trade marks or signs likely to be mistaken for trade marks. It is an offence for a person, with a view to making a gain for himself or another, or with the intent of causing a loss to another, and without the consent of the proprietor to make an article specifically designed or adapted for making copies of a sign identical to or likely to be mistaken for a registered trade mark; or to have such an article in his possession, custody or control in the course of a business, if he knows or has reason to believe that it has been or is being used to produce prohibited goods.

Naturally, a statutory defence is available if the defendant can show that he believed on reasonable grounds that the use of the sign in the way it was used or was intended to be used was not an infringement of a registered trade mark. On summary conviction for any offence against s 92, the defendant will be liable to a term of imprisonment not exceeding six months, or a fine not exceeding the statutory maximum. On indictment, the penalty increases to an unlimited fine, or imprisonment for up to ten years.

Trade marks and free movement of goods

Like other intellectual property rights, trade mark protection may conflict with the prohibitions set out in art 28 EC (previously art 30 of the EC Treaty). National trade mark law (and now the CTM) gives a proprietor territorial monopoly use of his mark and the possibility of keeping out the goods of others. Whether trade mark law (or indeed other areas of intellectual property law like patents and copyright) can be used by a trade mark proprietor to limit the freedom to 'parallel import' goods to maximise profitability or sales opportunities has long been an issue.

'Parallel imports' occur when someone, usually a third party, attempts to import articles from one country where they have been lawfully distributed to another country, usually against the intellectual property rights owner's wishes. Whether such imports are from one EC/EEA member state to another or from a country outside the EC/EEA area into the EC/EEA (the latter referred to as the 'grey market') considerable advantage can be made of price fluctuations internationally, whether it be because of currency fluctuation, governmental price controls on products like pharmaceuticals or simply because a brand leader has chosen to dispose of last season's premium luxury goods cheaply in some other corner of the world.

Courts dealing with interpretation of the law on this issue have not always been consistent. Trade mark protection has been justified as an indicator of origin (particularly in the UK) and quality and art 28 recognises that there can be public interest in monopolistic trade mark rights. As with patent rights this right must not constitute a means of arbitrary discrimination or disguised restriction on trade between member states. As with patent rights, the European Court of Justice has built up a body of case law to balance the sometime conflicting imperatives of promoting free competition and protecting the rights of trade mark proprietors, relying on the principles of '*exhaustion of rights*' (already explained in relation to patents above) and '*common origin*'.

Section 12(1) of the Trade Marks Act 1994 (implementing art 7(1) of the Trade Marks Directive) states that a registered trade mark is not infringed by the use of the mark in relation to goods which have been put on the market in the EEA under the trade mark by the proprietor or with his consent. Interpretation of the ambiguous wording in the Trade Marks Directive has led to much debate. Nonetheless, it has been possible for a trade mark proprietor to use trade mark rights to prevent parallel imports within the EC/EEA. In **Centrafarm BV _v_ Winthrop BV** (1976) (see **Centrafarm BV _v_ Sterling Drug Inc** (1975) in relation to patents) the American company Sterling Drug had subsidiaries in the UK and the Netherlands (Winthrop BV). Sterling granted both companies a patent licence to produce its drug 'Negram'. Each was also the registered proprietor of the mark 'Negram' in its respective country. Centrafarm bought Negram cheaply in the UK and marketed it for profit in the Netherlands. Winthrop BV unsuccessfully sued for trade mark infringement. The European Court of Justice decided that as the claimant had exhausted his rights by putting the goods into circulation for the first time in the UK, further circulation could not be prevented on the grounds that trade mark rights had been infringed.

However, art 28 EC (previously art 30 of the EC Treaty) has successfully safeguarded the rights of trade mark proprietors as long as this does not represent disguised restrictions on sales. In **Centrafarm BV _v_ American Home Products Corpn** (1978) American Home Products marketed Negram as Serenid in the UK and as Seresta in the Netherlands. Because of domestic price controls, the UK product was cheaper. Centrafarm bought Serenid in the UK and sold it re-marked as Seresta in the Netherlands. American Home products sued for trade mark infringement and the European Court of Justice found that a proprietor of a trade mark protected in one member state is justified under art 36 of the EC Treaty (now art 30 EC) in preventing a product from being marketed by a third party in that member state even if previously the product had been lawfully marketed in another member state under a different mark by the same proprietor. Thus it may be lawful for a manufacturer to use different marks in different member states to protect his interests as long as the practice is not intended to partition the market artificially (as that would constitute a disguised trade restriction for art 30 purposes). Here the European Court of Justice applied a _subjective_ test as to whether such a disguised restriction existed.

Of course, it is possible simply to repackage the goods without changing names and that would not be an infringement of the trade mark if it was _necessary_ to market the product in the country of origin, an _objective_ test as confirmed in **Bristol-Myers Squibb _v_ Paranova** (1996). The European Court of Justice also indicated that such parallel importers who necessarily repackaged had to notify the trade mark proprietor and that the repackaged product must not damage the reputation of the mark in the way it was re-presented in the market.

In **Pharmacia and Upjohn SA _v_ Paranova** (2000) the European Court of Justice revisited the topic and effectively reversed its decision in **Centrafarm _v_ American Home Products,** holding that the test for whether rebranding was non-infringing was an _objective_ one and not dependent upon the intention of the trade mark proprietor when selecting different marks for different countries. In doing so it applied the 'necessity' test to rebranding, permitting rebranding if it was objectively necessary to obtain market access. In **Glaxo Group Ltd** *v* **Dowelhurst Ltd** (**No 2**) (2000) it was argued that unnecessary repackaging was a trade mark infringement, even if it did no harm to the goods or the specific subject matter of the mark. The UK court held that the test of necessity only came into play if there was substantial damage to the specific subject matter or essential function of the mark. Other member states have interpreted the matter differently and the issue of the proper interpretation of 'necessity' has been referred to the European Court of Justice.

Common origin

The principles of exhaustion of rights (see explanation with regard to patents above) depend on the proprietor giving consent to first marketing in a member state of the European Union. What if there is no consent? In the much criticised case of **Van Zuylen Bros** *v* **Hag AG** (1974), the **Hag I** case, the Hag mark for decaffeinated coffee was originally owned by a German company, which sold the coffee in Belgium and Luxembourg. The right in the Hag mark was sequestered after World War I as enemy property and passed through assignment to Van Zuylen. The German company, Hag, planned to export coffee into Belgium bearing the 'Hag' mark and Van Zuylen alleged trade mark infringement. It was held that where trade marks have a *common origin* the rights of one trade mark owner could not be used to prevent parallel imports of goods bearing the same mark into its territory. This seemed to push the principle of exhaustion of rights beyond sensible bounds. In **Hag II, SA CnL-Sucal NV** *v* **Hag Gf AG** (1991), the German company sought to prevent the importation of coffee under the mark 'Kaffee Hag' into Germany by Van Zuylen. Effectively reversing its decision in **Hag I** the European Court of Justice found that trade mark protection could be used to prevent such imports; the trade mark could only fulfil its role if it could offer a guarantee that all goods bearing the mark had been produced under the control of a single undertaking accountable for their quality. Here the German company had not given consent and it had no control over the quality of the goods.

The **Hag II** position was radically altered in the case of **IHT Internationale Heiztechnik GmbH** *v* **Ideal-Standard GmbH** (1995) involving the mark 'Ideal Standard'. Here the trade mark proprietor was deemed to consent to use of the mark, having voluntarily divested itself of the mark in different territories. This has altered the level of consent required for common origin but not for exhaustion of rights. By separate routes, the cases concerning exhaustion of rights and common origin have reached a similar result. However, cases on exhaustion of rights emphasise a narrow interpretation of the protection of trade marks where there is interference with the free circulation of goods. In contrast, cases on common origin have emphasised the important function as a guarantee of origin which may limit the freedom to parallel import.

In relation to the 'grey' importation of goods from outside the EEA into the EEA, large supermarkets have recently been in the forefront of acquiring grey market goods and selling them at reduced prices against the wishes of the trade mark proprietors.

In **Silhouette International Schmied GmbH & Co KG** *v* **Hartlauer Handelsgesellshaft mbH** (1998) the European Court of Justice had to interpret whether the Trade Mark Directive provisions intended to limit exhaustion of rights to within the EEA or whether it intended to set a minimum standard which allowed separate countries to make their own rules relating to international exhaustion. Silhouette, an Austrian company, manufactured high-priced fashion spectacles distributed under its Silhouette mark. In 1995, it sold outdated spectacle frames to a Bulgarian company, which, Silhouette claimed, was instructed to sell them only in Eastern Europe. Hartlauer, based in Austria but not an approved Silhouette retailer, acquired the spectacles and sold them in their Austrian cut-price stores. Advocate-General Jacobs was satisfied that art 7(1) made clear that it introduced an unbending rule that a registered right could be used to prevent the movement of genuine goods into the EEA from outside, but the court did not go that far in its decision. The European Court of Justice ruled that, under art 7, countries are *not* free to maintain their own rules on international exhaustion while others do not as this would prevent free movement of goods. Community law prevailed. UK law has not followed this interpretation and in **Zino Davidoff SA *v* A & G Imports** (2000), which involved the parallel import of luxury cosmetics from outside the EEA, the court accepted that a trade mark proprietor may have legitimate reasons for objecting to further commercialisation of his goods. This would encompass impairment to both their physical (poor packaging, presentation, etc) or mental condition (for example, the manner in which the reseller advertised goods) which might leave an impression in people's minds that the goods or brand was inferior. However, such damage must be substantial. Emphasising the UK approach, namely that the function of a trade mark is as an indicator of origin, the court determined that this did not mean that *anything*, such as selling the goods at a discounted price, might undermine the mark's luxury image. In **Glaxo Group Ltd *v* Dowelhurst Ltd (No 2)** (2000) Laddie J appeared to narrow guidelines further, suggesting that 'sufficient damage' must constitute damage to its specific subject matter and not simply general damage to its image.

The UK cases go against the spirit of **Silhouette,** in which the emphasis of the European Court of Justice was on the importance of avoiding different rules on international exhaustion in member states as this would impede free movement of goods. The European Court has recently been asked to give a preliminary ruling as to whether the consent of the brand owner to EEA marketing of his goods has to be express or direct or can be given implicitly or indirectly. Further, it has been asked to decide whether consent to EEA marketing has occurred if the brand owner could have placed effective territorial restrictions on resale under the law of a non-EEA country in which the goods are distributed, but did not do so. On preliminary issues determined by the European Court of Justice, Tesco Stores Ltd, which sold Levi jeans imported on the grey market cut-price in its UK supermarkets against the wishes of the trade mark proprietor, have been held not to have infringed the mark proprietor's rights. Written judgment will not be available until later in 2001.

Whatever latest interpretation the European Court of Justice places on the ambiguous provisions of the Trade Marks Directive and on questions raised by its decision in **Silhouette,** the problems surrounding international exhaustion will need a political solution, a view expressed by the Advocate-General in that case. In essence, the question remains as to how far a trade mark can be used outside its basic function as indicator of origin to permit mark proprietors to control the market in their goods.

Question

Joe was the managing director of X Ltd, a small manufacturer. Joe's contract included a restraint of trade clause in which he agreed not to set up a competing business within five miles of X Ltd's premises for a period of two years. X Ltd was taken over by Y Ltd, who immediately sacked Joe. Joe started a new firm four miles away from X Ltd's premises and started to manufacture an item that he had designed while working for X Ltd and which X Ltd had patented.

Advise Joe about his legal position.

Answer

Joe wants to be able to use an item that he designed in order to set up a new company. The question raises a few issues: the existence of a restraint of trade clause, whether it is enforceable by Joe's new employer and his use of a patented item.

As discussed in previous chapters, restraint of trade clauses are enforceable if they are protecting some legitimate interest and are reasonable as regards both their duration and their geographic impact. This restraint of trade clause is *prima facie* valid.

The clause was between X Ltd and Joe. However, Y Ltd, who took over X Ltd and then sacked Joe, are seeking to enforce it. The decision of **Morris Angel & Son Ltd *v* Hollande** (1993) confirms that they can do this. Y Ltd have acquired all the contractual rights of X Ltd, including the right to enforce the restraint of trade clause.

Joe is producing an item that he created while working for X Ltd. As an employee invention the product belongs to X Ltd under s 39 of the Patents Act 1977, as is evidenced by the fact that they patented it. However, Joe would have been entitled to some compensation under s 40 of the Patents Act 1977. He cannot make the item without the patent holder's agreement as this would be contrary to s 60 of the Patents Act 1977. The company has a right to seek an injunction to prevent further abuse of the patent as long as the patent is still in force.

Further reading

Cornish, W R (1999). *Intellectual Property: Patents, Copyrights, Trade Marks and Allied Rights*, 4th edn (Sweet & Maxwell)

Bainbridge, D (1999). *Intellectual Property*, 4th edn (Pitman)

Davis, J (2001). *Intellectual Property Law* (Butterworth)

Keenan, D and Riches, S (2001). *Business Law*, 6th edn (Longman)

20 International trade

20.1 Introduction

International trade, in which goods cross national boundaries, forms an important part of the trading network of many companies, this being particularly true with the establishment of the single market in the European Union. Further, government policy exhorts producers to develop overseas markets as a means of earning foreign currency. However, international trade is not without its problems. Typically, the seller resides in one nation state while the buyer is based in another. This breeds difficulties as regards the transfer of title, the opportunity to inspect goods and, most importantly from the seller's perspective, the guarantee of payment. International trade law has responded by developing a range of contracts and payment methods specifically designed to deal with these problems.

The majority of cargo being carried in an international sale of goods will be carried by sea and thus be subject to the controls appropriate to such an arrangement. In most instances, goods leaving the UK will be governed by English law and hence by the Carriage of Goods by Sea Act 1971. This Act has adopted the Hague–Visby Rules, which establish a framework of rules governing contracts of carriage and the rights and liabilities of people interested in them, i.e. cargo owners and carriers. These Rules, which are a newer amended version of the Hague Rules, provide that there are three basic requirements that must be satisfied before the Rules are applicable to any individual contract of carriage: namely, that there must be a bill of lading or similar contract of carriage relating to the terms of the carriage, that the contract must relate to the transportation of goods between ports in two different nation states, and that the contract of carriage must either indicate that the Hague–Visby Rules or that legislation adopting them are to govern the contract or that the bill of lading must be issued in a contracting state or the goods be transported from a contracting state.

The Carriage of Goods by Sea Act 1971, while adopting the Hague–Visby Rules, also extended their impact by stipulating that the Rules will apply to goods leaving the UK irrespective of their port of destination. Thus, they apply to goods being transported from a UK port to another nation state but also for goods leaving a UK port and remaining in coastal waters. Further, the Rules can be adopted by documents other than bills of lading, for example sea waybills, and deck cargo will be included in a contract governed by the Rules.

The Hague–Visby Rules have been criticised as being too pro-carrier and a new set of rules, the Hamburg Rules, have been devised. To date, a significant number of nations have adopted the Hamburg Rules, but the UK is not among this number.

20.2 Bills of lading

In an international sale of goods contract, the seller and buyer are unlikely ever to meet. Consequently, documentary evidence of such contracts achieves an importance not generally found in domestic sales. Indeed, international sales of goods have been referred to as more of a sale of documents relating to goods. The three most common forms of documentation are bills of lading, sea waybills and a ship's delivery order. Of these, a bill of lading is the one in most common usage.

Potentially a bill of lading serves three functions: it can be a document of title, it may be evidence of a contract of carriage and it can be a receipt. As a document of title its significance lies in the fact that it can be used to buy and sell the goods while they are in transit. Whether the bill of lading actually constitutes a document of title depends on the wording of the individual bill. It should be noted that if title does pass under the terms of the bill of lading, the recipient will acquire only such title as was possessed by the transferor. In the absence of the passage of title, the bill of lading will, at the very least, give rights of constructive possession to the person who acquires it lawfully, with that person having the right to expect the carrier to deliver the goods up to him upon presentation of the bill. The contractual impact of a bill of lading arises from the inclusion within it of details of the contract of carriage under which the goods are being transported. Typically, this will comprise the standard terms of carriage subject to any acceptable variations agreed by the shipper (usually the seller of the goods) and the carrier. However, its contractual enforceability depends to some extent upon who is seeking to rely upon it. It may well be that the bill of lading does not stipulate all the terms of any contract of carriage agreed by the shipper and carrier. Where this is so, the agreement governing the parties is the main contract and the bill of lading acts merely as evidence of such a contract. However, at some stage the bill of lading will be endorsed and transmitted to the buyer to enable him to take possession of the goods at the port of destination. Naturally, the buyer will not be a party to the original contract of carriage between the shipper and carrier, although s 2 of the Carriage of Goods by Sea Act 1992 may provide him with some enforcement rights. The bill of lading is the only contractual document that the buyer will definitely have regarding the terms of the carriage. It is generally accepted that the bill of lading will constitute a contract between the carrier and the recipient of the bill of lading and will be enforceable as such. The role of the bill of lading as a receipt is crucial to the contract of carriage for it is good evidence as to the identity, quantity and condition of the goods loaded under it. The bill, if governed by the Hague–Visby Rules, must provide details of the following matters.

(a) *The leading marks on the goods* These are the identification marks which allow the goods to be identified as those to which the bill relates. This identifies them as the ones to be surrendered by the carrier to the holder of the bill of lading at the port of destination. The marks must be sufficiently permanent to prevent their obliteration during the voyage.

(b) *The quantity of goods loaded* The ship's master is under an obligation to account for the full quantity of goods to the buyer at the port of destination. Thus, his signed statement in the bill is important as it stipulates the amount for which the carrier accepts responsibility. If a lesser amount is delivered, the carrier is liable. Section 4 of the Carriage of Goods by Sea Act 1992 provides that a bill of lading signed by the ship's master or any other duly authorised person is conclusive evidence against the carrier of the shipment of the goods.

(c) *The condition of the goods when loaded* In an action by the buyer for the goods being damaged or not of satisfactory quality, the bill is proof of their condition at the time of loading. If the goods are in a good condition, the carrier will sign the bill to that effect, the bill being said to be 'clean'. However, if the goods or packaging are damaged at the time of loading, the carrier must detail those defects on the bill of lading, which is then described as 'claused'. This aspect of the bill is crucially important for it can be used as a means of allocating liability for goods delivered damaged at the port of destination. If the bill is clean, the carrier will be liable for the damage, which must *prima facie* have occurred during the voyage. He will not be liable though for any damage detailed in a claused bill, for which the buyer would need to seek redress from the seller. Whether the bill is clean or claused will also be vital to the ability of the holder of the bill to resell the goods during transit as a claused bill will militate against resale.

20.2.1 Obligations of shipper and carrier

The obligations of the shipper and carrier are stipulated partly by common law and partly by the Hague–Visby Rules. The main responsibility of the shipper is to pay the freight costs, i.e. the costs of carriage. The shipper is liable to pay these even though the cargo may have been lost or damaged at sea, any claim for such loss being subject to a separate action. The remaining duties on the shipper are to inform the carrier if any dangerous goods are being loaded and to arrange for the collection of all goods at their port of destination. Where the seller is transporting to an overseas buyer, this latter responsibility would be satisfied by ensuring that the buyer knows when and where to collect the goods. In an f.o.b. contract (see later) in which the buyer arranged the carriage, he would already be aware of these details.

The carrier's duties are threefold: to provide a seaworthy ship equipped to receive and stow the goods and thereafter put to sea, to take care of the cargo during transit, and to proceed without delay to the port of destination and not to deviate from the prescribed or agreed route except in an attempt to save life or property, or where the deviation is reasonable. Article III of the Hague–Visby Rules stipulates that the carrier is bound 'before and at the beginning of each voyage to exercise due diligence to make the ship seaworthy, to properly man, equip and supply the ship, and to make the holds, refrigerating and cool chambers, and all other parts of the ship in which goods are carried, fit and safe for their reception, carriage and preservation'.

While the shipper is under an obligation to pay the freight costs irrespective of loss or damage to the cargo and the carrier is under a duty to take care of the goods, obviously situations can arise where the cargo, or part of it, may be jettisoned deliberately. This might occur, for example, if a ship runs aground or if the cargo has shifted in a storm such as to endanger the stability of the vessel. In either situation, some of the cargo may be sacrificed in order to secure the safety of the ship and the remainder of the cargo. In circumstances such as these, it would be inequitable for the owner of the jettisoned cargo alone to bear the loss, which has benefited all the other shippers with cargo on the vessel. It is common, therefore, for shippers to pay a general average contribution to cover the cost of the loss from which they have all benefited. Any such general average contribution can usually be recovered via marine insurance.

20.2.2 Claims against the carrier

As explained above, the major conceptual difficulty with bills of lading has been their enforcement by the buyer. The bill of lading evidences a contract of carriage between the shipper (the seller) and the carrier to which the buyer is not a party. Normal rules of contractual privity clearly prevent the buyer suing to enforce this contract. This may be crucial if, as is usual, the risk in the goods passes to the buyer when the goods cross the ship's rail at the port of loading. Thus, while the contract exists between the seller and the carrier, it is the buyer who is affected by the performance of the contract.

Section 1 of the Bills of Lading Act 1855 was passed expressly to address this problem by providing that if certain criteria were satisfied the buyer should be able to enforce the contract of carriage as if he were a party to it. However, the wording of the section was seriously flawed as it appeared to limit its impact to those situations where the transfer or endorsement of the bill caused the property in the goods to pass simultaneously. The weaknesses of the 1855 Act have been addressed by s 2 of the Carriage of Goods by Sea Act 1992, which applies to all bills of lading, sea waybills and ship's delivery orders issued on or after 16 September 1992. In this context, s 1(2) of the 1992 Act states that a bill of lading does not include a document which is incapable of transfer either by endorsement or, as a bearer bill, by delivery without endorsement, but, subject to that, includes 'received for shipment' bills of lading.

Section 1(3) defines a 'sea waybill' as a document which is not a bill of lading but which is a receipt which contains or evidences a contract for the carriage of goods by sea and identifies the person to whom delivery of the goods is to be made in accordance with that contract.

Section 1(4) defines a 'ship's delivery order' as a document which is neither a bill of lading nor a sea waybill but which contains an undertaking given for the purposes of a carriage of goods by sea and is given by the carrier to a person identified in the document and promises to deliver the goods to that person.

Section 2, which encompasses the main provision of the Act, provides that the lawful holder of a bill of lading, the person entitled to delivery under a sea waybill or the person entitled to delivery under a ship's delivery order will be vested with all the rights to enforce the contract of carriage as if he had been a party to it. The advantage of s 2 over the Bills of Lading Act 1855 is that the new enforcement rights are not linked to the transfer of property (though they can be linked to possession) but arise merely by virtue of being the lawful holder of the appropriate documents, irrespective of the capacity in which they are held. This circumvents the difficulties posed by the Bills of Lading Act 1855. However, a demand for delivery under the documents or the exercise of the contractual rights makes the plaintiff liable on the contract as if he had been a party to it. He gains not merely the benefits but also the burdens.

Where a third party with an interest or right in the goods subject to a bill of lading, sea waybill or ship's delivery order suffers loss as a result of a breach of the contract of carriage, the person vested with contractual rights under s 2(1) of the 1992 Act may sue on their behalf although there is no obligation so to do.

There is a limitation on the person's ability to claim contractual enforcement rights under s 2(1). If the bill of lading does not give the lawful holder the right to possession of the goods as against the carrier, the holder will not acquire the right to sue on the contract of carriage unless he became the holder of the bill either as a result of a contract made before the bill lost its possession rights or as a result of the rejection of goods or documents delivered by him to another person under any contractual or other arrangements.

In addition to contractual rights, the holder of a bill may also have rights in tort, in conversion and possibly negligence. Conversion arises if the carrier delivers the goods to the wrong person at the port of destination. The difficulty arises if the goods arrive at the port of destination before the bill of lading. This is likely to happen if documentary credits are being used as the method of payment (see later) with the need for one and probably two banks to examine and approve the documentation. Any delay in the documentation can leave the buyer seeking delivery of the goods from the carrier at the point of destination but without the supporting documentation. Naturally, the carrier, wary of laying himself open to a claim for conversion, will be reluctant to surrender the goods. In practice, this is resolved by the buyer providing the carrier with an indemnity against any possible legal action, although the legality of this practice is not proven.

The other potential source of tortious liability lies in negligence if the goods have been lost or damaged in transit. However, the scope of this tort appears to be very limited in this context, with the decision of **The Aliakmon** (1986) confirming the traditional view that a negligence action can be brought only if the buyer has the property in the goods or, at the very least, an immediate right to possession.

20.2.3 Multi-modal transport

Transport has changed significantly in recent years with the advent of containerised transport. From the seller's point of view, containerisation has much to offer: a secure, easy-to-load method in which his goods are well protected from weather and theft throughout the whole of the journey from the seller's premises to those of the buyer. However, the contracts of carriage for such containers do pose some difficulties. If the sea voyage is subject to a bill of lading, it is impossible for the carrier to confirm the quantity or condition of goods in a sealed container at the time of loading. Thus, if the goods delivered to the buyer are damaged, it is virtually impossible to specify when the damage occurred. There is an obvious difficulty, as yet unresolved, of the conflict of the various rules and conventions which could theoretically cover the different parts of the journey. Thus, the Hague–Visby Rules would not apply automatically to the contract of carriage as they are applicable only to the sea leg of any such journey and would not be relevant to any road/rail transport to the port of departure or from the port of destination. Of course, *prima facie* there is nothing to prevent the contracting parties adopting the Hague–Visby

Rules. However, the road and rail parts of the journey will be governed by the CMR Convention and the CIM Convention respectively, with the CMR Convention stating that it applies to the whole of the journey, including any sea transit, thereby effectively seeking to disapply the Hague–Visby Rules. Such problems have given rise to four new multi-modal transport contracts which govern all aspects of the transportation from the seller's premises to the buyer's premises and thus include the road/rail transport to the port of departure and, if relevant, the road/rail transport from the port of destination to the buyer's premises. The various types of multi-modal contract may adopt the relevant INCOTERMS drafted by the International Chamber of Commerce (ICC). They can also cover the loading and unloading of the container from the ship. The need for such multi-modal contracts is obvious, the voyage part of which may be subject to some form of bill of lading, but it seems likely that any bill of lading would constitute only a receipt in these circumstances.

20.3 C.i.f. and f.o.b. contracts

As international contracts necessarily involve transporting the goods across at least one national boundary, it follows that seller and buyer must agree where the responsibility lies for making the arrangements and financing the carriage. A mere contract of sale of the type used for domestic sales is totally inadequate. The two most common forms of international contract are c.i.f. contracts and f.o.b. contracts, each of which may adopt the relevant INCOTERMS designed by the ICC.

20.3.1 C.i.f. contracts

A c.i.f. (cost, insurance and freight) contract is the more common type and places the responsibility on the seller to arrange for the shipment of the goods and to insure them against loss or damage during the voyage. Thus the price charged to the buyer is inclusive of these services. In a fluctuating market it is in the buyer's interests to agree to a c.i.f. contract where the seller bears the risk of any increase in transport or insurance costs.

A c.i.f. contract places duties on both the seller and buyer. Naturally, if the contract is governed by English law this will include statutory duties arising from compliance with the Sale of Goods Act 1979. The duties placed on the seller may be summarised thus:

1 To provide goods that conform with the contract as regards both description and quantity and that are of a satisfactory quality and fit for their intended purpose. A breach of any of these requirements would constitute a breach of condition justifying repudiation of the goods and termination of the contract.
2 To deliver the goods to the correct port of loading during the contractually specified period. Time is of the essence in this situation as it is a contractually agreed term, and thus to deliver the goods too early or too late will justify a termination of the contract.

3 To arrange for the necessary shipping to deliver the goods to the correct port of destination and to ensure that the vessel used can offer any special facilities needed, e.g. a refrigerated hold for the transport of some foodstuffs.
4 To insure the goods against loss or damage during the voyage.
5 To accept liability for the payment of the freight charges and the insurance charges.
6 To ensure that the appropriate documentation is available and forwarded to the buyer, or, if relevant, the bank, to enable the buyer to take delivery at the port of destination.
7 To arrange for any other necessary documentation such as export licences.

The duties placed on the buyer again include some terms that are derived from his obligations under the Sale of Goods Act 1979 and some that are peculiar to international contracts:

1 To take delivery of the goods when they arrive at the port of destination, assuming that they comply with the contract description and with the statutory implied terms.
2 To accept the bill of lading if it is in proper form and pay for the goods delivered under it.
3 To pay for any additional freight or demurrage (costs incurred through a delay in loading at the port of departure) if the contract so specifies.
4 To arrange for the transportation of the goods after their arrival at the port of destination if the contract so provides.
5 To inform the seller of the date and place of destination of the goods if the contract so requires in sufficient time to allow the seller to make the necessary shipment arrangements.
6 To arrange and pay for any necessary import licences/customs duties, etc.

20.3.2 F.o.b. contracts

The alternative form of contract is an f.o.b. (free on board) contract, which places the responsibility on the buyer to arrange for the shipment of the goods and their insurance cover for the voyage. Thus the responsibilities of the seller cease when the goods have been loaded. In some ways the duties placed on the seller and buyer by an f.o.b. contract are the same as under a c.i.f. contract. Thus the seller is under an obligation to deliver goods complying with the contract and with the statutory implied terms, while the buyer is under a duty to take delivery of the goods and the documents of carriage and pay for the goods. The duties placed on the seller and buyer relating to the transport of the goods differ, however, from those under a c.i.f. contract.

The duties placed on the seller are:

1 To arrange for the transportation of the goods to the port of departure.
2 To deliver the goods to the appropriate vessel during the contractually agreed period for loading.

3   To obtain a mate's receipt when the goods are loaded and hand it to a forwarding
    agent for transmission to the buyer.

The duties placed on the buyer are:

1   To book appropriate shipping space on a suitable vessel.
2   To inform the seller of the port and date of departure and the name of the vessel
    in sufficient time to allow the seller to make the transport arrangements necessary
    to ensure that the goods are loaded on time. A failure to do this will allow the
    seller to terminate the contract.
3   To insure the cargo against loss or damage during the voyage.
4   To pay the freight charges.

The potential advantage to a buyer of contracting on f.o.b. terms is that it allows
him the choice of vessel. If the buyer regularly imports goods he may have a block
insurance policy, or have his own shipping contacts who can provide cheaper
shipping. From a governmental point of view, f.o.b. contracts offer the opportunity
to use domestic ships, both encouraging the shipping industry and saving foreign
currency.

20.3.3   The passage of risk

As discussed in Chapter 10, the risk in goods under s 20 of the Sale of Goods Act
1979 usually passes with the passage of the property in the goods. However, s 20
provides that this presumption does not hold true if there is an agreement to the
contrary. In contracts for international trade it is usual to provide that the risk in the
goods passes to the buyer at the time that the goods cross the ship's rail during
loading irrespective of when the property in the goods passes. Therefore, if the goods
are damaged during loading but before they cross the rail the seller must bear the
risk. Equally, if there is a valid retention of title clause in the contract, or if the goods
have not been ascertained, the risk in the goods will pass to the buyer while the goods
are still owned by the seller.

20.4   Documentary credits

The financing of international sale contracts poses particular problems. The seller
will be reluctant to part with the goods until he is guaranteed payment of the
purchase price for, should the buyer fail to pay, the seller would be faced with the
difficulty of suing to enforce the debt in a foreign jurisdiction. While the position is
not as onerous if the buyer is based in another EU member state, because the
provisions of the Civil Jurisdiction and Judgments Act 1982 permit judgments to be
enforced throughout the European Union, it is still a situation which a seller would
rather avoid. The buyer for his part will not be prepared to part with the money for
the goods until he has received them and had the opportunity to inspect them. Both

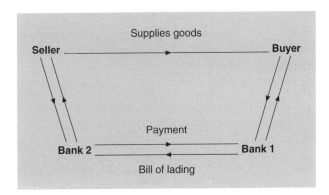

Figure 20.1   An irrevocable banker's documentary credit arrangement

parties are bound to be wary of dealing with a contracting party with whom they may not have dealt in the past and who is beyond the jurisdiction of the courts.

This potential breakdown has been addressed by the development of the irrevocable banker's documentary credit, which permits the sale to be completed while minimising the risk faced by both parties. Documentary credits are typically subject to the Uniform Customs and Practice for Documentary Credits promulgated by the International Chamber of Commerce (ICC).

Typically, the arrangement of an irrevocable banker's documentary dredit will involve the use of two banks, one in the buyer's country and one in the seller's country.

As can be seen from Figure 20.1, while the goods are sent directly from the seller to the buyer, the bill of lading or other shipping documents and the payment for the contract both pass through the hands of both banks. The arrangement works thus. Having agreed the terms of the contract of sale, the buyer instructs the bank in his country, Bank 1, to issue a documentary credit in favour of the seller. Once Bank 1 has confirmed to the seller that this has been done, the seller can safely ship the goods, certain that he will be paid. Bank 1 then instructs Bank 2, which is based in the seller's country, about the credit. Bank 2 will confirm the arrangement. The seller having shipped the goods will be in possession of the bill of lading. He presents the bill of lading to Bank 2, which after checking and accepting the documents will pay the seller. Bank 2 will, in turn, present the documents to Bank 1 and receive payment, Bank 1 forwarding them to the buyer for payment.

The system clearly has advantages for both seller and buyer. The seller is assured of payment as the documentary credit is irrevocable, but should any difficulties arise the seller has an identifiable defendant (Bank 2) based in his own jurisdiction. The buyer for his part acquires the bill of lading as soon as Bank 1 has paid the debt to Bank 2, thus allowing the buyer to claim delivery of the goods at the port of destination or even sell the goods while they are still in transit. This latter facility is important, for the buyer may need to sell the goods via the bill of lading in order to settle his indebtedness to Bank 1.

Because of the number of people involved in a documentary credit transaction, it is not uncommon for the goods to arrive at the port of destination before the buyer receives the bill of lading from Bank 1. This places the buyer in an invidious position. Naturally he will want to take possession of the goods as soon as possible to allow him to use them or arrange for their resale if that is his intention. However, in the absence of a bill of lading, the carrier may be reluctant to release the goods in case he is subsequently sued in conversion by anyone who has an immediate right to possession. The difficulty is resolved typically by the buyer providing the carrier with an indemnity against any claim in conversion that may be lodged against him.

Question

Virgo Ltd, a manufacturer of goods in England, agreed to sell them to Cancer, a company in France. The contract was a c.i.f. contract with the goods being transported by sea from Southampton to Le Havre. It was agreed that payment would be by documentary credit through Bank Aries in France and Bank Libra in England. Virgo Ltd arranged for the loading of the goods and gave a clean bill of lading to Bank Libra. The goods were damaged in a heavy storm during the crossing. The goods arrived at Le Havre before the bill of lading.

Advise Cancer about obtaining possession of the goods and claiming for the damage caused to them.

Answer

The goods are being transported c.i.f. Thus the obligation was on Virgo Ltd to arrange for the freight and insurance of the goods. They were duly despatched in good condition as evidenced by the clean bill of lading. The risk in the goods will have passed to Cancer when the goods crossed the rail of the ship on loading in Southampton. Therefore, when the goods arrive damaged the responsibility is on Cancer to arrange for a remedy.

The goods arrived before the bill of lading, which will have to pass through the hands of Bank Libra and Bank Aries before reaching Cancer. Cancer can actually obtain possession of the goods from the carrier by providing the carrier with an indemnity against any claims in conversion. Thereafter Cancer can make a claim against the insurer under the policy of marine insurance arranged by Virgo Ltd but which will have been transferred by endorsement to Cancer as part of the transfer of the bill of lading. They remain liable to pay the contract price for the goods to Virgo Ltd via Bank Aries and Bank Libra as the goods were in good condition when shipped.

Further reading

Atiyah, P S, Adams, J N and Macqueen, H (2001). *The Sale of Goods*, 10th edn (Longman)

Bradgate, R (2000). *Commercial Law*, 3rd edn (Butterworth)

Dobson, P (2000). *Sale of Goods and Consumer Credit*, 6th edn (Sweet & Maxwell)

D'Arcy, L, Murray, C and Cleave, B (2000). *Schmitthoff's Export Trade: The Law and Practice of International Trade*, 9th edn (Sweet & Maxwell)

21 Insurance

21.1 Introduction

Throughout this text we have referred to situations in which the supplier/manufacturer of goods or services would have civil law liability in circumstances in which it would be possible to protect himself from the full rigours of liability by the use of insurance. Thus, for example, this would include liability for damage caused by goods proving unsatisfactory or not fit for their purpose, injuries sustained from defective goods with consequent product liability, negligence, a failure to provide title to goods, accidental damage to goods and the loss of or damage to goods during transit by sea. It is noticeable that all the liabilities mentioned here refer to civil law liability. It would, of course, be contrary to public policy to allow the defendant in a criminal case to protect himself against the effects of such liability by the use of insurance.

Insurance has much to offer from the insured's perspective. It protects him from full liability for his actions by allowing him to contract with an insurance company for them to run the risk on his behalf. Further, the insured can spread the responsibility among his customers by treating the insurance premium, the cost of the contract, as another cost of production. This can be recouped from his customers through a marginal increase in the product price. Ultimately, therefore, insurance provides the insured trader with a means to avoid the financial implications of civil liability at minimal cost or inconvenience to himself.

21.2 Types of insurance

Insurance risks fall into two categories: indemnity insurance and contingency insurance. The former provides indemnity, i.e. full financial cover, if a particular situation arises. Thus, for example, fire insurance is an indemnity insurance which will pay for the full cost of fire damage, assuming that the property was fully insured. By comparison, contingency insurance occurs when the insurer promises to pay an agreed sum upon the happening of the contingent event. The most common form of contingency insurance is life insurance, under which the insurer agrees to pay a fixed sum upon the death of the person whose life was insured (not necessarily the policyholder). Life insurance is beyond the remit of this book and will not be considered in detail. The feature common to both indemnity insurance and contingency insurance is that there is a degree of uncertainty. With indemnity insurance the uncertainty is whether the event will ever happen. A company may have fire insurance on its factory and offices for 20 years and never have a fire. Similarly, it may have accident insurance on a company car and never have the car involved in an accident. With life insurance, the uncertainty is of a different nature. The contingent event, death, is bound to happen; the uncertainty is when it will happen.

Insurance can also be divided into first party insurance and third party insurance. First party insurance protects the insured from the damage that he will suffer if the event occurs. Fire insurance is a good example, where the insured person protects his own property against the risk of fire in order to receive indemnity against his own loss. Third party insurance provides compensation to third parties affected by the insured's actions. Thus, product liability insurance taken out by a producer to cover claims made by persons injured by defective products is third party insurance. It is possible to mix the two in one policy as, for example, where a company (or anyone else) insures a car 'fully comprehensive'. Such insurance protects the insured against the first party risks of damage to or loss of the vehicle itself through accident, theft, etc *and* protects it against third party liability owed to anyone injured by the car in an accident.

21.3 Insurable interest

In order to effect valid insurance the insured person must have an 'insurable interest' in the subject matter of the policy. The lack of any insurable interest will render the contract void under the Gaming Act 1845.

An insurable interest was defined in the landmark decision of **Lucena *v* Craufurd** (1806) as being 'a right in the property, or a right derivable out of some contract about the property, which in either case may be lost upon some contingency affecting the possession or enjoyment of the party'. The most obvious insurable interest is ownership of the goods or property insured, but any legal interest in the subject matter will suffice. Thus, in a contract of sale involving a retention of title clause the seller retains an insurable interest in the goods until the property in them passes although he may already have parted with the possession of the goods. The buyer in that situation, who has possession but not property, has an insurable interest as a person who has bought or agreed to buy the goods and who has a potential liability to the owner should the goods be damaged while they are in his possession. Similarly, both creditor and hirer in a hire-purchase agreement would have insurable interests. A lien over goods will suffice to create an insurable interest such that the unpaid seller of goods will have such an interest. A person has an insurable interest in marine insurance if he will benefit from the safe arrival of the vessel and its cargo and suffer loss by its failure to arrive safely. These examples all relate to first party liability but the same would hold true of third party liability. Hence the seller or manufacturer of goods would have sufficient insurable interest to cover liability to third persons should the goods prove to be faulty.

The insurable interest must exist at the time of the loss, an expired interest or one yet to mature being insufficient. Thus, in **Macaura *v* Northern Assurance Co Ltd** (1925), Macaura was the owner of timber on his estate in County Tyrone. He sold the timber to a company in return for 42,000 fully paid shares in the company, which made him the principal shareholder, all other shares being held by his nominees. He was also an unsecured creditor of the company in the sum of £19,000. He continued to insure the timber in his own name rather than in the company's name. Two weeks after the sale the timber was destroyed in a fire. The House of Lords held that although Macaura was the principal shareholder and creditor of the company and as such had a genuine interest in the well-being of the company, the timber was owned by the company and not by him in any capacity. As he had no legal interest in the property, he had no insurable interest and the insurance company was correct in refusing to pay upon his claim.

Macaura is also good authority for the proposition that mere possession of the goods does not amount to an insurable interest. A legal interest of some sort is necessary. Similarly, in **Glengate-KG Properties Ltd** *v* **Norwich Union Fire Insurance Society Ltd** (1996) the plaintiff, a property developer, was not able to recover for the losses that he suffered when architect's drawings being used in a site office at the plaintiff's site were destroyed in a fire. The Court of Appeal held that while the drawings were property and were in use on the plaintiff's premises for the purposes of his business, he did not have an insurable interest in them.

Lucena *v* **Craufurd** is evidence that a legal interest which has not yet matured does not constitute an insurable interest either and will defeat an insurance claim. In that case, some enemy ships were captured on the high seas by some British ships. The Crown Commissioners were authorised to take control of such ships when they reached a British port. Meanwhile, the Commissioners sought to insure the ships, some of which were lost at sea before reaching port. The House of Lords held that at the time of loss the Crown Commissioners did not have an insurable interest in the vessels and thus could not claim on the insurance policy.

The insured's ability to recover is limited to the extent of his own interest. However, in some situations it may be possible for the insured to claim the full value of the lost or damaged goods and hold the balance on trust for the owner of the remaining insurable interest. This is particularly so if the third party is named in the policy. In **Hepburn** *v* **A Tomlinson (Hauliers) Ltd** (1966) a carrier of goods insured them for the duration of carriage naming the owner of the goods as a party to the insurance and including some first party cover. The court held that the owner of the goods was entitled to recover when the goods were stolen from the carrier with the latter being in no way responsible for the theft.

21.4 The contract

A contract of insurance is at root a contract subject to the same rules as any other contract. Thus, there is a requirement for offer, acceptance, consideration, etc. In insurance, the contractual offer is made by the insured person presenting details of the insurance required to the insurance company. This is commonly done by the completion of a standard proposal form, which will include details of the party to be insured, the nature of the risk, the duration of the insurance and any special factors which are to be brought to the attention of the insurance company. As stated, this is done typically in a proposal form but there is no obligation to this effect. An offer made orally as, for example, where a motorist arranges for the insurance of a different car over the phone, is both legal and binding if accepted. If the proposal is the contractual offer, it follows that the insurance company is at liberty to accept or reject the offer, the contract becoming effective if the company accepts the offer. The consideration for the contract is the insurance premium.

An insurance contract is a contract *uberrimae fidei* and thus the parties are under an obligation to inform each other of all matters relevant to the insurance contract. This duty of disclosure is particularly pertinent to the provision of information by the insured person when proposing the contract. The insurance company obviously needs all the relevant information to enable it to decide whether to accept the insurance proposal and provide the insurance cover required. In practice, the crucial information will be almost exclusively in the hands of the person seeking the insurance cover, who is subject to an obligation to provide it to the insurance company. A failure to disclose all the material information will render the contract voidable at the behest of the insurer in the same way that any contractual misrepresentation affects the resultant contract.

The duty of disclosure begs the question what information must be disclosed. Clearly, any question on the proposal form must be answered fully and honestly, although it is clear from the Court of Appeal decision in **Hussain v Brown** (1995) that questions on the proposal form will be construed strictly and that answers will not necessarily impute promises by the insured as to his future conduct. In that decision a question on an insurance proposal form read 'Are the premises fitted with any system of intruder alarm? If "yes" give name of installing company'. The insured answered 'yes' and provided a specification of the alarm. The underwriters claimed that this created a continuing warranty that the alarm would be operational and would be set when the premises were empty. However, the Court of Appeal held that as the question on the proposal form was phrased in the present tense, it could not be used to create any warranty by the insured as to his future actions. If the insurance company wished to be certain of the insured's future conduct, appropriate questions should be asked.

The duty of disclosure requires that all material facts will be disclosed. The House of Lords in the 1994 decision of **Pan Atlantic Insurance Co Ltd v Pine Top Insurance Co Ltd** (1994) reconfirmed that facts are deemed to be material for this purpose if they would have had an effect on the mind of an insurer when deciding whether to insure the risk in question, although it does not require that a full and accurate disclosure would have had a decisive effect on the prudent underwriter's decision as to whether to accept the risk and at what premium. This approach was followed by the Court of Appeal in **Norwich Union Life Insurance Co Ltd v Qureshi** (1999) when holding that in determining the extent of the duty to disclose, the key factor is the extent of the risk. For an insurer to be entitled to avoid a policy for non-disclosure, he must show that the misrepresentation or non-disclosure was material and that it induced the making of the policy on those terms.

The duty of good faith naturally requires the insured to act honestly when disclosing material facts to the insurance company. But the requirement is honesty not infallibility. This approach was reinforced in the decision of **Economides v Commercial Union Assurance Co Ltd** (1997), in which the Court of Appeal held that while there is an obligation on the insured to act honestly when disclosing material facts and that there should be some reasonable basis for his belief in their veracity, there is no requirement on him to carry out specific inquiries to establish an objectively reasonable basis for that belief. Further, where a private individual is effecting insurance for non-business purposes, he only has to disclose those facts known to him and not inquire further into them.

It is a question of fact as to whether, in any particular case, a fact was material, but cases to date suggest that, for example, a previous conviction of the insured is a material fact even if the conviction is in no way related to the risk for which insurance cover is being sought. In **Woolcott** *v* **Sun Alliance & London Alliance Ltd** (1978) the insured arranged for insurance for his house. He failed to disclose that he had previous convictions for robbery but stated that, if asked, he would have disclosed details of the convictions. The house was subsequently destroyed by fire. The court held that the insurance company was entitled to avoid the insurance because of the insured's failure to disclose a material fact. The decisions of **Regina Fur Co Ltd** *v* **Bossom** (1957) and **Roselodge Ltd** *v* **Castle** (1966) would both support the above proposition.

The issue was further considered in the Court of Appeal decision of **Galloway** *v* **Guardian Royal Exchange (UK) Ltd** (1999), a case in which the plaintiff failed to disclose a conviction under the Theft Act 1968 for obtaining income support by deception when he applied for home contents insurance. Subsequently he was burgled and, in addition to claiming for the losses he genuinely suffered, he submitted a fraudulent claim for £2,000 for a non-existent computer, a fraud for which he was convicted of attempting to obtain property by deception. He attempted to claim from the insurance company for the genuine losses but the Court of Appeal held that the claim must fail as it was tainted by the fraud and that the duty of good faith on the insured was a continuing duty which would continue after the insurance contract came into force.

A refusal by another company to provide insurance for the insured is also a relevant material fact, as can be seen in the decision of **Glicksman** *v* **Lancashire & General Insurance Co** (1927), in which a firm of which Glicksman was a partner applied for some burglary insurance. The firm had never been refused insurance cover although Glicksman personally had been. It was held that the insurer was entitled to avoid the policy for non-disclosure of a material fact.

The duty of good faith and disclosure in insurance is a mutual duty and thus is also owed by the insurer to the insured. The House of Lords decision of **Banque Financière de la Cité SA** *v* **Westgate Insurance Co Ltd** (1990) confirmed this point although holding that the insured has no right to damages in this situation, his remedy being rescission of the contract.

An insurance contract can be assigned in the same way as any other contract. With insurance contracts, however, there must be compliance with certain criteria. As explained earlier, only a person with an insurable interest can insure goods. It follows, therefore, that if that person ceases to have an insurable interest the insurance policy will cease. The disposal of the goods, for example by sale, would defeat the insurance policy unless it is assigned to the buyer of the goods simultaneously with the passage of property in the goods. Further, as an insurance contract is a contract *uberrimae fidei* any assignment must be agreed by the insurance company.

The insured person cannot simply foist a new contractual party on the insurance company without its consent.

Contracts of marine insurance are assignable by endorsement. This flexibility is essential to the smooth running of international trade contracts, particularly c.i.f. contracts.

21.5 Terms of the contract

The terms of an insurance contract fall under three headings: warranties, conditions and terms descriptive of the risk. Rather confusingly, the use of terminology in insurance contracts is in direct opposition to its use in other contracts. Thus, in the insurance context, warranties are the most important and significant terms, the breach of which gives the insurer the option of rescinding the contract. Conditions are the lesser terms, the breach of which gives rise to an action for damages or perhaps the right to avoid liability for one particular claim. Terms descriptive of the risk are, as the name suggests, terms which add to the understanding of the risk insured but which do not give rise to any remedy if breached.

Warranties are often derived from the information contained in a proposal form with the form typically including a statement that such information will form the basis of the contract. It follows that if the information on the proposal is incorrect the insurer can terminate the policy. In **Dawsons Ltd** *v* **Bonnin** (1922) the proposal form for vehicle insurance on a lorry asked for the address at which the lorry would be garaged. The insured inadvertently gave an incorrect address. Although this mistake had no effect on the risk being insured the court nonetheless held that the insurers could avoid the contract for a breach of warranty as the proposal form clearly stated that the answers would form the basis of the contract.

Typically, the breach of a warranty will also allow the insurance company to avoid payment of a claim, but only if the breached warranty is relevant to the claim at hand. In **Printpak** *v* **AGF Insurance Ltd** (1999) the plaintiff sought to claim for fire damage to a factory. It transpired that, contrary to the requirements of the policy, the burglar alarm was switched off at the time of the fire. However, the Court of Appeal, finding for the plaintiff, held that while it was an individual contract, it contained several separate schedules, each of which related to a particular type of risk. The warranty regarding the burglar alarm was restricted in its effect to the schedule covering burglary and so did not effect a claim for damage caused by a fire.

Ultimately, it will be a question of fact in each case as to whether a clause is a warranty or merely a condition. The way that it is described in the contract will not necessarily be the way that the court will interpret it. Thus, for example, in **Kler Knitwear Ltd** *v* **Lombard General Insurance Co Ltd** (2000) the plaintiff's insurance policy contained a term in which it was 'warranted' that the sprinkler system would be checked within 30 days of the policy being renewed. The check was not done for three months. Subsequently, when the plaintiff claimed for storm damage to the property, the insurance company tried to avoid the claim on the basis that the contractual 'warranty' about the sprinkler check had been breached. The court held that the clause in question was a 'suspensive condition' rather than a warranty and found for the plaintiff.

Breaches of condition in this context refer to relatively minor breaches and may allow the insured to evade liability for one incident. A prime example would be the condition typically included in insurance policies which requires that the insured must inform the insurer of a likely claim within a specified period after the occurrence of the event. A failure to comply with such a term allows the insurer to avoid liability for that event while not interrupting the continuation of the insurance policy.

Terms descriptive of the risk are by way of being explanatory rather than enforceable, which may go some way towards mitigating the effect of a breach of warranty. Thus, in **CTN Cash & Carry Ltd** *v* **General Accident Fire & Life Assurance Corpn plc** (1989) the policy on the insured's premises stated that the cash kiosk would be attended and locked during business hours. The court held that this term was descriptive of the risk and that the insurer could repudiate a claim arising at a time when this term was not being complied with without repudiating the whole insurance contract.

21.6   The role of agents

A significant proportion of insurance business is conducted through independent agents or brokers registered under the Insurance Brokers (Registration) Act 1977. Much of the relationship is subject to the normal rules of agency but the key question in the insurance context is on whose behalf the agent is working. Is he the agent of the insurer to sell insurance policies or the agent of the insured looking for insurance cover? This is particularly important with regard to the insured's duty of disclosure for if the agent is acting for the insurer, disclosure to him will satisfy the duty. If, however, the agent is acting for the insured, disclosure to him will be of no effect. As a general rule of thumb, agents canvassing business on behalf of an insurer will be presumed to be acting for that insurer. Equally an independent insurance broker providing advice about possible alternative sources of insurance to the insured will be presumed to be acting as his agent. Both, however, would seem to act as the agent of the insurer for the purpose of issuing cover notes. Further, the decision of **Newsholme Bros** *v* **Road Transport and General Insurance Co** (1929) specified that if the agent of the insurer for the sake of convenience fills in the proposal form for the insured, this does not make him the agent of the insured, particularly if the insured signs the proposal form after it has been completed.

21.7   Claims

The insured party is entitled to make a claim under a policy when and if the event insured against occurs and causes damage or loss to the insured. Thus payment is due on a fire policy if the property insured is damaged by fire. Similarly, a life insurance policy is payable upon the death of the person who was the subject of the policy.

The policy typically provides that monetary compensation will be paid upon the occurrence of the event, but there is no legal requirement to this effect. Hence it would be perfectly legal to stipulate that the insurer is responsible for replacing a lost item or rebuilding a damaged property. The latter would be of particular value in the current economic climate, where the market value of property (which is the sum that the insured would be likely to receive upon destruction of the property) would not cover the cost of rebuilding it.

For indemnity insurance the insured will receive the market value of the property at the time of its destruction, this being so for both real property and goods. Thus second-hand goods will attract only their current value and not the cost of a new replacement. It is possible to obtain new-for-old policies whereby for an additional premium the insured will receive the cost of new goods rather than the market value of the old ones. Where the goods have not been destroyed, merely damaged, the insured will receive the cost of repairing them. It should be noted that total loss justifying payment under a marine insurance policy includes 'constructive total loss', in which the goods or vessel have been abandoned in a situation where actual total loss was inevitable.

These statements about payment have been made on the basis that the property is fully insured, i.e. that its full market value was insured. However, in practice property is often underinsured, either inadvertently because property values have risen without the insured making appropriate alterations to the insurance cover, or deliberately as a means of reducing the cost of insurance premiums. It would be inequitable to allow an insured person who is underinsured to recover the full cost of any damage that he suffers. It is normal practice for insurance contracts to contain an average clause, which provides that where the property subject to the policy is undervalued the insured person will receive only a proportion of the loss suffered. While there is no one average clause in universal use, one approach is for the insured to receive only a percentage of the loss suffered equivalent to the percentage of the risk insured. Thus, for example, if property worth £10,000 is insured for £6,000 the insured will receive only £6,000 if the property is totally destroyed as a result of an insured event. If the same property were to suffer damage valued at £5,000 (50 per cent of its market value) the insured would receive only £3,000 in compensation (50 per cent of its insured value).

With liability insurance, the insured person is entitled to receive the full amount to cover his liability to third parties injured by the insured item. Thus, for example, in product liability insurance the producer will receive the full amount of his civil liability to compensate the injured user of a defective product. This payment will be subject only to any maximum cover stipulated in the contract.

The right to full payment may be mitigated by the existence of an excess on the policy. Such a provision, very common in motor insurance, requires the insured person to accept liability for some of the damage – perhaps, for example, the first £100. If damage of less than the excess is occasioned the insured person is liable for all of it. If the damage exceeds the excess, the insured pays the excess with the insurer paying the remainder.

A basic tenet of insurance as stipulated in **Castellain v Preston** (1883) is that the insured will receive full indemnity but not receive more than the value of his loss. It may be, however, that the property or goods are covered by more than one insurance policy, with the net result that if all the relevant policies paid out fully, the insured would be overcompensated. In a purchasing and supply situation this could happen, for example, if the owner and the carrier of goods both insured the goods for the duration of the contract of carriage. If the goods should be lost or stolen during the carriage, payments could be claimed under both insurance policies. The same situation would occur with goods in storage if both the owner and the warehouseman insured them. When one of the insurers pays out the full claim in this situation, he is entitled to seek a contribution from any other insurer covering the same risk. This is so even if, as happened in **Legal and General Assurance Society Ltd** *v* **Drake Insurance Co Ltd** (1992), one of the insurers would have been able to avoid liability on the claim because the insured had not complied with the condition about the giving of notice of a claim.

21.8 Subrogation

Subrogation deals with the rights of the insurer to recover money from the insured if he has been overcompensated and to enforce the rights of the insured against any third party responsible for the loss.

The first part of subrogation, that relating to the opportunity for the insurer to reclaim some money from the insured, arises if the insured has been overcompensated. As explained earlier, the insured has a right to receive full indemnity for his losses, assuming that he was fully insured, but does not have a right to be overcompensated. This situation might arise if, for example, the damaged goods had been insured by two insurance companies, both of which, unaware of the existence of the other, had paid out full indemnity. The insured would then have received double indemnity. Similarly, it might arise if the insured receives full indemnity from his insurance company and then receives compensation from any third party responsible for the event, for example a negligent driver under motor insurance. In any situation in which the insured has been overcompensated, the insurer is entitled to recover the excess payment from the insured. However, the insurer may not recover more than the amount for which he was responsible under the policy. Any further excess is a windfall for the insured.

The second aspect of subrogation relates to the right of the insurer to adopt any legal action to recover compensation that would have been open to the insured. Thus, for example, if the owner of goods has received indemnity from his insurance company for their loss, the insurer could then sue anyone whose negligence caused the loss. This right of subrogation effectively means that the insurer steps into the shoes of the insured as regards legal claims. Therefore, the insurer is bound by any restrictions that would have applied to the insured. Hence, if any legal defence could have been raised against the insured, it can be raised against the insurer. Similarly, the insurer will be subject to any counterclaim of contributory negligence. Lastly, the insurer cannot sue any other party to the insurance policy as that would involve the insured effectively suing himself.

Question

Zeppo Ltd want to insure their factory against the risk of fire damage. Consider each of the three issues raised:

(a) Do they have an insurable interest?
(b) Must they tell the insurer that they were refused burglary insurance for the factory?
(c) Zeppo Ltd, being short of capital, can afford to insure the factory for only 80 per cent of its value. What is the inherent risk of this strategy?

Answer

Zeppo Ltd have raised three issues regarding the insurance of their factory:

(a) An insured person must have an insurable interest in the subject matter of the insurance. Where insurance of property is concerned this is most obvious if the insured owns the property. The facts given here mean that Zeppo Ltd will have an insurable interest, either as the owner or as the tenant of the property.

(b) An insured person is under an obligation to tell the insurer of any material facts that may affect the insurer's preparedness to accept the policy. The fact that Zeppo Ltd have been refused burglary insurance is clearly a material fact for it suggests that the property is at risk from burglary and therefore perhaps from arson. If Zeppo Ltd do not tell their insurer of this fact, the insurer can avoid the policy.

(c) Insurance policies typically contain an average clause. Thus, in the event of a claim, the insured receives the full value of the claim only if the property was fully insured. If it was underinsured the claim will be reduced by a corresponding percentage. Thus if Zeppo Ltd insure the property for only 80 per cent of its value they will receive only 80 per cent of any claim, whether the property is destroyed or merely damaged.

Further reading

Birds, J (1997). *Modern Insurance Law*, 4th edn (Sweet & Maxwell)
Bradgate, R (2000). *Commercial Law*, 3rd edn (Butterworth)

Index

ab initio 34, 35, 77, 78
abuse of dominant position 268, 274–6, 280–1
acceptable quality 102, 106
acceptance 9
  communication of 10–12
  by conduct 11
  of goods 131–4
  of offer 5
  postal 12
  sale of goods 113
  silence is not 11
accidents
  contributory negligence 167–8
  duty to warn 181, 182–3
  nervous shock 164, 169–70
  product liability 181, 182–3, 185
action for the price 135
actions, limitation of 70–1
Acts of God 27
actual authority 74–6
actual and commercial necessity 79
advertisements 300, 301
  false statements 203–5, 208–10
  food safety 238, 241
agency
  agreement (privity rule) 22
  authority 74–9
  breach of 74–5, 80–2
  –contractual relationship 73–4
  creation of 74
  duties arising 80
  law of 73–91
  of necessity 78–9
  by ratification 77–8
  termination of 86
agent
  bona fide actions by 79
  duties owed by 80–3
  financial settlement with 85

insurance (role) 323
  principal/agent relationship 80–4
  role 73–4
  third party relationship 86
agreement
  agency 22
  bilateral 65
  offer and acceptance 3
  termination by 64–5
  unilateral 65
agreements between undertakings 268–74
'all monies' clause 148
anti-competitive practices 47, 268–82
anticipatory breach 66–7
Anton Piller injunction 81
apparent authority 76–7
appearance (merchantable quality) 109
ascertained goods 141–2
ascertainment by exhaustion 145–6
assignment (privity rule) 22
authority
  actual 74–6
  apparent 76–7
  express 75
  implied 80
  implied actual 75
  necessity 78–9
  ostensible 76
  ratification 77–8
  usual 75–6
average quantity principle 245, 247–9

bailment 97, 121
bargaining power, inequality of 50
barter 120
batch system 249
battle of the forms 10, 28
Berne Convention 290–1, 293
'best before' date (food) 239
bidding authority 261

bilateral agreement 65
bilateral contractual offer 4–5
bills of lading 127, 308–12, 315–16
block exemption 272, 273, 274, 280
bona fide actions (by agent) 79
breach
    of agency 74–5, 80–2
    anticipatory 66–7
    of confidence 283–5
    of duty of care 167
    effect of 67
    fundamental 53
    of implied condition 113–14
    remedies 67–71
    termination by 66–7
    of warranty 96, 99, 113–14, 139
bribery 83
BSI Kitemark 195, 226
bulk 145–7, 149–51
buyer in possession 155–6
buyer's remedies 138–9
bypass procedure 206, 241

Cabinet Office Enforcement Concordat 206
car clocking 198, 199, 200, 206
car insurance 318, 324
care and skill 122–4
carrier
    claims against 310–11
    contract of carriage 128
    international rules 307–11
    obligations of 309–10
causation 167
caveat emptor 14, 34, 102, 108
certainty of terms (contracts) 9
children (duty of care) 165, 167
'Chinese Walls' 82
CIM Convention 312
claims, insurance 323–5
claims against the carrier 310–11
claused bill of lading 309
CMR Convention 312
co-ownership 150–1
codes of practice
    false statements 206, 210
    food safety 239
    product safety 216
collateral contracts 6, 21–2, 86, 118
commercial activity (product safety) 215,
    217
commercial agents 87–91

commercial agreements 17–18
commercial operations 230–1
commercial units (of goods) 133
commission 84, 88, 90
common law control 50–3
common mistake 35–6
common origin 302, 304–5
common ownership 150–1
communication of acceptance 10–12
Community Trade Mark (CTM) 297–8,
    302
compensation
    for false statements 193
    following termination 89, 90
    global limits 187, 188
    product safety 224
    punitive damages 69, 178
    for unfair dismissal 265
    see also damages
Competition Commission 269, 276, 277–9
competition law 268–82
competitive tendering 9, 253, 254, 260–2
component parts (defective) 185
compulsory competitive tendering (CCT) 9,
    253, 260–2
computer pricing system 209
computer software 180, 209, 291, 293
condition of goods (for shipment) 309
conditions 30–1, 96, 322
conduct, acceptance by 11
confidentiality 70, 81, 283–5
conformity (of goods) 115–17
consensus ad idem 3, 9
consent 168, 290
consideration 12
    executed 13
    executory 13
    past 13–14
    sufficiency/adequacy 14–17
    supply of services 124–5
    third party 13
constructive total loss 324
consumer goods 115, 218, 219, 221
consumer protection 116–18
    false statements 193–213
    food safety 229–44
    product liability 179–88
    product safety 214–28
    weights and measures 245–50
contact, impossibility of 78–9
contamination of food 232, 233

contingency fee system 178
contingency insurance 317
contra proferentum 52
contract clauses
   arbitration 27
   force majeure 26–7, 66
   liquidated damages 27, 68, 71
   penalty 27
   restraint of trade 46–7, 90–1
   retention of title 137, 147–9, 314, 318
   solus agreements 47
contract of sale 96–7
contracting authorities 256, 258, 259
contracts
   bailment 97, 121
   collateral 6, 21–2, 86, 118
   conditions 30–1
   cost, insurance and freight 312–13, 322
   employment 174, 263
   exclusion clauses 26, 50–62
   formalities 24–5
   formation 3–23
   free on board 309, 313–14
   of guarantee 24
   indemnity 24–5, 89–90
   insurance 319–23
   privity of 20–2
   standard form 28
   termination (remedies) 63–71
   terms 25–30
   void 34–49
   voidable 19–20, 34–5, 37
contractual capacity 18–20
contractual liability 56
contractual offers 3
   bilateral 4–5
   counter-offer 5–6
   precondition 6–7
   referential bid 8
   standing offer 8
   unilateral 5, 8, 254
contractual terms/formalities 24–33
contributory negligence 167–8, 186, 265, 325
'control' test 175
copyright 97, 283, 284, 290–4
'coronation cases' 65
corporate capacity 18–19
cost, insurance and freight (c.i.f.) contracts 312–13, 322
'cost of the cure' 69

counter-offer 5–6
counterfeit goods 183–4, 200–1
court jurisdiction, ousting 46
credit 136
credit-broker 110
credits, documentary 311, 314–16
criminal law controls (of exclusion clauses) 61
criminal liability for false statements 193–213
Crown Commissioners 319
cut-off period (product liability) 186–7

damaged goods (on bill of lading) 309
damages 67
   for breach of warranty 139
   exemplary 69
   liquidated 27, 68, 71
   for misrepresentation 41–2
   modification of remedies 113–14
   for non-acceptance 135–6
   for non-delivery 138–9
   punitive 69, 178
   recoverable 168–72, 185–6
   unliquidated 68–9
'day certain' 135
de minimis principle 246
dealing as a consumer 54–5, 57–8, 114–15, 122
dealings, previous course of 51–2
death 7, 187, 219
debt 15–17, 71, 85
deceit 172
defective products 133–4, 163–4, 177–89
defects (categories) 181–3
defences
   due diligence *see* due diligence
   false statements 204–6
   food safety 240–1
   innocent publisher 205, 210
   negligence 167–8
   product liability 183–5
   product safety 217–18, 226
   warranty *see* warranties
   weights and measures 247–8
defined authorities/activities 261–2
del credere agent 24
deliverable state 143–6
delivery 127
   date 128–9
   examination and acceptance 131–4

delivery (*continued*)
  in instalments 130–1
  non-acceptance 135–6
  non-delivery 138–9
  note 132, 147
  payment for 134–8
  place of 128
  time of 128–9
  wrong quantity 129–30
'DES Daughters' 178–9
description
  false statements 193–213
  falsely described food 238–9
  sale by 100–2
descriptive words (sale by description) 100–2
design
  defects 181–2
  registered 294, 295, 296
  rights 294–5
  unregistered 294, 295
development risk 184, 188
Direct Labour Organisation (DLO) 260,
    261, 262
Direct Service Organisation (DSO) 260,
    261, 262
Director General of Fair Trading 59–61,
    269, 270–4, 276–8, 279, 281
disclaimers 199–201
  on-screen 209
disclosure, duty of 320–1, 323
discriminatory trading 270, 275
dismissal, unfair 263, 264–5
distributive chain 95, 163, 272
distributors 214
  obligations of 216–17
divisible contracts 64
documentary credits 311, 314–16
documents, mistake in 39
domestic agreements 17
dominant position, abuse of 268, 274–6,
    280–1
drug industry 178–9, 182, 186–7
due diligence 205, 209–10, 212, 217–18,
    220, 240, 247–8
durability (merchantable quality) 110
duress 43–4
duties
  arising from agency 80
  existing (performance) 14–15
  owed by agent 80–3
  owed by principal 83–4

duty of care 163–4
  breach of 167
  owed to rescuers 170
  recoverable damage 168–72
  standard of care 165–6
duty of disclosure 320–1, 323
duty to warn 181, 182–3

e-commerce 4
economic, technical or organisational (ETO)
    reason
  for dismissal 264
  for redundancy 263, 265
economic duress 43–4
economic loss 171–2, 174
'eggshell skull' rule 168, 169
emergency control orders 234, 236
emergency prohibition notices 236
emergency prohibition orders 234, 236
employees
  employer's duty of care 174, 175
  inventions by 289
  redundancy 263, 265
  rights 262–4
  unfair dismissal 263, 264–5
  vicarious liability 175
employers (duty of care) 174, 175
employment
  contract of 174, 263
  tribunals 174, 264
environmental health departments 234
estimates 125
estoppel 76, 151–2
  promissory 16–17
ex gratia payments 13
examination of goods 131–4
exclusion (competition law) 271–2, 275
exlusion (product liability) 187
exclusion (supply of services) 125
exclusion clauses 26, 50–62
exclusion of liability (sale of goods) 114–15
executed consideration 13
executory consideration 13
exemplary damages 69
exemptions (competition law) 272–3, 274,
    280
exhaustion of rights 289–90, 302, 304
existing duties 14–15
expenses (owed by principal) 84
expertise 166
exports 220, 289–90

exposing for supply 199
express authority 75
express terms 26–9

fact, misrepresentation of 39–40
false statements 193–213
falsely described/presented food 238–9
faulty goods 133, 134, 163–4, 177–89
fiduciary relationship 147, 149
financial limits (product liability) 187,
    188
financial loss 171–2
financial settlement (with agent) 85
finish (merchantable quality) 109
fire insurance 318, 323
fitness for purpose 102, 106, 108, 109,
    110–12, 116
fixed term agency agreement 86, 88–9
flights (return tickets) 203
food
    definition 229–30
    labelling 238–9
    safety 165, 180, 218–19, 229–44
Food Standards Agency 236, 241–3
force majeure clause 26–7, 66
foreseeability 164, 168, 170, 215–16
forfeiture 224
formalities, contractual 24–5
forum shopping 179
fraud 152–4, 157, 172, 175
fraudulent misrepresentation 41–2
free movement of goods 256, 302–4
free offers 5
free on board (f.o.b.) contracts 309, 313–14
free on rail (f.o.r.) contracts 143
free trade 256
frustration, termination by 65–6
functional work 260, 261–2
fundamental breach 53
future goods by description 143, 145

General Agreement on Tariffs and Trade
    (GATT) 291
General Average Contribution 310
General Product Safety Regulations
    214–18
general safety requirement 214–16, 218–20,
    223
global limits (product liability) 187
good faith 38, 40, 79–81, 90, 154, 155,
    156–7, 320–1

goods
    ascertained 141–2
    delivery and payment 127–40
    durability 117
    false trade description 193–4, 196–8
    faulty 133, 134, 163–4, 177–89
    free movement 256, 302–4
    manufacturer's guarantees outsourcing
        253–67
    passage of title/risk 141–59
    sale of 57, 95–119
    specified 141–2
    supply of 57–8, 120–6
    unascertained 141–2, 143, 145–6
    unspecified 141–2
Government Procurement Agreement (GPA)
    257
grey market (imports) 302, 304
guarantee, contracts of 24
guarantees, manufacturer's 56–7, 117–18

Hague–Visby Rules 307, 308, 309, 311–12
Hamburg Rules 307
Health and Safety Commission 221
health and safety requirements 216, 219,
    221, 224–7
hire 121, 127
hire-purchase 57, 96, 98, 121, 127, 152,
    156, 157
holidays (false statements) 201, 202, 209
Honourable Pledge Clause 18
horizontal agreements 280

identity, mistake as to 37–8
illegal contracts 46–7
implied actual authority 75
implied authority 80
implied conditions (supply of goods) 32,
    120–2
implied terms 29–30, 122–5
imports 289–90, 302, 304
impossibility of contact (agency of necessity)
    78–9
improvement notice 234, 235
'inadequate package' 249–50
incorporation (exclusion clauses) 50–2
INCOTERMS 312
indemnity
    clauses (unreasonable) 56
    contracts 24–5, 89–90
    insurance 317–18, 324

indicative notice 257, 258, 260
individual exemption 272, 274
industrial goods (safety) 220–1
injunctions 67, 70
innocent buyer 152, 153, 154, 155, 157
innocent misrepresentation 41, 42
innocent publisher 205, 210
innominate terms 31–2
instalments, delivery in 130–1
insurable interest 318–19, 321
insurance 149, 181, 184
    brokers/agents 323
    claims 323–5
    contingency 317
    first party 318
    indemnity 24–5, 56, 89–90, 317–18, 324
    marine 310, 322, 324
    premium 317, 320, 321
    third party 318, 324, 325
    types 317–18
intellectual property 180, 283–306
intention to create legal relations 17–18
International Chamber of Commerce (ICC)
    312, 315
international trade 307–16
Internet 4, 12
interpretation of exclusion clauses 52
invalid contract 46–7
inventions 287–90
invitation to treat 3–4
irrevocable banker's documentary credit 315

jurisdiction of court, ousting 46
just-in-time system 129

Kitemark 195, 226
knowledge
    of the offer 11
    scientific and technical (unknowable
        defects) 184–5

labelling 238–9, 301
land agreements 272
lapse of time (termination) 7
leading marks (on goods) 308
legal relations, intention to create 17–18
letters of comfort 25, 255–6
letters of intent 9–10, 255
liability
    contractual 56
    criminal (false statements) 194–213

exclusion of (sale of goods) 114–15
    insurance 318, 324
    for misrepresentation 58
    negligence 56
    product 177–89
    for services 174
    vicarious 175
licences of right 288
licensing (food premises) 239
lien 136–7, 318
life insurance 317, 323
limitation of actions 70–1
limitation clauses 50–62
liquidated damages 27, 68, 71
liquidation 141, 147, 163
Lloyds Names 174
local authorities 193, 208, 117, 230–1,
    260–2
'lock out' agreement 6
locus standii 13

Madrid Protocol 297
manufacturers
    duty of care 163–7
    guarantees 56–7, 117–18
manufacturing defects 181–2
marine insurance 310, 322, 324
market overt 152–3
market share liability 178
material fact, misrepresentation as 40–1
Meat Hygiene Services 241
Memorandum of Association 19
mens rea 194, 201–2, 301–2
mercantile agent 154, 155, 156–7
merchantable quality 102, 105–10
mergers 268, 271, 276, 278–9
mileage readings (cars) 198, 199, 200,
    206
minor defects, freedom from 109
minors 19–20
misleading advertisements 238, 241
misrepresentation 39–42
mistake 34–9
    common 35–6
    in documents 39
    identity 37–8
    mutual 36
    unilateral 36–8
monetary loss 171–2
money-back guarantee 203
monopolies 268, 276–81, 289

Monopolies and Mergers Commission 269, 278
multi-modal transport 311–12
mutual mistake 36

National Consumer Council 120
nature offence (food safety) 238
necessity
  actual and commercial 79
  agency of 78–9
negligence 163–76
  goods lost/damaged in transit 311
  liability 56
  see also contributory negligence
negligent misrepresentation 41, 42
negligent misstatement 172–4
negotiated procedure (EU Public Procurement Directives) 257–8, 260
'neighbour principle' 164
nemo dat 98–9, 151, 152, 154
nervous shock 164, 169–70
new-for-old policies 324
non-acceptance, damages for 138–9
non-confidential information 285
non-delivery, damages for 138–9
non-disclosure (insurance) 320–1
non-owner, sale by 151–7
non-performance 64
non-prepacked goods 247, 248
non-purchasers 163
non-registration (trade marks) 298–300
non es factum 39, 51
notices
  emergency prohibition 234, 236
  of exclusion clauses 51
  food safety 234–7
  improvement 234, 235
  prohibition 222, 223, 226
  suspension 222–3
notification system (competition law) 274, 276

offer
  and acceptance 3
  knowledge of 11
offers
  contractual 3–8, 254
  special 204, 209–10
  standing 8, 255
offers to supply (goods with false trade description) 199

Office of Fair Trading 193, 275
Official Journal of the European Communities 258, 259
official secrets 284
on-screen disclaimer 209
open procedure (EU Public Procurement Directive) 257–8, 259
oral contracts 198
oral descriptions 198
oral snuff 221
orders (food safety)
  emergency control 234, 236–7
  emergency prohibition 234, 236
  prohibition 234, 235–6
ostensible authority 76
outsourcing 253–67
own-branding 181, 184, 219, 241
ownership rights 127, 150–1

packaging 181, 238–9, 298, 300–1, 304
  regulated packages 245, 248–9
parallel exemption 272, 273, 274
parallel imports 289–90, 302
Paris Convention 297
part payment (of debt) 15–17
part performance 64
passage of risk 141, 149–51, 314
passage of title 141–9, 151–7
passing off 184, 283, 285–6, 296
patents 98, 283, 286–90
payment
  of consideration see consideration
  following unfair dismissal 265
  quantum meruit 10, 51, 64, 84, 255
  redundancy 265
  right to 83–4, 128, 134–8
  time of 135
Pearson Report (1978) 177
performance
  impossibility of 65–6
  normal/proper 90
  part 64
  specific 67, 69–70, 138
  substantial 63
  termination by 63–4
personal injury
  false statements 193
  product liability 185, 186–7
  product safety 219
personal remedies (for seller) 135–6
physical injury 164, 169–71

place of delivery 128
possession
  buyer in 155–6
  seller in 154–5
  transfer of 127–39
post-tender negotiations 255, 260
postal acceptance 12
power of attorney 74
pre-incorporation contract 78
precondition, failure of 6–7
precontractual negotiations 3, 25–6
prepacked goods 247, 249
price 47, 124–5, 138–9, 246
  action for the 135
  fixing 268, 270, 275
  misleading indications 203–4, 207–11
  resale price maintenance 268, 270, 275
  scanning 209
primary victim 169–70
principal
  agency by ratification 77–8
  –agent relationship 73–4, 80–4
  duties owed by 83–4
  –third party relationship 84–5
  undisclosed 84–5, 86
  unnamed 84–5
prior information notice 259
privity 20–2, 73, 95, 163, 180, 310
pro-plaintiff juries 178
producer
  obligations of 216–17
  product liability 179–81
product
  insurance 318, 324
  liability 177–89
  recall 182, 217
  safety 182, 214–28
professional standards (duty of care) 166
profit (economic loss) 171–2
prohibition notices 222, 223, 226
  emergency 236
prohibition orders 235–6
  emergency 236
promissory estoppel 16–17
property
  damage 185–6, 219
  misdescriptions 194, 203, 211–12
  passage of title/risk 141–59
  rights 127
  transfer of possession 127–39
protection of intellectual property 283–306

psychiatric damage 164, 169–70
Public Procurement Directives 253, 255, 256–60
punitive damages 69, 178

quality
  acceptable 102
  food safety offences 237–8
  of goods when loaded 309
  satisfactory 102–10, 121, 122
quality control 167, 181, 183, 205, 229, 240
Quantitative Indications of Ingredients (QUID) 239
quantum meruit 10, 51, 64, 84, 255
Queen's Award to Industry 196
quotations 125

ratification, agency by 77–8
re-engagement (after unfair dismissal) 265
reasonable precautions 205, 209, 240
reasonableness (exclusion clauses) 55–6
rebranding 303–4
recklessness, false statements and 201–2
recoverable damage 168–72, 185–6
redundancy 263, 265
referential bid 8, 254
registered designs 294, 295, 296
registration of trade marks 298–300
regulated packages 245, 248–9
reinstatement (after unfair dismissal) 265
rejection (of offer) 5
reliance (fitness for purpose) 111–12
reliance on the representation 77
remuneration level (after termination) 88–90
replica goods 200–1
representation
  existence of 76–7
  reliance on 77
representations 25, 26
repudiation, right of 113–14
resale, right of 137–8
resale price 47
resale price maintenance 268, 270, 275
rescission 41, 42, 117, 321
rescuers, duty of care owed to 170
restraint of trade 46–7, 90–1, 284
restricted procedure 257–8, 259–60
restrictive trade practices 47, 268
retention of title 137, 147–9, 314, 318

revocation 6
rights
    intellectual property 283–306
    ownership 127, 150–1
    of resale 137–8
    to sell 97–9, 114
risk
    accidents 164, 167–70
    contributory negligence 167–8
    passage of 141, 149–51, 314
    product liability 178–9, 181–2, 184–5,
        188
    product safety 215–17, 219
    see also insurance
Rome Convention (1960) 291
Royal approval 195

sabotage (in food business) 232
safe product 215–16
safety
    defective products 182
    food 229–44
    merchantable quality 109–10
    product 214–28
sale (under food safety) 230–1
sale by description 99–102
sale of goods 57
    implied conditions 95–119
    by non-owner 151–7
sale or return 144–5
sample, sales by 112–13, 121, 131, 133
satisfactory quality 102–10, 121, 122
scale monopoly 276, 277
schools, food safety in 230–1, 233
sea waybills 308, 310–11
second-hand goods 220, 324
secondary victims 170
secret profit 83, 90
'sell by' dates (food) 239
seller's remedies (delivery) 135–8
seller in possession 154–5
services
    false statements 201–4
    implied terms 122–5
    liability for 174
    outsourcing 253–67
    supply of 120–6
ship's delivery order 308, 310–11
shipper, obligations of 309–10
short weight/measure 245–8
signed documents (incorporation) 50–1

silence (not acceptance) 11
sold note 52
solus agreements 47
special offers 204, 209–10
specific goods 141–2
specific performance 67, 69–70, 138
standard of care 165–6
standing offer 8, 255
statutory control (exclusion clauses)
    53–61
stock control 129, 185
Stock Exchange 82
stolen goods 153, 183
stoppage in transit 137
storage
    duty of care 165
    foodstuffs 239
    insured goods 325
strict product liability 177–8, 183, 186
sub-contractors 255
sub-sales/sub-buyer 132–3, 137, 139, 144,
    148, 150, 155–6
subrogation 325
substance (food safety) 238
substantial performance 63
suspension condition 323
suspension notices 222–3

tenders 7–9
    compulsory competitive 9, 253, 260–2
    outsourcing 253–5
    status of 4
Tenders Electronic Daily database 258
termination 63–6
    of agency 86, 88–9
    of offers 5–7
    remedies 67–71
terms
    of contract 25–6
    covered (in regulations) 58–9
    descriptive of the risk 322, 323
    implied 29–30, 122–5
    insurance contract 322–3
    mistake as to 36–7
    unfair 58–61
thalidomide 177, 182
third party 73–4, 77, 84–6
time
    of delivery 128–9
    lapse (termination of offer) 7
    supply of services 124

time limits
  product liability 186–7
  sale of goods 117
title
  passage of 141–9, 151–7
  retention of 147–9
  voidable 153
tolerable negative error (TNE) 249
tourism 211
toxic shock syndrome 183
trade
  international 307–16
  restraint of 46–7, 90–1
trade description 226
  applying offence 194, 197–8, 199
  definition/factors 195–6
  disclaimers 199–201
  false 193–5, 196–8
  offers to supply 199
  services 201–4
  supplying offence 194, 199
trade marks 181, 201, 214, 283, 286,
  296–305
Trade Related Aspects of Intellectual
  Property Rights (TRIPS) 291
trade secrets 47, 243, 284–5
trade unions (recognition) 264
trading standards departments 200–1,
  222–3, 234
transfer of goods 120, 121
transfer of undertakings 262–5
transit, stoppage in 137
transport (international trade)
  multi-modal 311–12
  shipping goods 308–14

uberrimae fidei 40, 79, 80, 90, 320–1
'ultimate consumer' 164
ultra vires 19, 35, 221, 223
unascertained goods 141–2, 143, 145–6
unconditional appropriation 145–6,
  147

unconditional contract (deliverable state)
  143
undisclosed principal 84–5, 86
undivided shares 150–1
undue influence 44–6
unfair competition 283, 285
unfair dismissal 263, 264–5
unfair terms 58–61
Uniform Customs and Practice for
  Documentary Credits 315
unilateral agreement 65
unilateral contractual offer 5, 8, 254
unilateral mistake 36–8
unknowable defects 184–5
unliquidated damages 68–9
unmixed foil 147–8
unnamed principal 84–5
unpaid seller 135–8
unreasonable indemnity clauses 56
'usability' test 106
'use by' date (food) 239
unregistered designs 294, 295
usual authority 75–6

vaccines (product liability) 187
vertical agreements 47, 272, 280
vicarious liability 175
vitiating factors 34–49
void contracts 34–49
voidable contracts 19–20, 34–5, 37
voidable title 153
volenti non fit injuria 168
voluntary organisations 184

warranties 30–1, 32, 247, 322–3
  breach of 96, 99, 113–14, 139
weights and measures 245–50
works contract 260–1
World Trade Organisation GPA 257
wrongful dismissal 263, 264–5

zeroising car mileometers 198, 199, 200, 206